fP

Also by Lee Eisenberg

Breaking Eighty
The Number

Shoptimism

WHY THE AMERICAN CONSUMER
WILL KEEP ON BUYING
NO MATTER WHAT

LEE EISENBERG

Free Press

New York London Toronto Sydney

Free Press
A Division of Simon & Schuster, Inc.
1230 Avenue of the Americas
New York, NY 10020

First Free Press hardcover edition November 2009

FREE PRESS and colophon are trademarks of Simon & Schuster, Inc.

For information about special discounts for bulk purchases, please contact
Simon & Schuster Special Sales at 1-866-506-1949 or
business@simonandschuster.com.

Illustrations by A. J. Garces

Manufactured in the United States of America

1   3   5   7   9   10   8   6   4   2

Library of Congress Cataloging-in-Publication Data

Eisenberg, Lee, 1946–
Shoptimism: why the American consumer will keep on buying no matter what /
by Lee Eisenberg.
p. cm.
Includes bibliographical references.
1. Consumer behavior—United States. 2. Consumers—United States.
I. Title.
HF5415.33.U6E47 2009
306.30973—dc22
2009002462

ISBN 978-0-7432-9625-0

To Linda, Ned, and Katherine: priceless

Consume or die. That's the mandate of the culture.
—Don DeLillo, *Underworld*

I gotta good mind to give up living and go shopping instead.
—B. B. King, "All Over Again"

CONTENTS

Part II: You Versus You

FOREWORD

SEVERAL YEARS AGO, ON AN UNREMARKABLE SATURDAY afternoon, my daughter, Katherine, and I, fighting cabin fever, decided to take a walk. No particular destination or plan. We just strolled down Michigan Avenue, Chicago's renowned shopping drag, the "Magnificent Mile" to Chicago residents and tourists with plastic in their pockets. We wandered into a few stores, not to buy, just to look. Now and then we stopped to examine things we neither needed nor wanted—a distinction that gets tricky, as we'll see. Occasionally we eavesdropped on snippets of conversations between shoppers or between shoppers and salespeople. At a department store men's grooming counter we listened in on a hulking man in shorts and flip-flops who, most amiably, asked the salesperson whether the store had yet received Tom Ford's new fragrance. I was unaware that Tom Ford was about to drench the market with a new fragrance, but I wasn't surprised. Every luxury designer licenses perfumers to create signature grooming products, and so do a lot of middle- or low-brow celebrities: J. Lo, the Donald, Paris, Beyoncé, Britney, Jessica, Celine Dion, even Scottish actor Alan Cumming, whose grooming line includes a soap called Cumming in a Bar. In any event, the salesperson told the man in flip-flops and shorts that Ford's fragrance hadn't yet arrived but would be in stock sometime in the next couple of weeks. The customer reacted with equanimity, saying he'd stop back because he was "dying to check it out."

A few days later, idly browsing the Web, I ran into a blog mention that provided details of Tom Ford's impending launch. Coming soon: assorted iterations of what Ford called his Private Blends, varieties that included, among other scents, Moss Breeches, Tuscan Leather, Japon Noir, and Tobacco Vanille. Each would cost a not-to-be-sniffed-at $450 per 250 milliliters—pricey, yes, but excusable if you buy into the notion that perfumes and other cosmetics deliver "hope in a bottle," as Revlon founder Charles Revson famously put it. As for Ford's marketing campaign, when it eventually appeared, it turned out to be precisely what one would expect: high-gloss, sensual, surreal, and soothingly pretentious. Tobacco Vanille: a "modern take on an old world men's club . . . with opulent essences of tobacco leaf," a scent that "unfolds with creamy tonka bean, tobacco flower, vanilla and cocoa, and finishes with a dry fruit accord, enriched with sweet wood sap"—all of which led me to wonder whether it would go better with meat or fish.

In the days that followed the encounter with that customer, I kept wondering what had made him so eager to slap on a dash of Tom Ford's forthcoming fragrance. Obviously, the man had his Buy hooter pressed to the ground. But who or what had turned him into an early adopter—an early dabber—of some superexpensive fragrance as yet unavailable? Was there an inside source, perhaps a friend at an ad agency or a professional sniffmeister who worked in the hope game? Maybe the man had learned about Private Blends online, browsing the consumer forums where grooming buffs gather. And what was he really looking to buy, anyway, that fellow? Hope in a bottle? If so, what was he hoping for? A smell that would make him feel rich, thin, suave? Or was he he simply longing to be pleasantly, unisexually self-scented in a tonka-beanish, tobacco-leafish sort of way? After all, according to a study in the *International Journal of Cosmetic Science*, a man's alteration of his natural body odor makes him feel self-confident, which induces others to perceive him as such.

A few weeks after that chance run-in, I decided to go looking for answers to some of these questions—to explore, however serendipitously, the major and minor mysteries that settle around why and how we buy what we buy. I would circulate no formal surveys. I wouldn't hide behind potted plants to videotape customers shopping. I'd commission no brain scans. There was already plenty of that out there. Rather, I'd take a determined walk down both sides of Consumption Street. There's the Sell Side, as I'll call it, where a vast army is aligned against you, me, and the big guy panting for Tom Ford's new fragrance: retailers, marketers, advertising agencies, consumer researchers, online buzz collectors, and academics, a conspiracy of manipulators, as some—I'll call them Buy Scolds—see them. After that I'd cross over to the Buy Side—that's our side, the customer side—where I'd search for some sort of Unified Theory as to what makes us tick. And I would keep at it until, as happens on every shopping expedition, I ran out of time and patience.

But Why Me?

To put my personal credit cards on the table: I am not now, nor have I ever been, a shopping junkie or a career marketing guru or a dyspeptic critic of consumption, the three usual suspects who churn out blog posts and books about shopping and buying. What I am is a husband and a father, a bread-winner, which means I take a proprietary and sometimes overbearing inter-est in how my wife and kids choose to disburse what hard-earned money I bring to the party. I am also, of course, a consumer myself, sometimes reckless, sometimes tight as a tick—my spending habits vary moment to moment. In fact, I actually think of myself as a more or less "typical" con-sumer—even though there's little reason to believe such a creature exists. I grew up—typically enough—in a middle-class Philadelphia neighbor-hood during the 1950s, the so-called Happy Go Lucky Years, when the Sell Side held out the promise that our collective future would be one long rib-bon of material prosperity, an endless skyway of unprecedented consumer abundance. Yet by the time the sixties rolled around, I came to question—typically—whether that highway wasn't in truth a treacherous toll road. Millions of people, minorities and the rural poor especially, were denied access to that endless skyway. And those fortunate enough to ride the road paid a heavy price for the privilege: soullessness, fueled by the purposeless acquisition of useless stuff piled on more useless stuff.

The seventies brought a turning point: I found myself working on the fringe of the Sell Side. As the editor of a glossy magazine (*Esquire*), my sal-ary was underwritten by advertising revenue—page after page of ads for men's apparel, cars, cigarettes, liquor, and grooming products. While I my-self didn't peddle those ads, I did spend a fair amount of time marching up and down Madison Avenue with the shiny-shoed, cunningly charming men and women whose job it was to sell "space." My role was to convince agency media buyers that their ad pages would be seen by hundreds of thousands of educated, opinion-shaping, trendsetting readers—Yuppies, remember?—whose affinity for literary nourishment was matched by their quest for a cool and affluent "lifestyle."

By the late 1990s, by now too old to recognize the twenty-year-old hotties featured in magazines such as *Esquire* yet still spry enough to quaff the advertised potables, I found myself, most unexpectedly, working in the swollen belly of the Sell Side beast. For nearly five years I served as creative director at Lands' End, the direct-to-consumer clothing company— no matter that I'd brought zero experience to the apparel, catalog, or retail business. My job was to oversee the creative execution of the company's large family of catalogs, manage its national advertising efforts, and help launch its fledgling e-commerce site. Lands' End knew early and shrewdly that selling online presented a formidable opportunity to expand its reach and was hardly the "black hole" into which corporate profits would disappear, as the head of a major media company once judged the Web. But despite a lofty title, I was a pipsqueak, a subparticle attached to a tiny molecule floating in the unbounded Sell Side universe. With annual sales of $2 billion, Lands' End represented all of five ten-thousandths (.0005) of the U.S. retail trade. Still, my time there—including eighteen misspent months in the wake of Lands' End's acquisition by Sears (more on which later)— gave me insight into how huge, complex, and bizarre the Sell Side is. Bottom line: the Sell Side is not nearly as ingenious as Marketing Gurus would have us believe, nor as dangerous as anticonsumerist Buy Scolds would have us fear.

Where, Then, to Begin?

Not entirely sure about where to dive in, I decided it would be prudent at first to snorkel just below consumption's surface. The first thing I did was talk to friends and family members about how they viewed themselves as buyers. Answer: they were all over the place. A healthy—well, maybe not so healthy—number of them confessed to being card-carrying shopaholics, alternately rejoicing over the thrill of acquisition and expressing guilt over the degree to which shopping had come to dominate their lives. Others sputtered in the manner of amateur Buy Scolds. They bragged about their penny-pinching strategies and breathed sighs of self-satisfaction as they recounted how liberating it was to downsize from a large house to a small apartment, how therapeutic to cart trunkloads of material waste to Goodwill or the town dump, thereby lightening the burden of their existence and clearing a path to spiritual discovery. Indeed, a few reached for the philosophical and metaphysical when they addressed the subject of consumption. My friend Michael Verde, a near-compulsive buyer of books, paused for a moment, then said, "I guess I never thought about it, but each book I buy comes with an opportunity cost: the time and money I spend, or waste, on one book is time and money that could be spent on a better one." Another friend, John Nelson, a man with a gentle disdain for conventional wisdom, said he agreed with the view that American shoppers were akin to Buddhism's "hungry ghosts": spirits with swollen, cavernous bellies, tiny mouths, and pinhole throats, always ravenous, impossible to satisfy.

During this warm-up phase, I browsed through textbooks that elite business schools use to educate eager-beaver MBAs about to spend their lives trying to sell us things. Buying, I learned from one of these texts, is a six-step process:

1. We decide we need or want something.
2. We then seek out information we use to narrow our choices: we pay attention to ads, scout around online, seek recommendations from people we trust, retrieve impressions of products and stores we've acquired through the years.
3. Next we zero in on the details of what we think we need or want. We need or want a new shirt—should it be striped, solid, or plaid?
4. We then weigh an assortment of finer variables—fit, size, price, brand, available parking.
5. We buy, often with a credit card.
6. Finally, we render a verdict (deliberation time varies). Did what we buy satisfy, fulfill expectations? Or did the Buy let us down, leaving us pissed at whoever or whatever conned us into buying it in the first place?

This tidy six-step process raised more questions than it answered. You know, I know, everyone knows, that much of what we buy we don't *rationally* decide to buy; we just happen to run into things we think we want or need. We buy on impulse. But what exactly accounts for our sudden urges, sometimes exciting, sometimes sick-making in the immediate aftermath of purchase? What is it that grabs our attention?

As for the difference between "wanting" and "needing"—well, what *is* the difference, anyway?

Where We Go from Here

To begin our journey, we'll take a brief, intimate shopping trip with my wife, Linda, who has graciously agreed to bare nearly all. The book then divides into two parts.

Part I, "Them Versus You," is about the Sell Side. What we'll find is that the Sell Side is exceedingly well financed. It harbors considerable research capabilities. It trains cameras on us as we shop. It stamps bar codes on everything—would stamp them on our noggins if it could—to keep track of inventory, change prices at a moment's notice, maintain a record of which things we buy in combination with other things, and track the progress of orders that begin with our mouse clicks and end with a knock on our door.

In Part II, "You Versus You," we'll ramble along the Buy Side. That would be us: gullible, confused, time-constrained, money-challenged, covetous, and yet—here's the good news—far better informed and "empowered" than ever before, thanks to easy online access to product and price information. Part II will also examine the masks we pull on when we're out shopping and buying. And it will explore what we're *really* looking for when we buy something. That man at the grooming counter, you, me, any of us—what are we after, anyway? Status? Quality? Value? A way to kill time, relieve boredom? "You Versus You" is about why many of us say we're in the grip of some sort of compulsive buying disease, even though most of us aren't. And it's about how each of us alternately engulfs (voraciously), nibbles (cautiously), or refuses to rise to the Sell Side's bait.

Oh, one last thing before we embark. Between the time I set out and the time I resurfaced, the world had changed on the Buy *and* the Sell Sides. Indeed, both sides had totally cratered. Credit markets collapsed. Home prices crashed. The government was trying with little success to glue broken banks back together. Consumer spending was running on fumes. Upmarket department store revenue was down by double digits. Day after day, bad news, then even worse news, on the doorstep. Thomas Friedman in the *New York Times*: "The equity crisis made people feel poor and metastasized into a consumption crisis, which is why purchases of cars, appliances, electronics, homes and clothing have just fallen off a cliff." Cosmetic surgery was now akin to the SUV, something one can well live without, a plastic surgeon told the *Times*. We had reached "the end of the affair," lamented *The Economist*. "The golden age of spending for the American consumer has ended and a new age of thrift likely has begun," said a Morgan Stanley analyst. "Sixty percent off is the new black," quipped a journalist at *The New Yorker*. Word spread that we were now living in the "Wal-Mart moment," which is likely to be a protracted but fashionable (sort of) moment. The January 2009 issue of *Vogue* sent a reporter to scout the "aisles and aisles of inexpensive finds" to be found at big-box discounters. Our long-standing fetish for bigger, faster, flashier, pricier had ebbed—temporarily or indefinitely, nobody knew for sure. "The tide is going out," said another retail analyst. (A riptide, more likely.) The *Wall Street Journal* opined in the summer of 2008 that "the about-face in consumer behavior could bring striking changes to the marketplace, as retailers revamp everything from the size of their stores to the way they stock their shelves, and may force manufacturers to trim niche products in favor of more reliably selling basics." The paper asked readers whether, in light of economic woes, they were cutting back on spending. More than 80 percent answered yes. As I write, the vacancy rate on the Miracle Mile is the highest it's been in over two decades.

What was, what *is*, going on out there? A mere speed bump on the ribbon of highway that leads onward to more spending? Or were we, are we, approaching the dead end of that putatively endless skyway? Gone, as the global meltdown unfolded, were the buyers from Europe and Asia who had marauded down Fifth Avenue loading up on shoes and handbags, and leaving American shoppers feeling like poor country cousins. Long-term, there was talk of a fundamental remapping of the global buyscape. The torch had been passed, some said, to billions of buyers who live and spend in faraway places where money is "young," where immense new shopping centers dot the map, many that dwarf the Mall of America in size and spectacle. "We don't do poor products for poor people," said Alain Evrard, who manages the L'Oréal business in the Pacific zone. "There are two billion people who are going to become middle-class citizens around the world. I believe those folks will live like we do in America," observed a Wall Street money manager who invests in overseas retailing stocks.

As for here and now in America—the cradle of the Buy—life goes on, albeit with far greater struggle, down and up the socioeconomic ladder (consumer spending by low-income households began to decline in 2001; everyone else has finally caught up). What's a shopping junkie to do? Scramble, redoubling efforts to find bargains, steals, and closeouts. And what are the Marketing Gurus up to, now that business is weak? They're working on ever more resourceful ways to capture our attention in the face of job losses and overloaded credit card balances. It's tough out there. So tough that once again, fearless leaders and economic seers of every stripe urge us to do what's fitting, proper, and necessary in times of crisis and catastrophe. Suck it up, people. Go shopping.

PROLOGUE

The world, stuffed into a little black dress

WE MIGHT AS WELL START, JUST TO work the kinks out, by going dress shopping with my wife. Now, if you're a man reading this, it's a safe bet that you're not thrilled about the prospect of going dress shopping with my wife, much less with your own wife, or going shopping for much of anything save for handheld electronics or a massive, high-definition video monitor. Chances are, if you're a man reading this, you're a grab-and-go sort of chap when shopping by yourself, or a wait-and-whiner when shopping with your wife. Either way, you're not likely to be wild about coming along on this foray. Grab-and-goers and wait-and-whiners have been subjected to serious academic scrutiny. I've looked at some of those studies, but they haven't told me much beyond what I already know. If you're a typical grab-and-goer, your overriding mission is to get into and out of stores quickly and stealthily. If you're a wait-and-whiner, you're crabby and impatient. You sit sullenly on a backless bench (if you can find a bench) while your partner picks over merchandise or tries things on, interminably. For now, if you're that kind of dude, hang in there. This first expedition won't take very long. And, happily, you can come along without leaving the comfort of your La-Z-Boy, with a caipirinha to keep you chill.

The reason for the dress-shopping trip was, on the surface, straightforward: Linda needed—maybe just wanted, the distinction gets tricky, as I've already mentioned—a little black dress. The occasion was the forthcoming annual fund-raiser at our kids' high school. It happens every spring. The

1

school draws up a shopping list of goodies not easily obtained through its annual operating budget: electronic SMART boards for classrooms, new computers for the library. The agenda is always the same: parents arrive and stand around chatting. Drinks are passed, lubrication for the main event, a Dutch auction. Besotted, we file into the auditorium, where we watch an upbeat video that depicts the school's students acting in ways they never do at home. The video portrays them bright-eyed and alert, paying rapt attention to teachers, not shirking assignments or zonked out on video games. They race across playing fields with joyful enthusiasm, not chewing Oreos with their mouths open and bingeing on Red Bull, as they do in the basement. The video is a well-wrought infomercial calculated to persuade parents that our kids are flowering, not floundering. When the video finally ends, there's lots of clapping, and then a professional auctioneer takes the stage to adroitly work the crowd. When the bidding sinks to a donation level you can live with—i.e., live with now that you're a little tipsy and worth a lot less than you once were—you raise your numbered paddle, a volunteer records your pledge, and that's it, save for a high-spirited raffle—*two tickets to a Bears game!* Then everyone files out for dinner and chitchat with other parents and teachers. Drink enough wine and the evening, while costly, turns out to be more festive than it sounds.

Dress Code

The invitation, in keeping with the tradition that this was no ordinary fundraiser, but a "gala" fund-raiser, calls for "cocktail attire," meaning that men are expected to wear business suits and women, well, cocktail dresses, that is, not long dresses with beads and excessive froufrou, just classy dresses, usually but not necessarily black. When the invitation arrived, Linda mentioned something about having worn the same thing to the past two fund-raisers and that she "wouldn't mind" looking for a new little black dress for the upcoming occasion. Now, normally she would just go off on her own and look for something like this, leaving me at home to fiddle around online. But given that I was beginning research on a book about why and how people buy, I asked whether I could tag along with her, an embedded reporter. There's a catch, I said. If I go, the reader goes, too. Linda was fine with that, or so she said. Deep down I knew she wasn't wild about having me—let alone you—play peeping Tom as she slipped in and out of dresses in a cramped changing room. I don't imagine this is anyone's idea of a pleasant shopping experience, not that shopping experiences are always pleasant to begin with, whether you travel solo or in a platoon of friends or total strangers.

We started out walking south on Michigan Avenue. Hundreds of shops line the Magnificent Mile, large and small, cheap and expensive, freestanding and tucked away in vertical malls, the majority in business to sell clothes and accessories to women. I intend to revisit the Mile quite a few times before this story ends, assessing stores that sell everything from American Girl dolls to Harley-Davidson dog collars. But for now the plan was strictly to look around for a little black dress at one of the Mile's large department stores. Why a department store? Linda is a pragmatic shopper. She knows, every woman knows, that department stores offer a generous selection of dresses at a suitable range of prices, and there are always—especially in crummy economic times—things on sale. Department stores practice what the trade refers to as Hi-Lo pricing, meaning that merchandise is initially marked up so it can be methodically marked down to give customers the idea that they're getting a deal. Because the Hi-Lo game has been played for so long, most of us are trained almost never to buy anything that *isn't* on sale. You know it and I know it: the Hi-Lo game is something of a scam, yet we fall for it again and again.

Our first stop was to be Bloomingdale's. But on the way there we passed a run of ultrachic designer boutiques. Impetuously, we stopped in at Chanel, if only to see how the fabled French fashion house defined that season's edition of the little black dress. At the front of the shop, where merchants display what they deem to be "impulse buys," we encountered a rack of Chanel sunglasses—more precisely, and especially at these prices, Chanel *eyewear*. Each pair sat in its own elegant Lucite cubby, dozens of cubbies in all. Between the columns of cubbies, in elegant typography (lest anyone forget she is looking at eyewear in a store called **CHANEL**, not Lane Bryant):

CHANEL	**CHANEL**	**CHANEL**
CHANEL	**CHANEL**	**CHANEL**
CHANEL	**CHANEL**	**CHANEL**
CHANEL	**CHANEL**	**CHANEL**
CHANEL	**CHANEL**	**CHANEL**

The repetition of **CHANEL CHANEL CHANEL** reminds us how the concept of product branding came to be: a red-hot iron searing (so as never to fade from living memory) a mark of possession into an animal's hindquarters.

Duly singed, we browsed the generous selection of eyewear styles, many in the form of immense, wraparound tortoiseshell frames with none-too-modest overlapping Cs anchored to the temples. (The iconic Cs were designed by CC herself, back in the midtwenties.) I gathered that on some of those frames the Cs were crafted in real leather, a level of detail that comes at a price: Chanel sunglasses cost $350 and up, a rather expensive impulse buy by any reasonable standard. But relative to other impulses that might grip us on a rainy-day lunch break or a Saturday afternoon when we need a mood lift, $350 is not an unreasonable price tag—*assuming* we're well enough fixed to buy our antidepressants at Chanel. At Chanel, $350 doesn't buy much more than what you'll find near the front door. Venture deeper into the shop and you'll encounter spirit-enhancing Chanel shoes that start at around $500; chase-the-blues-away handbags at $1,000 and up. Of course, the savvy shopper knows that Chanel knockoffs—sunglasses and handbags mainly—are available at considerably less cost on street corners in most major cities, *assuming* one is willing and able to live with Not The Real Thing. Asian shoppers, for example, are notoriously designer-brand fixated and demand the Real Thing. It's commonly reported that over 90 percent of Japanese women own something Louis Vuitton, having spent on average $247 per handbag. A great many teenagers also crave the Real Thing, though only teens in certain ZIP codes have any interest in, or can afford, Chanel. But even teenagers who live beyond Scarsdale, Greenwich, Lake Forest, or Beverly Hills happily pay a premium for the Real Thing, if the Real Thing is North Face, Juicy Couture, or Rugby, among other brands that, at any given trend nanosecond, impart a necessary *je ne sais quois* to the self-expression their hormones are aching for.

We arrived at Bloomingdale's on this chilly weekday only to find the store so empty you could shoot off a cannon without hitting anybody, as my father used to say. Department stores are facing stiff challenges in an age when buyers prefer to shop in specialty stores, spectacular flagship stores, and big-box discounters. Stepping off the escalator, I (we) followed my wife across the empty sales floor to a far wall, where a thicket of little black dresses clustered. They carried labels—ABS, Bianca Nero, Kay Unger, David

Meister, Laundry by Shelli Segal, Chetta B—that meant nothing to me and not much more to Linda. Maybe some were private labels masquerading as "real" brands, maybe not, who knows any more? Department stores are hell-bent on rolling out their own labels, because there's more profit to be made by cutting out the big-name middlemen and women—Ralph, Liz, Donna, Ermenegildo, and the rest. At JCPenney, for example, about half the chain's apparel sales derive from exclusive Penney lines: Arizona, Worthington, a.n.a., and so on. At Macy's and similar department stores, private-label sales have been increasing three times faster than sales of tried-and-true brands. In 2007, Macy's made Tommy Hilfiger a "strategic alliance" offer he couldn't refuse. Hilfiger agreed to sell his signature line exclusively at Macy's, in effect making Tommy a semiprivate label. New and instantly recognizable private labels are launched routinely in today's marketplace. Many carry the signatures of celebrity endorsers who have little hands-on involvement with design: Madonna's line at H&M on the lower end, Kate Moss's at Barney's New York on the upper—that is, before Kate went on to bigger things at Topshop.

Linda began to work her way through the acres of chrome racks, rattling hangers as she went, lingering a bit longer near dresses on racks with little SALE signs attached. The signs promised a further reduction of 25 percent should one of the dresses make it through the decision-making process and wind up at the cash register. Keeping a safe distance, I watched as Linda sifted through the lot, feeling fabrics with a thumb and forefinger to determine whether they have what the trade calls a "good hand." There was something a bit melancholy about those dresses on sale: wallflowers at the orgy, they seemed to me. Buyers had passed on them for whatever reason: bad lines, a bad "hand," or perhaps a bad Bloomie's buyer had simply bought too many of them. Out of compassion for the on-sale dresses, but also out of hope that we could save a few bucks, I secretly rooted for Linda to find a dress here worthy of marriage. A man for you, right? In any case, fifteen minutes of hanger rattling yielded results: a quartet of little black dresses, all priced between $200 and $300. Linda handed them over to a saleswoman who ushered us into a changing room, where we locked ourselves in.

Changing rooms can be grim, as everyone knows. A survey reports that seven out of ten shoppers want changing rooms to be big enough to accommodate two people; seven out of ten want to be left alone in the room, whatever its size, with no salesperson hovering outside. The changing room at Bloomingdale's seemed to have been spruced up recently. There was an enormous mirror, squeaky clean, and a comfortable leatherette bench for me (you, too) to slouch on as my wife slipped out of her street clothes and prepared to try on the four little black dresses lucky enough to have made it to the quarterfinals. Each seemed to be waiting, *dying*, to be the one asked to the cash wrap, then on to the gala.

For a lot of shoppers, particularly male shoppers, to get out of your clothes, try something on, take it off, try something else on, take *it* off, and so on until it's time to put your own clothes back on, is one of life's—that is, life in a consumer society's—most dreaded rituals. Many women, too, have told me they hate trying on clothes; others, not so much. Linda doesn't seem to mind, even with onlookers present. Those who dislike trying on clothes give several reasons for their dyspepsia. One: cramped, usually dingy, quarters. Two: you're not really sure what looks good on you to begin with— *does it make my ass look big?* Three: the dressing room feels like an isolation booth, just you and your insecurities trapped in a small space. Four: you're usually conflicted about spending money on whatever it is you're trying on. Five: there's all too often the annoying presence of the dreaded hoverer, who keeps coming to the door, calling out questions presumably meant to be helpful but that in fact rush the decision-making process and apply even more pressure:

"How ya doin' in there?"
"Everything OK in there?"
"Can I bring ya anything else in there?"
"How's it goin' in there?"

Linda shimmied into the first dress (the label read Laundry), zipped up the back, and with narrowed eyes took a good hard look in the mirror. Though no expert, I'd say the technical term for what she had on was "corseted"; that is, rather tight around the midsection and calculated to amplify what in my wife's grandmother's time was referred to as a "bosom." After staring at her reflection for a minute or two, turning left, turning right, checking out her legs, shoulders, and accentuated bosom, Linda rendered her verdict:

"I look like a dominatrix."

Hurdles

Quick color commentary: this much I know from personal experience—there's more going on here than meets the eye. Settling on a dress, a necktie, a pair of high heels or athletic shoes, is complicated business. The decision to buy has to do with far more than "I like it/I don't like it." Many of the things we decide to purchase—clothes for sure, but also home furnishings, cars, kitchen appliances—must surmount hurdles far beyond those relating to a product's practicality or, sad to say, its objective "value." The decision to buy something like a dress is a kind of puzzle. Multiple pieces need to fall into place before we, as buyers, cough up a yes. If a potential purchase crashes into one of the hurdles, or various puzzle pieces fail to fall into place, the Buy is rejected. In the case of dress number 1, which now lay rumpled on the floor, Linda decided it flunked the Appropriateness Test. You don't go to a fund-raiser at your kids' school dressed as if you are panting to take a riding crop to the headmaster.

Okay, back to the action—dress number 2.

This time my wife didn't step into it, she pulled it over her head (which, come to think of it, is another reason to hate trying on clothes: it messes up your hair). Until that moment, I'd never thought about why women sometimes step into dresses, while at other times they pull them on over their heads. I suspect many other men haven't thought about it either. But watch people shop, you learn things. If a dress has a zipper on the side, a woman pulls it over her head. If the zipper's in the back, she steps into it. The dress my wife was pulling on now, by Chetta B, was one she'd especially liked while rifling through the racks. One tiny problem; the store didn't have it in her size—Linda generally wears a 6, this was a 4. But she elected to try it on anyway because, as every woman knows, size matters, though not very much to clothing manufacturers, for whom "size" is fairly arbitrary. I happen to know this because when I worked at Lands' End I often heard merchants talk about how one label's 2 is another label's 6. Part of this has to do with shrewd marketing strategy: *let 'em eat cake, but if you want to sell 'em clothes, trick 'em into thinking that the cake they eat doesn't put on pounds.* The trade term for the ruse is "vanity sizing," which flatters customers into believing they're more svelte than they really are. The deception occurs worldwide, and authorities abroad are acting. In 2007 the Spanish government declared war on vanity sizing, decreeing that female store mannequins be draped in size 10 or larger. As far as I know, no such trailblazing legislation is pending in our own nation's capital, even though, according to an industry trade magazine, more than one out of two female shoppers in this country say they have a problem finding clothes that fit, with inconsistent sizing a prime reason. Over 40 percent say the sizes of clothes in their closets range widely, and nearly 20 percent say they have items they've never worn because they never bothered to have them altered.

In this case Linda elected to try on the dress anyway, because if she really loved how she looked in it, she could ask the store to order another in the next size up. Well, it turned out that the 4 *was* too small, but that's not what scotched the deal. What scotched it was that this little black dress had made a much better impression when worn by a cheap plastic hanger than by a living human being. The dress had, as Linda put it, "way too much going on"—waves of pleats running up and down the dress from the neck through the bosom, all the way to the hem. In other words, the dress had failed to clear the Aesthetics Hurdle.

Dress 3 was by Vera Wang, whose bridal shop on Madison Avenue has for years been where the affianced rich, or those who strive to be, order their wedding gowns and dresses for bridesmaids. But like just about every other luxury brand—Chanel, Gucci, Vuitton, Armani, and so on—Wang has over the past several years elected to go wide (not mass, darling, *wide*, or in Vera's case *double wide*) by expanding her product line in every conceivable direction. These days, buyers aren't so much fashion victims as brand victims. Or, more precisely, brand-*cum*-lifestyle victims—a brand such as Vera Wang isn't just about luxury, it's about a way of life. Result: if you're into Wang, bring on the Wang. A Vera Wang brand victim can now slip her painted toes into Vera Wang footwear, hide behind Vera Wang eyewear, sparkle in Vera Wang fine jewelry, spray Vera Wang fragrance behind her ears and under her breasts, write thank-you notes on Vera Wang fine papers, set out Vera Wang china and stemware when she entertains, even slumber on a Vera Wang mattress, which, however ludicrous a Vera Wang mattress might sound, is perhaps the most logical brand extension of all. Wear Vera Wang on your wedding day, sleep on Vera Wang that night (and, should you be so lucky, through the many years of blissful nights that follow). And now there's also SimplyVera, a low-price Vera Wang line that is to Kohl's what Martha Stewart Everyday was to Kmart: a Faustian brand-extension risk.

The (not Simply) Vera Wang dress Linda had by now slipped on bore little connection to a wedding day *or* night, save for a subtle hint of same: a couple of cream-colored buttons on the front, covered in fabric—brocade? Jacquard? Turkish taffeta? what do I know?—one associates with a wedding dress. I couldn't help but see those buttons, however, as anything but two wide-open eyes staring out from just below the bosom. I stared at them, they stared back. They unsettled me but didn't seem to bother Linda, probably because she couldn't make eye contact with them except in the mirror. After considerable reflection, Linda judged the dress to be simple and tasteful, "kind of cute," she said, a phrase women shoppers commonly murmur when they run across something they are, in fact, wild about. When Linda asked me what I thought of the dress, I hesitated for a moment. I'd resolved to be as invisible as possible throughout this expedition, a fly on the dressing room wall, better to observe things as they really happened without influencing the eventual buying decision. But discipline failed. I told Linda I didn't honestly think the shape of the dress was all that flattering, and hard as I tried, I couldn't take my eyes off the buttons that kept staring at me. So I told her so. That comment was, sorry to say, sufficient to kill the deal. The moments also illuminates yet another Buy hurdle: doubt—a reservation planted by a husband, a wife, or some other companion along for the ride.

(Hang in there, guys; we're almost finished.)

The fourth dressed turned out to be made by the same designer who gave us the dominatrix dress, only this one, in the words of my wife, was "flapperish": a dress to Charleston in, not that anyone does the Charleston anymore, not even at bar mitzvah parties. After turning left, turning right, walking to the mirror, then back to her original spot, Linda uttered the magic words— "but it's also kind of cute." It was also kind of—no, not kind of, *incredibly*— wrinkled. No one had bothered to give the dress even a cursory steaming when it was unpacked it from the shipping carton that carried it on its journey from a village in China, where it had—no surprise—been sewn together. But even wrinkled, the dress *was* cute, I had to admit. The skirt was short, just above the knee, a plus given that Linda has really nice legs. The dress came across as playful and kicky. Linda thought so, too, but therein was buried the seed of yet another potential reason to reject: the Projection of Self Hurdle. "I think it might be too young for me," she said, all the while examining the dress from every angle. Buying clothes gets especially tricky when you reach middle age, Linda remarks all the time. A woman of a certain age doesn't want to buy things that make her look frumpy, but she also doesn't want to buy things that make her look like she's trying to pass for a chick three decades younger or, just as bad, a bar-hopping cougar on the prowl. There's nothing less appealing than that, Linda says. But I could tell she truly *liked* herself in that particular little black dress, which is doubtless why she spent so much time in it, noting that she generally appreciates how she looks in a flared skirt, and that the dress would be knockout worn with black tights and slingbacks. Then—threateningly—the Age Cloud passed over again.

"Tell the truth, is it too young for me?"

"No," I said, by now dying to get the hell out of there. "I think you look really great in that dress. Young, but not too young. Not a hottie, no way."

After further reflection, Linda decided to buy the dress. And—cue the brass section—the chosen one turned out to be *on sale!* We had made it across all the hurdles, and my wife now had a new little black dress to wear to the gala fund-raiser. For those of us keeping score:

Price tag: $290
(Less) Hi-Lo discount (20%): $58
(Plus) Illinois sales tax: $20.88
(Bottom line) VISA charge: $252.88
Total time spent looking to buy little black dress: 1 hour, 45 minutes

Postgame Wrap

The excursion now in the bag, what are we to make of it?

Bluenoses out there—anticonsumerist Buy Scolds—would argue that dark forces conned my wife into thinking she needed a new little black dress in the first place. They'd point a damning finger at slick advertising carried in fashion magazines that, in fairness to the Scolds, Linda sometimes reads. More generally, Buy Scolds rail at the bloated, superficial culture that seduces women into thinking that it's what's on the outside, not the inside, that counts.

Others who comment on reasons we buy say that even if my wife wasn't exactly manipulated into purchasing the little black dress, she was conditioned by decades of media images. Armani suits, you'll recall, registered on men's radar with the release of *American Gigolo*, starring the impeccably

Armani-clad Richard Gere. As for the little black dress, movies and fashion retrospectives have relentlessly promoted it as an iconic wardrobe staple, a must-have. Credit belongs to Coco Chanel, who presented us with the LBD long before her trademarked interlocking Cs were seared into the hindquarters of our brains. Chanel's triumph was aided and abetted by *Vogue*, which in 1926 proclaimed the little black dress "a sort of uniform for all women of taste." Thirty-five years later, Audrey Hepburn etched the little black dress further into mass consumer consciousness. Remember the opening scene in *Breakfast at Tiffany's*, when Holly Golightly wanders the empty morning streets of New York City, lovely, lonely, vulnerable in a little black dress (designed not, as it turns out, by Chanel but by Givenchy)? Holly nibbles breakfast out of a brown bag and peers into the Tiffany store window on Madison Avenue. In fact, that very dress lives on, having turned up for auction at Christie's a few years ago, where it fetched close to a million dollars—or four thousand times what we paid for Linda's on-sale dress at Bloomingdale's.

Okay, maybe the movies helped write the script. But hand the little-black-dress dossier over to an academically accredited Buy sleuth and you'll get an entirely different explanation for what happened at Bloomingdale's that day. Academics who practice qualitative research—i.e., those who, armed with clipboards, cameras, or binoculars, either in full view of subjects or concealed behind pillars, watch people shop and follow up what they observe with in-depth interviews—would seek to decode a pattern of behavior in my wife's pursuit of the little black dress. I put the matter to Albert Muniz, who teaches marketing at DePaul University, specializing in how people form communities around the brands and products they buy. He told me he'd try to draw a finer picture of how the buying of the dress linked up with the occasion at hand—the fund-raiser—and what a woman such as my wife "desires to say about herself via the dress. To get at this," Muniz said, "I'd interview that woman before she went shopping. I'd want to know plenty about her background, her life story, to gain a better understanding of where she was coming from. I'd ask her to take me on a tour of her closet, identifying favorite outfits. I'd want to know what her goals were for the event in question. Does she want to impress and influence others? And I'd like to accompany her as she went shopping, asking her to explain her choices. Finally, I'd have a follow-up interview after the fund-raising event. I'd want to know how it went, who was there, and how she felt about her purchase afterward."

Muniz's approach parallels that of Americus Reed, a young faculty member at the University of Pennsylvania's Wharton School. Reed is a social psychologist by training. After I recounted the dress episode, he told me the impulse to purchase is related to our desire to obtain "feedback" in the form of social acceptance. Given that the evening was branded a "gala," that it called for "cocktail attire," and that Linda was inclined to dress appropriately, Reed said he would classify her a "high self-monitor"—one whose consumer choices enable her to "fit in," to adhere to the social cues and behavior one attributes to a particular event or environment. To be a high self-monitor is to possess a chameleon quality: you buy and wear what you judge to be right for the occasion. Low self-monitors aren't as much concerned with extracting positive social feedback. They buy and wear whatever they like to a school fund-raiser—mom jeans, if the spirit so moves.

Finally, a renegade anthropologist, Grant McCracken, who has taught at MIT and the Harvard Business School, offered me this elliptical response: "The Elizabethan Lord Burleigh removed his outer robes one festive occasion, saying, 'Lie here counselor, while I go off to dance.' An anthropologist runs the question in reverse and asks of a woman buying a new dress, say, what self do you take up with this dress, who will you now become?"

What McCracken was getting at: the little black dress, like so many things we buy, possesses a kind of transformative power.

Our journey had just begun, and one thing was already clear, at least to me: everyone has a take on what happened in that store, and no one knows for certain. When we look for all the possible explanations for why we buy what we buy, wear what we wear, drive what we drive, dine where we dine, or furnish how we furnish, we find ourselves adrift in explanations that range from the broadly trivialized—fashion victim! shopaholic! social climber!—to the truly arcane. There are those who would see Linda as a knot of sexual hang-ups, which we'll come to. And there are white coats in neuro labs who aren't the least bit curious about Linda the person but seek to understand her behavior in terms of switches and wires and electrical currents begging to be technologically scanned. There's *got* to be a buy switch amidst all that static and ooze, wouldn't you think?

PART I

Them Versus You

The Sell Side has us covered. It gathers intelligence. It watches us in stores, listens in online. It runs experiments. It knows where we live. It precision-bombs. Not to be paranoid, but what chance do we have?

1

A View from Within

The education of a floorwalker

Contrary to popular opinion, customers like to be sold, if, and when, they get in the hands of an authoritative salesperson who knows the stocks and shows an understanding of their needs.

—Stanley Marcus, *Quest for the Best*

 IN THE WEEKS FOLLOWING THE SUC-cessful acquisition of the little black dress, I toyed with the idea that the first half of this journey—our tour of the Sell Side—might handily take place within walking distance of my apartment. Just a few blocks to the south, on the Magnificent Mile, there's Nordstrom, Chanel, and Bloomingdale's, where we've already been. There's the Apple Store, Abercrombie & Fitch, H&M, Victoria's Secret, Macy's, and hundreds of other retailers. Why suffer through O'Hare's endless delays and cancellations just to fly thousands of miles to look in on the same stores we have down the road? Personal convenience aside, Chicago is rich in Sell Side history. Windy City mad men measure up just fine against their New York brethren. The fabled Leo Burnett agency is here, emblematic of the "Chicago school of advertising," birthplace of Tony the Tiger, Morris the Cat, Charlie the Tuna, Speedy Alka-Seltzer, the Jolly Green Giant, the Pillsbury Doughboy, Keebler's Elves. Not to name-drop—frankly, I don't recall his name—but not long ago I had drinks with a Chicago copywriter who announced proudly after a single martini that it was *he* who had conceived Nestlé tea's "Take the Plunge"

campaign. Sweet! "Which twin has the Toni?" "When It Rains, It Pours" are just two of the many classic slogans conjured here. Advertising, though, is but the tip of this town's Sell Side legacy. It was from Chicago that the Sell Side beat a path to front doors all across the land, even *mailed* those very doors directly to where they were installed. Sears, Roebuck and Montgomery Ward are native to Chicago. Pioneering Chicago merchants had so much to sell a growing nation that they banded together to build the world's biggest showroom, the Merchandise Mart, the riverside Deco hulk that spans two city blocks and stands twenty-five stories high.

Were I to stay planted in Chicago, I figured, ground zero would be the Magnificent Mile. It is, after all, one of the world's best-known and heavily trafficked high streets, the city's answer to Fifth Avenue, Rodeo Drive, Bond Street, Rue du Faubourg Saint Honoré, Via dei Condotti—so what if the shoppers you see on the Mile are typically less posh, generally more husky, and definitely longer in the vowel? Really, why leave home when, without changing out of my pajamas, I could slip on an overcoat and watch hungry hordes tromp through the usual specialty stores, luxury-brand shops, major department store chains, and an armada of showy flagships? The Magnificent Mile, so crowned in the 1940s, is graced by singular architecture. The beloved Wrigley Building, the neo-Gothic Tribune Tower, each dating from the early twenties, stand proudly at the southern end of the main shopping district. Just a short stroll to their north is the phallic yellow limestone Water Tower, a prominent landmark Oscar Wilde considered "a castellated monstrosity with pepper boxes stuck all over it." Most tourists, though, are enchanted by the limestone tower, if only because its plaza offers momentary respite from some really good shopping, sandwiched as it is between Ralph Lauren and Victoria's Secret.

I Know! I'll Work in Retail!

One weekend, while still mulling over whether to stay close to home or set sail for distant malls, a bright fluorescent light went on in my head. I wouldn't just visit stores, I'd get a job in one, if only briefly. Really, what better way to see hungry ghosts up close than to scuttle around a sales floor? So on a chilly Saturday morning I drove to a nearby Target store and applied for a seasonal position—the holidays were coming up. I was unshaven, dressed in dirty jeans and the T-shirt I'd slept in, which I thought didn't matter because I knew that at Target, you seek employment electronically, at a kiosk near the front door. Warily, I logged on and started to peck away at the application, which was more extensive than I had bargained for. Clicking through multiple sections, I fretted over how little about me matched what I presumed to be the prospective Target floor worker:

Age: Though grizzled enough to have grandfathered every other employee in the store, I didn't lie. No point in lying; someone would eventually lay eyes on me.

Previous salary level: The choices ranged from $5 to $12 an hour, or close to that. I checked the max and moved on.

Preferred position: I indicated that I was strictly interested in assisting customers, not working the register. Touching germy money, swiping credit cards, screwing up receipts, holding up the line—all of that was terrifying to contemplate.

The remainder of the application tried to pin down whether I was psychologically and ethically fit to serve you, the Target "guest." Plenty of multiple-choice questions on the order of: You spot another employee stealing. Do you: a) confront him/her? b) find a supervisor and rat out him/her? or c) pretend not to notice?

I reached the end and pressed SUBMIT, assuming that the application would in short order appear on the computer screen of a junior HR person in Minneapolis, where Target is based. Fair warning: if you ever apply for a job at Target, this is not what happens. What happens is that a fresh page appears on the screen instructing you to pick up the red telephone to your right. I figured there'd be a recorded message: *Thank you for your interest in Target—and have a nice day!* To my shock, there was a live, pleasant voice on the other end, a young woman who happened to be sitting in an office just a hundred yards away. Next thing I knew I was in that office, stared down by a cluster of associates three decades younger than me. Their boss had already printed out my application and greeted me with a smile. I studied her face for a sign of suspicion as to why this unshaven old guy in a rumpled shirt and imported Italian eyeglasses—wino? pederast?—was looking to work on Target's sales floor. I introduced myself, mumbled that I didn't expect to be interviewed just then and there, that I didn't want to work—no offense—at this Target but at the new, huge one, where was it again? Peterson Avenue, because it was closer to home. That was true. The fact that Oscar Mayer himself was buried in the cemetery across the street from the Peterson Avenue store had nothing to do with it. "Great!" said my never-to-be boss, taking no offense. "We'll send your application to Peterson right away."

Over the next several weeks, I wavered. It would be a lot easier to just drop in at Target from time to time and make like I was shopping for Christmas ornaments, taking furtive notes on who was dumping what into their capacious red shopping baskets. But I held firm. Store experience, I told myself, would serve as a good foundation for the expedition that stretched ahead. Then, one day, my cell phone rang. Could I come in for an interview? Uh, actually, tomorrow's not especially convenient, I said (which drew a chortle from Linda, who later explained that job applicants aren't supposed to be so blasé). Finally, on a blustery November afternoon, I surrendered. I drove over to the Peterson Avenue Target and checked in at the Guest Center, where I was told to hang around the Starbucks counter until someone came out to talk with me. A handful of other hopefuls also waited to be interviewed, including a huge guy, Ali G'd to the max, far more muscular than me, better qualified to move cartons and reach merchandise on upper shelves. Eventually an assistant manager walked over, carrying my application. I held my breath, but things went okay. She made no reference to my advanced age. She mostly wanted to know the hours I'd be willing to work. Then she ran me through a few more hypothetical questions about dealing with colleagues who may be thieves or pains in the ass (my terms, not hers). I blabbered about the importance of teamwork, that it's good to get gripes out in the open and rely on the judgment of seasoned supervisors. Minutes later, Target presented me with a "Conditional Offer of Employment"— conditional on my passing a drug test, which had to be administered within twenty-four hours or the offer would be summarily withdrawn, the interviewer noted ominously. I called Linda and explained that I might be late for a Human Rights Watch dinner that evening because I had to hightail it to a testing lab to deposit a urine sample.

"I hope they don't test for Lipitor," she said.

A week or so later the phone rang again: come in tomorrow afternoon for your orientation. "Oh, and don't forget to wear a red top," the caller said before hanging up. Red top. I didn't own a red top. So the next morning Linda and I scoured Michigan Avenue stores in search of an inexpensive red top, as close to Target red as might be available. Eddie Bauer? Filene's Basement? Gap? No red tops. Just as I was beginning to think the unthinkable—

I'd wear a blue top on my first day at Target—we found the perfect red top in the men's department at Nordstrom. Short-sleeved polo. Fit like a glove. And Target red. Well, almost perfect. There were two things wrong with that red top: first, it was considerably more expensive ($85, over ten times my hourly wage) than I wanted to spend on a shirt to wear to work; and second, there was an elegant little label—Façonnable—stitched on the breast pocket. But this was, after all, Nordstrom, a store known for its excellent customer service. The saleswoman offered to run the red top back to the tailoring room, where the fancy tag was promptly excised with surgical skill.

Target Takeaways

My brief life—barely a month—as a Target clerk would nonetheless prove useful. Here are a few of the things I learned:

1. However placid store life seems on the surface, a big retail chain has to work overtime to hold things together.
    While we customer-guests gripe about how there's never anyone around to offer help when we need it, the store is fighting a staggering rate of worker turnover. This is one of the reasons Target relentlessly and laudably tries to keep morale high and pushes the line that we workers aren't workers, we're "team members." I learned that it's a bitch to keep team members from hitting on each other, stealing merchandise, or sharing a joint behind the Dumpster when they should be offering guidance to us. A major portion of my orientation consisted of watching consciousness-raising videos that underscored the need for mutual respect and personal responsibility as regards sexual harassment, "asset protection" (shoplifting), racial tolerance, safety and security, and assorted threats to day-to-day team harmony. (Key Target employee credo: "The Strength of Many, the Power of One.")

2. Common sense is a store worker's best defense.
    At one point during my orientation, the trainer flashed a photo on the TV monitor: it showed a mock armed robbery taking place at a register. The miscreant had a handgun partially concealed in his pocket; the cashier was about to hand over a fat wad of bills. The trainer asked us to guess how much money was in the wad. Go figure. Were they ones, hundreds? You couldn't tell, so I took a guess: "Five hundred?" "Two thousand dollars," the trainer

responded. "Do you know how long it takes Target to take in two thousand dollars?" He paused. "Maybe half a second." Moral: team members are expected to be helpful to guests, not crime-stopping heroes. The goal is not to help catch a thief but to get the bastard out of the store as fast as possible.

3. Social and ethical issues preoccupy managers in retail stores, for which I give Target particular credit.

I especially admired the attention Target pays to teaching new team members how to deal with disabled guests. Never shout when talking to a hearing-impaired customer at the Guest Services desk—politely offer a pad and pencil, as needed. Never touch a disabled guest's wheelchair, which is no different from touching the guest herself. Never address a disabled guest's aide and ignore the guest; address the aide and the guest, bending down, if need be, to make sure the guest knows you're aware of his existence.

4. However praiseworthy all this consciousness-raising, no time was allotted to product training—none.

Stanley Marcus, who built Neiman Marcus and until his death in 2002 was the grandest of merchant grandees, would not approve. Target team members are not expected to hold court on why one crockpot outcrocks another. At Target, and at its competitors I can only assume, you are trained to be a human global positioning system. Again and again I was instructed not to say "May I help you?" but instead "Can I help you *find* something?" These six words—no substitutions allowed—are tantamount to a company trademark, no less critical to Target's identity than the big red bull's-eye. Why so mission-critical? A Target-sized store, as you doubtless know, is a very large place, and though it's well lighted, with wide aisles and excellent signage, it's easy for a guest to become lost, overwhelmed, confused, antsy, angry. If you're lost, overwhelmed, confused, antsy, or angry, there's an excellent chance you'll find Target in violation of the company's highest strategic priority: to make shopping at Target "Fast, Fun, and Friendly." "Fun" and "Friendly" are mission-critical to keep Wal-Mart—six times Target's size—at bay. "Fast" is first for good reason: shopper surveys cite "slow checkout lanes" as the predominant reason most of us choose to avoid a certain store, our waiting-time fuse being roughly four minutes long. (Compare that to how long, on average, we're willing to wait in a hospital emergency room: three and a half hours, by some accounts.)

Dutifully, I did what I could in the service of Target's mission statement. A smile on my face, I speedily price-scanned a jug of Clorox for an elderly guest dressed in a sari. Jauntily, I whisked a young, muscular Hispanic guest over to the kitchenware section, where he acquired a Jack LaLanne juicer with a 3,600-rpm whisper-quiet motor. I didn't actually know it came equipped with a whisper-quiet motor; I read it on the box as the guest was trying to decide whether he really needed a juicer or maybe just wanted one. And with that the curtain descended on my career as a floorwalker, which was fun, friendly, and over so fast I never once had to work the register.

Maybe it was the endless Chicago winter that lay ahead. Maybe it was spending those long afternoons and evenings stocking shelves. But in the aftermath of my stint at Target, I was more than ready to get out of town. Chicago's retail shoulders are broad, yes, but we live and shop in one big, hairy land of Buy plenty. I'd need to spend time in New York, for sure, where marketing gurus and retail experts abound, maybe do a little shopping myself. I'd need to visit business schools and psych departments around the country. I'd need to travel hither and yon to capture even a fractional sense of how cosmic the Sell Side universe is. Our nation's Buy numbers are immense: retail rings up $4 trillion worth of sales annually (80-plus percent of which is spent by women). U.S. stores emit a collective *ka-ching* of deafening sonic magnitude—that's the sound of money moving from our pockets into the Sell Side's gaping maw. Personal consumption accounts for over 70 percent of the nation's gross domestic product. We drop close to $300 billion each year just at Wal-Mart and Sam's Club.* Wal-Mart isn't merely the biggest retailer in the U.S. (around 4,100 stores), it's the biggest or second biggest company in the world, depending on how well the oil companies are doing. One out of every five other U.S. businesses traffics in retail, making this the largest market in the world, nearly four times greater than runner-up Japan and five times greater than third-place China, which is moving up fast on the outside and will likely streak past Japan by 2012. Some 15 million of us work in the retail industry (median hourly wage $8.92), about a

---

*My annual spending at Wal-Mart is typically zero. Chicago has restricted Wal-Mart's presence to a single store, a local-trade protection policy praised by some, condemned by others.

million just in apparel retailing. So employed, we cultivate professional folding and stacking skills. In 2008, the *Wall Street Journal* ran a story about the growing segment of Americans who, *at home*, obsessively fold and stack, organizing their sweaters and socks according to color and style.

My Target experience notwithstanding, I remain a truly lousy stacker and folder. Still, my years at Lands' End and Sears taught me a great many other things. The semiotics of "vanity sizing" I've already noted. I also learned about inventory control; how warehouses and call centers function; how the Sell Side operates on specialized lingo that a newcomer must master to get the job done: "casual bottoms," for example, refers not to J. Lo's or Jessica Alba's but to jeans and chinos. I also learned that it's difficult to coordinate multiple sales channels: catalog, online, bricks-and-mortar. I learned that successful selling is a complicated team sport requiring players with specialized skills: merchandising, product sourcing, marketing, distribution, the need to keep innumerable data bases tidy and up-to-date.

Here's something else I learned at Lands' End: how challenging it is, despite gung-ho books written by self-appointed marketing gurus, to win and keep the hearts and minds of customers. While nearly every company on the Sell Side boasts that it is "customer-centered"—viz., they do it all for us—many retailers are just blowing smoke. They say that our calls are really, really important, then put us on hold for an eternity. Precious few go out of their way to satisfy. Amazon, to which I am personally and fanatically devoted—breadth of assortment, great deal on a year's worth of two-day shipping—deservedly rules the University of Michigan's American Customer Satisfaction Index. Zappos, the online shoe retailer, is also a dogged customer servant. The company offers prospective customer-service reps a $1,000 bonus to *quit* after their initial training, the presumption being that a juicy reward weeds out those not committed to serving us with care beyond the call of duty. A high level of customer service pays off: past buyers account for three-quarters of Zappos' sales. Lands' End also delivered on the pledge to place its customers first. The company's unique selling proposition is *Guaranteed. Period.* Dog gnawed your attaché case? Summon the chutzpah to ask, and Lands' End would send you a brand-new bag. The person who accedes to this sort of brazen request, the woman on the other end of the line, is likely a moonlighting Wisconsin farm wife, friendly and accommodating, working in the phone center because it provides extra income and health benefits for her family. The people in the Lands' End call center really *do* do it all for you. Years ago, one of the operators followed through on a request to place a wake-up call to a woman about to be married and who was worried about sleeping late on her wedding day. The bride rightly assumed that a Lands' End order taker would never let her down. Another phone operator drove home in the middle of the day to pick up and send to a customer a pair of her husband's cufflinks, the particular style being temporarily out of stock.

It's a Jumble Out There

Given the enormity of the stakes, it's a store-eat-store world, which is something else I learned as a Sell Side insider. In the spring of 2002, Sears bought Lands' End in the hope that a respected clothing brand would perk up what had long been its dismally performing "softer side." This in turn would enable Sears to compete more effectively against mall rivals JCPenney and Kohl's, both of which had years ago caught Sears with its rugged pants down. Happily for us, Sears paid a premium for Lands' End, not because it had worked out a clear strategy for how it would roll out the brand in stores, but mostly out of delusive wishful thinking. Sears execs must have been hearing weird voices in their heads:

"Oh, I *adore* your swimsuit!"

"Thank you, I bought it yesterday at Sears!"

"Wow, it matches the garden hose—cool!"

Though I was dubious about the cultural fit between little old friendly Lands' End and lumbering, sclerotic Sears, Roebuck, I agreed to work for the merged company for a time. This magnanimous gesture required me to spend a day or two a month suffering through senior-executive meetings at Sears headquarters outside Chicago. It was a self-imposed sentence that carried cruel and unusual punishment: long hours staring at bar graphs charting the explosive growth of powerful competitive retailers who had been scarfing up real estate in concentric circles around Sears's down-at-the-heel, mallbound stores. In just three years, a grim-faced presenter told us during an especially glum review, six top competitors—Home Depot, Lowe's, Best Buy, Kohl's, Wal-Mart, and Target—had opened a couple of thousand new stores across the country. Aside from tinkering with a new format here and there, Sears had opened *no* new full-line stores. Even more depressing was the realization that the aforementioned chains had at least two huge advantages over Sears: (a) depth of merchandise assortment, which made them "destination" stores whenever, say, you needed home improvement supplies or electronics; and (b) breadth of merchandise, that is, vastly broad inventories that give you reason to return to them frequently. How many times a year do you buy a garden hose, let alone a swimsuit to go with it?

But life can be a bitch even for those come-lately behemoth chains. Market by market, Home Depot and Lowe's go at each other with two-by-fours, Home Depot projecting a manly face to attract builders and contractors, Lowe's cozying up to women. Target brandishes those designer teapots to hold off Wal-Mart. Even in good times it's never easy being a retailer. All selling chains—from Abercrombie & Fitch to Zara—battle price, profit, and market-share pressure. Their merchants are forever missing out on trends or betting on ones that fizzle and pop: the notorious Nehru jacket, the bubble skirt, the poncho as basic wardrobe staple. Even when store merchants do nail a hot product, they order it in the wrong sizes and colors.

And were all of this not headache enough, retailers have to put up with *us:* impulsive, impatient, price savvy, each of us operating out of an individual value system, even if we were spawned in the same gene pool. Take Danielle and brother Guy Crittenden. Danielle, married to the conservative commentator David Frum, hates Ikea so much she was moved to post an anti-Ikea rant on the Huffington Post, here liberally abridged:

> Ten minutes passed. The line crept forward. Finally it was my turn. The euphoria of my imminent savings had not yet worn off, and I was still hopeful about the Ikea experience. I handed the employee my sofa document. He examined it like a surly immigration official and typed some things into his computer. Then the Milan Kundera* comedy began:
>
> "Not in stock."
>
> "My sofas?"
>
> "One sofa. The loveseat."
>
> "Oh. When will it be in?"
>
> "It usually takes five days."
>
> "Okay. So I'll order it and then you guys can ship it, right?"
>
> "No."
>
> "No?"

---

*Sounds more like Beckett to me, but whatever.

"No."

"So what do I do?"

"You check with us in five days to see if it's come in."

"If it hasn't?"

"You can check back with us a few days after that."

"And then you'll ship it?"

"No."

"So how do I get my sofa?"

"When it's in you come back and pay for it."

"Wait a minute: You mean I have to drive all the way back out here just to pay for a sofa I am going to have delivered? I can't pay for it now? I can't give you my credit card number over the phone?"

"No."

"Okay. So what's the number I call to check when it's in stock?"

"Check the website."

"The website? You don't have a phone number?"

"It's better to do it online."

"Wait—can I order the sofa online?"

"Yes."

"Then why wouldn't I do that?"

"Because they'll charge you more for shipping."

"How much more?"

"I don't know."

Danielle Crittenden's brother, Guy, editor of an environmental magazine, *loves* Ikea:

For me, [Ikea offers] an efficient way to quickly furnish a modest apartment. . . . The energy-efficient flat-pack distribution methods and use of (mostly) recyclable paper and cardboard packaging, and the "do-it yourself" experience of buying and assembling the items, converged in my mind with the international flare of the stores to make me feel I was consuming in a sort of Third Way that blends global capitalism with populist thrift and eco-efficiency. . . . I can't help feeling that my Ikea experience offered me a glimpse into a more desirable future wherein people consume wisely and reduce their ecological footprint, but also live comfortably.

The Crittendens are solid evidence that herding loyal customers is much like herding developmentally challenged kittens: who can predict our whims and demands? We buy here today, who-knows-where tomorrow. Remember, in the eighties, when we all thought Gap was superhip? How seductive those nifty portraits of noteworthy celebrities by top photographers: Joan Didion by Annie Leibovitz, William Burroughs by Herb Ritts, Dominick Dunne by Albert Watson? Today, Gap struggles to climb out of a pit of iffy sales and declining cachet, having ceded significant market share to some of the same competitors who wounded Sears: Kohl's and JCPenney, as well as others. What's a flagging brand to do? In Gap's case, go back to the well. Years after that great photo campaign, the company mounted a déjà-vu advertising blitz that featured a fresh generation of celebrities—Lucy Liu, Liev Schreiber, Sarah Silverman. And, more recently, there was a campaign featuring T-shirts designed by artists—Marilyn Minter, Kiki Smith, Cai Guo-Qiang, Barbara Kruger, Ashley Bickerton—who'd exhibited at the Whitney Biennial (as if millions of shoppers know or care). What happened to Gap? Well, it's a huge challenge for an apparel retailer to be all khakis to all people. Says a Wall Street analyst, "Everyone who is successful at the mall today has a laser focus"—meaning if you're a teenager, you seek the true Outer You at American Eagle; when you grow a bit older, you address your presentation-of-self issues at American Apparel and Urban Outfitters; older still, you step up to Anthropologie; until, eventually, you find yourself trying on tops at Ann Taylor. Meanwhile, Gap does what it can. I recently read it had hired a new chief designer and, according to the *New York Times*, ordered store personnel to pin back the clothes on store mannequins to project a hipper, more tailored, Gappy look. Minding the Gap isn't easy.

2

Lost in Retail Space

*Giant sponges, swarming algae, and a
magic mirror that reflects the future*

Not only is shopping melting into everything, everything is melting
into shopping.
—Sze Tsung Leong, *Harvard Design Guide to Shopping*

STORES COME AND GO, A FACT OF LIFE ON
the Sell Side. Same-store sales are up, they're
down. Retailers are in, they're out, they're
out of business. Lord & Taylor has up and
vacated the Magnificent Mile—poof. A few
blocks to the south, the huge, loud, thump-
ing Virgin Megastore has also vanished,
replaced by a garish, cheap-chic Forever
21. Chicago stalwart Marshall Fields is no
more, ingested by Macy's. The year 2008 was
annus horribilis on the U.S. Sell Side, and 2009 will be far more *horribilis*.
Some 6,000 recognizable chain stores went dark in 2008, the largest percentage drop in a decade and a half. Starbucks announced the closing of nearly
1,000 stores; Foot Locker, Home Depot, Ann Taylor, Zales, hundreds more.
Penney's and Kohl's and Home Depot and countless others reported that
they are scaling back expansion plans. Linens-N-Things is threadbare. Cir-
cuit City has been liquidated. The nation's second-largest mall developer, a
billion dollars in debt, likewise threw in the towel.

Not to worry—even with a tanked economy we won't exhaust store supply anytime soon. The Sell Side isn't about to let us off the hook. There are—

I've given up trying to obtain a reliable count, nor does it much matter—at least a million stores in this country: mom-and-pop stores on the corner; convenience stores along the highway (150,000 nationwide, one out of ten of them in Texas); stores full of old junk or precious antiques; specialty stores with fine wood fixtures and halogen sparkle; spectacular flagship stores, Cathedrals of Brand; 200,000-square-foot supercenters and hyper-markets and warehouse megastores that stock everything from soy milk to USB cables under a single flat, steel-trussed roof; supermarkets intent on passing themselves off as purveyors of the authentic, the artisanal, the organic, and the locally grown; "pop-up" stores that spring up overnight, only to go away days or weeks later; plus other disappearing acts that come and go in the guise of concept stores or as promotional showcases for new products and brands. There are still, yes, department stores, which look more and more like white elephants, paler than their former selves but still palatial compared to the big-box stores hauled in on flatbed trucks, then bolted together. There are stores that never left, and stores that eventually moved back to, big-city downtowns; stores in crumbly strip malls; stores entombed in marble-tiled, climate-controlled malls with roaring fountains and concierges who gamely try to be of service, or at least make themselves heard over the thunderous cascade. There are the countless stores within zero driving distance from home or office, reachable via fiber optic cable, phone line, or wireless signal. How many sites are there, selling merchandise on the Web? Nobody has an accurate count. No matter, e-commerce is huge and growing huger year after year. In 2009 the Sell Side's online stores will do close to $200 billion of business, increasing at a rate far faster than sales at bricks-and-mortar stores. Web-*influenced* in-store sales amount to some $650 billion a year.

Shopping has melted into everything, according to an essay in the *Harvard Design School Guide to Shopping,* a phone-book-thick compendium of musings, maps, blueprints, and photographs that trace the rise and further rise of shopping over the course of human history, the past century in particular. The book devotes a generous chapter to the escalator, judged to be retail's most useful mechanical achievement, though I'd argue the honor ought to be shared with the revolving door. Retail, the book reminds us, has oozed its way into airports, office buildings, even rural villages (there's a Wal-Mart in tiny Dodgeville, Wisconsin, pop. 4,840, where Lands' End is headquartered). What had been a New Orleans funeral parlor, and before that the house in which Tennessee Williams wrote *Suddenly Last Summer*, is today a Borders bookstore. Shopping has melted into—utterly swamped—whatever patches of vacant scrubland or desert existed a decade ago. Untold acres of those patches are now home to thousands of those boxes that became the principal cause of agita for those Sears execs hunkered down at corporate HQ. Why would anyone of sound mind fight traffic to drive forty-five minutes to Sears when big-box category killers have melted into the space that lies between your house and the once appealing Sears mall, the one that now has all the cachet of a concrete bunker designed to withstand the blast of a daisy-cutter? A 2008 survey showed widespread dissatisfaction with malls. Our biggest complaints: same-old, same-old merchandise; same-old, same-old food selection. Indeed, Americans are so disenchanted with old-style suburban malls that over the past decade their numbers have steadily declined.* In 2005, the nation's top mall developer announced it would build no more of them, opting instead to erect "lifestyle centers," or "faux villages," as Paco Underhill, the prominent retail consultant, calls them. Until the economic meltdown turned off the jets that power thousands of gushing outdoor fountains, the lifestyle center was considered the Sell Side's hottest format. Not long ago I visited one such in Palm Beach County, Florida. This particular iteration of faux village is known as a "power hybrid": a lifestyle center anchored by a big box, in this case a massive Whole Foods complete with requisite boutique seafood counter. There was a twenty-one-screen multiplex that towered over a ring of upmarket restaurants and dozens of small shops, with condos all around the perimeter. It was, to quote a developer's pitch for a similar conglomeration: "a great place . . . that combines the sensory of hardscape, landscape, light fixtures, music, hanging baskets, architecture, storefronts, trees, banners [that] when woven together creates not a singular reaction but a total experience."

The purported appeal of such "town centers" is that they approximate what shopping *used* to be—kind of—back when our moms took us to

---

*For anyone inclined to celebrate America's de-malling or to pay respects to the very mall they aimlessly roamed as a teen, there's a Web site (Deadmalls.com) devoted to their passing. For mall necrophiliacs, the site is pure porn, offering a comprehensive glossary of terms for degrees of deterioration ranging from "dead malls" (high vacancy rate, decaying conditions) to "sealed malls" (closed to the public) to "shuttered malls" (literally boarded up with plywood, as if waiting/hoping for a Category 5 storm to put them out of their misery).

real downtowns for our school clothes, then a tongue on a kaiser roll sandwich, then maybe a movie if we behaved ourselves. A day in the life of a faux village offers many of the same amenities, as tailored to a post-Yuppie, "mixed use" sensibility. A Buy plus *primi platti*—penne alla vodka, hold the tongue. A Buy plus shooting the breeze with chums under a brightly colored market umbrella. At the Florida center I visited, there were so many market umbrellas you'd think you'd landed in Marseilles, except for the over-the-top water sculptures and fountains and gravelly New York accents booming out of the mouths of snowbirds. What exactly is the Sell Side selling with these lifestyle centers? It's selling the idea that the Buy is not just about buying but about feeling connection to a neighborhood, however ersatz. It's about experiencing a place that nods to what the great urban activist Jane Jacobs deemed the essential ingredients of a true, vibrant neighborhood: buildings designed on a human scale, a place dotted with cafés, bars, and theaters that encourage social interaction. Not that Jacobs would think much of lifestyle centers: she liked her neighborhoods organic, not prefabricated. She liked streets filled with diversity: kids, people of different colors and origins, longhairs and suits intermingled. That's not exactly what daily life in a faux village is about. It's usually about Talbots and J. Jill customers, women for whom shopping seems kinder and gentler when staged amidst cobblestones and reproductions of antique lampposts, where the only challenge to serenity is the forgotten art of parallel parking.

Sponges and Algae

Power hybrids, standalone shops, suburban malls, catalogs, e-commerce sites, all these are merely the Sell Side's front line. My time at Lands' End and Sears taught me that a company that exists to sell you things directly or indirectly—Amazon, Starbucks, Fidelity Investments, it doesn't matter—is an extraordinarily complex organism. To compete, it must be agile, shrewd, and sufficiently well-managed to be able to synchronize a host of complicated internal systems, or bodily functions: Product development. Supply chain. Distribution. Financial services. Technology services. Sourcing services. Store management. Asset protection. Merchandising. Communications. Packaging and design. Customer service. Advertising and marketing.

The failure of any of these functions can cause even the biggest and strongest Sell Side company serious harm in the marketplace, including slow, or surprisingly sudden, demise.

For now, let's ignore the tangle of those many departments and systems, all geared to sell us things we may or may not need or want. Instead, just to make it easy, think of a company that exists to sell us things—Crate and Barrel, H&M, Apple, Home Depot—as the simplest of organisms. Think of it as a sponge, not a Tuffy or a Scotch-Brite, but a real sponge, the sort that lives on the seabed and whose chief claim to anatomical fame is the capacity to pump water through its cells, filtering out the nutrients that enable it to live. A retail sponge also exists to pump. It pumps gross sales through its cells, from which it ultimately (with luck) filters out some bottom-line profit.

Like real sponges, companies that exist to sell us things need more than a little help from other life forms. Biologists call it "mutualism": a relationship between organisms by which both parties derive benefit. In the case of a marine sponge, benefit comes in the form of algae. Although algae turn sponges green, verdancy isn't the chief benefit a sponge derives from taking algae along for the ride. Algae provide sponges with what sponges need to grow to be big and strong: oxygen and sugars. In return, sponges keep algae alive by offering them surfaces to cling to. The Sell Side swarms with its own forms of algae, otherwise known as consultants, who specialize in systems that stores and Web sites depend on in order to be optimally performing sponges: bank check verification systems; ATMs, cash registers, and currency handling systems; collection services systems; wireless data transmission systems; in-store communications systems; customer-relationship management systems; "decision support" systems (customer satisfaction surveys, and so on); sales forecasting and inventory control systems; vendor assessment systems; labor scheduling systems; business intelligence systems (store traffic counters, for example); data mining and storage systems; in-store video and music systems; scanning technology systems; labeling and printing systems; marketing campaign management systems; gift certificate and gift card systems; price, promotion, and markdown optimization systems; alarms, safes, and hidden-camera security systems; distribution and warehouse systems.

Again, what chance do we have?

A Really BIG Show

The optimum time and place to observe the mutualism between Sell Side sponges and Sell Side algae is in January on the west side of Manhattan. It's here that the National Retail Federation holds its annual convention and expo, "Retail's BIG Show." It was to the BIG Show that I made my first pilgrimage beyond the Magnificent Mile. The convocation takes place in the mammoth Javits Center, with some 675,000 square feet of exhibition space. How big is that? A bit smaller than the size of the average regional shopping mall. Retail's BIG Show is overwhelming in scale and scope. Draped above the main hall are immense corporate banners belonging to the show's principal sponsors: systems-spewing algae such as IBM, Microsoft, Oracle, SAP, JDA. Less imposing but hardly modest are the company colors of many other big players who've paid significant premiums to unfurl their logos high above the exhibition floor: heavy hitters from the tech world (Cisco, Intel, Epson), financial services companies (Goldman Sachs, Amex, MasterCard). This is the power we're up against when we stroll into Macy's, the Gap, Pier One, Lowe's, or the Cheesecake Factory.

That the Sell Side gathers at the beginning of each calendar year has much to do with the fact that, for retail, January is the pits, which is another thing I learned at Lands' End and Sears.* With the all-important fourth quarter behind them, sponges and algae have a bit of downtime and they can get out of the store for a few days, take stock, celebrate strong holiday numbers or lick their wounds, take a gander at what's coming down the pike. January is also the time the rest of us take stock. We resolve to pay off, or at least pay down, credit card balances we ran up in the previous month or two, vow that we'll pare restaurant and vacation spending in the year ahead, promise to make healthier consumer choices, maybe lose twenty pounds. In January we join health clubs and buy elliptical trainers and treadmills, which we typically abandon the instant the weather breaks and we decide we could use some midwinter pick-me-ups (a flowery top, a hardtop convertible) to add a touch of spring to our step.

Armed with a hefty spiral-bound events program, I picked my way

---

*December is the biggest month for buying. November usually comes next, but not every year—global warming can play havoc with sales of sweaters and winter outerwear. May, June, and August are also heavy buying months, which isn't to say that we keep our powder completely dry in March, September, October, or, weather permitting (i.e., warm and sunny), in April. February, like January, is generally tepid.

through the BIG Show's endless maze of display booths, squeezing past 18,000-plus attendees, including several thousands who'd come from sixty-odd countries around the world. Having little reason to test-drive the latest and sexiest sales forecasting and inventory-control systems, I decided to sit in on a few presentations that promised to shed light on what all this mayhem has to do with how, when, where, and why we buy. By the end of the third day I'd distilled my impressions into a list, a miscellany of BIG Show takeaways:

1. We buy because the Sell Side has industrial-strength tools to monitor and adjust, continuously, the zillion variables that influence our decision making.

That's what all these systems at the BIG Show were about, all the immense computing power sitting under the Javits Center roof, why IBM, Microsoft, Intel, and hundreds of software development firms were in attendance, their minions uniformed in logo'd polo shirts. Ever advancing technology enables the Sell Side to test price promotions; project sales on the basis of long-term weather forecasts; calculate how many salespeople ought to be on the sales floor and at what time of the day and week; and match optimum merchandise mix to the ZIP code you live in, all of which—in theory—makes retailers more efficient and you and me more Buy vulnerable. Big winter storm about to roar through? Thanks to high-tech systems, a battalion of shiny new snowblowers are ready and waiting, surrounded by salesguys—not too many, not too few—ready to explain how the adjustable chute director is one sweetheart of an option given that long, sloping driveway of yours.

2. We buy because, even though most of us are inveterately impulsive and some of us hopelessly compulsive, the Sell Side knows that it helps to keep track of our unpredictable and bizarre behavior.

Trekking through the Javits Center, I took particular note of the weird lingo that echoed through the hall. "Clienteling," for example. According to a glossary maintained by a Sell Side algae firm, clienteling refers to "using data about an individual customer's buying habits and preferences during interactions in the store." It's but one of multiple entries in the retailspeak lexicon (another is "customer-centricity") that are stand-ins for what we used to call customer service, as in, back in the good old days: "Hi, Lee. You look terrific. How's the family? How's Ned's music coming along? Katherine applied to college yet? They grow up fast, don't they? Oh, before I forget. I know you really liked that maize windowpane sportcoat you bought last year, and I know you're pretty well stocked now that you're not punching the clock every day, but if you've got a minute, let me show you something that just came in and I think you'll love."

That old-style, one-on-one customer service "has long since disappeared," says an IBM brochure I picked up at the BIG Show. "[It] offered benefits to the customer and the retailer" but fell victim to "the interests of scale and growth." In its stead, the Sell Side hires IBM and others to deploy systems known variously as Customer Relationship Management, Customer Data Integration, and Customer Experience Management. Clienteling was a hot-button concept at the BIG Show. Understandable. It's hopeless for a big retail operation to try to keep track of us on anything like an up-close-and-personal basis, not least because retail salespeople turn over at such a fast clip. A big retail chain, however, endeavoring to record our past purchases and preferences, requires advanced computer technology and data storage. Consulting algae sell all sorts of tools to aid in this: database software, letter and e-mail templates, telephone scripts, policy guidelines pertaining to birthdays and special occasions, customer-segmentation programs, customer sales projections, salesperson evaluation models.

The clienteling brigade was out in force at the Javits Center, promising, as one consulting firm says in its mission statement, to "enable the sales associate to strengthen his/her relationship with their best customers by personalizing each encounter and taking responsibility for the customers [sic] satisfaction throughout the 'want-it, buy-it' use-it' [sic] experience." Taking a coffee break, I sat in a corner musing on the distinctions between "clienteling" and traditional one-to-one "customer service," and even drew a chart on the back of a media handout:

Traditional Customer Service	"Clienteling"
Middle-aged or really ancient salespeople.	Dynamic, cutting-edge sales force.
Human relationship–based. Tastes, preferences observed firsthand, jotted down for future reference.	Data-based. Past purchase history stored in hard drive/server. Keystroke retrievable.
Flows from the inside out. Owner-manager-employees drink the Kool-Aid.	Installed, serviced by third-party algae.

3. We buy because—notwithstanding all the clienteling systems, the hardware, the sales tracking and reporting software on display at the BIG Show —we are prisoners of desire.

A Sell Sider's success depends on accurately forecasting the directions in which our desires run, long and short term. A large subset of the Sell Side devotes itself to sniffing at new, seasonal concepts blowing in the wind, new ideas, products, styles that waft in from places that used to be far away but are now tightly bound into one big global Sell Side ecosystem. Trade publications wallow in seasonal and international trends. They wax poetic over them, or try to, as in this timely dispatch excerpted from a 2008 report published in *Chain Store Age*:

> Currently influenced by the green movement, global awareness and all things Asian, retail spaces are evolving to express the meaningful experiences shoppers seek.
>
> Color palettes are being taken from nature—grassy greens, spicy reds, fresh tones tempered with neutrals—along with natural forms, imagery and organic materials. Blond wood and Zen-like minimalism are the choice of upscale brands such as TSE and Jil Sander.
>
> Shoppers continue to place a high value on authenticity, which plays out in store materials . . . Segmented spaces rather than wide-open floor plans intrigue customers, as seen in Gilly Hicks and J. Crew's much buzzed-about Madewell . . .
>
> The Asian invasion is represented by MUJI, with its sleek simple household products . . .
>
> The urban influence is very much alive. Malls are welcoming Metropark, already 50 stores and growing, a hip and stylish destination that blends fashion, music, and art for the young.

At the BIG Show, trend sucking as furiously as I could, I attended a talk given by Brian Dyches, a top-billed presenter at Sell Side conferences worldwide. Dyches is a VP at Watt International, a Toronto-based global design and strategy firm. His BIG Show bio noted that he's an expert in "customer behavioral traits central to sales and retention strategies." In simpler terms, Dyches trend-hops through the zeitgeist of retailing *now*. He delivered a smooth PowerPoint show, video rich, graphically lush, dusting Sell Siders with insights into how susceptible we are to taking eye candy from strangers. His central theme was that design and packaging are the crucial triggers that spark our spontaneous decisions to buy. This was hardly news. For years, industry-leading marketers such as those who toil at Procter & Gamble have advanced the idea that there are serial "moments of truth" that influence *whether* we buy, whether we *like* what we buy, whether we buy what we buy *more than once*, and whether we *recommend* what we've bought to others. How many "moments of truth" there are depends on whom on the Sell Side you ask. Some Sell Siders say there are two moments of truth, some say there are three, and some say there a half dozen or more. The two moments of truth on everybody's list: the one that occurs when we make sensory contact with a product (does the product make a favorable first impression?) and the one that occurs when we take that something home and use it (does the product meet expectations?).

4. We buy because what we buy confers instant membership in a community or, more fashionably, a "tribe" consisting of other customers who for whatever reason impress us as hip, rich, sophisticated, or whatever we aspire to be.

Dyches devoted a portion of his talk to how stores and products need "attitude"—an "attitude" that reflects a customer's own "attitude." Apple gets it, Voss bottled water gets it, he said, flicking through his slides. Without attitude, bottled water is, you know, just water in a bottle, albeit a $15 billion industry. Dyches rhapsodized over how Voss sets its bottled water apart from the 10 billion gallons of bottled water Americans buy each year. The trick: Voss' ultrasleek bottle. It's plate-glass thick, with a blingy platinum cap, a bottle fit for superpremium vodka or designer fragrance—no accident given that the Voss bottle was designed by the former creative director at Calvin Klein. Here is bottled water glammed to the max, possessed of an attitude that may or may not prompt us to buy it but an attitude that certainly prompts us to take notice. Personally, I've never bought Voss water but I've certainly registered it, meaning I've had moment-of-truth collisions with it and even sampled it (it tastes exactly like water). The reason I've had these run-ins with Voss is because certain high-profile restaurants stock it and because Voss is often found in ultratrendy boutique hotels where I occasionally, and regrettably, find myself staying, hostelries in which the guest rooms are so chicly minuscule and minimally furnished that the Voss bottle on the tiny dresser effectively doubles as the room's most prominent appointment. But as I say, I've never actually *bought* a bottle of Voss water and doubt I ever will, no matter that the Voss Web site is so dedicated to driving home Voss's attitude it has a tab labeled Gossip. *Gossip? Bottled water?* Click the tab and you'll see dozens of photos of the rich and famous awash in Voss, the official bottled water at New York's Fashion Week, the Sundance Festival, the Emmy, SAG, and Golden Globe awards. Oh, and Miami Polo World Cup, where buff Argentine players quaff Voss between chukkers and bottles are freely dispensed to spectators cooling their Jimmy Choos in VIP tents.

5. We buy because buying is a way to assert our identity (real or idealized). We buy to express ourselves.

Brian Dyches devoted yet another section of his BIG Show talk to a roundup of other trends that algae firms routinely pass along to client-sponges so as to keep them tight with What's-Really-Happening-Out-There-This-Second. These trends included, at the time of the BIG Show I attended, "hobbynomics" (consumer spending on materials that enable customers to make things for themselves or to give as gifts); "hygenia" (which, if I understand it, is a global trend whereby we share information about locally produced goods, stripped bare of hype); and "snobmoddities" (once taken-for-granted commodities such as salt, rice, or lettuce cognoscenti now demand in dozens of specialized varieties which, needless to say, carry premium prices). And then there was "gravanity," a trend Dyches stressed was superhot, though it may well have come and gone by the time the ink dries on this page. Gravanity flitted onto consultants' radar a few years ago when the term popped up on Trendspotting.com, one of the many online sites the marketing community turns to when pulling together PowerPoint shows for retail clients. "Gravanity," a conflation of "graffiti" and "vanity," refers to our weakness for slapping our own name, face, or pearls of wisdom on consumer products and packaging. In 2008, for example, the Scion division of Toyota offered buyers the chance to paste their family's coat of arms—just choose from hundreds designed by graffiti artists—on the side of its odd-looking vehicle. The *New York Times* also brought news of CreditCovers, a Web site that sells "skins" for credit cards, graphic designs to paste over the front of your plastic. (Alternatively, you can log in at Capital One and upload a family portrait onto your card.) One of the more popular CreditCovers is a rendering of a whacked-out eagle and the words BLOODSUCKING FINANCIAL INSTITUTION. Timely, no? "Gravanity" is cousin to "mass personalization," which is now offered by numerous online sites: Nike.com, Converse.com, Oakley.com, to name just a few. These Sell Side brands invite you to choose among a range of product styles and color palettes that you can mix and match to create quasi one-of-a-kind pairs of sneakers and sunglasses. If "gravanity" is here to stay, think of it as further extension of what anthropologist Grant McCracken, in his perceptive *Culture and Consumption*, refers to as the "possession ritual": the "attempt to transfer meaning from [our] own world to [a] newly obtained good."

6. Finally, we buy because, well, unless you're a grab-and-goer or a wait-and-whiner, buying is fun, sociable, and diverting, an escape from boring, predictable existence.

This last takeaway was evident at what was clearly the biggest draw at the BIG Show that year. In an exhibition space dubbed "The Store of the Future," an installation addressed how shopping is rapidly melting into social networking. In other words, "social retailing," or "Facebook meets the mall," as Joseph Olewitz described it to me. Olewitz is a senior VP at IconNicholson, a New York–based "digital agency" that brings hot new technology to bear in back offices and on sales floors throughout the retail universe. Indeed, a broad range of high-tech, Buy-related R&D is being launched as we speak (e.g., search and IM services that enable us to check inventories while walking around a mall, seeing what's in stock where, and at what price). IconNicholson collaborated with Rem Koolhaas on the slick Prada store on the edge of SoHo in New York, where sales associates are wired—radio-frequency enabled—so they can ascertain in-stock sizes and styles without leaving you alone for a second to contemplate whether you, weak in the knees, are prepared to drop $500 on a pair of achingly adorable gold gladiator sandals.

What IconNicholson brought to *this* BIG Show was a supercool shopping tool in the form of a magic mirror. The little black dress shopping trip we took with my wife? Well, let's say Linda wasn't all that enamored of the prospect of us all crowding into that changing room yet still wanted third-party feedback on how she looked in the dresses she was trying on. Wait—not a good example. No offense to Linda, but the magic mirror is aimed chiefly at younger customers. So, take two: let's say that your daughter or mine needs a prom dress. While your daughter or mine is more than happy for us to *pay* for the dress, she would just as soon go shopping for the dress with friends, not us. But what if the right coterie of friends wasn't around? Here's where social retailing and the magic mirror race to the rescue. The magic mirror, Joseph Olewitz explained as I stood in front of it, is a three-paneled, interactive mirror installed just outside a store's changing room. A wall-mounted Webcam points in its direction. When your daughter or mine—say she's trying on a $300 Tadashi stretch satin prom dress with a neckline that gives us pause and a nervous-making side-slit skirt—steps in front of the mirror, she can not only look at herself in the mirror but, using a touch screen, instantly broadcast her image directly to friends' PDAs, cell phones, and computers, even to her parents', if only as a courtesy, given that she's toting our charge card in her purse.

But that's just the beginning of what the magic mirror can do. The device is connected to the store's Web site, which has been programmed to flash other prom dresses onto the screen, along with recommended shoes, bags, and jewelry judged to go well with each dress. Anyone who's plugged in via the Web can "vote" thumbs-up or -down on the dresses, send text messages ("u look weird☹" or "SWEEET!☺") and/or recommend that the young customer check out any or all of the other dresses suggested by the mirror. *Plus,* anyone who is signed in can place her own order for the onscreen merchandise. I asked Olewitz whether this IconNicholson technology could transform a customer into an electronic paper doll by enabling her to "try on" properly sized clothes beamed into the mirror—that way no one would ever again have to mess up her hair. He told me it was feasible, not a big deal. If and when the magic mirror is widely deployed, he said, a customer's exact physical specs would be programmed into the system via the store's VIP card program.

How many customers will want to social-shop electronically remains an open question. Management guru Peter Drucker observed that the only thing we know about the future is that it will be different, which goes double for the season-to-season, ever changing face of retail. A couple of months after the BIG Show, the magic mirror was demo'd for actual customers who happened to be passing through the Nanette Lapore boutique at Bloomingdale's on New York's Upper East Side. Linda, Katherine, and I walked over there one slushy winter morning. Stepping off the escalator, we saw a cluster of women gathered around the magic mirror. "Awesome!" one teenager exclaimed to a friend, then bravely stepped in front of the device. She punched in her height as a Canon HDV Webcam drank everything in, then dispatched the image through cyberspace to a site where, if the system were up and running for real, it could be viewed by selected address-book pals. Various other dresses were then digitally clienteled onto the mirror, but they didn't conform to the girl's size, and it was difficult to get a sense of how they would look in real life. But the kid did what she could to get a better sense: she stood on tiptoes to make herself taller, then flexed her knees to make herself shorter. It seemed to me that without the custom-sizing component, the magic mirror was not yet ready for prime time. The older women who had crowded around were somewhat intrigued, but with season after season of dressing room experience under their belts, they expressed doubts about the magic mirror. One middle-aged woman was particularly nonplussed. Turning to a friend, she wondered whether the magic mirror would prove to be more trouble than it was worth. "It might *lull* you into buying stuff," she said to her friend, "because it gives you a lot of suggestions and, yes, maybe because somebody out there tells you something looks good. But it wouldn't surprise me if those distractions resulted in a lot of returns."

I asked Katherine, who of course is Facebooked and MySpaced to the max (which is why advertisers have followed her into those once commercial-free sanctuaries), what she thought of the mirror. She pondered for a moment, then replied with a classic teenage shrug. And with that she turned and headed farther into the juniors department, nothing virtual about it.

3

How We Got Here

The coming of Gen Buy and the selling power of S-E-X

> The most serious offense many of the depth manipulators commit . . . is that they try to invade the privacy of our minds.
> —Vance Packard, *The Hidden Persuaders*

TIME NOW TO TAKE A STEP BACK, WAY back, from the magic mirror, if only to gain our bearings. To appreciate how the Sell Side brought us to where we are today and where it might be taking us—social retailing? a wonder drug to cure compulsive shopping?—it helps to look into a time-tested mirror, that is, the rearview mirror. There's no need in our journey for an exhaustive history of how the modern Buy came to be, but a detour now and then will help us keep things in focus.

Our daughter, Katherine, soon to enter college, and our son, Ned, now a college junior, are fourth-generation American shoppers. The first generation, Katherine and Ned's immigrant great-grandparents, fresh off the boat in the New World, didn't know from supercenters or magic mirrors. They knew from pushcarts. Come the weekend, they'd ride the trolley from the Lower East Side to a world newer and more improved than they ever bargained for. Imagine what it must have been like: to hop on at the corner of Scarcity and Subsistence and then, ten minutes later, hop off at the intersection of Abundance and Glitz. There they gazed in wonder as they walked through immense, astonishingly grand department stores filled with goods from around the globe—this was, after all, the dawning of the age of *choice*—where floorwalkers in white gloves served customers amid marble staircases and crystal chandeliers. These first-generation modern American shoppers pressed their noses to the display glass, gaped at the soaring skylights, and no doubt hoped to return one day not just to look but to buy. When they finally did join the party, material abundance would be hailed as the great social leveler, the American stand-in for socialism, as sociologist Daniel Bell would observe in *The Cultural Contradictions of Capitalism*.

Katherine and Ned's grandparents, second-generation modern American shoppers, also shopped from pushcarts, but only as little kids. Then they moved to a better neighborhood. Not to the suburbs, which were still around the corner, but to a part of town where stores were cleaner and more fully stocked than in the old neighborhood. Then came the Crash—the one before this one—that left everyone without the carfare to trolley over to the grand shopping palaces. Everybody was stuck, and for a good long while, at the corner of High and Dry.

The saga of third-generation modern American shoppers—that would be us, Linda and me—is by now all too familiar. Much as I'd like to move the story along and bring us back to the Sell Side of today and tomorrow, it's a good idea to linger here for a bit. In the fifties the Sell Side as we know it kicked into gear. The American economy exploded, but in a good way compared to now. More babies were born between 1948 and 1953 than during the prior thirty years, sociologist Todd Gitlin has pointed out. The Sell Side, well, it simply *adored* kids: strollers, cribs, car seats one day; hoop skirts, hot rods the next; breakfast cereal now and forever. In the ten years following World War II, new auto sales quadrupled. The Sell Side loved cars as much as it adored kids. "Shopping and leisure," Gitlin noted, were "retailored for an age of easy access. The [suburban] shopping center represented the possibility of consumption without limits." Suddenly America sparkled (chrome blenders)! America roared (dual carbs)! America hummed contentedly (air-conditioning)!

Haul out the family album and you'll see all of the above, preserved in now faded Kodacolor: the postwar family at play in a new nation, conceived in affluence and dedicated to the proposition that there was nowhere to go but higher and higher still. You'll see all-electric kitchens, Mixmasters, closets jammed with poodle skirts and saddle shoes, rec rooms strewn with bowling balls and hula hoops, garages full of Schwinns and Radio Flyers. You'll see an inflatable pool in every backyard, and not one but often two cars the size of *Queen Marys* parked in every driveway. You'll see a festival in "Populuxe," a term propagated by Thomas Hine, who published an illustrated retrospective on the era. Hine's book rings the usual bells: how ever more giant corporations created a bulging middle-class workforce; how shopping malls and supermarkets spread as rapidly and indiscriminately as crabgrass. It is this version of American "progress" that passes for what is by now the happy-face view of the 1950s.

But it was also in the fifties that America underwent a bloodless coup that transformed us from engaged citizens into self-indulgent consumers. We became, in the words of historian Lizabeth Cohen, a "Consumers' Republic." In this new political and economic order, to be middle class and white was to inherit a freshly minted, unalienable right: the pursuit of *stuff*. Indeed, to acquire more and more of it was tantamount to a patriotic imperative, so it's not surprising that merchants and Madison Avenue came to regard the postwar period as America's Great Leap Forward. Consumption ruled. Americans didn't have to *make* things to feel rich and happy, we just needed to buy things, whether we could afford them or not.

There were, however, some holdouts. Party poopers emerged, usually from behind ivy-covered walls, and tried to prick the Sell Side balloon. Prior generations, the poopers reminded us, had made it through Depression and war by virtue of their collective sacrifice, by making do. In the fifties, the poopers said, virtue was suddenly at risk. The fifties, they argued, was not a golden age so much as a fool's gold age of artificially induced spending and social insecurity. Close the photo album and imagine the landscape as seen through the poopers' eyes: ticky-tacky houses on the hillside; crowded commuter train platforms with faceless men in hats—perhaps your father among them—lined up to ride to the salt mines in the city; narcotized housewives—your mom, maybe?—pushing their new vacs; grinning dads—your dad, home from the mines?—in aprons and chef's hats, flipping the steaks. These images, the poopers contended, were symptomatic of a culture on its way to hell in a shopping cart. Mindless buying was turning society homogenous, rootless, something close to what Orwell had foreseen. John Kenneth Galbraith (*The Affluent Society*) underscored how high levels of production, abetted by Madison Avenue, conned us into consumption that made *the Sell Side* fat and happy, not us. William Whyte (*The Organiza-*

tion Man) and David Reisman *(The Lonely Crowd)*, the Bobbsey twins of postwar alienation theorists, lamented how mass marketing and corporate culture were sucking the air out of individuality, the result being a society of outer-directed, spendthrift conformists. "Thrift is now un-American," Whyte famously declared in a 1956 issue of *Fortune*. Sociologist C. Wright Mills *(White Collar)* piled on, addressing the issue of why the long faces on the guys waiting on that suburban train platform. Their Brooks Brothers suits, Hathaway shirts, and Worth & Worth fedoras were mere disguises. Those poor Joes were far from successful execs with power and authority to drive companies; they were uniformly outfitted and interchangeable cogs performing monotonous tasks within bureaucratic machines. How could they *not* down three martinis by noon or, when the weekend finally arrived, restore their flagging manhood by buffing, stroking, and Simonizing jutting tailfins? Galbraith and the others labored to make sure we understood that unchecked consumption would take a big bite out of the American spirit. They sent up warning flags that continue to flutter (listlessly) in contemporary classroom debates about how corporate interests and marketing propaganda play havoc with our values and psyches.

And yet, as I go around asking people of a certain age what they remember about the nervous-making side of fifties consumerism, I'm struck by the fact that all they remember are the ancient rumors about how movie theaters projected subliminal messages for three-thousandths of a second, every five seconds, as the feature played:

DRINKCOKE!EATPOPCORN!DRINKCOKE!EATPOPCORN!DRINKCOKE!

Or, a few years after that, how the Sell Side slyly retouched the ice cubes in liquor ads, spelling out S-E-X. They remember, sort of, that the Sell Side was rumored to be working on all sorts of weapons of mental disruption ("sneak pitches," they were called, prompting lawmakers to introduce bills to keep us safe from mind control).

Could it happen here? Did it happen here?

The movie theater rumor, of course, was a hoax—perpetrated by a man named James Vicary, a marketing guy, natch. In the early sixties Vicary fessed up to the *DRINKCOKE!EATPOPCORN!* prank, admitting that he did it—why else?—to drum up new clients. S-E-X in the ice cubes? Likewise the work of an overactive imagination. Yet in the fifties, such manipulations were imaginable. "Mind control" had been in the headlines for years. Stalin and Mao used it in the name of the Party. Captured GIs in Korea refused to return to the States even when free to do so—brainwashed, obviously. Orwell's *1984* and Koestler's *Darkness at Noon* reinforced the fear that "they"—in the persons of Communist tyrants or even Madison Avenue slick biscuits—had means and motive to mind-control every one of us into helpless submission. Science, after all, could do just about anything. If concerted R&D could produce the Bomb, cure polio, unravel the double helix, and eventually launch men into space, why couldn't it, in the wrong hands, induce Joe Six-Pack to switch from Pabst to Budweiser? Or turn a sane suburban housewife into a stay-at-home junkie hooked on Miltown, the so-called "Happy Pill" marketed by Wallace Labs, the era's tranquilizer of choice?

Hidden and Forbidden

If people remember this scary business at all, it has little to do Galbraith, Whyte, Mills, Reisman, and other Ivy League party poopers, and much to do with a self-described "backwater farm boy" educated at Penn State, a mere journalist. Vance Packard, more than anyone, planted the seed that dark forces conspire behind the Sell Side's drawn Venetian blinds and that the Sell Side's scheme was to voodoo rational beings into buying goods for no reason beyond its own insatiable interests. Packard's investigations caused consumers to raise their defenses a notch or two. In today's terms, Packard put us on alert—threat level orange, give or take.

I was too young to be much interested in Packard's books, but I do remember leafing through a few. My parents had a number of his titles, mostly paperbacks, lined up neatly on the knotty-pine shelves recessed into the knotty-pine paneling in the basement of our Philadelphia row house. Our house was far from a perfect expression of Populuxe interior design. No Jetson furniture, barely a stick of Scandinavian. We did of course have a black-and-white TV embedded in a mammoth mahogany cabinet, and a *partially* all-electric kitchen in the form of a portable, automatic dishwasher. My father had it delivered one Mother's Day, a state-of-the-art scullery maid on wheels with a Formica wood-grained lid. Every evening after dinner we rolled it over to the sink, attached a rubber hose to the faucet, and exulted—or at least my mother did—in the brave new world of convenient living.

As for those knotty-pine shelves in the basement, they held solid evidence to support Todd Gitlin's view that in the fifties people were transforming into middle-class "cultural omnivores," spending more and more money on books, magazine subscriptions, prints and posters, and LPs, from Belafonte to Bach. Our knotty-pine-paneled *bibliothèque* housed, alongside Packard's books, a set of the World Book Encyclopedia and a seemingly priceless (to a kid) collection of Reader's Digest Condensed Books pretentiously designed to pass for leather-bound literary classics, even if all they bound were abridgments of such literary luminaries as Cleveland Amory and Irving Stone. Oh, and also on those shelves—these I remember vividly because I read the dirty bits over and over—were a number of steamy novels by writers such as James Gould Cozzens (*By Love Possessed*), Grace Metalious (*Peyton Place*), and John O'Hara (*Butterfield 8*).

The television, the dishwasher, and the potboilers are long gone, no doubt buried deep inside a landfill that now lies beneath a shopping complex or Sell Side distribution warehouse somewhere in the Delaware Valley. Inexplicably, I still have my parents' old copy of Vance Packard's *The Hidden Persuaders*—though I can't begin to understand how it survived multiple moves and my once- or twice-a-decade purge of books no longer wanted. The paperback sits on my desk right now: a little red Cardinal edition (price thirty-five cents). The spine is cracked. Its pages turned a sickly yellow many purges ago. When Katherine picked it up the other day, she looked at it as if it were the paperback edition of the Dead Sea Scrolls.

A Vance Packard exposé—a drumbeat of damning evidence conveyed with indignation that stops just short of hysteria—hewed to a formula that left readers squirming in their Jetson chairs. From the midfifties to the early seventies, cultural omnivores gobbled up Packard's trademarked brand of investigative reporting. Three of his books, published within a three-year span, made it to the top of nonfiction best-seller lists: *The Hidden Persuaders* (1957), *The Status Seekers* (1959), and *The Waste Makers* (1960). Then came *The Pyramid Climbers* (1962), *The Naked Society* (1964), *The Sexual Wilderness* (1968), *A Nation of Strangers* (1972). They delivered a common message: American values and ordinary folks were under siege, for reasons observed by those erudite party poopers. Packard made the same points, but in a voice middle-class readers found more convincing. America, once the land of opportunity and fair play, was riddled with greed, plundered by fat cats. To reread Packard today is to detect trace elements of Upton Sinclair, Rachel Carson, Ralph Nader, Betty Friedan (who decried advertising's thought control of women), plus a soupçon of Lou Dobbs. Certainly more than Galbraith and the other intellectual fancy pants, Packard knew how to push the mass market's panic button.

I open the brittle paperback and try to imagine myself sipping Bosco, snug in a Naugahyde lounger. Packard lays it right on the line, page 1: " . . . large scale efforts [are] being made, often with impressive success, to channel our unthinking habits, our purchasing decisions, and our thought processes by the use of insights gleaned from psychiatry and the social sciences." Then, in little more than two hundred breezy pages, Packard persuades us that the modern Sell Side is far from benign. To the contrary, it's sophisticated, cynical, and scheming. It possesses an array of ingenious methods, and it's not afraid to use them. The Sell Side toys with our senses, pokes at our low-self esteem, exploits our hypochondria, stokes our fear of aging and death. It's all right here in my crumbling copy of *The Hidden Persuaders*. Carefully turning the pages, I find a welter of reasons why we harbor distrust of Sell Side motives and slippery tricks:

1. *Sell Side operatives won't rest until they have broken through to the fundamental* why *of why we buy.* Why? "So they can effectively manipulate our habits and choices in their favor."

2. *The Sell Side knows that (a) we are hopelessly gullible, and (b) consistently irrational, which only serves to incite marketers' methodical efforts to snare us in their web.*

3. *The Sell Side looks down on us as trifling "bundles of daydreams, misty hidden yearnings, guilt complexes, irrational emotional blockages. We are image lovers given to impulsive and compulsive acts."* This the Sell Side likes about us. What it doesn't care for is how our emotions flit about like hard-to-swat moths. "We annoy them," Packard says, "with our seemingly senseless quirks."

4. *The Sell Side, undeterred by our fecklessness, attacks us with an arsenal of weapons, including hired guns.* Packard yanks up the

shades to expose the Sell Side's backup force of mercenaries. There are conspirators he calls the "depth boys," a principal focus of *The Hidden Persuaders*. Depth boys are social scientists who test and tinker with our emotional hang-ups. Then there are the "nose counters"—quantitative researchers—who work up elaborate statistical profiles of us based on gender, age, geography, and household type. Many of these mercenaries are recruited from our leading universities and medical schools. *"Whiskers,"* Packard calls them, *"buck happy"* whiskers who'd caved in to the bonanza of money and recognition gained by renting out their labs and consulting services to Madison Avenue.

5. *The Sell Side harbors secret insights into us (and our kids). We don't always know what we want, and even when we do, we don't know how to communicate what we want.* By way of example, Packard cites a survey of men who express a preference for "a nice dry beer." When asked what makes for "a nice dry beer," the dolts just sit there with their teeth in their mouths. The Sell Side is onto how we don't always tell the truth about why we buy what we buy, even when we *do* know why we buy what we buy. We lie like rugs. We puff ourselves up. The Sell Side exploits the fact that we are a confused mass of fears and insecurities, profoundly repressed. Here *The Hidden Persuaders* hits its stride. The Sell Side preys on these weaknesses with everything it's got: through the wording of its ad copy and the visual imagery it disseminates to deceive us via print, radio, and that hulking cyclops that squats in the corner of the living room.

The evil mission—when you add all of this all up—is to dangle the promise of relief from the emotional conflicts and insecurities that wrack us. To sell soup, they invoke the comfort of the womb. *Soup! It's warm, protective, nourishing.* To sell prunes, they avoid any association with "prune face" and any association with prunes' principal utility. No, they celebrate *Prunes! The wonder fruit! A healthy alternative to candy!* In this manner, the Sell Side— whether it's selling cake mixes or motorboats or feminine hygiene sprays— exploits our seemingly unquenchable need for:

- Emotional security
- Reassurance of our own worth
- Ego gratification
- Creative outlet
- Love objects
- Power
- A sense of place
- Immortality

I carefully return the paperback to its place on my bookshelf. Packard's allusion to immortality is curious, it strikes me. The point he's making here is a narrow one, just a few pages devoted to the selling of life insurance. He quotes an adman who contends that men buy life insurance because, *deep down*, a life insurance policy will enable them "to dominate their families; to control the family standard of living, and to guide the education of their children long after they are gone." But the more I think about it, the more I sense that Packard has stumbled onto something important here. The Buy = immortality? Something fetching in that. In the rush to crank out another best seller, however, Packard didn't stop long enough to think it through, to realize that the reach for immortality may have much more to do with the Buy, the ultimate *why* of it, than he or any brainwasher ever imagined. I make a note to look into the relationship between the Buy and immortality, but I do so on a clean sheet of paper, not wanting to deface my departed parents' copy of *The Hidden Persuaders*.

Seeking some fresh insight into Packard and his influence on the times, I looked up Daniel Horowitz. A history professor at Smith College, Horowitz published an admirable biography of Packard in 1994, two years before the muckraker's death. Over the course of nine years, the two spent innumerable hours together in Packard's comfortable home in New Canaan, Connecticut, a wealthy and WASPy suburb, the prototypical adman's bedroom community of choice. Packard was eager to cooperate, Horowitz told me, providing forty boxes of materials and a copying machine, and opening doors by introducing Horowitz to friends and former colleagues. Packard was, Horowitz said, an exceedingly warm and generous man but keenly concerned about his place in American social history. He never made peace with the fact that he hadn't achieved the public-intellectual status accorded to Galbraith and the other celebrated party poopers, no matter that *his* books sold in the tens of millions and that he lived prosperously in a $3 million suburban house and also owned a fifty-acre property on Chappaquiddick Island, a clam toss from Martha's Vineyard. Packard, Horowitz recalled, was somewhat uncomfortable with his wealth, a populist farm kid to the end, a liberal who would have voted for Obama. I asked how Packard would view the Buy world of the past couple of decades.

"He'd be horrified," Horowitz replied. "Horrified and fascinated, too. He'd probably see this as a New Gilded Age, utterly astonished that so many millions, the middle class in particular, take granite countertops and Sub-Zeros completely for granted."

S-E-X on the Brain

Maybe it was the brittle little book, maybe it was the ice cubes in my highball, but lately I've had little more than S-E-X on the brain whenever I look at advertising. I'm not the only one, of course. The other night my wife and I, along with some friends from Wisconsin, were driving to a restaurant in Chicago. The Wisconsin woman asked how this book was coming along—what's it about, anyway? I said that it's about how people shop and buy, and that the first part deals with how the Sell Side gropes at customers from various angles. The woman—intelligent, progressive, committed to preserving native prairie grasses—launched into a diatribe worthy of a Victorian Buy Scold: "It's all about sex, isn't it? Every commercial: sex, sex, sex. They use sex to sell everything. That's what they use to hook us—sex."

Well, there's certainly reason to look at it that way, I answered, not mentioning that earlier in the day I'd spied a billboard advertising Effen vodka at the exact instant a kid in a FCUK T-shirt shuffled by. Nor did I cite a research tidbit that indicated that young adults were 65 percent more likely than adults to encounter ads with models wearing sexually revealing clothes, and 128 percent more likely to encounter sexual activity going on in ads. Instead, I reminded her that Vance Packard warned us of the Sell Side's filthy dirty tricks half a century ago, that advertisers allegedly used, still use, techniques designed to tap into deep-seated impulses that supposedly motivate us to buy. I explained that there are Sell Side consultants out there, a ton of them, who specialize not in the what, the when, or the where of the Buy, but the *why* of it. They're called motivation researchers, I told her. For decades they've been interviewing us, delving, probing, recording our free associations and especially our subconscious fantasies, fetishes, and sexual hang-ups. Once we'd been seated at the restaurant, I was tempted to hold court with anecdotes about how motivation research came into its own—juicy dinner conversation—but a wifely under-the-table kick told me to save it for the book, so here goes:

In *The Hidden Persuaders*, Vance Packard's leading no-goodnik was a balding, bow-tie-wearing, more-jaunty-than-mad social scientist by the name of Ernest Dichter. He operated out of a twenty-six-room stone house overlooking the Hudson River a few miles north of New York City. The castlelike pile had eleven bathrooms and a sixty-five-foot living room. From this house, Packard reported, at the end of a (cue the lightning) "rough, winding road," Dichter's Institute for Motivational Research conducted hush-hush experiments underwritten by a plethora of leading consumer companies, including General Mills, American Airlines, and Lever Brothers. Packard took us on a tiptoe tour through Dichter's Transylvania-on-the-Hudson headquarters, past a TV room filled with kids, where there are "concealed screens behind which unseen observers sometimes crouch, and tape recorders are planted . . . to pick up the children's happy or scornful comments." Elsewhere on the grounds there were "psycho-panel" files on hundreds of local families "charted as to their emotional make-up. The institute," Packard revealed, "knows precisely how secure, ambitious, realistic, and neurotic each member is [and] by trying out various subtle advertising appeals can purportedly tell what the response might be to a product geared, say, to the hypochondriac and social climber."

Dichter, the lord of this mysterious manor, was born in Vienna. In the mid-1930s he worked his way through university, picking up a bit of Sell Side experience and a few schillings decorating the windows of his uncle's department store. Before fleeing Austria and the eventual Nazi occupation, Dichter maintained a modest, at-home psychoanalytic practice notable only for the fact that he saw patients in a flat directly across the street from Freud's famed office at number 19 Berggasse. Once in the States, Dichter wrote letters to numerous companies not so subtly associating himself with Freudianism. The letters suggested he could help companies become more effective selling agents through a keener understanding of the hidden emotions that drive our behavior.

The publishers of *Esquire*, still in its early years, were among the first to take a meeting with Dichter. Back then *Esquire* offered male readers an intoxicating brew: stories by the likes of Hemingway and Fitzgerald sandwiched between amply bosomed, impossibly long-legged, achingly gorgeous and not-quite-naked pinups. It wasn't Hemingway or Fitzgerald Dichter wanted to talk about when he finally sat down with the magazine's sales execs. His pitch was that *Esquire* had an opportunity to gain greater advertising share, a "finding" he'd arrived at after "extensive research." The research indicated that when men look at pictures of nudes (or, in this case, near nudes, but nude enough), their pupils open wide, which in turn makes men "more attentive to visual stimuli" of any sort. Facing what I can only imagine to be a roomful of blank stares, Dichter explained that when a man is visually aroused, he is far more likely to pay attention to advertising, advertising being visually intensive. *Zees ees your competitive advantage*, Dichter told the *Esquire* team. "It pays to advertise in *Esquire* because [advertisers] will be appealing to readers whose eyes are more widely open than when they read other publications."

Indeed, and to say the least, Dichter would not be the only researcher to draw the connection between sexual stimuli and the urge to buy. Just a few years ago, a large-scale, eyeball tracking study indicated that men do pay greater attention to ads featuring female sexual imagery. It found that breasts, legs, and exposed skin serve to raise a man's *intention* to buy products featured in ads oozing female pulchritude. But there was a caveat, overlooked (or conveniently ignored) by Dichter that day in the *Esquire* conference room: when the eyeball-aroused subjects were later asked to identify the *logos* of the products featured in the sexy ads, their brand recall was, at best, flaccid. Their attention had been directed elsewhere.

For Dichter, the notion that we buy in response to motivations buried in our cranial muck set him on the path to a remarkable career. In no time he had Madison Avenue eating Sacher tortes out of the palm of his hand. Through the fifties America experienced an abiding infatuation with Freudian theory, which posited convincing psychological explanations for why company men in the city and housewives in the suburbs downed martinis and gobbled Miltown. Numerous sources of angst festered beneath the bucolic surface of white-collar tranquility—Rat Race Angst. Finger-on-the-Button Angst. Too-Damn-Many-Kids-Underfoot Angst. Dichter sold the

Sell Side on the idea that it should hire him to burrow into the strata beneath what he described as "the smooth, lush, green fertile lawn of the human personality." Through psycho-aeration of that lawn, he could get at what was "hollow, rotten, and cavernous underneath." Thus would Dichter drag American shoppers to the couch, pull up a chair, adjust his horn-rims, and proceed to pry us open. His "in-depth" interviews were built on the conviction that our Buys have less to do with what we *say* we do in stores and almost everything to do with underlying issues, mainly repressed desires and anxieties concerning our sexual identity.

Throughout his voluminous and shamelessly self-serving writings, Dichter variously referred to himself as a "detective," a "cultural anthropologist," and a "social engineer." He was no less a determined swordsman. His memoir, *Getting Motivated*, might well have been titled *Getting Laid*. He confessed to a "half-open marriage" with his beloved wife, Hedy. Between accounts of the many brilliant ad strategies inspired by his relentless probing, Dichter took time to chronicle an episode with a young prostitute in Zanzibar, an encounter ruined because the woman yawned just as Dichter was ready to get down to business. He recounted how he liked to "play" with his "very sexy secretary," a woman given to low-cut blouses who was more than delighted to accede to the good doctor's request that she lean over suggestively when proffering dictation notes. The couple consummated "on top of a very uncomfortable desk in an unoccupied conference room," Dichter reported.

Mostly, though, Dichter's memoirs focused on how he was able to brilliantly channel Freud to convince Madison Avenue that effective selling is selling that pokes at customers' nerve endings, sexual ones, for the most part. "I am absolutely not compulsive about seeing [sex] in every product and every analysis," he declared, and yet:

- Men favor a crease down their trouser legs because it smacks of an erection.

- Women buy lipstick because lipstick is an antidote to "pale blue lips [which] are the sign of old age and death." And because "lips are a sexual organ." In some so-called primitive tribes, Dichter related, "not only are the . . . lips of the face painted, but also the lips of the vagina."

• We buy soap—or can be induced to buy *Ivory* soap, a Dichter client—"to get rid of [our] psychological dirt and guilt feelings."

• We don't—or didn't—buy the Edsel because a clueless Ford designer had "castrated" the car before it hit the streets. In *Getting Motivated*, Dichter wrote: "[The Edsel] had a gaping hole at the front end. Our survey showed that the otherwise inhibited Americans were referring to this oval shaped opening either as a lemon or, the more outspoken ones, as a hole which needed a bit of pubic hair around it to make it more real."

Lipstick = labial adornment?

The Edsel = castrato? A Brazilian wax job on wheels?

Even if Dichter and his many disciples were occasionally full of Austrian baloney, their message was profound: effective selling is selling that attacks Puritanism at its roots. Effective selling is selling that gets us to unzip, to slip out of our emotional hang-ups into something that promises to be more comfortable, powerful, and sexy. This message proved particularly persuasive in two major Sell Side shopping arenas: the car showroom and the supermarket.

On the automotive Sell Side, Dichter's rise came at a time when America was still wed to Detroit, notwithstanding early indications that a marriage breaker loomed across the Pacific. In 1957, CBS news correspondent Robert Pierpoint, reporting from inside a vehicle the *New York Times* referred to as "oddly small," predicted, "someday, you too may be driving a car made in Japan." It's far from fair to ask Dichter and other early motivation researchers to take the fall for how American carmakers blew it. Prominent among Detroit's other deficiencies, wrote Theodore Levitt in the *Harvard Business Review*, has been a congenital marketing blind spot: a knack for *not* asking customers about the kinds of cars they want, but asking them instead to choose among the cars Detroit already offers. An industry, in other words, hopelessly product oriented, not customer oriented.

But Dichter didn't do Detroit any favors, either. His views on the psychosexuality of automobiles reinforced Detroit's long-standing macho delusions, a case of the brainwasher brainwashing the braindead. In Dichter's view, as surely as a man's home was his castle, the car in the castle's driveway was his Johnson. He sold Detroit on the idea that a showroom is alive with erotic signals and muffled fantasies, practically a red-light district. He told carmakers that when he flicked open the hood of the male psyche, he saw that a man shopping for a car is a highly conflicted beast. When a man looks at a boxy sedan, he sees his wife. When he looks at a sporty, top-down convertible, he sees someone akin to the secretary Dichter mounted in the conference room: a high-gloss, high-performance doxy with zero guilt emissions and requiring no emotional upkeep. So, even if you want to sell sedans, Dichter told auto dealers, make sure there are always peppy ragtops—tarts, hookers, busty secretaries, in effect—featured in your ads or parked out in front to keep the car buyer's hormones pumping.

The other principal arena, the supermarket, likewise provided a generous slab of business for Dichter and other motivation researchers. Dichter tirelessly advanced the idea that certain foods emit specific sexual signals. Red meat screams "male." Baked goods purr "female." Soup, Dichter wrote, "is the brew of the good fairy. . . . It protects, heals, and gives strength, courage, and the feeling of belonging." The cereal aisle in particular was paved with interpretive opportunity, the fifties being the golden age of all grains flaked, shredded, toasted, and puffed. Dichter was expansive on the subject of rice. In a memo to the Leo Burnett agency, he referred to "unmistakable" evidence that rice—to include Rice Krispies—was inherently female and declared that many of his subjects "subconsciously associate it with biological phenomena." Just think about it: "Rice gains life as it cooks. It expands and swells . . . ready to burst with new life at any moment. The babbling, boiling water contributes added realism to this . . . pseudo-birth." Moving over to the dairy department, Dichter was onto moving milk long before "Got Milk?" came along. Men know that milk is nutritious, but if you want to get them to drink *more* milk, he suggested, prompt them somehow to think "breasts." Finally, over in the produce section, Dichter expounded on the psychosexuality of assorted fruits and vegetables. In his *Handbook of Consumer Motivations*, he notes that Europeans have "almost a fetish" for asparagus, their pleasure enhanced by the fact that asparagus stalks are "handled by hand without fork and knife, dipped into sauce, and plunged into the mouth."

Thanks to Dichter's indefatigable self-promotion, motivation research became, and remains, a fixture in the Sell Side's toolkit, with sex its most favored, multipurpose sales tool. By the late fifties, according to David Bennett in a paper titled "Getting the Id to Go Shopping," more than eighty registered MR firms were peddling assistance to marketers. And the Advertising Research Foundation came out with an industry dictionary that included entries for "anal eroticism," "mother-fixation," and "abreaction," a Freudian term that refers to catharsis gained through "reliving" a traumatic experience (as in, say, "I can't believe I ate the whole thing").

Drill, Baby, Drill

Motivation research is widely practiced today, much as it was in Dichter's time. It remains a mining operation. There's gray muck in your head awash in emotional needs and repressed desire. Motivation researchers, working at the behest of those intent on selling us things, maintain that if they can penetrate the muck and get their mitts around those needs and desires, they can extract marketing gold:

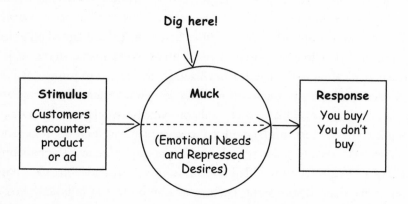

And so even today, on college campuses and in office buildings, at the end of the workday motivation researchers usher willing participants into stuffy, windowless rooms, ply them with Skittles and Fanta, subject them to sentence-completion games, inkblot tests, and free-association exercises. Then they turn what muck they collect over to ad agencies whose assignment is to come up with a jingle or a slogan that hits the B-spot, i.e., our Buy impulse.

With all its digging and sifting, motivation research is more time-consuming than quantitative, or numbers-based, research. But it offers up leads that simple surveys can't. Milk producers want to sell you more milk, but before they hit on a solution they need to figure out the problem. The quantitative approach calls for hiring researchers who collar you in the mall and ask whether you buy and drink milk. You say no. The questioner checks the "No" box, asks a few more straightforward questions, then moves on to ambush others. Each encounter yields data points that tell the Sell Side what percentage of you, say, between ages twenty-five and forty-nine, drink little or no milk. An ad agency team then sits down in a conference room to figure out what to do with that knowledge.

Motivation researchers don't let you off the hook nearly so easily. They lead you into a room, offer you Skittles, then probe your innermost *feelings* about milk. You tell the inquisitor that while you know milk is good for your kids, as far as your own consumption goes, you don't drink regular milk because it's too high in fat, and skim milk, in your opinion, is watery and tasteless. Milk is boring, you tell the researcher, except when you chugalug it to wash down a chocolate chip cookie or a peanut butter and jelly sandwich, both of which you crave though you try to resist. "Hmm, just curious," says the interviewer, "but you seem a little anxious—can you tell me why?" You confess that you're trying to lose weight, that the tire around your middle hangs like a dead manatee around your self-esteem, that you'd like to be fit and sexy. The motivation researcher excuses you and you go home, feeling guilty about how many Skittles you ate.

An analysis of your "in-depth" input now goes to the folks back at the ad agency. What they come up with is "Got milk?," considered one of the most effective ad campaigns of the past decade. Millions see and enjoy the ads and, thanks to your input, the campaign successfully motivates people to drink more milk. Initially the "Got milk?" ads and commercials played on your weakness for cookies and peanut butter and jelly. One of them depicted how deprived you feel when you go to wash down a chocolate chip cookie only to open the fridge and discover that you've got no milk. Another ad showed a chocolate chip cookie with a bite taken out. Next to it, only two words: "Got milk?" Linking milk to deprivation turned out to be a winning message, and the sale of milk rose.* Over time, "Got milk?" evolved to tap into those other comments you made at your "in-depth" interview: the desire to be fit, look healthy, stay vital—the way Serena Williams comes

---

*Not all consumers react the same way, however. There are ethnic, cultural, and social differences among us. For example, milk as deprivation relief doesn't fly in the Hispanic community. Says one Hispanic advertising exec, "There's already enough deprivation."

across in one of the later "Got milk?" ads. Serena's photographed in a sleek white Nike tennis dress and matching white milk mustache ("Serve by Serena. Body by milk."). A subsequent ad likewise connected with your desire to be fit and sexy: Glenn Close, no worse for wear at age sixty-one, photographed in a smart white shirt, white vest, matching white milk mustache, shimmering black tights, and four-inch heels. Fatally attractive, Close leans back languidly in a director's chair, her eyes gently closed as if recalling a moment of supreme ecstasy, one rarely associated with a peanut butter and jelly sandwich. The accompanying copy reiterates what the motivation researchers found buried in your muck. It reads: "To perform my best, I need to give my body the attention it deserves. That's why I eat right, exercise and drink milk."

Dichter Lives!

Now that I've got S-E-X on the brain—it'll pass, I fear—I can't help but discern Ernest Dichter's influence on many ads I now see, not to mention classic campaigns that ran for years and seemed quite innocent at the time. The other day I came across a 1999 special edition of *Advertising Age*, the leading Madison Avenue trade publication. Like many other magazines, *Ad Age* had pulled together a retrospective of the passing century. Among the many lists and timelines was the editors' choice of the ten top jingles from the solid gold century of advertising-jingle writing:

1. You deserve a break today.
2. Be all that you can be.
3. Pepsi-Cola hits the spot.
4. M'm, m'm good.
5. See the USA in your Chevrolet.
6. Oh, I wish I were an Oscar Mayer wiener.
7. Double your pleasure, double your fun.
8. Winston tastes good like a cigarette should.
9. It's the Real Thing.
10. A little dab'll do ya.*

---

*That is, a little dab of Brylcreem, for those too young ever to have dabbed it.

Now, consider those jingles again, this time through Ernest Dichter's horn-rim specs. Hear what I hear? Nine of the ten flirt salaciously with S-E-X. Seven of the ten connect to a longing for oral gratification. The only jingle that doesn't nod to fore-pleasure or end-pleasure has S-E-X already built in—bosomy, blond Dinah Shore belted out "See the USA in your Chevrolet" every week on TV. Here are those jingles again, this time with their hidden psychosexual cues added:

1. You deserve a break today (*orgasm*).
2. Be all that you can be (*buff*).
3. Pepsi-Cola hits the spot (*uh-huh, that spot*).
4. M'm, m'm good (for you and me *both!*).
5. See the USA in your Chevrolet (see Dinah Shore, above).
6. Oh, I wish I were an Oscar Mayer wiener (*self-explanatory*).
7. Double your pleasure, double your fun (*ménage à trois*).
8. Winston tastes good like a cigarette should (*cylindrical object inserted in mouth*).
9. It's the Real Thing (*as opposed to faking it*).
10. A little dab'll do ya (*lubricity*).

So, you tell me: were these merely puerile little ditties? Or were they orchestrated attempts to sell mundane products by appealing to the repressed buyer's inner tar pit?

4

Downtown

In the land of merchant princes, there lurks a master spy

One feels as if under a microscope when walking down one of those broad aisles.

—Anonymous female department store shopper, 1891

WE WALK INTO ONE OF THE MILLION OR so stores in the country. What we're shopping for doesn't matter: wieners, a red doxy of a sports car, a little black dress. Ernest Dichter would have us believe that some sort of magma is gurgling inside our skulls. Maybe it is, maybe it isn't. As far as we can tell, we're just shopping. Maybe we're on the lookout for something new and different. Maybe we're just trying to escape boredom, the condition that stems from the "lack of a *personal* connection with the external world," as Saul Bellow described it in *Humboldt's Gift*. Maybe we're shopping for something that expresses personal identity. Or maybe we're on the prowl for something that will induce others to think well of us: a smart deal, a flattering accoutrement, an advertisement for ourselves. Well, maybe we're not exactly *thinking* about any of this. What's going on inside is a flow of shards, snippets, half-thoughts, and images adrift in a stream of consciousness. Sort of the way critic James Wood describes stream of consciousness on a page: a "movement of the mind," "a gesture to what cannot be said." That's often how *I* feel when I'm wandering around a store. *Hot in here. Monkey-puke yellow. What time's the game? Should walk the dog. Not me. Cool.*

While all this rattles around inside, on the outside we're naked and exposed. Sell Side eyeballs are trained in our direction. We don't relish this scrutiny; we may not deserve it. Still, to the Sell Side, each of us is a person of intense interest, which is why the Sell Side has put us under surveillance:

1. We're security breaches waiting to happen.

High-resolution video cams track our progress up and down the aisles, sending digital images through a relay server to faceless agents hunkered down in undisclosed locations. An oft-delayed, proposed new shopping complex in New Jersey—The Meadowlands Xanadu, complete with Pepsi Globe, America's largest Ferris wheel—boasts that it will have three hundred fixed and "pan-tilt-zoom" cameras indoors and out, assuming the mall ever opens.

More commonly, as we enter smaller shops we get a once-over from the guy at the door, who's big as a mountain, has a shaved head, wears a black suit and thick rubber-soled butt-kicking Oxfords, a stud in one ear, an earpiece in the other. Salespeople, if there *are* any damn salespeople, also shoot glances our way, something they've been trained to do. Management has pounded them—as Target pounded me during my orientation—with facts about the high cost of shoplifting, a major component of what the Sell Side calls shrinkage. Target made sure I understood that shrinkage in general and shoplifting in particular take huge bites out of wages and benefits (assuming team members have benefits). My eyeballs were key weapons in the Global War on Shrinkage, the first line of defense when it came to "asset protection." Retailers show recruits videos with charts that indicate how five-finger discounts account for $45 billion worth of "lost" merchandise annually. A big chunk of in-store theft is perpetrated by what the Sell Side calls Organized Retail Crime, whose operatives steal goods averaging $100 to $150 a day not for personal consumption but to sell to third-party fences. At supermarkets, baby food is hit frequently by ORC. According to the FBI, there are about a million cases of *reported* shoplifts a year, a mere sliver of the actual total. It's hard to profile shoplifters, racially, ethnically, or otherwise. The training video at Target featured well-groomed and respectable models: if Winona Ryder, Courtney Love, Farah Fawcett, Jennifer Capriati, Olga Korbut, and a former secretary of the army can rip off stores, why not someone who looks like you? But if this sour economy is encouraging you to strike, think twice. The National Retail Federation reports that a majority of retail outlets are fortified by closed-circuit video cams.

2. Everybody's nosy.

It isn't just the Sell Side that's watching. Shoppers themselves—including you and me, let's admit it—sneak peeks into each other's baskets, as if the items therein offer insights into our innermost lives (which, to some degree, they actually do). People check out our hair, the clothes we've got on, how we choose to deal—verbally, physically, not at all—with our kids, for whom shopping issues permission to go crazy in public, just when we're entirely exposed, our arms full of boxes, cans, and bags.

3. Finally, we're of high strategic value. We're lab rats.

Nearly everything we do while half-thinking our way through a store holds potential bottom-line significance: the instinctive way we snake through departments; the product displays that capture our attention; the things we pick up, hold in our claws, look at, sniff, only to put back on the shelf; the mix of items we offload onto the checkout belt. A number of Sell Side companies—Kimberly-Clark, Coca-Cola, General Mills, Kroger, Wal-Mart—now employ virtual reality tools and eye-tracking technology to ascertain how we take in items as we walk down store aisles, data that help Sell Siders refine just where to place those items to boost packaging punch. And there's always the old reliable surveillance tool: an unobtrusive, casually dressed human being, partially obscured by a pillar or potted plant, charting our moves on her clipboard, pecking details of our behavior into an electronic handheld. IBM, one of the many companies that provide the Sell Side with technology systems that gather and store data, recently distributed a survey to potential clients: "*The Shopping Tribe*: Understanding your shopper's behavior to leverage dynamic digital merchandising." IBM isn't bashful about the Sell Side's advanced ability to snoop: "We probably know as much about the behavior of the human shopper in its natural habitat, the mall, the grocery, or the department store, as we do about the activities of any species of animal in the wild."

While all this is going on, you, the shopping animal, are just you. You may be in a hurry or you may be killing time. You may be on a specific buying mission or simply browsing. You may be a regular customer or a one-time drive-by. You may be young, old, in between. You may be rich or trying hard to scrape by. You may be somebody or nobody. Check that. To the Sell Side, nobody's nobody. Everybody amounts to actionable intelligence: precious, detailed, and copious. So the Sell Side keeps its eyeballs fixed. There's nothing seriously threatening about it, nothing untoward. For the Sell Side, it just pays to snoop.

If the Sell Side can snoop, okay, then so can I. Not long after the BIG Show, I returned to New York for another round of surveillance. The first morning in town, I slipped into a pair of jeans, threw on a sports coat, jumped on a subway, and headed downtown. I'd arranged a session with Paco Underhill, the best-known and most widely cited retail snoop on the planet. Underhill operates out of a warren of cluttered rooms in a narrow nineteenth-century building on the west side of Broadway, between Twentieth and Twenty-first streets. This is hallowed Sell Side ground, itself worth a snoop. It was here in the Flatiron District where those first-generation modern American shoppers, Katherine and Ned's great-grandparents, came to gape a century ago, which is why I'd left myself some time to take a twirl around the neighborhood. Here is where America shucked off a culture of frugality and fell in love with the soft caress of material luxury. Here is where it became abundantly clear that somebody up there loved us, or at least wanted us to love to shop incessantly. In a single year, for instance—1879—three acts of divine intervention occurred that would lead us out of the pushcart wilderness and into the Buy's promised land of plenty:

- *Let there be light*: Thomas Edison delivered unto us the incandescent lamp to fire up signs, parking lots, display cases.

- *Let there (eventually) be mass advertising*: William Crookes delivered unto us the cathode-ray tube, auguring the day that our lives would be filled with TV commercials.

- *And, from this year forward, let there be buying on a scale so splendiferous that it will be hard to keep track of it all*: James Ritty delivered unto us a machine he called the Incorruptible Cashier, an ingenious device that kept a precise tally of transactions. The machine had little keys that signified denominations, had a built-in adding device, and was equipped with a bell that, when one pressed a key, issued a sound—*ka-ching*. The entire world would come to recognize and clamor to hear it for themselves, but it is a sound that remains most loudly and proudly made in the USA—even in these unfortunate times.

* * *

It wasn't as if I was a stranger to these streets. In the late 1980s I lived just a few blocks east of the Flatiron Building at a time when the handsome, cast-iron façades of many buildings were coated with grime. In the years following, the area had been scrubbed and polished, not to the level of its original glory but spiffy enough. Today, the Flatiron District is one of Manhattan's hipper residential and shopping areas, an unplanned, urban power hybrid: condos and lofts amid the usual specialty stores—Zara, H&M, Sephora—holding their own in the wretched economy. Standard-issue shopping. Apart from the Gilded Age architecture, the retail scene here is no more enticing than it is at Any Mall, USA, maybe even a notch below what is easily accessible to me along the Magnificent Mile. If there's anything like an outlier, it's a store called ABC Carpet and Home, Broadway at Nineteenth, worth a look if only because it suggests the scale of what shopping was once like down here. ABC Carpet and Home is a fine example of how stores can evolve. It started out as a pushcart on the Lower East Side in 1897. The immigrant who pushed the cart, Sam Winerib, newly arrived from Austria, peddled floor coverings. Sam's son, Max, eventually took the business over and recarpeted it into something bigger and better. He upgraded the pushcart into a discount carpet store—still in the old neighborhood but a few steps up the stairway to the American Dream. In 1961, Max's son, Jerome, moved the store from the old neighborhood—only poor people and winos lived there at the time, people with little to carpet—to its present location, the building that was once the grand W&J Sloane department store. Here Jerome, later joined by his daughter Paulette, elevated ABC into something quite special: a "*destination* store," one that draws people from all over, and drags in other stores in its wake. Today ABC is a self-described "six-floor emporium of rugs, furniture, antiques, home textiles and accessories—a dynamic mixture of old and new, East meets West, formal and country, traditional and modern, classic to funky," a statement that, however self-congratulatory, captures how far ABC Carpet and Home has come from its pushcart beginning.

But long, long before ABC moved in to revitalize the neighborhood, the Flatiron District was home to America's most regal retail establishments. It was along the so-called Ladies' Mile that the great American department store, gussied up as a palazzo, gained its footing. No wonder Ned and Katherine's great-grandparents were transfixed when they walked these streets.

Unless they had shopped in the great European cities, Paris and London notably, first-generation modern American shoppers had never seen anything remotely like this. On weekends the Ladies' Mile attracted throngs of factory hands and working-class girls, over from Brooklyn or across the Hudson from New Jersey. Here was retail as never before imagined, a breakthrough Sell Side business model. Department store advertising trumpeted a revolutionary new concept: "customer service." There was no haggling over price. And if you bought something, you could take it home only to change your mind and bring it right back, few or no questions asked.

By all accounts it was quite a scene along the Ladies' Mile. The district had a "champagne sparkle"; it was where "all the world came to . . . shop, to dine, to flirt," in the words of a curator at the Museum of the City of New York. Understandably, temptation was rife. In a study of how turn-of-the-century women used and abused department stores, historian Elaine S. Abelson reviewed women's diaries and concluded that "shopping dwarfed all other activities. Women shopped constantly. . . . For many of [them] the stores provided a use for leisure time that necessitated neither rationalization nor apology." And for this they earned no small degree of masculine ridicule, as captured in a couplet of the day: "*From Eighth Street down, the men are earning it / From Eighth Street up, the women are spurning it.*" Stores had the capacity to loosen not only women's purses but their moral fiber, according to Abelson's *When Ladies Go A-Thieving*. Salespeople therefore kept close watch, even on the best-dressed, most respectable lady customers. Cops moonlighted as store detectives. Not infrequently, they busted socialites whose transgressions were splashed all over the papers. The miscreants' evil deeds, Abelson tells us, were attributed to rampant "female hysteria and mental degeneration."

Most notably, it was here, on the Ladies' Mile and the streets to the south, that America's first generation of merchant princes ascended to their thrones. Among the earliest was an Irish immigrant named Alexander Turney Stewart, whose store, the Marble Palace, had shelves carved of curly maple and mahogany, and was illuminated throughout by overhanging crystal. Mary Todd Lincoln haunted Stewart's emporium, lavishing Abe's limited income on clothing and knickknacks, according to Stewart's biographer, Stephen Elias. Were Mrs. Lincoln alive today, she'd be adjudged a raging shopaholic, a depressive who sought temporary emotional relief by blowing her White House furnishings allowance on imported frocks and millinery. Her profligacy was routinely disparaged by a disapproving press corps and decried by her husband.

While A. T. Stewart deserves credit as the founding father, there were others, retail being retail, never too proud to knock off a good idea when they saw one. Across the country a slew of merchant doges emerged from their own ornate woodwork: Marshall Field in Chicago; John Wanamaker, Strawbridge and Clothier, and the Gimbel brothers, in Philadelphia; Joseph Hudson in Detroit; David May in Cleveland and later St. Louis.

But that was then. The Ladies' Mile, while a cool place to live and shop, ain't what it used to be. The landmark Siegel-Cooper department store ("A City in Itself"), with its twenty-two marble columns under a central rotunda, along with a thirteen-foot-high replica of the *Statue of the Republic* commissioned for the World's Columbian Exposition, is now home to Bed Bath & Beyond, Filene's Basement, and T.J. Maxx. Today's Man operates at Eighteenth and Sixth, where B. Altman built a grand emporium before moving uptown and then, in the late 1980s, to the department store hereafter, never to return.

Master Spy

At the appointed time I trundled over to Paco Underhill's offices, where I took the tiny, creaky elevator up to Envirosell, the company Underhill founded thirty years ago. Given that Underhill is the best-known retail snoop in the world, I wanted to hear his current thoughts on the state of the Sell Side. Underhill is known for getting around. He travels the globe pitching retail clients and stopping to snoop around stores and malls whenever he has a free hour before heading to an airport.

Paco Underhill is a big guy—not ideal for a snoop, but he'd raise no suspicions were you to catch him following your movements as you shopped. Bearded, balding, rumpled, in a white oxford-cloth shirt and a sleeveless sweater vest that has seen more than few fashion seasons come and go, Underhill is garrulous notwithstanding a slight stutter. He's also opinionated, even borderline quarrelsome, yet he was warm and welcoming as we introduced ourselves—an outsized and engaging teddy bear of a snoop. There's nothing glamorous about Envirosell's offices on the old Ladies' Mile, little to suggest that the company's snooping operation has global reach, with outposts in Mexico City, São Paulo, Milan, Bangalore, and Tokyo. Envirosell's headquarters are of uncertain provenance. From behind the massive wooden worktable he uses as a desk and a resting platform for his ursine torso, Underhill gestured to the room's thick window frames and a disused wood-burning fireplace in the corner and speculated that back in the neighborhood's glory days the building had likely been a hotel, a place to kick back after a day of shopping.

Underhill is best known, not just on the Sell Side but to general readers, for his two best-selling books, *Why We Buy: The Science of Shopping*, which came out in the late nineties, and *Call of the Mall: The Geography of Shopping*, published a few years later. He refers to himself as a "retail anthropologist," a claim that rankles some academics, who earn far less respect and remuneration when consulting for deep-pocketed Sell Siders. Some of them pooh-pooh, gently or snidely, the "soundness" of Envirosell's methodology, but this seems like sour grapes to me. Underhill's writing is chock-full of tidbits that illuminate what makes shopping in stores repellent or seductive —why some stores are easy and pleasant to shop in, how others shoot themselves in the foot with lousy floor plans or merchandise display:

- Supermarkets are egregiously stupid when they stock pet treats on their uppermost shelves when the buyers likely to reach for them are old people and children.

- Stores waste opportunity and woodlands when they (almost always) place circulars just inside the front door. Shoppers tend not to look down as they enter stores. If a store wants its circulars to circulate, it should position them ten feet farther in.

- Signage and product displays inside and outside stores are all too often misplaced. Given that shoppers lack eyes on the sides of their heads, signs and displays would be more effective if "canted to one side so . . . they can be more easily seen from an angle."

Underhill's work attracts a steady stream of media attention that often takes the form of a journalist tagging along as he sleuths through retail establishments. The now defunct *Mirabella* magazine accompanied him to the Galleria mall in Dallas, where he uncovered creepy dressing rooms. In 1996, Malcolm Gladwell published a *New Yorker* piece about him. Gladwell poses a question in that piece: *Should we be afraid of Paco Underhill?* "One of the fundamental anxieties of the American consumer," Gladwell says, "has always been that beneath the pleasure and the frivolity of the shopping experience runs an undercurrent of manipulation." And not just American consumers, either, nor just since the Consumers' Republic was founded. Old folk proverb: "If you are buying a cow, make sure the tail is included."

However intriguing Underhill's take on the specifics of endcap optimization (prime real estate, don't waste it!), the need for front-door "landing strips," a woman's innate fear of "butt brush" in too-narrow store aisles, these things were not what I came to talk to him about. What I wanted was the Big Picture. But Paco, knowing how visitors lap up his company's detective work, was eager to show me around the operation, so we climbed a spiral staircase to the second floor. There, seven or eight associate snoops were at work, Gen Yers mostly, every one attached to an aging iMac or video player. They smiled brightly when Paco emerged from the hatch. There was lots of easy banter. Shepherding me from one workstation to the next, Underhill introduced me to his young analysts and invited them to explain what they were doing before they were so amiably interrupted.

One of the junior snoops, a young woman who had been with Envirosell for six months, had been coding a tape showing a male shopper (early twenties, I'd say) who was footloose in the video game section of what looked to be a big-box discounter. Envirosell makes no special attempt to hide its in-store cameras; it just keeps them more or less out of our sight lines, and shoppers rarely notice them. The guy in the games section was entirely unaware that he was being watched. In the center of the frame: an elaborate and obviously expensive product display designed to showcase the Microsoft Xbox 360. Xbox had been out for the better part of a year but now faced what was—in the estimation of clear-eyed industry analysts as well as those who truly know what they're talking about, i.e., glassy-eyed teenage video-game freaks—serious competition from two more recent launches. There was the long-awaited and apparently overpriced Sony PlayStation 3 and, more ominously for Microsoft, Nintendo's Wii, the game box that had rapidly moved from long shot to dark horse, to practically Seabiscuit, judging from the chatter online and in school lunchrooms from Queens to Orange County.

"Here, look at this," said Paco's analyst, turning back to her monitor and hitting the play button. The young man strides right past the imposing Xbox display and without a sidelong glance walks directly—I mean, *directly*—over to the Wii demo machine. He picks up its controller, or its much applauded motion-sensing nunchuk (the camera angle doesn't afford a clear view), then goes to town on the Wii.

Xbox display? What Xbox display?

Granted, Envirosell's video cam had captured but a solitary episode—one day, one guy, one store—perhaps not representative of what would happen were you or I to encounter the display. And, yes, it's possible that the elaborate display indeed had something to do with the fact that five million-plus Xboxes had by then wound up at the cash register while sales of the rival PlayStation 3 had been so soft that Sony had slashed prices more than once. On the other hand, maybe this episode recorded and coded by Envirosell revealed a colossal waste of promotional dollars; that the display, in fact, packed the customer stopping power of a giant invisible rabbit.

The colleague next to the Xbox snoop was taking detailed and meticulous notes while screening an interview with a man—midthirties—trying to decide whether he wanted a tablet PC with integrated Verizon wireless broadband technology. Another Envirosell hand perused behavior patterns (*human* behavior patterns) in the health care aisle at PetSmart. Next to him, a more seasoned Envirosell snoop was putting the finishing touches on a PowerPoint pitch to a prospective client. All this was happening in a room where there are shelves of clear plastic storage boxes filled with tapes and notes—for all we know, you or I may be caught on tape in those boxes—gathered on behalf of Envirosell clients. Collectively, these clients represent a large hunk of the global Sell Side: retailers (Blockbuster, BP, CVS, Disney Stores, Godiva, LensCrafters, Lowe's, the US Postal Service, Sunglass Hut, Wal-Mart, to name a few); food services (Burger King, Denny's, Einstein Brothers Bagels, McDonald's, Starbucks, Subway, Taco Bell, plus many others); consumer products (Adidas, Coca-Cola, Pepsi, Gillette, Hallmark Cards, Revlon, Upjohn, Quaker Foods, the list goes on); and banks (Citibank, Chase Manhattan, Wells Fargo, just for starters).

Global Intelligence

When we returned to his office, Paco was more than happy to share his thoughts on the Big Picture. He settled back behind his big worktable, voice rising, hands waving. There was no declaiming about how shoppers typically turn right, not left, when entering a store. Instead, he made sure I understood that Envirosell sells its services to one out of two of the fifty largest merchants in the world. He noted that he was consulting with Adidas on a new venue in Moscow, with Carrefour on a prototype department store in Belgium, and with H&M on its unremitting expansion throughout Europe. Store prototyping—built around how retailers put data into play—had become the significant and growing part of Envirosell's business. Why the changeover from straightforward snooping? Because there are now hundreds of snooping algae firms out there that do exactly the same thing: keep an eye on us.

Today, *collecting* data is easy, Underhill explained. "You can gather it up as fast as you like. But unless you have the ability to process it, give it back to the merchant or marketer in a usable form, it is what it is: just data. Someone tells you that a suburban mom driving a minivan, in a household making sixty thousand to eighty thousand dollars a year, prefers Jif to Skippy two to one. Fine. What can you really do with that?" The hard part, he said, is helping stores configure data into passkeys that actually open our credit card cases and unlock our spending through improved store layout and sales training. It's not *that* a guy walks past a fancy display. It's how do you *use* the captured video to come up with a display that *will* stop him, you, me, cold in our tracks.

Underhill then offered a summation on how topsy-turvy the Sell Side currently is and how erratic we, the customers, have become. "We've gone from a time when brands competed within their separate categories to what is basically a bar fight," he said. "Everyone competes with everybody. Whole Foods is worried about Trader Joe's, even though Whole Foods is a *high*-end, *high*-price provider on a large scale, and Trader Joe's is a lower-end provider on a much more modest scale. Also, someone who goes to a shopping center with two hundred and fifty dollars might spend it at JCPenney or she may just as easily spend it at Williams-Sonoma. Why? Because seventy percent of what people spend in a mall, or a grocery store for that matter, they had no intention of buying when they walked in the door."

Mindful that consultants aren't in business to give away for free what deep-pocketed clients pay for, I pressed gingerly to get Paco to send me back down to the Ladies' Mile with a master snoop's X-ray of what he sees when he looks our way at this moment in Buy time.

What he's been seeing for years, he responded, is not the Buy world as depicted in anticonsumerist manifestos or in the media generally: the conventional wisdom that American shoppers have eyes bigger than their wallets. "The picture we've gotten of how and what people buy has been exaggerated," he said, leaning across the table. "Take the kids working upstairs, some of whom have six-figure incomes. They can't afford to live in this city. Compare that to my father's time. When my father bought his house in nineteen sixty-five, it cost roughly what his annual salary was then. Today it's different. Take monthly expenses. We now have a mobile phone bill, an Internet access bill, a cable television bill, an inkjet printer that eats cartridges, none of which drew down our disposable income a few years ago. The average American household spends more a year on technology-related products and services than it does on clothes, health insurance, prescription drugs, or entertainment." Paco paused. "The poignancy of our era, Lee, is that a significant part of the population worries about downward mobility, which is why the Dollar Stores of the world are winning." And why, he continued, "if you'd asked me what the big headline is in the early twenty-first century, I'd tell you this: the brand war is over. Period."

"Meaning what?" I asked him.

"Private labels have won, though consumers may not be fully aware of it yet. The same factory that manufactures Huggies is likely to be the same factory that makes diapers for Walgreen's. Shoppers who walk into H&M or Whole Foods don't think of those places, or what they sell, as private labels, but that's exactly what they are."

The headline, in other words, is that while we are certainly aware of Listerine, Lancôme, and Ralph Lauren, their hold on us is evaporating in the face of comparable and cheaper alternatives. They're cheaper because a layer of profit—Ralph Lauren's, say—has been removed from the pricing equation. As this trend expands, we'll have less reason to talk ourselves into believing, or allow the brand to talk us into believing, that Huggies fulfill their diapering responsibilities any better than Walgreen's nappies. Widespread generic substitution is but one sign that we now live in the Age of Cheap, so dubbed by David Bosshart, a Swiss consumer think-tanker whose conclusions Underhill heartily endorses. Chalk it up to the low (though rising) cost of Third World labor, retail sponges with streamlined operations and/or economies of scale (Wal-Mart, Zara, the warehouse clubs), plus wider acceptance by everyone that "mass" is no longer at odds with "class" (witness the "Tarzhay effect"). Food prices and the cost of air travel may spike, health care costs go up and up. Details, blips. Overall, we live in the Age of Cheap, and it's here to stay.

To drive home his point—that in this Age of Cheap, brands aren't what they used to be—Paco demanded that I show him the label inside my sport coat. My guess is that he was betting the label would say Men's Wearhouse, or some made-up, department-store brand that sounds Neapolitan: a fictitious Italian tailor's name ending in "i": Flangini, Bronzoli, Tonelli. But I fooled the master spy. The label read Canali, a high-end brand, a *perfetto* example of what I presume Paco considers the sort of overpriced, lah-dee-dah brand that more and more of us, fretting over our downward mobility, will abandon over time.

"OK, so I got one wrong," Paco said. A store man, not a brand hypester, he didn't appear the slightest bit chastened, not for a moment inclined to retract the headline.

Back down on the Ladies' Mile, I had something to chew on. Why, if one's reluctant (I am, are you?) to buy merchandise with logos displayed on the outside—jackets and handbags and sunglasses of dubious superiority that announce "I am this brand, this brand is me"—do we shell out for a pedigree undetectable by the human eye? This is the Age of Cheap, right? Wal-Mart, as journalist Charles Fishman has pointed out, sells lawn mowers cheap enough to throw away after a single season. The cost of a Brooks Brothers suit is about the same as it was in 1998. So—why *did* I shell out for Canali? Why buy anything so dear when there's a reasonably comparable something that costs much less? Am I fooling me? Or is Barneys New York fooling me? Or both?

5

Midtown

The Sell Side can see your house from up here

Hair removal skews higher with teens. Twenty-six percent of the usage is with girls between twelve and nineteen, [who represent just] 13 percent of the population.

—Senior vice-president, marketing, Nair

Once you label me, you negate me.

—Søren Kierkegaard

PACO UNDERHILL WAS NOT ESPECIALLY charitable about what retailers accomplish with the profusion of data at their disposal and the equations they draw about our household buying behavior—*suburban mom, drives minivan . . . household income 60K . . . prefers Jif to Skippy.* His skepticism, however, hasn't put a dent in the tens of billions spent each year on profiling buyers. To get a better look at how the data game works, I trekked two miles north of Underhill's office, up and over to the east side of midtown, then took an elevator to the fifty-eighth floor. I'd arranged a meeting at one of the world's largest data collection firms. My contact was running late, which left me biding my time in one of the biggest conference rooms I'd ever been in, absurdly vast given that one other person would be joining me. I was atop the Citigroup Center at Fifty-third and Lexington, the distinctive silver tower with a slanted crown.

The delay left me ample time to gape at unobstructed views to the south and west: the Chrysler Building due south, the Empire State to the southwest, and moving west, Rockefeller Center, then north of that the Philip Johnson–designed Sony Building, with a pediment that's been compared to a Chippendale highboy. Below me lay what Sell Siders designate the New York "metropolitan trading area" or "shopping radius" or, if you're in the business of selling advertising, "designated market area." Some 19 million people live within the shopping radius, the most populous district in the land.

I was here to learn how the Sell Side puts us and our household members in categories casually designated "consumer buckets." Fifty years ago the Sell Side focused mostly on a single bucket, the Mass Market bucket, which was filled to the brim with "average customers," millions upon millions of interchangeable "Mr. and Mrs. Consumers." The Sell Side blasted away at this monster bucket via commercials on the three TV networks and in high-circulation national magazines such as *Life, Look,* and *Reader's Digest.* "Spray and pray," the strategy was called. The Sell Side doesn't spray and pray much anymore. Today there are so many mini- and microbuckets that the Sell Side fires with far more precise nozzles. There's the Suburban Single Mom bucket, the Small-Town Traditional Values bucket, the Millenial bucket (a huge bucket where my kids are to be found, even when it's two in the morning and I personally have no clue as to their actual whereabouts). Once the Sell Side has placed you and yours in the appropriate bucket(s), it can—in theory—use its marketing hose more efficiently. Nair, the hair removal product, for example, places ads in magazines and on Web sites favored by those in the Teenage Girl bucket, which is why you'll never see ads for Nair in *The New York Review of Books.*

Consumer bucketing is a highly advanced science. For our purposes, I'll try to keep things simple. In essence, consumer segmentation is how the Sell Side keeps tabs on who we are, where we live, when we might be in "purchase mode," the kinds of products we most care about, and the sorts of selling offers that positively influence our buying decisions. There are basically two kinds of buckets used to accomplish all this: the demographic and the psychographic. The demographic bucket buckets us on the basis of age, sex, income, occupation, level of education, marital status, and ZIP code. According to a Carnegie Mellon study, the Sell Side can identify nearly 90 percent of us—*by name*—using as few as three of those personal data points. And it's a snap for the Sell Side to collect this straightforward data. Details about our age, address, income, and so on are easily obtained from customer surveys, banks, credit card companies, and the Census Bureau, which is the demographic mother lode.

The psychographic bucket buckets us according to squishier, more subjective criteria: factors such as our personality type and belief system (relax, it's in there somewhere), our media and entertainment preferences. Once it draws a bead, the Sell Side assigns a "lifestyle" moniker to us. Even if you don't think you *have* much of a lifestyle, a psychographic researcher can come up with an interesting term to describe how he perceives your pattern (say, the Aspiring Contemporary Transgender Urban bucket). How does the Sell Side gather psychographic info? It snoops into the magazines we read, notes our preferences in movies, considers the television programming and Web sites we favor, judges our political leanings, factors in whether we attend church.

Hey, You Down There!

While we're cooling our heels in the conference room, let's take a demographic tour (data courtesy of the Federal Reserve) through the five boroughs of New York City. Roll that posh office chair over to the window and together we'll explore the urban trading area that, on a clear day, stretches all the way to the horizon:

Manhattan: Looking directly down, we observe the most densely populated county in the United States. One and a half million people dwell on Manhattan island. Over 2.4 million people *work* down there, which is why stores get so crowded at lunchtime and why Starbucks has seen fit to open more than 150 stores from the Battery to the border of the Bronx. There's an extraordinary degree of income disparity in Manhattan—no other concentrated geographic area in the nation comes close. This means that marketing to Manhattan residents is immensely tricky, demographically speaking. On paper, if you average out the residents of Manhattan, the place looks fairly normal. Median family income ($56,000) is just a tad higher than the national average. But if you're a high-end store or product or one on the low end, or if you sell merchandise with a specific ethnic appeal, you need to place your advertising and locate your stores precisely. If you're looking to sell to customers in the Highly Educated bucket—regardless of income, though there's a correlation—Manhattan should indeed be high on your list. Fifty-seven percent of adults over twenty-five years old have a college degree here, more than twice the national average. Still, you'll need a ZIP code filter, given that 15 percent of Manhattanites in this age range fall into the Did Not Complete High School bucket.

Brooklyn: Median household income across the fabled steel-wire bridge is two-thirds what it is in Manhattan. Demographically, Brooklyn resembles most other urban areas around the country, though the borough ranks rather low in owner-occupied housing. Still, there's no shortage of upmarket neighborhoods here, where condos are priced high enough to make a Chicagoan or Atlantan blanch. Brooklyn has an above-average representation of minorities: 20 percent Hispanic, 7.5 percent Asian, a sizable segment Chinese. Most notably, 36 percent of Brooklyn's population is African American or West Indian, a fact not lost on the marketing directors of the vast number of brands aimed at specific ethnic communities —e.g., the honchos who, especially at Kwanzaa time, market Hallmark's Mahogany line of greeting cards, stationery, and gift wrap tailored to the African American bucket. (Kwanzaa, initiated in 1966, is celebrated by an estimated 13 percent of African Americans, who on average spend around $900 each holiday season, a good portion of it on greeting cards, food, candles, and flowers.)

Queens: Here there are about the same number of people as in Brooklyn, but Queens is far less densely inhabited: "only" 20,000 people per square mile, compared to Brooklyn's 35,000. If you're selling home improvement products, look to Queens; nearly one out of three Queensians is an owner-occupier. Most notable, though, is the fact that 18 percent of Queens residents are Asian, three times the national percentage. If you're in business to sell products to Asians, that's very good news. The challenge, though, is that you can't, or shouldn't, try to advertise to one big Asian American bucket unless you're selling computers or broadband connections, categories in which Asian Americans have among the highest usership rates in the nation. Otherwise, owing to language and cultural differences, Chinese, Japanese, Korean, Filipino, Vietnamese, and Asian Indians have highly distinct buying habits and product preferences, particularly in the food category.

Bronx: Home ownership (above 20 percent) is among the lowest in the nation: nine out of ten people live in multifamily dwellings. Median income is $29,000, well below the U.S. average. For marketers seeking Hispanic customers—and few these days aren't—the Bronx offers excellent opportunity. The borough has witnessed a significant population boom over the past two decades, mostly the result of Hispanic immigration. Today, nearly one out of two Bronx residents is Hispanic, which is why, if Wal-Mart ever launched a major assault on New York City, it should choose the Bronx as its Omaha Beach. Given that the U.S. Hispanic market consists of over 40 million people with spending power of $800 billion a year, it's little wonder that Wal-Mart aggressively stocks stores in heavily Hispanic neighborhoods with a deep inventory of specialty foods, effectively turning those Wal-Marts into superbodegas.* Hispanics shop *mucho*. Relative to other ethnic groups, they tend to forgo packaged foods and prepare dinners from scratch. This means they go food shopping significantly more often than most other ethnic groups—on average twenty-six times a month. Hispanic women, on average, also spend more in-store time shopping for apparel than either Caucasian or African American women.

Staten Island: With just under half a million residents, Staten Island is as small-town as a New York borough can possibly be. It's the most affluent of the five boroughs (median household income $63,000), and over the past two decades has enjoyed (or lamented) the greatest population increase of any county in the state. Racially, SI roughly parallels national averages. There's not much industry there, but the health care business is solid, accounting for a third of the jobs and 40 percent of personal income. About half as many people commute to Brooklyn as commute to Manhattan, though it would take a marketer savvier than me to know what to do with that fact.

Okay, that's New York City in a demographic nutshell. What are some of the ways the Sell Side uses demographic profiling? It isn't nice, and not always productive, to make sweeping generalizations about people based on their race, income, and ZIP code, but the Sell Side doesn't stand on ceremony. If you're a marketer and you see folks clustered in a bucket, you spray away. Imagine you're a marketing director. Here's a little quiz to test your aptitude for getting the products you sell to the people in the right bucket:

---

*Wal-Mart, to a lesser degree, is similarly testing the sale of Middle Eastern specialty foods in a heavily populated Arab American neighborhood in Michigan.

- Those in the Jewish bucket patronize nightclubs more often than those in either the Protestant or Catholic buckets. Taking that fact into account, imagine you have a blank check to be used for marketing a particular establishment or a service that has something to do with nightclub attendance. How and where would you use it?

- African Americans buy a lower percentage of ground and whole-bean coffee than non–African Americans. Is it better to a) accept the status quo and try to sell more instant coffee in African American neighborhoods, or b) initiate marketing schemes designed to change customer behavior?

- Those in the Gay and Lesbian bucket cite Apple, Absolut, Levi's, and Bacardi, as among the most "gay-friendly" brands in the country (Gillette, Sears, Frito-Lay, and Dunkin' Donuts among the least friendly). Gay respondents cite a number of reasons for their likes and dislikes, among them the opinions of friends and the tenor of a product's advertising. Say you're marketing Levi's 501 jeans. Should you create special gay-friendly advertising and place it nationally, or seek existing gay-oriented print and cable TV outlets? (I'll give you this one: in 2008, Levi's 501 jeans bought a hefty block of advertising on the Logo cable network, an MTV-owned channel aimed at gay viewers.)

The 1.14 Percent Solution

The vast conference room we're loitering in belongs to a company called Experian. It is headquartered in London but operates in sixty-five countries. You've probably heard of Experian. Along with Equifax and TransUnion, it's one of the three major U.S. credit bureaus that keep score and issue reports on how well you pay your bills, which in turn determines your credit-worthiness. As you may know from unpleasant experience—identity theft, a retailer's mistake, or, most commonly, buying off more than you could chew—your credit score affects the interest rates you pay on everything from revolving accounts to home loans (remember those?). A lousy score can prevent you from getting a loan altogether, though rarely will it kill your chances of obtaining a credit card, and even if it does, you can always borrow the one a card company inadvertently mailed to your dog. But I didn't take the long elevator ride up to this conference room to examine credit card spending—we'll get to that later. I came here to find out what was new and exciting in Experian's "Marketing Solutions" division, the company's bucketing operation. Experian is a major player in this arena, along with other companies with names that sound more like prescription drugs than Sell Side research outfits: Axciom, Claritas, Synovate.

A market research firm such as Experian needs to be a sophisticated marketing machine unto itself, since it continuously pitches its services to clients who are themselves major-league sellers. Accordingly, bucketing outfits are forever coming up with fetching names for their proprietary profiling platforms. Experian maintains what it calls a BehaviorBank, "one of the nation's largest repositories of consumer-supplied lifestyle data." Other companies have handles such as National People Meter, AdVantage, Mega-View, IDEAZ, InfoScan, MindField. A big research firm based in Chicago, GolinHarris (this is an industry that disdains the space bar), touts a methodology it dubs *anthrographics*, which it describes as a high-octane blend of "demographic, psychographic and ethnographic insights into Predictive Personality Profiles of your target audience that draws a picture of the real, 'live' person we need to reach, motivate and inspire." *Impactful!*

By the time my contact finally entered the conference room, the people in the shopping radius down below were heading out to lunch. Richard Holt wore an open-collared yellow dress shirt with a blue Polo pony on the front. His pants were gathered at the waist, a study in Economist Chic. A likable, down-to-earth guy with a sense of humor about himself, Holt told me he'd recently been appointed the new president of business strategies at Experian, dispatched to the States from the UK to help the company play catch-up with a couple of giant competitors who'd been eating Experian's bucket lunch. He told me sheepishly that he wasn't much of a pitchman and that he volunteered to see me only because the really good pitch guy had been unexpectedly called away to make a presentation to a major client. He apologized that the slides he was about to walk me through might seem dry. "After all," he said, "I'm an economist." With that he began an hour-long briefing that illustrated just how far giant market researchers have advanced the science of bucketing, while offering a blizzard of details showing how comprehensive demographic bucketing has become:

To arrive at the Lee Eisenberg or the (Your Name Here) Mosaic House-hold profile, Experian uses four basic "data inputs":

- *Personal data:* Straightforward info about your age, your children's age(s), and everyone's level of education.

- *Household data:* Your ethnicity, size of your dwelling "unit" and its market value, whether you rent or own it, whether you own a business, your receptivity to direct-mail solicitations, tendency to use mail order.

- *Census block data:* Including, among two hundred variables, where you live according to urban/rural indicators and how your census area breaks down vis-à-vis marital status, income, income sources, employment industries, occupations, languages spoken.

- *ZIP+4 data:* Your city or town size and how it receives package and postal delivery. The latter is important because much of the above data is culled from, and on behalf of, Sell Side direct marketers. Buy something from a catalog or online or over the phone and you've given the Sell Side a small but highly treasured piece of actionable evidence.

Holt then guided me through a series of slides that touted Mosaic's "key features." Foremost among them, "highly descriptive, *household-level* classification" designed to help Sell Side clients know a) who you are, b) what you buy, and (c) where you're hiding, intelligence that enables them to target ads and direct-mail pieces and, in so doing, improve their return on investment. Astoundingly, Mosaic claims to update its profile of you monthly, you being *105 million* American households. The program's "key advantage," Holt said as he moved to the next PowerPoint slide, can be summed up rather succinctly: "*Forget* 'birds of a feather flock together.'" He showed me a slide that drove home the point: sappy photos of four fictitious next-door-neighboring households, which the presentation declared to be "different neighbors, same ZIP+4, but *different household types.*" At 42 Elm Street, a young family with kids. At 43 Elm Street, a married couple without kids. At 44 Elm Street, middle-aged empty nesters. And at 45 Elm Street, a retired couple. (It occurred to me that Experian surely knew my neighbors far better than I do.)

Taking into account all of the above, Holt explained how Mosaic USA puts 105 million American households through a series of data grinds that yield a set of "lifestyle groups." Here's a sample of them, including the percentage of U.S. households each represents:

Affluent Suburbia (11.19 percent)
Upscale America (13.26 percent)
Small-town Contentment (7.64 percent)
Blue-collar Backbone (6.57 percent)
American Diversity (9.73 percent)
Metro Fringe (10.63 percent)
Aspiring Contemporaries (11.18 percent)
Rural Villages and Farms (4.77 percent)
Struggling Societies (6.58 percent)
Urban Essence (8.63 percent)

Holt elected not to drill into the sixty *subgroups* nested within the buckets listed above, but if you're a Experian subscriber, you'll get pages and pages of details about any and all of the subbuckets. I did steal a look at the subgroup that tops the top bucket (Affluent Suburbia). It's called "America's Wealthiest" (1.14 percent of American households), and if you're signed on with Experian you'll receive a detailed profile of the lifestyle and media choices favored by this fortunate 1.14 percent. You'll discover that the 1.14 percent are forty-five to sixty years old; that they live in places like Saddle River, New Jersey; Potomac, Maryland; and Beverly Hills; and that when you plot their concentration on a map of the country, the biggest, densest blotches are in California, Nevada, Florida, and the Northeast Corridor. The 1.14 percent are highly educated and predominately white. They're among the first to buy BlackBerrys and satellite radios. When they watch TV, they favor cable news. When they read magazines, they read titles such as *Barron's* and *The Economist*. They consider themselves "careful about money" and are willing to spend a good deal on financial planning. Preferred cars are the Acura MDX, the Audi A4, the BMW X5, and the Mercedes-Benz E and S Classes. They own life insurance. Marketers who subscribe to Mosaic have ready access to the names and address of those who comprise the 1.14 percent thanks to the fact that just about everybody in this cohort places orders, on the phone or online, for computers, home furnishings, clothes, sporting goods, appliances, books, flat-panel TVs, boats, pet food, cameras, wine, flowers, artwork, and audio equipment, and has them shipped to their home address. Book air travel, car rentals, resort accommodations, order theater and sporting-event tickets, trade stocks via the Web, and they'll find you that way, too.

The Psychographic Bucket

Okay, so much for the demographic bucket. The Sell Side's other principal bucket, the psychographic bucket, came into vogue in the late sixties. Its foundation was laid decades earlier, however, by a Brooklyn-born son of Russian Jewish immigrants who started out with a degree in primate psychology and left behind an enduring theory of human potential. In 1943, when he was in his midthirties, Abraham Maslow famously outlined how our behavior is driven by the quest to satisfy a series of needs. Once we address what Maslow called one "lower-order needs" we move on to ascending "higher-order needs." Some of those needs can be more material than others, meaning that the Buy comes into play as a way to satisfy them. Our need for safety and security is first, followed by our need to belong—our need for love and friendship and all that. Then there's our need for self-respect and dignity. And finally there's our need to "self-actualize," to realize our full, individual potential. Rendered diagrammatically, Maslow's needs form a pyramid, one that predated but resembles the USDA food pyramid found on cereal boxes. Maslow's classic pyramid has been reproduced in a million textbooks, but since it's not to be found in our kitchen cupboards, I'll supply it here:

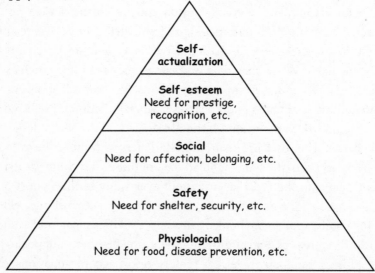

While Maslow didn't construct this geometric representation so the Sell Side could come along and hijack it, he was indeed aware that the Buy figured heavily in the pyramidal scheme of things. He wrote, " . . . the American value system—the American dream—is typically expressed in lower-need terms . . . and almost entirely in materialistic terms. That is, personal success is generally defined in terms of the amount of money one receives and, along with it, the number of symbolic, status objects that one has attained in life, such as a fancy automobile, a boat, a big house in an upscale neighborhood, lavish vacations, and fine clothes."

Maslow's pyramid was, as I say, integral to the advancement of psychographic or lifestyle bucketing. Here I bear minor but personal witness. In the late 1980s, when I was working at *Esquire*—the same magazine to which, a half century before, Ernest Dichter pitched the notion that aroused men with pinup-dilated eyeballs are receptive to advertising—a personable fellow named Jay Ogilvy flew in from California to unveil a hot new market research tool. The program was called VALS (as in lifestyle *values*). At the program's core was Maslow's pyramid of needs as reconstrued by a would-be poet named Arnold Mitchell, who wound up working at SRI (formerly the Stanford Research Institute), a cutting-edge consulting firm in Palo Alto. Mitchell had published his findings in an influential book called *The Nine American Lifestyles: How Our Values, Beliefs, Drives, and Needs Combine with Social Trends to Shape Our Future*. SRI has over the years refreshed what it deems to be America's principal lifestyles, but in Mitchell's time they encompassed:

- "Survivors and Sustainers": those whose lifestyle revolved around Maslow's lower-order needs and who, as Mitchell described them, tended to be distrustful, rebellious, and harbor strong feelings that society doesn't give a damn about them.

- "Belongers," "Emulators," and "Achievers": those who collectively comprise Middle America. If you belonged in the Belongers bucket, you were someone who likely stuck to the rules and played fair. If you were an Emulator, you searched for your lifestyle cues in mass-market movies and magazines. And if you were an Achiever, you were probably a Republican, lived in the suburbs, and drove a humungous sedan.

- "I-Am-Me's": Those who chose to dress flamboyantly, were energetic, opinionated, and enthusiastic about the games and cultural activities they favored.

- "Experientials": Those with a "deep personal involvement in ideas or issues," such as ripping off their clothes and jumping into a hot tub full of other naked strangers at Esalen—or going off to the Himalayas to meditate.

- "Integrateds": Those who were "open, self-assured, self-expressive, keenly aware of nuance and shadings, and . . . possessed of a world perspective."

Esquire's audience, Jay Ogilvy explained to me, consisted of clumps of readers whose lifestyles ranged across all of the above; and a big opportunity lay in the fact that the magazine could, through reader surveys, quantify which lifestyle types predominated, information we would then share with advertisers whose products best fit a given segment's profile. In other words, for example, our salespeople could approach purveyors of outdoor gear with evidence that *Esquire* reached an especially high proportion of, in this case, Experientials.

Today, VALS remains a viable Sell Side tool but only one of many psychographic bucketing methods that flow from Maslow's pyramid of needs. Marketers love Maslovian reasoning, since it helps them turn virtually every superfluous *want* into a defensible *need*. Gatorade, for example, positions itself as a high-performance "survival" drink, i.e., it satisfies a *physiological* need. Gatorade's copywriters make sure we know that "sweat loss reduces blood volume and increases the concentration of sodium in the blood. This stresses the cardiovascular system and contributes to a faster increase in body temperature." Moving one step up the pyramid, Michelin marketers play on our need for *safety*: "Because so much is riding on your tires." And so it goes, all the way up to the apex. Maslow says we need affection: how better to garner some good feeling than with a Frank Gehry Torque tag pendant in 18-karat rose-gold, a Tiffany exclusive? Maslow says we need the respect of others: how better to cop some of that than sliding behind the wheel of an Audi Q7 in Bahia Beige, tagged with vanity plates GR8-LVR?

Maslow's pyramid was on my mind one evening when I was out gabbing with New York friends. One of my pals leaned over and told me under her breath that her husband spends way too much money on model trains and accessories, whereupon the husband overheard and took vigorous exception. He countered that his expensive hobby was one of his few diversions from the pressures of a sixty-hour work week. It underpins his sanity and allows him to let off—no pun intended—steam. I sat for moment, poking at my polenta. What would Abe Maslow think? I concluded that Maslow would conceivably confer his blessing on the husband. Model trains don't supply much in the way of sustenance or physical security, but the railway buff is already pretty well set on his lower-order need fulfillments. As we get into Maslow's higher-need categories though, a case can be made for why the man does "need" all those boxcars, cabooses, illuminated bumpers, trestles, snow-speckled mountain tunnels, crossing flashers, passenger stations, semaphore block signals, yard lights, smoke fluid, automatic gatemen, and additional sets of farm animals and plastic townsfolk:

1. Model railroading addresses his need for love and belonging.

Our hobbyist feels great affection for the plastic universe he painstakingly assembles on the plywood platform in his basement. In all likelihood this enthusiasm harks back to cozy winter evenings spent with his father or favorite uncle or grandfather, or to nostalgia for a time when neighbors gathered at their town's station platform to greet sons and daughters arriving home for the holidays, before America turned into a cheap carnival that goes berserk on Black Fridays.

2. The miniature rail world is a ticket to real-world connections.

There are mutually admiring club members out there, fellow buffs in their own basements wearing vests festooned with commemorative patches and collectible pins, dorky-but-sweet gray-and-white engineer caps or poplin baseball caps embroidered with the insignia of the rail lines that ran through their hometowns when they were boys with big dreams and full heads of hair: Lackawanna, Canadian National, Burlington Northern.

3. The hobby fills the need for self-esteem.

The make-believe world our hobbyist has created elicits not only private pleasures but begs for applause (notwithstanding the ridicule levied by his otherwise devoted and affectionate spouse). His suggestions and expert tips are enthusiastically received at swap meets. Friends, neighbors, and kids gape in wonder at what he's assembled: hand-fluffed cotton snowbanks, a tiny wireless video camera mounted on the nose of a diesel locomotive that gives a train's-eye view. Wow, you did all that yourself? (Sheepish nod.)

4. Finally, model railroading even addresses the need for self-actualization.

The railway buff admits he's obsessive and is quick to laugh at the time and the money he invests in his hobby. But he offers no apology for it. The train platform is the plywood canvas on which his art flourishes, where tricky technical problems are solved resourcefully. Others can make all the nerd jokes they want; this is his fully integrated world, and a legacy of sorts.

Buckets: What They Can and Cannot Do

One can make the case, as Paco Underhill does, that the nits-and-gnats of market segmentation lead the Sell Side around by its nose, often down blind alleys. Experian's Richard Holt counters that "demographics hold the gold." They're both right.

On the plus side, demographic and psychographic profiles help point the Sell Side to promising store locations and suggest future product-line extensions. Wal-Mart became Wal-Mart by hewing to the proposition that price, *everyday-low* price, conquered all buckets. And yet the bigger it grew, and after more than four decades of unremitting expansion, Wal-Mart came to realize that some of us belong to customer buckets for which everyday low price doesn't wash. According to a story in the *New York Times*, these underexploited buckets included "brand aspirationals" (those with low incomes who are nonetheless infatuated with names such as KitchenAid) and "price-sensitive affluents" (those who have a lot of money but can't resist a great deal). In response, Wal-Mart marketers weighed alternative positioning statements, from "Low Prices, Always" to "Look Beyond the Basics" to "Saving People Money So They Live Better Lives."

Over at Best Buy, psycho-sifting is no less intense. One day I sat in on a Web seminar hosted by Harte Hanks, a consulting firm. A senior analyst offered a summary of how Best Buy was tinkering with the configuration of its stores, refining what merchandise specific locations carried based on the psychographically informed conclusion that there isn't one all-purpose Best Buy customer, there are at least four of them. There's "Barry" (Hi, Barry!), an affluent professional who seeks a top-of-the-line technology experience; there's "Buzz" (Wassup, dude?), who's younger than Barry and chases "cutting-edge" technology, spending a nice hunk of his disposable income on CDs and DVDs; there's "Ray" (Good to meet you, pal!), a well-meaning dad keen on providing his family with the technology lifestyle it deserved; and there's "Jill" (Greetings, Jill!), a mom whose chief interest in technology is how it might "enrich" the lives of her kids. Since Barry-Buzz-Ray-Jill are not proportioned evenly across all cities, towns, and ZIP codes, Best Buy was working on how it could adjust individual layout, signage, and inventory so that each store matched its neighborhood's cast of aforementioned psychographic characters.

In these ways Sell Siders harness the power of psychographics to make sure that you and a store are lifestyle soul mates—i.e., you share the same values. This poses a challenge for certain types of stores. Paco Underhill told me that consumer electronics stores, appliance stores, and car dealerships have long been viewed as "hostile environments" for female shoppers, but many are now taking steps to correct the situation. Numerous psychographic-based retailing studies conclude that we prefer to shop where our aspirations and values are mirrored. Mirrored by what? By what we think of fellow customers, how the sales staff meets and greets us, the overall "atmospherics" we encounter. All of these considerations come into pronounced play—often to the point of wretched excess—in the case of expensive flagship stores, or "spectacular consumption sites," in academic parlance. What typifies a spectacular consumption site? A store that is highly "interactive" (lots of stuff to test and handle); rich in a specific lifestyle fantasy; full of visual stimuli in the form of over-the-top displays (trade term, *entertailing*), all of which reflect your favored lifestyle values. In other words:

If you are, psychographically...	...you're right at home at:
Fit, active, athletic, vital, hero worshipful	Niketown
Sports-loving, TV-loving, beer-burger-and-fries loving	ESPN Zone
Design conscious, creative, freethinking	The Apple Store
Adventurous, rugged, "green"	REI

* * *

Today, few self-respecting retailers risk a major move without considering the mid- and long-term demographic fallout. More and more subscribe to the notion, as one consultant puts it, that "retailers [need to] define themselves by the customers they serve, not by the *products* [they sell]."* Drugstore chains, for example, consider how best to exploit the aging baby boom bucket: they should "stop thinking about being in the drugstore business," one consultant says, "and think instead about being in the health delivery business." Thus do Sell Siders keep one eye on us as we move through the aisles, the other peeled for valuable nuggets buried in Census Bureau reports. For instance, the bureau predicts that in a few years there will be a 5.2 percent rise in the number of Americans ages twenty-five to thirty-four and a nearly equivalent *decline* in those aged twelve to eighteen—indeed, my own kids just slammed the door on the latter segment. Five percent here, 5 percent there, what's the big deal? It's a huge deal if you're the marketing director at American Eagle, Pac Sun, or Abercrombie & Fitch, all of which are currently planning ways to avoid getting caught with their cargo pants down when so many of their prime customers are a year or two older than they are today.

Demographic shifts can be an *immense* deal for retailers. For all the attention the media bestow on the baby boom, there's now a groundswell of obsession on the Buy impact of Millennials, aka Gen Y, Echo Boomers, or simply the Boomlet (a misleading tag given that there are 70 million-plus of them). Born over the final two decades of the past century, Millennials will soon outnumber baby boomers owing to the cruel—for boomers—inevitability of actuarial tables. Implications abound. While the boomers built the high-end luxury brands we know and love and now can't afford, Millennials have been aware of these brands since birth, which means, as the *Wall Street Journal* has pointed out, they will either keep Ralph Lauren and Tory Burch and Kate Spade in clover, or they'll tire of them and move on to newer, fresher labels. Indeed, Millennials have already substantially redrawn the global buyscape. Millennials are all-cell-phones all-the-time. My kids, late Millennials, have barely touched a landline telephone

---

*This tenet, often ignored by marketers, was one of Peter Drucker's principal convictions, reinforced time and again throughout his voluminous writings on the proper role of management.

in their lives, have never opened a phone book, don't know the difference between the Yellow and White pages. The other day Linda suggested to Ned that he dial directory assistance for the number of the Illinois Department of Transportation—he needed to replace a lost driver's license. "What's directory assistance?" he replied. Millennials are also, obviously, heavily into e-commerce, prompting discussion among psychiatrists that excessive Internet use might soon be officially designated a compulsive-behavior disorder. Surveys indicate that Millennials spend more time online than with television, print, and radio combined. It's not surprising that when BMW launched its 1-series, it did so on Facebook and other Web sites, "the highest concentration of nontraditional media of any BMW launch," crowed the carmaker's marketing director.

Yet bucketing, for all its enabling, is not surefire. Just because the Sell Side manages to put us in our more or less rightful places doesn't mean it can predict our actual buying behaviors. This gives the Sell Side fits. I can be a sixty-two-year-old SWM, subscribe to the *New York Review of Books*, and *still* be a heavy Nair user. Or I may never have graduated from college but love to shop at Brooks Brothers, even though Brooks Brothers selects merchandise and places advertising on the assumption that customers are almost certainly to be netted in the Highly Educated bucket. Or I may be a high-net-worth, white-collar beer drinker whose brew of preference is Old Milwaukee and wouldn't think of trading up to Grolsch or Heineken. In this case, a common bond is at work, one that defies easy bucketing—both beer and beer drinker are cheap.

Overreliance on the message in the bucket, as Paco Underhill suggested, can be highly risky for Sell Side retailers. In 2005, Gap announced it would pounce on an "underserved" demographic slice of the pie: women over thirty-five and getting older all the time, a substantial segment notably underrepresented among Gap customers. In a grab for this beckoning demographic, Gap announced a retail concept it called Forth & Towne. The strategy: compete with Eileen Fisher and Chico's, women's apparel stores already positioned to exploit the thirty-five-and-over sweet spot in the market. Media and industry trumpets blared—*farsighted! shrewd! way to go, Gap!* Within eighteen months Gap management had pulled the plug on Forth & Towne. What went wrong? The demographic reading was sound, but the company misfired into the Older Women bucket: separate and confusing sections for moms, grandmothers, suburbanites and city dwellers, the press eulogized; too little regard for the vast differences among women over thirty-five. Just who are you, anyway, thirty-five-year-old-and-up woman? *Slate*'s Julia Turner wondered. Sarah Jessica Parker? Madeleine Albright? Anna Wintour? Oprah Winfrey?

Finally, Mea Culpa

During my time at Lands' End, I, too, learned at least one hard lesson about how well-meant bucketing efforts can get a Sell Sider into trouble. The merchants had decided that there was considerable potential in launching a catalog specifically designed for "plus-size" women. These buyers represented a significant chunk of the company's customer base—indeed, the Center for Disease Control and Prevention estimates that two-thirds of Americans are overweight. At Lands' End, plus-size customers were easily identifiable by past-purchase history. So why not give them their very own catalog? Lands' End would hire plus-size models to show customers how its clothing actually looked on "real" women, not waifs. The new catalog would group all plus-size offerings in one place. Well, this sensible experiment went over like the proverbial pregnant pole vaulter. More than a few customers let us know, and in no uncertain terms, that they wished to be treated like everybody else, and sales of plus-size offerings in the regular catalog consistently outpaced sales of the same items in the special edition. A touchy subject, this. Although many women justifiably excoriate the use of too-thin fashion models, many independent studies confirm what we learned at Lands' End. A finding published in the *Journal of Consumer Research*: " . . . exposure to thin models does not necessarily have a negative impact on one's self-esteem. On the contrary, exposure to moderately thin (but not extremely thin) models has a positive impact on one's self-esteem."

At Lands' End, the customers' message was heard loud and clear: take your bucket and shove it.

6

Brain Wave

The search for the elusive Buy Button

It would be arrogant to say we could stick someone in a machine and understand everything.
        —Brain scientist quoted in *Forbes*, 2003

FOR THE SEVERAL MONTHS AFTER THAT trip to New York City, I stayed close to home. The holiday season came and went, and it was now late January, when there's not much to do except wait for the Buy burst that attends the Super Bowl. In the days leading up to the game Americans crawl out of their demographic and lifestyle buckets to buy twelve million pounds of avocados, enough for eight million pounds of guacamole. We also buy carloads of chicken wings, pizza, and salty snacks, and shell out $500 million for beer and soft drinks. Super Sunday long ago eclipsed New Year's Eve as the biggest in-home party excuse of the year. Come game day, we kick back. Malls are empty and forlorn, as if painted by Edward Hopper. But if Super Sunday isn't a Buy day for us, for ad agencies it's the most anticipated, scrutinized, overhyped *Sell* day on the calendar. Super Sunday marks a return to the days when TV commercials mattered, before cable atomized the ABC-NBC-CBS wasteland into hundreds of arid networks, before the Internet came along to steal ad revenue and provide a broader choice of news, commentary, entertainment, and hours of endless distraction. Super Sunday is when, if only for hours, the big old American Mass Market bucket reconstitutes itself: 150 million-plus pairs of eyeballs focused on the same thing at the same time. Super Sunday is when we crawl out of our cozy demographic and psychographic segments, settle into living rooms and bars, and come together in a Consumers' Republic family reunion, an immense, doughy, captive audience.

If you're a marketing director or an advertising exec, if your company sells overnight shipping, pickup trucks, cell phone services, beer, soft drinks, or other male-oriented products, or if you are, even at this late date, a fledgling dot-com looking to make a splash with a crazed frog, monkey, or hand puppet, Super Sunday is your best shot at mass consumption's center stage, even if it means putting an entire year's ad budget on the table. Why? Because "*It's the Super Bowl!*" in the trenchant opinion of the president of Soloflex, maker of machines that turn flab into rock and a Super Bowl sponsor back when, twenty years ago, a single thirty-second spot cost $525,000, or $17,500 a second. Today, a half minute costs $3 million, or $100,000 a second. Superexpensive airtime is just a slice of the spend. Adding to the Super Sunday Buyfest are partnership arrangements with the NFL, ancillary PR campaigns, coupon and direct mail promotions, not to mention the $300 million a year that ticketholders and corporate boondogglers shell out to eat, drink, sleep, and carouse in the host city.

While Linda and I enjoy a tub of buffalo wings as much as the next couple, one cold morning I gently broke the news that we were going to take a pass that year. For some time I'd been keeping an eye out for a chance to spend some time on a college campus with those who are entrenched in, or on the fringes of, the Sell Side Academic Complex—scholars who think, research, and expound on matters that illuminate the deeper cognitive, emotional, and, of late, neurological forces that attend selling and buying. This is, after all, a leading social scientist told me, "consumption's moment" on campus. In fact, it has been consumption's moment on campus for the past thirty or so years, when it became apparent that the Buy was too important—socially, culturally, politically, economically, and scientifically—to be ignored. Before that revelation hit, academic condescension was the order of the day. Most scholars held their noses when the topic turned to consumerism, intent on keeping the ivory tower "commercial free." Shopping and shoppers—women squeezing melons, guys slobbering over power tools—was piffle.

* * *

Vance Packard deserves credit for spotting early signs of what would constitute a mighty shift in academic attitude. As we've seen, in *The Hidden Persuaders* Packard announced that the Consumer Express had left the station and that a growing number of what he called "whiskers" were climbing aboard. Whiskers were not just sex-on-the-brain "depth boys" like Ernest Dichter but a diverse band of social scientists curious to poke their noses into the why of everyday buying decisions. In time no aspect of consumption was beneath academic attention. In 2001, Gerard Prendergast, a marketing professor at a Hong Kong university, interviewed two hundred people about their relationships to shopping bags. The goals of the study:

• To investigate the reasons for using and reusing shopping bags
• To investigate the attributes consumers expect from a shopping bag
• To investigate the reuse frequency, and storage time, for shopping bags

Prescient though he was, Vance Packard had little clue as to just how many academic boxcars would eventually become attached to the Consumer Express or how far and fast it would chug down the line. No longer would the Buy be left to traditional economists, who for too long held fast to the delusion that buying decisions are essentially rational, that we buy in accordance with the laws of supply and demand, for reasons of utility and practical need. The new breed of don recognized that the Buy was driven by emotion, not reason, by cognitive processes nobody fully understands. There was research to be done on all fronts.

Today, from Swarthmore to Stanford, academics of nearly every persuasion swarm over issues that relate to buying and selling. Over in the neuro lab, subjects are rolled into $3 million scanners that record brain activity triggered by images of products and thirty-second spots. Over at the social science and marketing departments, an immense camp is devoted to qualitative research and another to quantitative, and the two are forever shooting spitballs at each other. The Quants think the Quals lack methodological purity—all they do is look, ask, take notes, interview, reinterview. They might as well be—ugh—journalists. The Quals think the Quants don't get out of their labs nearly enough. They stare at their own navels and conduct precious experiments whereby students—young Millennials with minimal "real world" experience—play games to win pennies or coffee mugs, experiments designed to shed empirical light on what might actually happen when people visit a store with a pocketful of credit cards. The titles of their studies reflect how abstruse it gets ("Context Effects in Diverse-Category Brand Environments: The Influence of Target Product Positioning and Consumers' Processing Mind-Set"). The Quals are not amused. "The Quants are doing so many controlled experiments they're running out of things to test, pure and simple," one marketing professor told me with a weary sigh, she being a Qual who specializes in a methodology known as "SWC" (Shopping with Customers).

Hey, all of you—stop bickering! Vance Packard had no idea how right he was when he referred to the "big bucks" available to underwrite Sell Side–related research. Today there's plenty of grant money and corporate giving to go around, so everyone should play nice. There are consulting gigs, boardroom seats, endowed faculty chairs, even entire schools devoted to scholarly exploration of why and how we buy.

For instance, the Center for Brand and Product Management at the University of Wisconsin–Madison sprouted in 2003, thanks to a $6.4 million gift from Signe Ostby and Scott Cook, wife and husband, she being a UW alum and former P&G marketing exec, and he being the founder of Intuit, the software company that markets Quicken. The advisory board includes executives from Procter & Gamble, Johnson & Johnson, General Mills, Kraft, and Kimberly-Clark, among others. It's but one example of how hundreds of millions of Sell Side–related dollars annually rain down on the U.S. campus, every corner of it. At med schools Big Pharma funds new drug research and clinical trials for antidepressants that are potentially effective in the treatment of compulsive buying disorder. The Sell Side flies (front cabin, a rare treat) psychology profs to corporate headquarters, where they present their latest findings to senior executive marketing teams. The number of corporate sponsorships displayed on business school walls rivals the number of logos at a Nascar event and maybe exceeds them now that car companies and advertisers have begun pulling back or eliminating their auto-racing spend. It's estimated that marketing profs make up more than half the faculty members in U.S. B-schools. In many of those schools there's hardly a faculty chair, a lounge, a media lab, a library, a conference room, a cafeteria that doesn't carry the name of a beneficent Sell Side company or alum who made it to the top of the corporate ladder. The University of Missouri had a hard time recruiting for its Kenneth L. Lay chair in economics, endowed by the late Enron chief for a million dollars-plus. No problem—there are a lot of other seats at the two hundred or so B-schools across the country, including the Anheuser-Busch Chair at the Howard University business school, the Kmart Chair of Marketing at Wayne State, the McLamoree/Burger King Chair at the University of Miami, and, next to the *I-ain't-sittin'-there!* Kenneth Lay chair, my second-favorite endowed chair, the PetSmart Distinguished Marketing Chair at Indiana University.

Anyway, Back to Super Sunday

The specific impetus behind forgoing the buffalo wings was a story that had just hit the wires:

Researchers Use Brain Scans To
Predict When People Will Buy

PITTSBURGH—For the first time, researchers have used functional magnetic resonance imaging (fMRI) to determine what parts of the brain are active when people consider whether to purchase a product and to predict whether or not they ultimately choose to buy the product. The study appears in the journal *Neuron* and was co-authored by scientists at Carnegie Mellon University, Stanford University and the MIT Sloan School of Management.

This story interested me on several levels. As I said, I'd been looking for a chance to meet researchers at the cutting edge of scientific research into consumer-related behaviors. But I was especially interested in the fact that the research team in this case was composed of neuroscientists and behavioral psychologists, a nice example of how disparate academic disciplines now routinely merge around issues concerning consumption. I eagerly e-mailed one of the study's coauthors, George Loewenstein, an esteemed professor of economics and psychology at Carnegie Mellon. Loewenstein graciously agreed to see me in Pittsburgh. What I didn't realize, nor did Loewenstein—not that he'd remotely care, as it turned out—was that our initial session, a Sunday evening dinner, would fall smack in the middle of the Super Bowl.

Arriving in Steel City several hours early, I hunkered down with a drink and a bowl of peppery tortilla chips at the Marriott bar. The opening kickoff was at least an hour away. On the wall facing the bar, two flat-panel screens beamed a steady stream of made-for-Super-Sunday commercials. Otherwise the place was dead quiet, as you'd expect in a business travelers' hotel on the biggest home-party day of the year. At the bar it was just me, the bartender, and a food-service employee engaged in her own pregame ritual: she sat on the floor rearranging beer bottles in the refrigerator beneath the liquor shelves so that the better-selling brands were in front, the less favored ones in back: sensible, if not exactly superbrainy, retailing science.

"Yo, what's more popular, Amstel Light or Corona?" the bottle arranger asked the bartender, who looked barely older than the legal drinking age.

"What do you mean?" he answered. "Like, what do *I* like better?"

"No, which do we sell more of?" she said, with some exasperation.

"Well, I'd say it's kinda mixed," the young guy replied. "Some nights it's one, other nights the other. It sort of balances out."

"Kinda mixed" is not an expression that bespeaks knowledge of advanced retailing science. From Wal-Mart on down, inventory control and in-store placement are too important to be left to casual observation, let alone a disengaged barkeep. Big-time retailers know better. They apply bar codes and radio-frequency ID tags to the thousands of SKUs they stock, to determine which items deserve full-frontal facings on the shelves, on which specific aisle, shelf, or endcap.

Turning back to the ads, I quickly concluded that this year's endless reel posed no creative threat to Apple's famed "1984" commercial or Coke's classic "Hey, Mean Joe." Commercial after commercial found a creative wellspring in locker-room pranks, jiggly boobs, Southwest moonscapes with cliffs that amount to little more than speed bumps for a parade of brawny pickup trucks. The commercials were predictably testosterone-juiced and fairly brainless, only fitting given that they were aimed almost exclusively at the American male buyer. Suddenly there appeared a shockingly fresh grope at the male Buy switch, wherever that switch might reside—in the brain or groin—courtesy of the Mars Candy Company. If you missed that by now infamous Snickers spot, it's really too bad. The commercial never again saw the light of plasma (though it's yours to enjoy time and again on YouTube): two hairy auto mechanics gnaw at a Snickers bar from each end, only to find their lips meeting in the middle. "Did we just kiss?" one grease monkey says to the other, with an expression that suggests he may have bitten into a dog turd. To expiate the sin of their unintended smooch, the duo desperately performs an act of penance: each rips out a clump of his own chest hair.

Our little Marriott focus group—the fresh-faced bartender, the bottle arranger, me—reacted with mild revulsion and controlled amusement. Nobody *laughed* exactly, just a fleeting ripple of guffaws. I chomped my chips and tried to decode the spot. By what marketing logic would a commercial like that induce anyone to buy a Snickers bar next time they're standing in a checkout line? Did the spot pander to homophobia, or was it a spoof of same? Still pondering, I paid the check and left to meet the man for whom I'd willingly sacrificed an entire day's scarfing of buffalo wings and guacamole.

My Dinner with George

George Loewenstein turned out to be a tall, nice-looking, soft-spoken fellow, every inch a college professor: bushy, salt-and-pepper hair and requisite whiskers, in his case a mustache. He wears hiking boots and drives a fuel-efficient compact car with a manual transmission littered with books and papers. We drove over to a cozy, candlelit Moroccan restaurant Loewenstein favors not far from the Carnegie Mellon campus. Over a bottle of good red wine, Loewenstein, who's not very comfortable talking about himself (okay, he's *almost* every inch a college professor), indulged my curiosity about how he came to nestle in the crevices between traditional economics, psychology, and neuroscience. He had grown up in Boston and came from a line of preeminent psychologists. This was why, "somewhat neurotically," he noted with a small smile, he chose a graduate program in a field other than psychology, enrolling at Yale as a doctoral student in economics. The rebellion was short-lived. Straight economics didn't set Loewenstein's neurons ablaze, so he requested that he be allowed to pursue a joint program in economics and psychology, a flourishing hybrid today but then unheard-of. He explained how a breakthrough paper had inspired his move—it was "transformative," he said. The paper's author was Richard Thaler of the University of Chicago, who was among the first to conceive the field now known as behavioral economics. It's a discipline that wrestles with what Thaler calls our "mental accounting": how the interplay of our emotions, prejudices, beliefs, biases, and ability to reason lead us to make personal financial decisions. Why do we throw good money after bad? What determines our bizarre behavior when we're swept up in an auction? Why do we buy on the installment plan when we know we can save a lot of money by paying up front and in full? How do we determine what a "fair price" is? Why do we fancy ourselves shrewd investors when we consistently trail the market by taking the advice of our idiot brother-in-law?

Behavioral economics is dedicated to the proposition that irrational decision making is not just human, it's pretty much the human norm. Richard Thaler provides a helpful example: You buy a pair of shoes, but the first day you put them on you discover that they hurt your feet. The next time you wear the shoes they hurt your feet even more. What do you do about it? Thaler predicts the following: 1) the more you paid for the shoes, the more times you'll try to wear them; 2) after a while, you'll stop wearing them but you'll be loath to throw them away; 3) eventually you *will* throw them away because your "mental accounting" has by that point fully "depreciated" the price you paid for the damn shoes.

It's not surprising that behavioral economics—in demystified form— receives a steady stream of media coverage. Newsmagazines routinely report on the findings of Daniel Kahneman at Princeton, who won the Nobel Prize for laying bare the assorted anomalies and self-delusions relating to our Buy decisions, how we tend to be overconfident when we pick stocks, a process invariably driven by unwarranted optimism. There's Robert Shiller at Yale, a frequent go-to guy for the press when the subject turns to Big Bursting Bubbles—tech, home prices, subprime lending—that occur with sufficient frequency that his books (*Irrational Exuberance, The New Financial Order, The Subprime Solution, Animal Spirits*) reliably make it onto bestseller lists. There's Dan Ariely, whose entertaining *Predictably Irrational: The Hidden Forces That Shape Our Decisions* was a 2008 best seller, with chapters entitled "The Fallacy of Supply and Demand," "The Problem of Procrastination and Self-Control," and "The Influence of Arousal." And there's Thaler himself, the founding father, who in 2008 coauthored a book aimed at general readers: *Nudge: Improving Decisions About Health, Wealth, and Happiness.* It explores what Thaler calls our mental "choice architecture"—the process by which we make decisions, often misguided ones, such as buying extended warranties (almost always a bad bet, says Thaler) and why we neglect to read the fine print on mortgage and credit card applications.

George Loewenstein, for reasons of his own, has opted not to go commercial with his abundant scholarship, though he works closely and amiably with those who have. An A-list behavioral economist, his work, too, revolves around the intricacies of decision making: the trade-offs we make between a product's benefits (including the emotional) and what it costs. But he also spends time working in that hybrid that brought me to Pittsburgh, a hybrid of hybrids actually: a field originally called *neurobehavioral economics*, later and wisely abridged to "neuroeconomics." The news story, remember:

Researchers Use Brain Scans
To Predict When People Will Buy

After dinner I asked Loewenstein about the route he took to arrive at the junction of psychology, economics, and the geomapping of the brain. He told me he'd been introduced to brain research in the early 1990s, when he settled in at Carnegie Mellon and started lunching with members of the university's renowned neuroscience department. He and a young colleague named Colin Camerer (now at Cal Tech) had concluded that standard economic theory had little success explaining why we do the unfathomable things we do when we buy. The brain boys, they agreed, might have something to contribute. In 1997, Loewenstein and Camerer reached across the divide and organized what turned out to be a fateful conference. "It was obvious to us that neuroscience had a huge amount to offer to the understanding of economics," Loewenstein recalled. "So we invited a bunch of neuroscientists and economists, started the day with a tour of the campus. Right away the economists became very upset when they saw monkeys with wires attached to their heads. Not a great beginning, but things quieted down. A few neuroscientists presented talks, which were followed by the economists' reactions to what they'd heard." The conference thus opened a dialogue among economists, psychologists, and brain researchers, and the rest is neuroeconomic history, right down to the brain scan experiment that had brought me to Pittsburgh.

That study, in brief: Loewenstein's co-researchers, neuroscientists at Stanford, hooked up twenty-six adults to functional magnetic resonance imaging machines and gave the subjects money to spend on a variety of goods. Subjects were told that if they elected to purchase products, the goods would be shipped to them after the experiment ended. They also had the option of not buying, in which case they could keep the money. Subjects were then shown a series of products. The scanning machines revealed increased activity in a region known as the nucleus accumbens, a part of the brain associated with pleasure that's likely to flicker when, say, you boogie into a hip clothing store. The prospect of an appealing purchase triggers neural pleasure. But when researchers flashed especially high prices for desired products, a different region of the brain—the insula—grew restive. The insula is the part of the brain that typically reacts to painful stimuli, including offensive smells, social snubs, and, apparently, nosebleed pricing.

For the Carnegie Mellon team, the observation that uncomfortably high prices set off alarms in the insula represented "an electric moment." Loewenstein, wearing his neuroeconomic mortarboard, had already been researching the differences between tightwads and spendthrifts. Standard economic theory maintains that when we hold off on spending money, we do so mainly because we're rational enough to know that if we spend money now, we won't have money to spend later. Accordingly—remember, this is in theory; we'll get to credit cards later—we might decide against sailing the Greek isles this summer in order to put the money toward a Japanese car. But while that's a perfectly good reason not to spend now, it may not be what fundamentally distinguishes those who easily refrain from spending from those who have no problem throwing money around. Indeed, the true answer may lie in what our nucleus accumbens and insula are signaling. Loewenstein and team contend that it's the *pain* of paying—as signaled by the insula—that discourages penny-pinchers from reaching into their pockets to pay for the trip to Greece or much of anything else. Cheapskates feel particularly *intense* pain when contemplating a purchase, and characteristically hold back. Spendthrifts, on the other hand, feel less pain. *Two weeks in Greece? Why not? I'll worry about the car in the fall.* And even if you're not a classifiable tightwad or spendthrift, the "pain of paying" might explain quite a lot about your everyday spending behavior, such as why most of us are likely to order fewer drinks when paying by the round than when running a tab. By running a tab, we keep our insulas at bay, at least until the tab finally comes.

Even before the brain scan study results, Loewenstein and his research colleagues, notably a doctoral candidate named Scott Rick, had been doing a lot of probing—neuroimaging, experiments, and surveys of married couples—on the general differences between spendthrifts and tightwads.* Whatever neurological activity may be at work, their findings are interesting enough to pass along:

- Tightwad behavior seems to be more prevalent among men than among women. It also correlates positively with age and level of education. PhDs (engineers in particular) feel the pain of paying with greater intensity than those with bachelor's degrees.

- Neither tightwads nor spendthrifts particularly *like* being tightwads or spendthrifts. This leads them into ill-advised mixed marriages—who wants to live with someone with qualities they dislike? This turns out to be a huge mistake in many cases: endless sparring (or worse) over each other's spending/not-spending habits. Sound like anyone you know?

- Tightwads say they *want* to buy more, and sometimes grit their teeth and indulge. When they do, though, they fail to extract much enjoyment—the pain of paying outthrobs the pleasure received.

- Given that tightwads wish to minimize their pain, they are more likely than spendthrifts to succumb to what researchers refer to as "situational factors" when they run into them in stores or through advertising. Tightwads, for instance, will spring for expedited shipping when the cost is soothingly described as a "*small $5 charge*," as against a "$5 charge." Spendthrifts couldn't care less—they'll pay the $5 either way.

---

*"Spendthrift," should you be wondering, derives from a Norse word, *dingthrift*, *ding* meaning "thump" or "thwack," or "ding" as with a hammer, according to the OED. *Thrift* denotes prosperity or good fortune. A *dingthrifter* is one who thwacks his own good fortune with a mallet. "Tightwad" was first used in Britain around a hundred years ago, and is a direct allusion to "one who keeps his wad of paper money tightly rolled." To Loewenstein et al., to be a tightwad is not the same as being a frugal person. Tightwads find spending money painful; frugals find saving money pleasurable.

- The purchase of clothing is a particularly strong differentiator. Spendthrifts buy tons of clothing, tightwads as little as possible. But tightwads also underspend spendthrifts when they go shopping for preventive health measures and life insurance. For tightwads, *everything* is painful to pay for.

How spendthrifts might differ from cheapskates is only one of a vast number of experiments going on these days in the hope that neuro-imaging will deliver more definitive clues as to why we buy. Indeed, at the exact moment George Loewenstein and I were breaking *matlouh* at the Moroccan restaurant, another brain-imaging study was underway on the West Coast. It, too, employed fMRI technology and was conducted at the Ahmanson Lovelace Brain Mapping Center, part of the Neuropsychiatric Institute at UCLA. For the second consecutive year, researchers at the center, in partnership with a private lab, had chosen to put fMRIs to work to study what exactly happens in our brains when we watch, say, two guys in a candy-bar commercial rip out their own chest hair. Five men and five women between the ages of eighteen and thirty-four were instructed to put on goggles and watch Super Sunday commercials not from a comfy couch but from inside a bagel-shaped fMRI. The idea was to observe how various commercials generated blood flow through the brain; in particular, how blood pulsed through a diddlybob called the amygdala, which is shaped like an almond (hence its name) and located in the front of the temporal lobe. The amygdala, commonly referred to as the brain's "threat detector," is often likened to a smoke alarm. When its activity is intense, it alerts us to assorted dangers, downers, and discomforts, and prompts us to react appropriately (assuming it's working properly): it summons anger, avoidance, defensiveness, fear. An intensely activated amygdala instructs our palms to sweat and the muscles around our mouths to tighten; it suggests that we back away from people who scream obscenities in our faces and run like hell from people, things, or animals that might hurt us. If the amygdala is on the fritz, or if it has been removed surgically, we fail to recognize unpleasant cues such as bloodcurdling shrieks and menacing growls. What does the amygdala have to do with commercials? The assumption is that when our amygdala is flashing red, we're probably thinking about self-protection, not about whether to buy a Coke, a cell phone, or a candy bar.

What were the subjects' amygdalas telling them on that Super Sunday? Well, some of the commercials put the subjects on alert—*be careful!*—and some didn't. For instance, one of the commercials that caused amygdalas to spike was a Nationwide Insurance spot, in which Kevin Federline spirals down from pop-music-idol status to burger-flipper status at a fast-food joint. *Yo, that could be you!* the subjects' amygdalas seemed to be yelling. Even more unsettling to many amygdalas was a GM spot that featured a robot who'd been canned from his job at an assembly plant (he accidentally dropped a screw onto the assembly line floor), then found himself working at a series of increasingly dead-end jobs, only to wind up a mechanical-depressive whose only task was to lift and lower the barrier at a parking ramp. A UCLA researcher commented, "That one got people's attention. But they did not feel good about the message. It produced big spikes of anxiety and perhaps . . . feelings of economic insecurity."

All Buttoned Up

Some compelling questions surround the growing interest in how brain mechanics may influence, or even determine, why, when, and how, we buy. The this-is-your-brain-on-advertising experiment was precisely the sort that science reporters swallow whole—*Flash! Researchers Locate Consumer On/Off Switch!* Indeed, it's a rather familiar story by now, dating back at least to a *Forbes* magazine cover in September 2003. The headline: IN SEARCH OF THE BUY BUTTON. The reporter's own brain seemed hyperkinetic:

> What makes some products irresistible? [Neuroscientists] are racing to find the answer to that question—and to pass it along to consumer marketers. [They] say that by peering inside your head they can tell whether you identify more strongly with J. K. Rowling's Harry Potter, say, than with J. R. R. Tolkien's Frodo. A beverage company can choose one new juice or soda over another based on which flavor trips the brain's reward circuitry. It's conceivable that movies and TV programs will be vetted before their release by brain-imaging companies. . . . All this is moving toward an elusive goal: to find a "buy button" inside the skull and to test products, packaging and advertising for their ability to activate it.

It's getting so that each week brings news of yet another "breakthrough" that purportedly draws a tighter circle around the parts of our encephalas where Buy Buttons may be planted. Just moments ago I opened *The Economist* to find an article titled "The Way the Brain Buys: Retailers are Making Breakthroughs in Understanding Their Customers' Minds. Here is What They Know About You." The piece offers meager pickings: mostly warmed-over Paco Underhill stuff about how we gravitate toward merchandise placed at the ends of aisles and how we disdain standing in long checkout lines. The article contains spotty and hardly groundbreaking references to the brain itself—unless you count the observation that people with certain kinds of brain damage "find it hard or impossible to make any decisions at all. They can't shop."

In 2008, inspired by that enduring *Forbes* cover story, marketing guru Martin Lindstrom published a book called *Buyology: Truth and Lies About Why We Buy. Time, Newsweek,* and *USA Today,* among others, jumped on Lindstrom's spirited account of the connection between neural activity and the Buy, including a few examples I'd turned up in my own foraging. An impish, Danish-born branding consultant who always seems to dress in marketing-chic black, Lindstrom was invited by the *Today* show to elucidate what Meredith Vieira referred to as the "groundbreaking study," "using cutting-edge technology," that constitutes the heart of the book. Apparently a couple of thousand subjects—"The Largest Neuromarketing Study Ever Conducted," per the opening of chapter 1—were scanned, 197 of them by fMRI, the rest with a less expensive technology called SST, which Lindstrom describes as an "advanced version of the electroencephalograph."

The key finding, Lindstrom told Vieira, is that 85 percent of our buying decisions take place in the subconscious. Then he talked a bit about how warning notices on cigarette packages activate the nucleus accumbens, the brain's "craving spot," he called it. Because we're so used to seeing those warnings, he explained, our brains unconsciously filter out the negative message attached to them, which in turn reduces the warnings to nothing more than associative prompts *to* smoke—in other words, they act as ads *for* cigarettes. It's but one example of how brain circuitry is thus the ultimate hidden persuader (some selling hooks never go out of fashion). Behold, then, the insidious power of neuromarketing. Or, as it says on the back flap of the book, the "shocking"—more shades of Vance Packard—attempt "to win our loyalty, our money, and our minds."

While morning talk shows and newsmagazines buy into gee-whiz claims such as those served up in *Buyology,* there are dissenters. The head of the

Advertising Research Foundation, Bob Barocci, scoffed when asked about Lindstrom's premise that neuroscience had the Buy all but figured out, telling *Advertising Age* that *Buyology* "falls under the category of pop books that purport to be serious books but they're not." A professor at the Harvard Business School noted that neuromarketing was still too formative a field from which to draw conclusions about how brain-imaging data correlate with behavior. Seeking further expert opinion, I sent a copy of *Buyology* to Scott Rick, who'd worked on the fMRI-based tightwad-spendthrift study with George Loewenstein. Rick found a few problems with the research, questioning whether the work was indeed "groundbreaking" and "revolutionary." *Buyology* and the claims it made about the connection of brain activity to buying behavior, Rick said, were "at least a decade premature."

Which doesn't mean that the Sell Side researchers won't keep scanning and poking. The *Wall Street Journal* reported that a member of a Boston ad agency team, a woman with a PhD in cognitive science who wears a lab coat at the agency, argued successfully that an Ocean Spray diet cranberry juice commercial should feature a group of women who were exercising, not having fun at a party as in the original scenario. The brain, she contended, would be better able to "connect" exercising and diet cranberry juice. Furthermore, the on-site PhD suggested that viewers should see the women exercising *before* they learned that this was indeed a spot for diet cranberry juice, the point being that one's brain needs a second or two to process images. All of this makes sense, of course, and hats off to the adwoman in the lab coat, but really, is a PhD in cognitive science a prerequisite for common logic?

The fact remains, however, that a good many of us, not just marketing gurus, television producers, newsmagazine editors, and newspaper reporters, find irresistibly compelling this idea that there's some kind of Buy toggle switch entombed in our heads. They persist in the belief that it's only a matter of time before neuroscientists put their finger on the precise location. Why does this possibility so intrigue us? My guess, with not a drop of data to back it up, is that we accept, subconsciously or otherwise, the idea that we haven't a clue as to why we do what we do when shopping, and wouldn't it be nice if someone, especially a *neuroscientist*, came along and solved the mystery once and for all? Meanwhile, let's not hold our breath. Around the time Martin Lindstrom's *Buyology* hit the bookstores, Deena Skolnick Weisberg and a team at MIT published a paper titled "The Seductive Allure of

Neuroscience Explanations." The researchers tested two sets of subjects, one consisting of "experts" in neuroscience, the other of those who knew precious little about the field. Each group was given a series of "explanations" about various psychological phenomena. Some of the explanations specifically cited "brain scans" or "frontal lobe circuitry" as the supporting basis for the assertions, while others omitted any mention of scans or regions of the brain. Finding: those who were not expert in neuroscience consistently favored explanations that invoked neurological "evidence." Those who actually *knew* something—a lot, in fact—about how the brain works favored just the opposite: they bought into explanations that omitted reference to neurological evidence.

The day I said good-bye to George Loewenstein at Carnegie Mellon, the day after Super Sunday, everyone in America was Monday-morning quarterbacking the commercials we'd watched the day before. A handful were taking swipes at the imaging study that measured the responses of those Californians who watched the commercials from inside the fMRI scanners. One analyst who worked in the advertising industry, whose own amygdala seemed to quiver at the idea that *she* could be replaced by an advertising analyzing thingamajig, told a reporter, "I think [brain scans] tell the truth, but we've found we get similar findings with paper-and-pen research." And adman Donny Deutsch—he, like Martin Lindstrom, had been invited to opine on *Today*—cut to the chase. Pooh-poohing brain scans as predictive Buy signs, he noted that one thing and one thing only matters when assessing the cause and effect between a commercial and our decision to buy: does it or does it not get us to set aside the guacamole and haul our lazy butts into a store?

7

Bombarded

Four ways to think about advertising

20,679 Physicians say Luckies are less irritating.
—Lucky Strike ad, 1930

 THE EXACT RELATIONSHIP BETWEEN the amygdala and advertising remains elusive, but it's for certain that advertising hogs, some would say clogs, our brain circuitry. It's hardly a stretch to say that most of every waking hour calls on our hundred billion neurons, assigned to their respective lobes, to process—not to mention derive pleasure or pain from—advertising's constant assault. Really, what chance do our beleaguered neurons stand against a Sell Side that carpet bombs American households with roughly (accountings vary) $65 billion of television advertising annually? Dumps another $28 billion into newspapers, $30 million into magazines?* Spews more than $12 billion around the Web, where advertising growth has been, at least until 2009, white-hot? Throw in radio, billboards (aka "litter on a stick"), bus shelters, toilet stalls, classrooms, doctors' examining rooms, the backs of ATM receipts, and all the rest and the U.S. ad spend is roughly equivalent to the GDP of Ireland, Finland, Hungary, or Israel. Procter & Gamble alone spends close to $4 billion a year. AT&T, Verizon, and Time Warner $2 billion each,

---

*2008 was the first year TV ad revenue surpassed newspaper ad revenue, the latter experiencing a much-discussed, dramatic freefall.

give or take. These huge numbers don't capture what such companies *really* spend on advertising; they refer strictly to what those companies allocate to so-called measured ad placements: media purchases that can be more or less accurately toted up by external auditors. P&G spends an additional $1.5 billion on *unmeasured* advertising: in-store ads, product placement on TV shows, online search engines; Time Warner, another $1.2 billion on "untraditional" ad buys.

Point taken? There's just too damn much advertising? Ad agencies and their clients are quick to concede that their greatest challenge is bulldozing through the clutter of their own making. Studies show that on average each of us is exposed to between three thousand and five thousand advertising impressions a day. Most ads whip by so fast we don't register them as impressions. Think of how swiftly we browse the Internet, how link after link lands us on pages where advertising crowds the info we seek, flash-dancing across the screen. Our mouse clicks give Google and others tracking info with which to sell space to Sell Siders whose commercial interests align with our own. As Nicholas Carr noted in a 2008 *Atlantic* cover story—"Is Google Making Us Stupid?"—our clicks leave behind tasty "crumbs" for advertisers, "the more crumbs the better," Carr says. "The last thing these companies want is to encourage leisurely or slow, concentrated thought. It's in their economic interest to drive us to distraction."

Beyond the fact that there's too damn much of it, there's little everybody agrees on about advertising. Buy Scolds would have us believe that advertising compels us to buy things, more things than any sane human being could possibly need. For them, advertising is, in effect, *injectable*: having been pricked by a print ad or commercial, our nervous system succumbs to a ravaging Buy virus. Others take a less deterministic view. Advertising, they say, doesn't *make* us buy; its principal task is simply to alert us to the existence of products and services we may (or may not) need, to differentiate one product from the next, even if those products are identical (bottled water) or virtually identical (toothpaste, aspirin).

Either way—whether advertising *infects* us, or just *affects* our decision making—our susceptibility to it depends on the attitude we bring to advertising in the first place. This is why the Sell Side undertakes a vast number of studies to determine how we personally feel about advertising, and under what circumstances we might respond to its myriad forms. That is, we may be easy marks for certain kinds of advertising but blind, deaf, or hostile to other kinds. Say you buy your clothes at Lands' End. If so, and consistent with solid demographic evidence, you're likely middle-aged, reasonably affluent, and well educated. Your customer bucket is one that watches considerably less television than do other demographic segments. But does this mean the Sell Side is willing to write you off as hopelessly advertising-phobic, that it waves a white flag, and won't somehow try to get its smelly foot in your door? No, it means the Sell Side will look for an alternate way to tromp in. In your case, this would seem to point to the mail slot. A catalog is, after all, nothing *but* advertising. Based on your captured and stored and rentable Buy history, you are a certified catalog customer, which signifies to all direct-to-consumer marketers that you're attitudinally open to advertising masquerading as a catalog. This is why, if you buy a fleece jacket from Lands' End, you'll soon have a mailbox full of— to throw out just a few of the Bs—Bean, Bauer, and Bose mailings. These Sell Siders assume there's a fair chance you'll glance their way while leafing through their offerings before having your junk mail into the recycling bin. (Lands' End customers—responsible, earnest, and well-educated people— tend to be conscientious recyclers.)

Researchers who study attitudes about advertising uncover interesting insights into how we delude ourselves. For instance, there's the "Third Person Effect." It goes like this. Were I, interviewing you for this book, to ask what you think of certain questionable commercials—e.g., those that tout the gambling casinos down by the river, or the appeal-to-teens Captain Morgan rum commercials on Comedy Central, or the funky Visa spots with break-dancing teens whipping out their plastic to buy clothes and cell phones with reckless impunity—you might bluster that you strongly believe that these advertisements run counter to society's best interests. But—you might be quick to add—*not* because these ads present any clear and present danger to *you*. No way. *You* know gambling's a sucker's game. *You* drink responsibly. *You* pay your monthly credit-card bills on time and in full. The problem, in your view, is that *others,* less sophisticated and more gullible, are at risk. The Third Person Effect holds that the better educated you are and the more money you have, the more likely it is that you'll tell yourself you can withstand advertising's tricks. Madison Avenue can try to stick its hypodermic into you all day and it won't penetrate.

Let's admit it: few of us are fortified enough to withstand the right ad at the right moment. You may *tell* yourself that advertising dissembles and corrupts, and then one evening as you're watching Wolf Blitzer, CNN cuts to a commercial for a new drug that promises to lower blood pressure. Because you or someone you love suffers from hypertension, you put down that V. S. Naipaul novel and turn up the volume on the tube. Third Person Effect? What Third Person Effect? Suddenly it's as if a drug company has attached a jumper cable to your amygdala. You're all eyes and ears. Next thing you know you're logging onto WebMD for further details about the drug, or phoning to share the news with your hypertensive dad, or leaving a voice mail for your doc (not that he'll return it anytime soon). Thus does the Sell Side play advertising gotcha. When it manages to marry the right message—*new and improved! clinically tested blood pressure medicine!*—with the right media buy—*Wolf Blitzer in the Situation Room!*—advertising clicks. It's hardly an accident that pharmaceutical companies buy so many thirty-second spots on CNN: the network draws heavily from the Fifty-Plus bucket, a market segment prone to high blood pressure, not least when it's trapped in a room with Wolf. Studies confirm that the overwhelming reason (80 percent) people pay attention to drug advertising is because they, or those they care about, are afflicted with whatever a specific drug is supposed to help. This in spite of the fact that fewer than half of us say that drug commercials adequately describe side effects and about a third of us say we find drug ads confusing in some way. And that one in four of us believes drug advertising has no business being on television in the first place, that it should be confined to doctors' magazines. But tell that to your amygdala.

Having spent a considerable amount of time thinking hard about advertising and how it affects us, I've come to the following conclusion: it depends. Many people tell me they're fine with advertising; many say they loathe it; many say they're so accustomed to inhaling it they barely notice it anymore. So it seems to me that almost everyone can be dumped into one of four Advertising Attitude buckets. Two of the four—I'll call them the Advangelist and Adbasher buckets—contain people with extreme views on the role advertising plays in their lives, one pro, the other con. The remaining two—I'll call them the Agnostic and Ambivalent buckets—are home to those who occupy a middle ground:

Advangelists say . . .	Adbashers say . . .
Yes, advertising matters, *and* it works, *and* it's good for both seller and buyer.	Yes, advertising matters, *and* it works, *and* it totally sucks.
Agnostics say . . .	**Ambivalents say . . .**
Yes, advertising matters (some-times), *and* it works (sometimes), but even when it doesn't matter or work it's culturally interesting or significant.	No, advertising doesn't really matter because there's so damn much of it that nobody pays serious attention, nor need they.

Advangelists

Those who argue that advertising matters (and generally works) hold the view that advertising performs a useful service for the Sell Side and consumers alike. Advangelists are, in the main, those who make their living from advertising. To cleave to the Advangelist point of view is to accept the following textbook premises about what makes advertising effective and potent:

1. It reaches those for whom it's intended—e.g., people who have, or know others who have, high blood pressure.

2. Having been reached, we pay attention to advertising—we set down *A Bend in the River* and turn up the volume on Blitzer.

3. Having paid attention, we interpret the advertising message— *new and improved! clinically tested blood pressure medicine!—* correctly.

4. Having understood it, we retrieve the message under the appropriate circumstance—e.g., "Hey, dad, listen. Would you calm down for a minute? I was just watching TV and there was this ad for a new blood-pressure pill. . . ."

Advangelists maintain that advertising's chief task is to lead us to the Sell Side's trough, in this case to a doctor's office, then straight to the drugstore. Even the most rapturous advangelist—an agency business-development exec, for instance—will concede that getting us *to* the trough is always a challenge. A study in the *Journal of Marketing Research* sheds light on the ways advertising can spook us, to hell with stopping at any trough. Example: a car dealer runs an ad that touts a particular model as "well equipped," with "lots of options." Sounds good! So you hightail it to the showroom only to discover that the dealer is, in fact, hawking a crummy base model equipped with nothing more than standard options. The study offers evidence that such an episode poisons not only your regard for the jerk dealer who ran the ad, but for car dealers in general (the Better Business Bureau fields over a million inquiries a year pertaining to car dealers' reputations). Over time, your eyes and ears grow ever more alert to misleading advertising. This morning, while I was at the gym, a commercial came on for Charmin toilet tissue. Its premise: young kids are always tearing off more toilet paper than they need, which of course drives parents crazy. But Charmin, the commercial says, is more *absorbent* than those bargain brands, and therefore—get ready for a not so subtle leap of logic—young kids will tear off a lot *less* toilet paper when they go potty. Kids know from "more absorbent"? Kids tear because kids are kids: borderline uncivilized, and besides, tearing is fun!

The Inside Pitch

Advangelists, those who defend the value of advertising, remain indomitable in the face of consumer attitudes that range from leery to hostile. An adman or -woman is, after all, a salesperson, from the top of his head to the tips of his Gucci slip-ons. While you and I may have toilet-tissue-thin skin, the adman's/woman's is as leathery as those Italian loafers. Ours would be, too, if we were rejected so frequently by demanding clients. The advangelist, calloused by clients' rude behavior, is good at taking no for an answer. At a pitch meeting, the adman (or adwoman) keeps plugging away, dealing concepts from a stack of face-down storyboards to the poker-faced client at the other end of the table. A curious ritual is at work here. The concepts the adman/woman secretly favors, his/her aces in the hole, are always tucked away at the bottom of the deck, while the likely losers are at the top. The adperson plays the cards one by one, setting up each with a beguiling sentence or two, building suspense. When pitching ideas, advangelists have a remarkable oral facility: they can blow smoke—flattering the intelligence of the client and the client's customers—while simultaneously tooting their own horns.

The reason I'm familiar with how this game works is because at Lands' End I *was* the stony-faced guy at the end of the table. It was an unexpected turn of events, to say the least. The chap who'd offered me the Lands' End job had almost forgotten to mention that, in addition to the other duties he'd outlined, I'd be responsible for the company's national print and TV campaigns. He knew I'd never created advertising and had no training in how to measure its effectiveness. I'd been a magazine editor who, often as not, jousted with the ad guys. (We were always bickering. Me: "*Esquire* is a journalistic and literary magazine!" Owner: "No! *Esquire* is a men's fashion magazine with a few articles thrown in!") Who better to run the advertising at Lands' End? Anyhow, not knowing what else to say, I asked my recruiter how much Lands' End spent each year on magazine and TV ads. "Twenty million," he replied. This struck me as a breathtaking amount to entrust to a neophyte. What I didn't know then: $20 million is ad-budget peanuts, an anemic .0006 percent of what the big-time players at Procter & Gamble throw at the wall every year.

Once I'd arrived at Lands' End, I soon convinced myself that I had reasonably good instincts for the ad game, if only because the client's role isn't all that complicated. You sit impassively at the end of the table, listen to pitches by thick-skinned salespeople, spend a day or two with the storyboards they left behind, then reach the inescapable conclusion that you have to fire the whole sorry lot of them as soon as practicable. And so I did. I took no particular pleasure in the task—nearly everyone I fired was someone I liked. In spite of whatever poison they crop-dust on the culture, ad folks are generally great fun to be with. They make terrific dinner companions (they pay). They dress in cool black clothes and wear funky glasses. And, best of all if you're the client, they're the most accomplished brownnosers in the business world. Still, I had no choice but to fire them. First I fired Lands' End's long-standing ad agency—its work was literate but snoozy. Our advertising, I explained gently, needed more zest. I then retained a new agency, a big shop in Chicago. Sadly, I fired them after a while—their work was too much like everybody else's. Lands' End had to be more than a "me-too" brand, I explained with a heavy heart. Convinced that there had to be somebody out there who could create advertising that was smart *and* lively *and* distinctively our own—not just pretty pictures of casually dressed families on the beach, with watered-down electronica pulsing in the background—I hired a search firm to find a full-time replacement agency. The winner turned out to be a small firm based in North Carolina. Had I not decided to leave Lands' End, I probably would have fired those people as well—their work was hip but also predictable, advertising for its own sake.

None of this should suggest that the advertising we produced at Lands' End wasn't, at least on occasion, intelligent and brand-appropriate, possibly even effective. I say "possibly" because it's often hard to know for sure how much advertising has to do with sales. During my years posing as a mini ad mogul, Lands' End enjoyed record revenues and profits. Among the products that contributed to our success were dorky-looking but versatile rubber-soled shoes marketed as "All Weather Mocs," and which we advertised for brief spurts on bucket-appropriate cable networks. One of the best All Weather Moc spots featured a row of multicolored All Weather Mocs arrayed as piano keys. The happy mocs plunked up and down, beating out a catchy Fats Waller–like tune. I screened the commercial at companywide employee sessions and at board meetings. Huge laughter and applause! And sure enough, just as the campaign kicked off, those mocs began flying out of the warehouse. A vast addition to our already giant warehouse was hastily built, extra storage space for our growing shoe business. The plunking All Weather Moc piano spot had ignited it all, everyone seemed to agree on that. As for me, while I was delighted to take credit for the success of the All Weather Moc, I was never convinced that the commercials had done the trick. First, the audience we reached was relatively small, and the campaign had a limited-engagement run. Second, the commercials' airings were deliberately timed to coincide with the mailing of our catalogs, which prominently featured All Weather Mocs on their back cover, highly valuable selling space.

In other words, it was difficult to know whether the commercials or the catalog presentation deserved the credit. (Yes, these things are testable—withhold the commercial from certain markets and compare sales results to those where the commercial in fact ran. But we didn't bother with that.) On top of everything else, it wasn't as if *we* were the ones who'd created customer awareness of this hot, rubber-soled tromp-about. A well-known outdoor footwear company (Merrill) had successfully introduced similar rubber-soled mocs the season before, so customers were already familiar with the look and utility of the shoe. In the end, maybe our enormous success came down to—are you sitting down?—*price*. Our All Weather Mocs cost just $29.95, Merrill's about twice that. Who knew whether the plunking shoe commercial had hit the winning notes; whether our media buy had reached the optimum audience; whether the commercial captured and held people's attention and etched those Mocs into buyer consciousness, there to be retrieved under the appropriate circumstances? Only a true advertising advangelist, a person of dubious veracity, would claim to know that for sure.

Adbashers

I sincerely don't think I did lasting harm to society during my time as an ad honcho or contributed to the inexorable decline of civilization. Adbashers would beg to differ. (Later on we'll listen to major-league Buy Scolds who are "out to reverse America's consumer binge," to quote the cover of *Culture Jam*, Kalle Lasn's diatribe against global capitalism in general and advertising in particular.*) Adbashers reject any notion that advertising is benign, that it exists merely to help us "differentiate" one product from the next. What advertising does, adbashers argue, is bamboozle us into mindless buying. Sure, those All Weather Mocs were a good deal for the money, but did anyone really need two pairs, one brown, the other green, or any of the other colors that plunked on the piano, just to walk the dog or take out the garbage? (Which, by the way, according to Buy Scolds, the Sell Side generates in prodigious quantity and wraps in excessive amounts of paper, cardboard, and worse, non-biodegradable materials—which, come to think of it, are exactly what those shoes were made of.) The most ardent adbasher sees the devil in Prada and every other brand that chooses to litter the good earth with advertising, thereby corrupting the spirit and fracturing the social order. And not just here, everywhere. The mayor of Beijing, a Buy Scold with an ideological agenda, announced prior to the 2008 Olympics that he was banning billboards in certain sections of the city. Why? Because "many [advertisements] use exaggerated terms that encourage luxury and self-indulgence [that are] not conducive to harmony."

---

*Lasn is the founder of *Adbusters*, a magazine by and for committed adbashers.

Some adbashers are shrill, others less so. To the more tepid objectors, advertising isn't a scourge, it's just irredeemably sleazy. A few years ago a Gallup survey reported on the public's perception of "honest professions." Advertising scraped the bottom of the list. Gallup found that Americans rank Madison Avenue flimflammers just below insurance agents and barely ahead of car salesmen. Movies and books routinely portray the adman as manipulative and self-loathing. Instead of becoming the great American novelist he aspired to be when he was in college, the adman's a broken spirit who churns out a profusion of simple-minded taglines and jingles that, like mayflies, flutter for the briefest of time, their purpose on earth being to find someone to screw. The portrait lives on: see *Mad Men*, the hit AMC network series that's set on Madison Avenue circa 1960. Here are the prototypical boozers, unregenerate skirt chasers, and ethical losers who comprise the advertising world.

It hardly seems necessary to recite in full the bill of indictments handed down by the adbasher lobby, but here are five:

1. Advertising exists to con us into thinking we're too fat, too poor, too old, conditions for which it provides instant amelioration.

2. Advertising exists to legitimize the superfluous.

3. Advertising exists to praise products, services, and therapies which, if they work at all, don't work as advertised.

4. Advertising exists to corrupt the minds, hearts, and souls of our children, even as it makes them obese and destroys their teeth and gums through glorification of everything high in fat and sugar. Personally, I agree with this one. How can you not? In 2005, a study published in *Pediatrics* concluded—after researchers watched fifty thousand commercials—that 97.8 percent of ads aimed at kids two to eleven touted products high in sugar, fat, and sodium. Even more frightening, the study didn't include fast-food restaurants.

5. Advertising exists for the same unfathomable reason that Canadian thistle exists. Left unattended, advertising is to the culture what thistle is to a pristine meadow: an ineradicable scourge that plants itself in every tiny patch of available space. In

the case of advertising, that includes movie theaters, gas station pumps, bathroom stalls, elevators. In 2008 a 7,500-square-foot ad for Chanel, in the form of a temporary art pavilion inspired by a Chanel handbag, arose in the middle of Central Park. On a more mundane level, I recently spent several days at a convention hotel in San Diego, where flat-panel screens are mounted in the elevator cars. Installed by a company called Televator (its slogan, "Elevating Vertical Transportation"), the screens continuously beamed ads for products (contact-lens solutions, eyedrops) targeted to the groups meeting at the hotel, the American Society of Cataract and Refractive Surgery and the American Society of Ophthalmic Administrators. For the advangelist, a slick idea. For the guest, an inescapable irritation.

Agnostics

Those who are less bilious about advertising, who fall into the agnostic category, tell adbashers to calm down. A couple of decades ago, some thirty years after Vance Packard's *Hidden Persuaders*, sociologist Michael Schudson wrote an influential rebuttal to the notion that advertising has the power to accomplish all the nasty things adbashers criticize it for. The fear that Madison Avenue practices "precision microsurgery on the public consciousness" was, to Schudson, a lot of phooey. Winking at Packard's book, Schudson titled his *Advertising, The Uneasy Persuasion*. Packard looked at advertising and discovered "dark forces"; Schudson looked at it and saw a lot of "*stabbing* in the dark"—which aptly describes my MO at Lands' End. Nevertheless, Schudson argues that advertising deserves serious attention because it reveals a great deal about the culture. But that's no reason to freak out: "The most avid watchers of commercials are the men and women who created them, the preschool children who [don't] distinguish them from regular programming, the important but inevitably small segment of the audience . . . in the market for the advertised product [and] students of popular culture looking for deeper meanings."

Agnostics, while they shunt aside fears that advertising corrupts absolutely, press the case that it's worth paying attention to because it's a barometer of the culture. Sometimes they go overboard here, giving copywriters and art directors more credit for cultural influence than they warrant. Consider one of more bizarre examples of overanalysis: it concerns a certain member of the family Leporidae, portrayed as a puckish and hyperactive creature with a pink nose, highly elongated ears that more or less bend in the middle, arched black eyebrows, a cherry red tongue, and a fiendish grin. If you guessed Trix the Rabbit, you guessed right. At first blush it wouldn't seem that Trix offers an agnostic scholar anything to munch on in terms of significant cultural meaning. It was, after all, just a dopey cartoon conceived at a time (the fifties) when the sale of breakfast cereals enjoyed an explosive snap, crackle, and pop. Cereal was convenient: quick from cupboard to bowl to belly. Cereal appealed to buyers of all ages. Best of all, if you were a Sell Side marketer, cereal was deliverable via a versatile advertising medium: the box it came in. Marketers leveraged the box to provide breakfast-time games and reading; they stuffed it with offers for toys and prizes (in my day, decoder rings and bathtub submarines powered by baking powder); and used it as a billboard for health claims, recipes, and celebrity endorsements. They also found the box to be an effective platform on which to launch cartoon characters who instantly became brand avatars, as recognizable and long-lived as any Disney character: L'il Abner was Grape-Nuts; Mighty Mouse was Sugar Crisp; Quick Draw McGraw was Sugar Smacks; Katy the Kangaroo was Frosted Flakes, though she was heartlessly shoved aside when Tony the Tiger, Mrs. Tony, and Tony Jr. moved in on the box.

As for Trix the Rabbit, I was recently surprised to learn that he wasn't just an inane cartoon creature dreamed up by admen following a martini-soaked lunch. Thomas Green, writing in the *Journal of Popular Culture*, contends that Trix the Rabbit bears more than a passing resemblance to what Carl Jung and others refer to as a "trickster," a character who appears in ancient myths and folk tales, part human, part beast, and is generally up to something strange and sometimes taboo, a something that usually has to do with acquisition. "Tricksters," Green writes, "are often depicted as participating in some kind of trick, theft, or sacrifice that results in the gift of the useful technology or plant to humanity." Trix, of course, fits the legend perfectly. Green points out that he's comparable to the harelike Wakjunkaga, a prominent trickster from Native American (Winnebago) folklore and a character of considerable interest to Jung. Wakjunkaga, Green tells us, "made plants that are useful to humans out of his penis," but that's not all:

[Trix the Rabbit] exhibits the insatiable hunger typical of Wakjunkaga, but not for foods typically associated with rabbits. He desires only the Trix brand breakfast cereal, and is willing to cheat and deceive in order to get it. In the early days of Trix, the variations on the specific disguise that the Rabbit adopted were still closely identified with the plot premise: He was attempting to appear as something other than a rabbit, so a little old lady or astronaut disguise would do. In more recent years the disguises have begun to take on the form of whatever the advertisers perceive as popular with kids at the time, so in the 1980s the Rabbit disguised himself as a breakdancer, and, most recently, a karaoke singer. In any case, the Rabbit is using these disguises to appear more human than rabbit, which empha-sizes the way in which the Trix Rabbit most closely corresponds to the archetypal . . . trickster.

And we, silly us, back when we were kids, thought we liked Trix cereal because it tasted good and set off little explosions in our mouths. Not close. They *conjured* us into eating Trix by milking the power of enduring myth.

Ambivalents

Those who shrug off advertising's influence, mythical or not, believe that advertising is not a science, rarely an art, and that when all is said, done, and broadcast, nobody can say with certainty why some ads prove more ef-fective than others. Accordingly, tons of research is conducted to try to nail down just what it is about an ad that sticks in our mind, assuming it does. One of my favorites is a study that sought to determine whether we're more likely to respond to an ad if we see a reflection, literally, of ourselves in it. The answer carries implications. Billions a year are spent on storyboard-ing, pitching, casting, shooting, and running ads with human faces featured in them. Sometimes it's the face of an annoying celebrity (William Shatner comes to mind), sometimes the mug of an Average Jane or Joe. Whoever the faces belong to, ad agencies choose them with great care, often after hours and hours of focus-group discussion. *You, you eating the Skittles. Do you like this face? Is it a trustworthy face? A friendly face? The face of someone whose opinions and tastes you respect? Would you marry this face?* Ronald Faber, Brittany Duff, and Yulia Lutchyn at the University of Minnesota conducted an interesting study concerning how we relate to faces we see in advertisements. The team showed a number of people an ad in which the face (female in the ad women subjects looked at; male for the men) of a model (in the example below, Sam Waterston) who was digitally morphed with the subject's own features (in this case, mine):

Among the findings:

- Not one of the subjects detected even a trace of themselves in the morph, not consciously anyway.

- Women tended to find nonmorphed faces, i.e., the models', more interesting than the ones morphed with their own eyes, nose, mouth, and hair.

- Men responded the other way. They commented more frequently, and more favorably, on the morphed faces that bore traces of their own features.

When it came to *buying* the product featured in the ad—in this case a fictitious face cream—"you-ish" features made not a dime's worth of difference for either gender.

Notwithstanding whose facial features pop up onscreen, most of us unthinkingly reach for the remote when a commercial comes on. We moisten index finger with tongue when we flip through the pages at the front of magazines. These are nonverbal indicators that we likely hold an ambivalent view of advertising. As Michael Schudson put it a couple of decades ago, "Advertising is propaganda and everyone knows it." During a recent NFL telecast, I saw back-to-back spots for a Bristol-Myers Squibb cardiovascular drug and Burger King. Last night an ad for Wendy's and the antacid Prilosec ran sequentially. Take advertising seriously?

Ambivalents don't take advertising remotely seriously—they've been sensitized by too damn much of it. Trix the Rabbit could be the reincarnation of Maimonides for all anybody knows. Who cares? In the ambivalent's view, the Buys you make are expressions of free choice. You are, as characterized by one marketing guru, a "*pro*sumer." *You're* in charge. You, not the adman, determine what's good, bad, worthwhile—you've been doing it all your life, even when you were a tyke, the age when the Buy Scolds say we're most vulnerable to advertising's assault. What a crock! You watched years of Saturday morning television, but Trix the Rabbit could never in a million Saturday mornings make you eat Trix. You could barf from Trix. You ate Rice Krispies (even though you were a boy and rice, as Ernest Dichter posited, is feminine). And—before anyone jumps to the conclusion that advertising deserves any credit—your love of Rice Krispies had nothing to do with the blandishments of Snap, Crackle, or Pop, who you thought were total dorks even back then.

8

You

The new Them

The days of sitting behind the focus-group wall are going the way of the buggy whip.

—Word-of-mouth marketing consultant

WE NOW APPROACH THE END OF OUR walk down the Sell Side. Soon we'll cross over to the Buy Side, taking care not to be flattened by a bus, taxi, truck, or stock car plastered with too damn much advertising. To recap: there are retailers, gurus, whiskers, snoops, techno-geeks, advangelists, and platoons of others arrayed against us. They lure us into cramped changing rooms where, all but naked, we wrestle with hopes, fantasies, and insecurities. They track our movements through stores, noting whether we turn left or right as we enter, how we shy away from narrow aisles lest a customer or clerk brush us in the butt, intentionally or with perversity aforethought. They scoop us up by the millions—our families, neighbors, everybody—and dump us into industrial-grade sifters, deposit us into appropriately labeled buckets, then douse us with Buy offers. They slide us under expensive scanning machines to observe how our nervous systems respond to thirty-second rat-a-tats of calculated lust or longing. They churn out young recruits by the thousands, MBAs who take up posts as tyro brand managers and marketing researchers with starting salaries of $85,000. They marinate us in vats of advertising to soften us up. They try to seduce our kids with pointy-eared pests bearing mythological powers. *And yet*, spend even a little time wandering along the Sell Side and you'll hear over and over that certain Sell Side weapons are losing their firepower. I heard this way back at the beginning of my Sell Side tour, when Paco Underhill stared me in the eye and declared: "Look, Lee. Here's the thing. Merchants and marketers in the twenty-first century are nervous. They're worried. What are they worried about? They're worried that their traditional and reliable tools—advertising strategies, brand promotions—don't work the way they used to." And it's true. Advertising agencies are especially nervous. They're worried about Google and other new technology-driven marketing and advertising models. Google, a former agency CEO told the *New York Times*, "clearly wants to replace the advertising industry in its totality."

If old-style advertising doesn't work the way it used to, you can make the case that the late 1960s marked the beginning of the end. A so-called Creative Revolution had gotten under way. All of a sudden there was less talk about how advertising played on our sexual hang-ups. The chitchat around the water cooler now was about how the commercials were far better than the programs. Advertising had become sharper, and "told it like it is," its champions boasted. Why the change? Well, for one thing, Madison Avenue's long-standing WASP barricades had been breached by a guerrilla force of JIGS (Jews, Italians, and Greeks), a gang of art directors and copywriters who were unusually gifted and irreverent. They drew inspiration from advangelist Bill Bernbach, visionary-in-chief at Doyle Dane Bernbach. Advertising, Bernbach said, is "fundamentally persuasion"—and the best way to persuade is not through cheap huckstering, subliminal sexual cues, or paint-by-numbers commercials based on market research. Persuasion was best achieved through art, through humor, commercials that honored the consumer's intelligence. Good advertising was advertising that shared an understanding with us: *We know that you know that advertising is mostly crap.* "The customer is not a moron. She's your wife," David Ogilvy famously declared. Ogilvy was another leading auteur who rode advangelism's new wave. As if overnight, Madison Avenue began treating us with respect. In a smart retrospective essay on the Creative Revolution, Randall Rothenberg recounted how the BBDO agency greeted the arrival of color TV with a Pepsi spot that paid homage to the opening scene of Fellini's *8½*. There was VW's classic "Think Small" campaign: black-and-white images of the weird-looking little car floating in white space, a "stark contrast to the iridescence of Detroit's advertising offerings," Rothenberg writes.

A pal of mine, Bruce McCall (now a regular contributor to *The New Yorker*), typified all that was admirable on Madison Avenue in those last-gasp glory days of advertising, the late sixties into the seventies. McCall turned out superbly crafted ads that positioned Mercedes-Benz as the finest car in the world, premium priced but worth it. McCall's typewriter brought the Mercedes marque to life. He made sure to explain precisely why the car was superior. The German carmaker took McCall's prose and ran it full-page, in sumptuous ads with nary a bombshell in stilettos in sight. These ads informed. They didn't talk down to readers, but provided persuasive evidence about the particulars of Mercedes engineering. It was copywriting as finely calibrated as the product it celebrated.

The Creative Revolution also deftly hitched a ride on the counterculture's distrust of advertising. Thomas Frank, in *The Conquest of Cool*, comments that Madison Avenue itself acknowledged the charge that fifties' "consumer culture [had been] a gigantic fraud [that sought to] sell you shoddy products that . . . fall apart or [went] out of style in a few years."*

Decline and Fall

Within a decade, the Creative Revolution faltered. Advangelists weren't worried at first, just unsettled. Creeping despair set in. Hot-shot creative shops congealed into a handful of global holding companies: Needham Harper, BBDO, and Doyle Dane Bernbach merged to become Omnicom Group, the largest agency in the world; Saatchi & Saatchi bought Ted Bates, then combined Bates with Backer & Spielvogel; a Brit named Martin Sorrell, having gone public with his own WPP empire, acquired J. Walter Thompson in a hostile takeover. These international advertising firms were anything but fertile breeding grounds for creative expression. Morale sank. Talented writers and art directors opted out to write movies. Meanwhile,

---

*The Sell Side has always been adept at ripping off, then repackaging, fringe culture. Joseph Heath and Andrew Potter's *Nation of Rebels* provides an estimable account of how advertising co-opted jazz, rock, hip-hop, body piercing, long hair and facial stubble for men, red, blue, and orange hair for teenage girls, torn jeans, tie-dyed T-shirts, and skinny ties. Today these are all widely available to buyers in Peoria. In other words, products and styles don't just trickle down, as Thorstein Veblen and sociologist Georg Simmel made clear back in the era of the Ladies' Mile. Products and styles also trickle *up*.

back at the big conglomerates, clients came and went through furiously revolving doors. Those well-crafted, intelligent VW and Mercedes campaigns devolved into car ads that are banal and predictable, as described in a recent *Wall Street Journal* story: "In the opening shot, a gleaming car hugs the curves of a sinuous road, the soaring Rockies filling the background. (Or perhaps it's the glimmering Painted Desert or maybe the twinkling Pacific.) Next, we see the once-roaring auto at rest, basking in the sunshine." Then: big numbers and small print detailing not the engineering but financing terms.

Any wonder we're not paying as much attention? What do they take us for, morons? A despondent advangelist admitted to the *Journal* that nowadays "most car ads are lame [and] boring." Commercials for pickup trucks, beer, and candy bars pull out the stops: computer graphics, special effects, B-list celebrities out for a buck. The harder commercials try, the more lame they seem, the more lame and loud, the more lame and prurient, the more lame and outrageous—viz. two grease monkeys ripping out their chest hair. Anybody here have a better idea? *Wait! How about . . . citizen ads! Let customers write the ads!* Flash back to that Super Bowl Sunday, the Marriott bar where I killed time before visiting George Loewenstein. Doritos airs two amateur spots submitted via the Web, and they attract a lot of press. Madison Avenue pats itself on the back for how daring this is—*Let customers write the ads!*—and in so doing raises the risky proposition that anyone, even a moron with a video cam and a laptop, can create advertising as effective as, if not better than, the pros.

As for copywriting that informs and enlightens, read any good selling paragraphs lately? The world's gone visual. The long copy block is dead. Studies point to an "endangered reading brain," the result of our overexposure to digital media. It's all about eye candy now. I open my wife's copy of *Vogue*. Oscar winner Jennifer Hudson is on the cover, aglow in a burgundy duchesse-satin dress by Carolina Herrera and Fred Leighton diamond earrings. Her face bears an assortment of hopes-in-a-bottle: Blushing Blush Powder Blush in Sunset Glow; Colour Surge Eye Shadow Soft Shimmer in Enchanted Sugar Sugar [*sic*]; Cream Shaper for Eyes in Black Diamond; High Definition Lashes in Black/Brown; Brow Keeper in Almost Black; Full Potential Lips Plump and Shine in Blackberry Bloom—all from Clinique (BTW, a major *Vogue* advertiser). I leaf through the magazine and find that the first 487 pages are fashionably mute. Hundreds of pages of photos, no words, spread after spread after spread of bronzed, long-legged, plump-lipped, sultry, unsmiling, icy hot, and scary-skinny models dressed in a sumptuous variety of shorts, day dresses, gowns, thongs, slinky tops. Nearly every one wears Fuck-Me-But-Only-in-Your-Dreams-Buster four-inch heels. These women never smile, they scowl. This, too, is the result of methodical investigation. Scowls signal higher social standing, says a professor who runs experiments on the nature of smiles: "While we typically think of a smile as displaying our emotional state (happiness), it also appears that smiles convey information about the signaler's status. Specifically, lower status individuals appear to smile more than higher status individuals." My wife's copy of *Vogue* confirms this. No smiles, no copy. The only ads with smiles and copy are ads for midmarket brands such as Gap, Dillards, Cole Haan, and DisneyParks.com. As for the others, there's hardly a grin, not a headline, not a product-positioning line, hardly a sentence that tells of benefits or features.

Is there a subliminal message here? Of a sort: if you don't know what Prada (or Dior or Dolce) is, or what makes the brand chic and worth a month's take-home pay—a handbag, killer shoes, or gotta-have cigarette pants, no matter that they're made in Asia, not Italy or France—then we're under no obligation to tell you, even if we *knew* how to write.

As Paco Underhill said to me that day on the Ladies' Mile, the mainstream Sell Side was anxious even before the vicious economy blindsided us in 2008. The Sell Side acknowledges that traditional advertising is hit or miss and it's expensive. There's got to be a better way to go, clients mutter. They run return-on-investment analyses. Customers are time-pressed, money-pressed, and clutter-*oppressed*, so what's the optimum way to use a precious marketing buck? Knowing that customers seek refuge in movies, music, video games, and other entertainment platforms that are, on the surface, "commercial-free," Sell Siders understand that to make their way through your ad-cluttered mind field, it helps if their message is camouflaged. And there are plenty of ways to do just that:

Advertising camouflaged as editorial. Magazines and newspapers roll out special sections they call advertorials—"content" commissioned expressly to complement the surrounding advertising (as if readers don't get what's going on when a "travel story" about Aruba faces—*oh, kismet!*—an ad for

Aruba). Magazine publishing companies, scrambling to hold on to ad dollars fleeing to the Web and other new media, launch lighter-than-air "magalogs" in which, yes, there is a nominal distinction between "edit" and "ad," but it's perfunctory. Magalogs come and go, though lately far more have gone than come: *Lucky: The Magazine about Shopping and Style* (the luckiest and ad-fattest of magalogs); *Shop* (a *Lucky* knockoff that expired after two years); *Cargo* (a *Lucky* for him that also expired after two years); *Sync* (a *Lucky* for tech-heads that expired after a year and a half); *Vitals Man* and *Vitals Women* (*Lucky* and *Cargo* knockoffs, each of which expired in less than a year). Okay, back to the drawing board.

Advertising camouflaged as news. In 2002, Al Ries and Laura Ries published a contentious best seller, *The Fall of Advertising & the Rise of PR.* "Public relations has credibility, advertising does not," they declared. Advertising can't play offense—it can't *create* brands you like—it can only play defense to prevent predators from encroaching on brands you already favor. Ries and Ries point to monster brands that came out of nowhere (Starbucks, Amazon, eBay, Harry Potter, Red Bull, BlackBerry) to capture a share of your wallet without spending tons on advertising. Had the Rieses' book come out a year or two later, it would surely have pointed to the greatest of all who-needs-advertising? triumphs: Google. One of the world's best-known brands, Google has sold tens of billions of dollars' worth of advertising, along the way creating a major revolution in ad selling, without buying much of anything to promote itself, thanks to word of mouth and extensive media coverage. PR is timelier and cheaper than advertising. It can turn on a dime and jump on the next news cycle. TV, radio, print, and Web outlets are now so thinly staffed that many are happy to publish unedited stories filed by the Sell Side. Switch on local news stations and you'll be treated to "B-rolls," video news releases fed by satellite to stations coast to coast. B-rolls look and sound like real news segments complete with suitably coiffed on-air reporters, but they're merely television's answer to the print advertorial. As reported in *The Economist*, journalism has "come to depend on a drip-feed of information and products from the PR industry. Journalists focusing on electronics, fashion, travel, beauty and food have a huge appetite for free samples."

Advertising camouflaged as entertainment. In 2001, BMW came up with a nifty concept: BMW Films. The automaker commissioned an all-star team of international movie directors—Ang Lee, Alejandro González Iñárritu,

John Frankenheimer, and others—to create videos to be broadcast exclusively online. The series starred Clive Owen as "the Driver" and featured Madonna, Don Cheadle, Forest Whitaker, and Marilyn Manson, plus a smashing supporting cast of ultimate driving machines. The campaign grabbed attention: some hundred million online viewings.

Within a year *Advertising Age* proclaimed that so-called branded entertainment heralded a major industry upheaval; perhaps not another Creative Revolution, but certainly a Convergence Revolution. It dubbed the trend "Madison & Vine." *Epochal! Transformational!* Advertising married to entertainment, entertainment stuffed full of advertising. The idea wasn't new. Back in the twenties, when radio ruled, we had the *Maxwell House Hour* and the *General Motors Family Party*. There were "soap operas" sponsored by Oxydol and other detergent brands, which carried into and beyond the early days of television. But this new iteration—collaboration, conspiracy, call it what you will—goes beyond transparent sponsorship, says *Ad Age*'s Scott Donaton in his book *Madison & Vine: Why The Entertainment & Advertising Industries Must Converge to Survive.* Madison & Vine means shameless product placement in sporting events, movies, television, video, and electronic games. In 2007, 7-Eleven, coincident with the release of *The Simpsons Movie*, went so far as to transform a dozen of its stores into "Kwik-E-Marts," Springfield's fictional convenience store chain. *Chain Store Age* called it "the cleverest promotion of the year." Last summer, within sight of our Chicago apartment, Red Bull sponsored a "Flugtag" competition—hokey "flying machines" piloted by loopy costumed people who took not-so-long flights off a short ramp into Lake Michigan as seventy thousand people looked on. Nor can we fail to notice the imposing red Coke cups, in the shape of old-fashioned soda fountain glasses, sitting on the judges' desk on *American Idol*, nor the "NetJets" logo stitched down the sides of jockeys' pants at 2008's Triple Crown races, where the UPS logo was strategically placed atop the starting gate. Go, Big Brown!

As I say, none of this is new. Unabashed product placement abounds in Ian Fleming's Bond books, and the Bond movies, of course. At first, an Aston Martin here, a bottle of Dom Perignon there—small potatoes, really. Hollywood took the concept and ran with it. Successive Bond flicks increasingly looked as if they'd been inspired not by a Fleming novel but by a catalog lifted from an airline seat pocket. By *Tomorrow Never Dies* (1997), the eighteenth in the series, it was hard to tell just who the hero was: 007

or the product-placement hack who'd lassoed Visa, Avis, BMW, Smirnoff, Heineken, Omega, and L'Oréal. Today, well, it's *way* out of control. In 2008, Procter & Gamble entered into a partnership with Island Def Jam records to create a pop music label called TAG, after the body spray. Cisco sponsored a *single line* of dialogue in an episode of *CSI: NY* (a character summons colleagues to a conference call on the TelePresence network owned by Cisco). Then BMW struck again, this time sponsoring an entire episode of *Mad Men.* Shrewdly, the company ran but a single spot in the sixty-minute episode: a mockumentary interview with the *real* madman who'd come up with BMW's "Ultimate Driving Machine" line.

Madison & Vine means that underwriting advertisers now have a seat at the table when programming ideas are pitched. It means promotional and licensing tie-ins between entertainment companies and sponsors that range from McDonald's to Hewlett-Packard. Donaton quotes the former marketing chief at Coke, one of the biggest corporate players at the corner of Madison & Vine: "At the Coca-Cola Company we're thinking about marketing in a radically different way. Economic and social developments demand a new approach to connecting with audiences [and their] unrivaled ability to . . . avoid advertising." Dario Spina, who heads up "integrated marketing" for the MTV networks, didn't even bother to camouflage his intentions. He told the *New York Times* in 2008, "We want to blur the lines between the commercial breaks and the entertainment content."

Peer Power

Paco Underhill and Coke's marketing honcho are spot on: traditional advertising and promotion strategies have been exhausted. The spotlight now shines on *us*. Just think about what we typically do when we decide we need, or want, a digital camera, a blood pressure monitor, a Caribbean all-inclusive package, an espresso machine; or where we turn when we wish to assess competing claims about product reliability or customer service; or need an idea when planning a Saturday night out for that special someone; or want to know how much profit a car dealer is squeezing out of his "best offer." We turn to worldly wise Uncle Internet, have been for years now. Nearly two out of three online buyers say they read peer reviews of products before proceeding to purchase, scoping out what buyers and users say about a product's or store's quality, value, reliability, service, or cool factor.

Are you a woman who likes to dish about clothes? Then maybe you shop around at TheBudgetFashionista.com ("Be Fabulous for Less"), which claims a million page views a month, its growth fueled entirely by word of mouth and free PR. *Real Simple* rated the site the #1 Fashion Blog (2008). Its founder, Kathryn Finney, turns up on the *Today* show and E! The *New York Daily News* runs a photo of Kinney lounging on a bed with her Mac laptop, which nicely coordinates with her basic-black skirt and top, dramatically accessorized with a silver beaded necklace and fire engine red boots. Finney launched her site in 2003 and remains its "Chief Shopping Officer." One day I gave her a call. Articulate and cordial, she told me she'd gone to graduate school at Yale, was on a career track to epidemiology, never had a thought about a career on the outskirts of retail. She was blindsided, she said, by a "love of fashion and a lack of cash." A light bulb clicked. Build it—a shopping enthusiast's blog—and they will come. Ever expanding, TheBudgetFashionista now hosts forums where shopping tips are exchanged: *Cost per wear? I love that idea—helps me stay focused!" "Having a friend or two with you is a must—mirrors don't show the real thing!"* Coupon links transport users instantly to Target, Zappos, Urban Outfitters, even Sears. "News alerts" are culled from *Women's Wear Daily* and other sources: *Bonwit Teller, the once venerable, now deceased, upscale women's department store may be coming back!* There are podcasts: *We chat with Measha Brueggergosman, acclaimed Canadian soprano, about hair products, cold weather, and shopping in New York.*

A conversation with Finney foretells that she's no flash in the pan. She has a firm take on how the new Sell Side works, and she's a classy and effective promoter. "In her free time," her site reports, Finney "plots ways for Marc Jacobs to premier a clothing line at Wal-Mart [and] shops at her local 'Sally's Boutique' (aka Salvation Army)." Her official bio informs us that she "lives in the New York Metropolitan area with her husband Tobias, a drawer full of Spanx, and 36 pairs of shoes." A team player, Finney's quick to give credit to a strong bench of contributing fashionistas: Angela Shultis, who "spends her off hours as a walking advertisement for Marshalls, for which she someday hopes to be compensated handsomely"; Kate Noonan, who "spends her free time bargain-hunting at her favorite store, Loehmann's"; Robin Tolkan-Doyle, who "when not blogging about beauty trends and her favorite new finds, can be found at her home away from home, Target."

Or maybe you have zero interest in clothing, you're a gadget geek in the market for a smart phone and a cellular service plan to go with it. You log on to HowardForums.com. Only chumps take Buy direction from fast-talking goofballs in cell phone commercials, while only old fogies read *Consumer Reports*, where guidance comes from a group of gearheads in a testing lab capable of reviewing only a fraction of the phones and fine-print service plans out there. No, if you want the real skinny on phone products and carriers straight from the mouths of those with day-after-day, hands-on experience, HowardForums is the place to go. It has hundreds of thousands of registered users and some eight million postings dedicated to mobile phones and calling plans. Here you can compare notes not just about reliability, price, and customer care; you can get down and dirty on every arcane query, emotional quandary, or pet peeve you might have on the subject of handsets and plans. Want the scoop? Just register and ask:

- *What's the longest uptime, what's the average uptime, on a Sony Ericsson P990i?*

- *I was wondering if it was possible to use a blackberry without subscribing to a blackberry plan. I only need to use it as a phone and to send text messages—that's it. No emails. I just wanted a keyboard. I found a 7290 which is quad band. It seems to fulfill my needs. What do you guys think?*

The other guys, never bashful, tell you *exactly* what they think, sometimes with reassuring consensus, sometimes with impassioned and fractious disagreement.

This all represents a turning point in Sell Side history. *We* have become valuable selling assets. When did it begin? Pretty much around the dawn of the new century, when a different species of Sell Side snoop started sidling up to us in bars, chatting us up at our kids' playground, striking up conversations as we sat minding our own business at Starbucks. Chance encounters? Maybe, maybe not. I can remember reading a spate of stories back then about how person-to-person exchange of information was Topic A at Sell Side strategic retreats. In 2001 an issue of *Business Week* reported on what it termed "the Summer of Buzz." It described how we might be strolling down to the dry cleaner when a "sleek, impossibly attractive motorbiker" pulled over to ask directions. We thought we were just being polite when we complimented her on that powder blue Vespa, but in response she pulled out a piece of paper and wrote down the name and location of the nearest Vespa "boutique." Or, maybe we were watering our roses when a member of a neighborhood "mom squad" stopped to offer—for free!—a string of Hebrew National hot dogs to throw on our backyard Weber. Or, if we had a grade-school child in the house, we may have been unaware that a fifth-grade "secret agent," possibly our kid's best friend, had been effectively deputized by Hasbro to infect our little boys with an aching desire for a new P-O-X device, a much hyped and stealthily marketed attempt to marry Pokémon trading cards with handheld gadgetry.

Incidents such as these were on the rise, according to reports in *Business-Week* and elsewhere. Whether pushing dungarees or cars or Guinness Stout or Cheer laundry detergent, Sell Siders had warmed to the idea that word of mouth—the combined power of diaphragm, lungs, and trachea overlaid with the power of suggestion—could be weaponized. A pretentious term came into play: "diffusion marketing," otherwise known as "buzz." *Buzz: More powerful than a television commercial. Faster than a speeding sales promotion. Able to leap over tall objections—"I can't afford it!" "I don't need it!"—in a single bound.*

Listening In

Right now I'm looking at a PowerPoint presentation still in progress, a study commissioned by a big American retailing chain. It was prepared by a small agency that snoops in a way altogether different from Paco Underhill's anthropological, in-store look-sees. The company doesn't mount cameras in stores. It doesn't dispatch live secret agents. Based in Evanston, just north of Chicago, MotiveQuest is in the chatter collection game. It harvests and analyzes online buzz, what you and millions of your closest consuming friends say about the products and services on your mind. Like the other snoops in its field, MotiveQuest uses search engines to trawl the Internet, looking for specific references: a product name, a keyword. A huge haul of customer buzz, your buzz and mine, is then digested and regurgitated, in the hope that the by-product will be of some nutrient value to the sponges who underwrote the harvest.

The folks at MotiveQuest are so young they'd already mastered Power-Point at the age their parents were playing with Magic Slates. Aware that a slide show in the wrong hands amounts to a deadly weapon, they work hard to give good presentation at pitch meetings. The slide I'm looking at now is called a Passion Peak graph. It's a computer-generated "mountain range" that depicts two things going on at once: the degree to which you and others are buzzing about a specific retailer, and whether your buzz is tepid, lukewarm, or inflamed. The base of the "mountains" is colored blue, or cool, meaning the chatter isn't especially passionate; the slopes start out red but gradually turn orange, meaning we're now getting worked up about something. The peaks of the highest mountains are a smoldering yellow, meaning a high degree of intense feeling, positive or negative. Many factors determine how high and how hot a mountain of buzz can be. During the holiday selling season, when the nation's shopping activity rocks and rolls, the buzz mountains soar to towering heights: the more shopping, the more thinking about shopping and the more chatter about shopping. A prominent news story can swiftly turn a hillock of buzz into a mountain of chatter: Rat Poison Found in Cat Food! Janitors "Jailed" in Stores Overnight! Passion Peaks aren't prescriptive; they simply geo-map what you and I have judged to be a retailer's slippery slopes. Filthy bathrooms? Out-of-stock sale items? Rip-off prices? A Passion Peak graph gives the retailer a nod as to where to start climbing.

MotiveQuest is but one of many forms of algae that help sponges by trawling the Web, collecting and assessing our raves and rants. Another is Nielsen Online, which started up as a listening post known as BuzzMetrics. Like the folks at MotiveQuest, the Nielsen people proselytize that they're on the cutting edge of a marketing revolution. A *New York Times* story confirms that the business of monitoring consumers' online opinions is big and getting bigger. Major players on the Sell Side are paying attention. Procter & Gamble, the nation's preeminent mass marketer and home to huge consumer brands such as Tide, Pampers, and Crest, has its ear cocked to what you and I are saying about its products. The *Times* piece points out that a few former P&G brandmeisters abandoned their gigantic mother ship—at P&G, more than *twenty* brands have annual sales of least a billion dollars—to work at BuzzMetrics. It was no accident that BuzzMetrics set up shop in the shadow of P&G world headquarters in Cincinnati, if only to catch the crumbs. For a company like P&G, which spends all those billions on advertising, hiring a MotiveQuest or a Nielsen Online represents only the teeny-tiniest rounding error in a giant sponge's go-to-market spend.

Just a few years ago, the buzz collection business model might have seemed fanciful, certainly ominous. Vance Packard would have had a field day with buzz collecting; there's more than enough here to give everyone the willies. Imagine: strangers tapping into millions of private conversations around the clock. And, yes, today there *is* concern about privacy, or the "creepiness factor," as watchdogs call it: the Sell Side's ability to track our online moves, which in turn leave a trail advertisers use to stalk and ambush. In 2008 a company called comScore calculated the number of "data transmission events"—data collected from searches, ads, page views, and so on—we unwittingly trigger whenever we visit big Internet sites such as Yahoo, Google, AOL, MySpace, and others. More than six hundred billion DTEs a month are generated just on those sites. The resulting data are then used to direct where the Sell Side places advertising. In this way we draw bull's-eyes on our own backs—who needs market researchers to pin labels on us? True, sites such as Yahoo, Google, and Microsoft permit us to opt out of targeted advertising, but few of us know we can do that or go to the trouble, even though a majority of us, when asked, say we would if we could. A current survey on "behavioral tracking" reports that over 70 percent of those asked were "aware" that their browsing is collected and likely turned over to those who want to use our click history to sell us something. Only 57 percent of respondents said they were uncomfortable with the practice. A survey by the Annenberg Public Policy Center reports that 75 percent of those who notice the privacy statement at the bottom of a Web page take it to mean that customer data won't be shared with other companies. Maybe Vance Packard could vigorously stir up the willies were he still around, but in his absence few of us seem to be losing sleep over buzz-collecting efforts. After all, the buzz trackers assure us that they don't know, and don't need to know, our actual names, they only know our IP addresses. Still, says the director of TrustE, a nonprofit that issues *Good Housekeeping*–type seals to companies with acceptable privacy policies, they *do* know a great deal about us: what we do and where we traipse online, and in real time.

No wonder, then, that companies such as MotiveQuest themselves get quite a lot of chatter. It's easy to get carried away by all the buzz about buzz and overlook the fact that, as one student of the new marketplace told me, "there's still a huge power discrepancy between a lot of little people plugging away on their blogs and the marketing power of the Nikes and Apples of this world." Details, details. Rumors flit around the Web that Google might jump into the buzz-collecting biz, where it could leverage its massive search-and-storage capacity to capture your I-like-its and I-don't-like-its, not just your search queries. The *Wall Street Journal,* under the headline "The Wizards of Buzz," describes how "a new generation of hidden influencers is taking root online, [which] has implications for advertisers shelling out money." The socio-mercantile significance buzz is routinely trumpeted in marketing trade publications, the *Harvard Business Review,* and in numerous books written for marketers major and minor: *The Anatomy of Buzz: How to Create Word of Mouth Marketing; Buzzmarketing: Get People to Talk About Your Stuff.* Author and public speaker Jackie Huba, who preaches what *Forbes* called "the word of mouth gospel," said in a 2007 industry colloquium: "Brands have already lost control now that anyone can blog or podcast messages about them to a worldwide audience. Citizen marketers are publishing and broadcasting about brands they love and brands they hate today. And as more and more people, especially Millennials, adopt social media tools, the amount of multimedia word of mouth on the web is only going to increase. Smart companies are embracing and reaching out to these vocal constituents and establishing a dialogue with them."

Buzz remains a hot topic at retail and marketing conferences, fanned not only by the gatherers themselves, with their press releases and slick B2B Web sites, but by yet another form of algae that exists to analyze and rate companies like MotiveQuest and BuzzMetrics. At Forrester Research, technology analysts are bullish on the future of companies that plant listening bugs online, and they say so with conviction: "The power shift from media institutions to consumer communities means that marketers must track a diverse and growing range of influential voices." Forrester has created special buckets to classify online users: not demographic or psychographic, but *technographic,* based on your participation in online social networking. It then rates chatter collection firms on how well they suck data out of those technographic buckets. It gets pretty hairy. A Forrester's report card issued high marks to BuzzMetrics and Cymfony for "comprehensive technology platforms and extensive data source coverage"; to Biz 360 for how it monitors online public relations campaigns; to Umbria for its ability to segment online talkers into target groups at which a sponge can take aim; to Brandimensions for its targeted expertise in listening in on automotive, entertainment, and pharmaceutical industry chitchat; and to MotiveQuest for the quality of its services and strategy.

Ergo, business at MotiveQuest has been brisk, which is why, on the day I visited, the company was preparing to move out of its headquarters, a funky, refurbished tool-and-die plant located among a scattering of mom-and-pop plumbing and roofing companies, and into larger digs several blocks away, not far from the Northwestern University campus.

Sucking It Up

Down in MotiveQuest's basement there was a roomful of HP and Dell servers—garden-variety, nothing fancy. These servers don't rake the entire online universe, just immense stretches of it where you and millions of others go to shoot the breeze: blogs (some hundred million of them, give or take), consumer discussion forums, and product-related newsgroups. Motive-Quest's servers suck up terabytes of buzz from these sites, and while that might sound like a lot of computing power, a techie informed me that it doesn't come remotely close to the *petabytes* Google would throw at the web should the Monster of Midvale decide to plunge into the buzz-tracking business. Still, MotiveQuest feels it has more than enough server strength to do its thing for a growing roster of client sponges. It even has enough computing power left over to retrieve big bytes of the conversations we leave behind in "off topic forums": sites where we sound off not about smart phones or food processors or pills that reset erectile dysfunction, but our thoughts on the state of the nation, what good or evil lies in organized religion, the ethics of cloning cows and gerbils. MotiveQuest grinds these exchanges into what it calls "General Mood" data sets, which it considers "proxies for national water cooler conversation," in the words of one staffer. A General Mood data set reassures a sponge that MotiveQuest has a bead on the whole zeitgeist, not just on the Sell Side. This bead, the firm contends, enables a retailer or product company to broaden its worldview (and serves as welcome distraction during an otherwise somnolent marketing meeting). Motive-Quest doesn't claim to measure, scientifically or otherwise, public opinion. It's not a newfangled Gallup or Yankelovich survey—it just wants to be that friend in high school who, in the absence of hard evidence, you dispatch to the lunchroom to listen in on who might have the hots, or the colds, for you.

A typical MotiveQuest client report is generated from a handful of questions conceived to help a Sell Sider do a more effective job. Are your tongues wagging about the in-store experience? How do you feel about the policies and ethics of the company? Is your patter in line with how the store wants you to perceive its brand, or is there some disconnect? What are you saying about the store's advertising campaign? Is there anything in your jawboning that might help the retailer better serve the community?

The harvesting of raw buzz (literally millions of posts are represented in the report I've been looking over) is only a part, the less interesting part, of what MotiveQuest does on behalf of clients. After the harvest comes the scrub. Once our online chatter is captured, the servers in the basement X-ray it using proprietary analytics. MotiveQuest's software—in theory at least—assesses the mood we're in when we discuss the standards and practices of a Sell Sider. The folks at MotiveQuest produce graphics they refer to as MotiveMeters. They look like this:

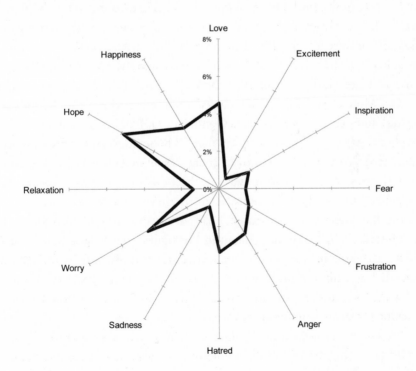

This spidery MotiveMeter plots the emotions we express about a given product or service or store: positive emotions are indicated at the top, negative emotions at the bottom, active emotions on the right, passive emotions on the left. In this example a good many of us are quite pleased with our store experience, while a smaller number of us express worry, frustration, or unalloyed hatred. To humanize graphs such as these, a MotiveQuest report includes a few pages of actual snippets from posts deemed to be representative. They range from the adoring ("I LOVE this store. My only complaint is that their cute boy clothes sell out too quickly!") to the utterly pissed off ("I hate that shit hole").

Free at Last

The senior players at MotiveQuest, starting with the company's founder and president, David Rabjohns, are mainly refugees from the mainstream ad biz. Stressed out, they sailed from the old Sell Side to the new digital world in search of personal liberty and marketing freedom. When I asked why they're now content to work in funky offices surrounded by plumbing and roofing contractors, they told me it's because they "saw the writing on the wall," or were fed up with "the usual bullshit" on Madison Avenue. They are sold on the fact that technology in general, and the World Wide Web in particular, are wholly transfiguring the Way We Buy Now.

The MotiveQuest execs introduced themselves: there was Rabjohns, Australian born, in his early forties, a former EVP of brand strategy at the Leo Burnett agency, whose bio notes that his honeymoon was a four-month safari across Africa in a Land Rover. There was senior strategist Ebru Majoo, early thirties, who prior to moving to the Midwest spent four years selling apparel to Hasidic Jews in Brooklyn. There was Kirsten Recknagel, just turned thirty, director of research, a University of Chicago MBA who is a self-described "Brazilophile," fluent in Portuguese. There was Mark Witthoefft, early thirties, another senior strategist, late of Boston-based Arnold Advertising, who told me that over the past five years he had lived in four cities with seven different addresses, which is indicative of how tenuous working for ad agencies has become.

We sat in a circle, eating sandwiches. The group was eager to help me understand how the Web has reconfigured the way we shop and buy: how the Internet enables us to join new communities around shared interests in the things we need or want and to exchange information about those things. And how it enables the Sell Side to reach, with hitherto unimaginable efficiency, those among us who are in the market for an electric toothbrush or a Bentley. It's all about you, you, you. Indeed, the first of my several conversations with Rabjohns occurred just a week or two after *Time* magazine in 2006 selected You as its person of the year. The magazine proclaimed the Web "a tool for bringing together the contributions of millions of people and making them matter." It noted how Facebook, MySpace, and YouTube, the big three early winners, signaled a new era: "the many wresting power from the few." You and your camcorder could now capture, then broadcast worldwide, headline-making or inane personal happenings as readily as any mainstream media organization. You can lay down tracks and distribute your own music and video programming. And, to bring it all back to the Buy, by sharing reviews of products and stores, and by ordering directly from e-commerce sites worldwide, you can make and execute buying decisions without having been assaulted by agency-produced ads and all the fluff—celebrity endorsers, slick slogans, nerve-jangling jingles—that attends them.* (The phenomenon by now has its own buzzword, "groundswell," defined by two Forrester Research analysts as "a social trend in which people use technologies to get the things they need from each other, rather than from traditional institutions like corporations.")

Rabjohns had also suggested that I check out another magazine story, one that ran a few months prior in *The Economist*. It proclaimed that online social media were reshaping the world no less dramatically than Gutenberg managed with movable type. "People no longer passively consume media"—and their lifeblood, advertising—"but actively participate in them," the article said. "This has profound implications for traditional business models in the media industry, which are based on aggregating large passive audiences and holding them captive during advertising interruptions. In the new-media era, audiences will occasionally be large, but often small, and usually tiny." Meaning, *you*. For a century and a half, the Sell/Buy equation was "we talk, you listen." Now it's *you* talk, *they* listen, say the apostles of buzz, who have an ear pressed to a glass pressed to the Web. What you say drives business.

---

*Well, not quite. Within a year of the *Time* cover story, news broke that Facebook, for one, was intent on pursuing multiple stratagems by which advertisers could find you and give you a stiff poke: they could build user profiles of themselves, place ads targeted at demographic communities within their target range, and plant cookies that will let Sell Siders know how often you visit specific e-commerce sites. Bottom line: not even the Person of the Year can hide.

The MotiveQuest crew informed me that over the ten days following Apple's unveiling of the iPhone, the device received more blog mentions than George W. Bush's decision to send additional troops to Baghdad, which was the biggest front-page news story at the time. (Wikipedia had an iPhone entry within *minutes* of Steve Jobs's announcement from the stage at the 2006 MacWorld conference.) And they made sure I understood that when one talks about the power of buzz, one isn't just talking about acne-faced adolescents debating the merits of guitar amps and animé releases. The MotiveQuesters projected slides from studies commissioned by powerful global companies that sell everything from mutual funds to osteoporosis medicines. At least somebody is listening to gramps.

I asked the assembled group if MotiveQuest software was able to distinguish among the *types* of people who participate in forums and chats. The group conceded that, for now at least, the profiling of chatterers was an inexact science, but that those of us who buzz online fall into certain categories:

Mavens: The best-informed and most influential participants in a consumer forum. The word "maven" derives from Hebrew and Yiddish terms that denote "understanding" or expertise. "Maven" has been rattling around in the popular lexicon for decades but was brought to the fore by the ever-alert Malcolm Gladwell in *The Tipping Point*. Gladwell defines mavens as those who "aren't passive collectors of information [but rather] obsessed with how to get the best deal on a can of coffee. What sets them apart is that once they figure out how to get the deal, they want to tell you about it too." He wasn't specifically referring to those who mavenize via the World Wide Web, but a maven is a maven, regardless of channel. In consumer forums, a maven posts with impressive frequency and is treated with the respect once reserved for the village elder.

Lurkers: Most of us hide out here. We register to access online consumer discussions, maybe ask a question now and then, but for the most part, we just listen in, often while we're doing something else—checking stock quotes, eating pizza. You might be a regular lurker, i.e., you maintain an ongoing passion for a given product or brand—a camera buff, say, or a *Canon* camera buff. Or you might be a one-time lurker who happens to be in the market for a digital camera and shows up to absorb the wisdom of the crowd before making a final decision on what to buy.

Trolls: Unlike the real trolls found in Swedish folklore, a consumer-forum troll isn't a person who lives in a cave or a hollow tree trunk, isn't suspected of having a tail hidden in his pants and has no history of abducting innocent wayfarers and turning them into slaves. If you're an online troll, you're judged to be a pest or, to borrow again from the Yiddish, a *nudnik*. For whatever psychological need, a troll is one who likes to make trouble. He posts messages that are indelicate or politically incorrect, even deliberately wrong: for example, he'll kvetch about a lousy feature on a highly regarded camera just to bait people. While troll-like behavior is disparaged by an online community, it is not necessarily cause for permanent exile.

Flamers: Far more incendiary than trolls, flamers range from the simply rude to the deeply sociopathic. A flamer is to a consumer chat room what a bad drunk is to a decorous hotel bar. If you're a flamer, you trample accepted standards of civility. Rather than take polite exception to an opinion expressed in a post, you launch an ad hominem attack. You spew epithets, impugn the honor of people's mothers and sisters. Nobody likes a flamer, and usually at the first flicker they're told to go away, stay away, and go screw themselves for good measure.

Moles: Here we reach the lowest of consumer-forum lowlifes. Moles are shills who are paid or otherwise compensated to infiltrate discussion groups in order to promote specific products or companies and, while they're at it, dump on the competition. This practice is also known as sock-puppeting. In 2007 the CEO of Whole Foods, John P. Mackey, gained induction into the Sock Puppet Hall of Shame when news broke that for several years he had used a made-up screen name (an anagram of his wife's name) to post over a thousand messages extolling the virtues of Whole Foods while trashing a competing food chain, Wild Oats (which Whole Foods eventually acquired). The outing of the hitherto widely admired Mackey made him the object of widespread outrage, including the charge that he was "just plain nuts" to do something so stupid. One message-board post, as reported in the *New York Times*: "What a hoot! It's so Nixonian! Maybe he needs some animal fat in his diet. I've known vegans who suffered from teeth and gum disease; now we know a vegan who's suffering from 'foot-in-mouth' disease."

There's a general assumption that most moles sooner or later get caught by scam-sensitive online communities. Not necessarily, one marketing professor told me. He described a classmate who helped pay tuition costs by shilling online and explained that there were clumsy moles and highly skilled moles. A skilled mole, the professor said, is furtively fiendish: his posts are neither blatantly positive nor ferociously negative, but "nuanced."

A skilled mole will dole out four stars instead of five, making sure to include a quibble or two about a minor feature.

So, is this where the Sell Side ends? With *you*?

The grand palazzos on the Ladies' Mile are history. The suburban mall is dead or dying. The S-E-X in the ice cubes melted away decades ago. Advertising doesn't work the way it used to. But consumer product reviews, *your* I-like-its-I-don't-like-its, are ubiquitous: Amazon, iTunes, Trip-Advisor, Chowhound, the list is endless. A couple of years ago Petco retained a firm to figure out how best to solicit consumer feedback on its online offerings. Then it pooper-scooped customer favorites into a "Top Rated" category, awarding stars in the form of paws *(Let's hear it for Nutro Max Weight Control Formula for Overweight Less Active Dogs!)*. The company's president was immensely pleased with the results, boasting to the *New York Times* that Petco had created a "shopping experience that's driven by the voice of other shoppers." And the reason for this? "Consumers will trust the voice of another customer before they trust the retailer or manufacturer," he said, wagging his own tail about how shoppers spend 35 percent more when sniffing out goods on the Top Rated pages than when just clicking here and there.

The latest Jonathan Kellerman novel, the new Andrew Bird release, the Canon EOS Digital Rebel XTi, the AeroPress Coffee and Espresso Maker, Olay Definity Pore Redefining Scrub—thumbs up or thumbs down? According to *them,* the Sell Side sponges and the algae along for the ride, *you* are the decider, dead smack in the middle of the action.

So, does this make you *you,* or does this make you *them*—and whose side are you on, anyway?

PART II

You Versus You

We're stooges, Buy Scolds say, manipulated by Sell Side come-ons.
We're out of control, impulsive. We've got credit cards, plenty of them.
But how about a little credit for personal judgment?

9

Poor Ewe

Are you a sheep, constantly grazing, easily fleeced?

Do not trouble yourself much to get new things. . . . Sell your clothes
and keep your thoughts.

—Henry David Thoreau, *Walden, Or, Life in the Woods*

ENOUGH ABOUT RETAILERS, MERCHANTS, snoops, advangelists—what about us? Sharks swim in water, we swim in consumption. As predators, sharks are much better equipped. A shark's vision, while anatomically similar to ours, is in certain ways more acute. The eye of a shark has what's called a nictitating membrane that protects the eye from damage during violent food fights. We have no such membrane. When the doors are unlatched, a predawn feeding frenzy begins on Black Friday, the day after Thanksgiving, when up to ten thousand ravenous shoppers swarm to get a jump on the best deals. Our eyes have no defense against flying elbows. On Black Friday there are fistfights and worse: in 2008, two men shot each other dead at a toy store in California; three thousand miles away, a clerk at a Long Island discount store was trampled to death.

A shark's olfactory equipment is likewise superior to ours. A shark, when it's cruising around for a bite to eat, can smell an appealing morsel up to a quarter mile away. Our homing signals are rarely received through our snouts, save for the intense waft of cinnamon rolls pumped into a corridor at the mall—nasal marketing, not viral—and the smell of fresh coffee at giant bookstores that awakens our appetite for books.

A shark hears better than we do. Its inner ear can detect an object of interest several miles away. We get the word through commercials—grating, nonstop, ubiquitous. A shark has electroreceptor organs that detect prey even when it's buried in sand. We rummage through bargain bins, hoping to luck out.

Finally, a shark won't spring for what doesn't taste good, or when its belly is full. Our closets, attics, basements, and garages are crammed with items we gobbled up but never needed or used. One reason for this is that we have something that sharks don't. We have credit cards—no matter that the cards levy interest rates only a loan shark could love.

Buy Scolds charge that our senses have deteriorated because we're bewitched (by advertising), benumbed (by abundance), and befuddled (by too much choice, too many stores). There's nothing new about those indictments. Let's go back a decade or so, to 1998, a very good year for American consumers. Low inflation. High employment. Housing demand at record levels. The U.S. economy owed 85 percent of its growth to our determined buying. We were doing our civic duty and then some. The powers that be—the Sell Side and elected leaders—lauded our selfless-selfish efforts. But there were, as always, party poopers to spoil the fun. Harvard's Juliet Schor came out with a book that year, *The Overspent American: Why We Want What We Don't Need*, a diatribe on wretched excess. Rather than applaud our contributions to the happy state of the nation's economy, Schor accentuated the negative. Our debt level was shocking. The disinclination to save, horrifying. The heart of the problem, she said, was our penchant for "competitive acquisition." She argued that we buy not to keep up with the Joneses, but to keep up with the Images—"reference groups," she called them—that advertisers and the media ram down our throats. These groups—the friends from *Friends* at the time Schor was writing, celebrities fawned over in magazines, skeletal temptresses sprawled out in designer clothing ads, well-to-do urbanites who commission six-figure chef's kitchens featured in the Style Section—tickle our Buy bone. Reference groups are affluent, alluring, chic, hip. They travel a lot, wine and dine, and spend mighty sums on clothes and cosmetics. Their living rooms, media rooms, and bathrooms are outfitted with extras nobody needs but are nice to have. Following the Images' lead, we fall into line: a phone for the bathroom, souvenirs from the Louvre museum shop—if only to prove we were there. Breast implants. Schor takes to task Nicole Brown Simpson and her surviving sisters, all of whom, apparently, were implanted. I suspect Schor would have indicted *my* family's choice of pet: Woody, a tawny, elegantly conformed vizsla, a breed frequently cast in fashion shoots. Woody's sleek appeal was not, I swear, what drew us to him. And yet—I admit—we spent a lot for that dog ($900).

Schor's point here, a not unreasonable one, is that reference groups sharpen our Buy appetite. In *The Overspent American* she issues a prescription to cure our slavish emulation of media-promoted trendies: pare down, live small. Easier said than done, of course, especially when times are good. As Thorstein Veblen told us in *The Theory of the Leisure Class:* "It is notoriously . . . difficult to recede from a high standard of living." In 2001, British installation artist Michael Landy gave it a go. He rented an abandoned department store in London, where he meticulously cataloged every single one of his worldly possessions: art, clothing, electrical equipment, furniture, kitchen contents, leisure gear, perishables, reading material, motor vehicle. Then he and a few helpers systematically destroyed every last item, 7,227 objects in all, 5.75 tons of personal *stuff.* If Landry's solution strikes you as drastic, Schor's book offers alternatives. If you must keep up with anyone, forget the reference groups the media shove down our throats and emulate the penny-wise millionaire next door or even the less affluent "downshifter" down the block. Drive a compact, fuel-efficient car. Better still, walk or bike to work or the grocery store. Avoid designer rip-offs. Better still, sew your own clothes. Learn to love the breasts God gave you. Choose a four-legged companion who slobbers love and can be yours for far less than what we shelled out for Woody. Better still, visit the pound, leave a small donation.

McAmerica

Modern-era Scolds such as Juliet Schor hail from a long line of moralists who've not been shy about telling us to roll back our acquisitiveness for our own and the collective good. Several years after he wrote his biography of Vance Packard, Smith College professor Daniel Horowitz broadened his inquiry into twentieth-century Buy Scolds. The book was called *The Anxieties of Affluence*. Galbraith, Reisman, Whyte, Mills, those fifties party poopers, make their appearance. So do Buy Scolds who even earlier railed against the perils of modern-day consumption: Robert and Helen Lynd, pioneering sociologists and authors of the classic *Middletown* (1929), a book that suggested there was a silver lining in economic adversity, a relief from "our irrelevant strain of endless competitive acquisition for its own sake." Post-fifties, Horowitz surveyed the warnings of Ralph Nader, Betty Friedan, Michael Harrington, Paul Ehrlich, and others, who showed us the connections among rampant profligacy, shoddy product quality, the oppression of women, the growing disparity of wealth, and the threat consumerism posed to social justice. Horowitz also chronicled the preachy tendencies of Jimmy Carter, who, making like the president next door, carried his own garment bag while campaigning, sold off the presidential yacht *Sequoia*, and banished fancy tablecloths in the White House mess. While writing his self-destructive "malaise" speech—cut your wasteful energy spending, turn down your thermostats, invest in cozy cardigans—Carter consulted an assortment of respected Buy Scolds, a less-than-all-electric kitchen cabinet. There was sociologist Daniel Bell, who believed that modern capitalism encouraged instant gratification and undermined the work ethic. There was sociologist Robert Bellah, who urged the president to bring a certain religious fervor to the call for thermostatic sacrifice. And there was Christopher Lasch, historian and social critic, best known for *The Culture of Narcissism*, a jeremiad that identified overconsumption as a principal cause of our spiraling adoration of celebrity, our frenetic search for eternal youth, and the emergent "do your own thing" ethos—all of which run counter to the contemplative pursuit of life's deeper satisfactions.

Carter came, Carter went, but the Scolds kept right on coming. In the early nineties, a professor named George Ritzer wrote *The McDonaldization of America*, a sharp indictment of a society and culture that had become deep-fried in the fast and the fake. Artery-clogging food was just the beginning of the high cost of living under Golden Arches. "McDonaldization" sped the rise of superficial media (McPaper), inspired the too large, ill-built spaces we called home (McMansions), and legitimized the meaningless work we perform in Dilbertian cubicles (McJobs). No less than Juliet Schor, Ritzer didn't shrink from telling us how to escape the despair of everyday McLife in America:

- Avoid living in tract houses. Try to live in an atypical environment, preferably one you have built yourself or have had built for you. If you must live in a tract house, humanize and individualize it.

- Lubricate your own car. If you're unwilling or unable to do so, have it done at a local, independent filling station. Do not frequent one of those franchised lube businesses.

- Instead of popping into H&R Block at income tax time, hire a local accountant, preferably one who works out of her own home office.

- Next time you need a pair of glasses, use a storefront optometrist and avoid Pearle Vision Center. Next time your hair needs cutting, go to a local barber or hairdresser, not a franchised clip joint.

- Use cash rather than credit cards—it'll raise the consciousness of department store clerks.

- Return all junk mail to the post office, especially pieces addressed to "occupant" or "resident."

- If you are a regular at McDonald's, develop personal ties with the counter people; try to get to know them. Do what you can to humanize the place. Just because the food is fast, *we* don't have to be. Relax. Read the paper. Hang out.

O Cursed Day!

Today happens to be a day of particular infamy on the Buy Scold calendar. It's Black Friday, when an estimated 150 million people, fueled by a huge portion of the fourteen pounds of (mostly inorganic) turkey the average American scarfs down a year, storm the retail barricades, refueling on the fly at McDonald's and Chick-fil-A. Black Friday, as everyone knows by now, marks the "official" beginning of the holiday shopping season, but the early-warning signs and preholiday specials and twinkling lights have been in evidence since late summer. Black Friday is, to a Buy Scold, the ultimate nightmare on high street. In good economic times the average shopper spends around $350 on this day. Nearly a third of us visit Wal-Mart, 20 percent drive to Target, Sears, or JCPenney. As far back as the late eighties, Buy Scolds launched a rebranding campaign to try to protect us from our own worst impulses on Black Friday. They renamed it Buy Nothing Day: a day when they urge us to take our hands out of our pockets and purses and hold them palms up where the Sell Side can see them. Some activists go even farther and encourage us to engage in acts of retail disobedience: push empty shopping carts through the throngs at a big chain store, the better to add to the congestion and mayhem.

Buy Nothing Day has been promoted in the media by a loose consortium of Scolds under the baton of Kalle Lasn, whom we've already met briefly. Now in his midsixties, Lasn charts attacks (mostly verbal) on corporate-made cultural pollution from his base camp in Vancouver.* Like Juliet Schor, he has a few things he'd like us to understand about the Sell Side's rampant destructiveness. Marketing, as practiced on today's global scale, is for all intents and purposes totalitarianism and must be defeated. He urges that we rise up and take back a culture owned and operated by the oligarchs of international branding. The stakes are high, the consequences dire:

- We no longer live in a country so much as a multi-trillion-dollar brand: "America™"—with motives, values, and an agenda no different from McDonald's or Marlboro's.

- We're no longer capable of "free, authentic lives." Instead, we lead "designer" lives. "A continuous product message has woven itself into the very fabric of [our] existence."†

- We're addicted to a "narcotic" otherwise known as "cool," which America™ cranks out and dispenses in endless supply— new this, trendy that—thus perpetuating our need for stronger fixes.

Overwrought? Well, perhaps, especially coming from one who lives and rails in the country a fellow Vancouverite once referred as the "vichyssoise of nations": cold and difficult to stir. Lasn, though, is an inveterate stirrer, a

---

*If Buy Nothing Day has escaped your attention, it's because mainstream media won't run BND advertising. A few years ago MTV rejected a commercial featuring a burping pig. For Lasn, the network's decision was neither unexpected nor unwelcome, given that he thrives on riposte: "Gangsta rap and sexualized, semi-naked school girls are okay," his Web site comments, "[but] not a burping pig talking about consumption."

†Recent example: Chicago was said to be weighing the sale of naming rights to municipal attractions. Coming soon—*Old Navy Pier!*

provocateur. He lays no particular claim to civility, not when the fate of the culture and the planet hang in the balance.

Civility, now, that's something we might reasonably expect from Benjamin Barber, professor of civil society at the University of Maryland. But Barber, no less than Lasn, is madder than hell and resolved that none of us need take it anymore. In 2007 he published *Consumed: How Markets Corrupt Children, Infantilize Adults, and Swallow Citizens Whole.* The message: advertising and the media aren't merely content to induce us to keep up with reference images or addict us to cool. The plan is far more insidious: promote "adult regression in the hope that it might rekindle in grownups the tastes and habits of children and thus offload a useless cornucopia of games, gadgets, and myriad consumer goods for which there is no discernible 'need market' other than capitalism's frantic need to sell." Big Brother—or, in this case, Big Baby Maker—offers us mind-numbing candy from every direction, particularly from Hollywood, Barber says, where media companies make up a collective (Wet) Dream Factory. Philistine studio heads snuff out any project that doesn't pack wallops of "comic-book action, branded characters, numberless sequels, extensive product placements, and commercial tie-ins with fast food and other global enterprises, minimal plots, and still more minimal dialogue." While civilization burns, in other words, we fiddle with game controllers and slide *Die Hard 4* into our DVD trays.

Aided by researchers armed with scissors and search engines, Barber offloads a welter of articles that support the charge that the Sell Side, not content to arrest the development of our kids, is hell-bent on stunting ours as well. He finds support in a *New Yorker* profile of Shaquille O'Neal. The piece describes how Shaq relishes food fights with an entourage of cousins from Newark. He maintains a fleet of motorized vehicles, some of them cacophonous ATVs. He engages in idiotic horseplay with his homies and idles away time with a huge library of action flicks. Why? *Just for the fun of it!* Barber declaims, noting that Shaq's behavior might be excusable "at thirteen, but [he] was over thirty at the time." Harsh? I can't help but counter with a passage from *Nation of Rebels*, which takes a dim view of Buy Scold ranting: "Whenever you look at the list of consumer goods that (according to the critic) people don't really need, what you invariably see is a list of consumer goods that *middle-aged intellectuals* don't need."

But beyond that, Shaq is hardly representative of the American consumer universe: he's a seven-foot-one-inch superathlete making close to

$39 million a year, who works an eleven-month schedule of bruising physical contact, suffers from occasional injury and tedious business travel. So—just my opinion—the big guy is entitled to kick back now and then. It's also a bit uncivil of Barber not to point out that between *Die Hard* screenings and towel-snapping hijinks with his buds, Shaq has earned an MBA (okay, *online*) and says that he one day plans to pursue a doctorate. No matter. If Barber *is* onto something, if watching blood-and-guts movies, playing video games, and bouncing around in a mud-splattered ATV can turn grown-ups into overgrown toddlers, he'll have uncovered the first anti-aging claim that actually delivers on the promise.

Buydeological Conflict

Modern Buy Scolds take a mostly secular approach to moral reproach. Their ideology holds that we're not sinners so much as sheep, hapless ewes narcotized by capitalist excess, then sheared by global marketing giants. If you're like many people I've interviewed, you may find offensive these sourpusses who give you no credit for rational judgment, even if you admittedly lapse into Buy-silly now and then (last Christmas, when you couldn't resist that gift pack for your purebred accessory-in-fur, complete with suede stocking, odor-eliminating soy candle, and dog-spa kit, all for only a hundred bucks). Yes, we transgress, and we look for excuses. Consumer researcher Russell Belk has traveled the world, asking folks how they judge their own rampant materialism. Turks tell Belk that it's okay to spend because they're giving their kids a better life. That's not "materialism," it's parental devotion. Western Europeans tell Belk that "stupid Americans" give materialism a bad name, because we waste money on lousy food. They, on the other hand, have a finer appreciation for quality. And we, here in the Consumers' Republic, tell ourselves it's not materialism, really; we're just doing our patriotic duty.

Plenty of people spring to our defense. James Twitchell teaches English and advertising (an oxymoronic double major?) at the University of Florida and is the author of *Lead Us Into Temptation* and other writings that seek to de-demonize materialism. "We live through [material] things," Twitchell writes. "We create ourselves through things. And we change ourselves by changing through things." Reason enough, he points out, that we call goods "goods" and not "bads." In an essay titled "Two Cheers for Materialism," Twitchell strikes back at the Buy Scold ethos:

Our commercial culture has been blamed for the rise of eating disorders, [the] epidemic of depression, the despoliation of cultural icons, the corruption of politics, the carnivalization of holy times like Christmas, and the gnat-life attention span of our youth. All of this is true. Commercialism contributes. But it is by no means the whole truth. Commercialism is more a mirror than a lamp. In demonizing it, in seeing ourselves as helpless and innocent victims of its overpowering force, in making it the scapegoat *du jour*, we reveal far more about our own eagerness to be passive in the face of complexity than about the thing itself.

Twitchell heaps disdain on Scolds who maintain that our one true way out of involuntary ensheepment is a life of voluntary simplicity—an ideology called "freeganism." A freegan is one who observes No Buy Day and keeps it holy, who maintains that we are put on this earth to live life not as common mall rats but to "embrace community, generosity, social concern, freedom, cooperation, and sharing in opposition to a society based on materialism, moral apathy, competition, conformity, and greed."

Odds are that most of us fall between the cracks of these competing ideologies—anticonsumerism, freeganism, *anti*-anticonsumerism. Odds are we're neither total ciphers in sheep's clothing nor libertines who believe our buying promotes the march of civilization. Odds are we're neither shopaphobes nor shopaholics. More likely we think of ourselves as everyday people who, Buywise, alternately indulge and beat ourselves up for spending on things we often don't need. But for now, let's not quibble with the Buy Scolds or with those who'd like the Scolds to stuff a sock in it. Let's just agree that nearly every one of us buys things we really don't need, things we only just want. Let's agree to agree on these three points:

1. The Sell Side, whether evil or not, has the resources to capture our attention: a ton of money, a mountain of data, access to the clever and talented whiskers, consultants, and image makers.

2. The Sell Side, even if it's fallible, knows how to seduce us with the right "want" at the right moment at the right price: the well-aimed mailing, the perfectly placed display, the fetching image of the romantic vacation, wedding party, or retirement dream house.

3. The Sell Side is adept at blurring the line between *need* and *want*—not that we don't do a pretty good job fooling ourselves.

$64 Questions: What's a Need? What's a Want?

In quasi observance of Buy Nothing Day I decided to sit out Black Friday and devote the occasion to further examination of the needs-versus-wants conundrum. I headed down to Michigan Avenue, where Tom Ford's new fragrance was now in ample supply, along with mountains of other merchandise awaiting the holiday hordes. I wrapped a Paul Smith scarf around my neck—yes, I need a scarf but, no, I don't need a *Paul Smith* scarf—and zipped up my trusty Lands' End Squall parka (hardly reference-group inspired, or else it would carry a North Face logo on the outside). I didn't get far before it became crushingly apparent that many more people were participating in Black Friday than honoring the precepts of Buy Nothing Day. Black Friday is commonly assumed to be about Christmas shopping. It isn't. A retail study reports that over 80 percent of Black Friday shoppers say they're battling the crowds on behalf of themselves. I elbowed my way into Victoria's Secret, the Apple Store, then Macy's. I stood around watching people fondle things, pick things up, put things back, and consult with compatriots in the rapture of early "holiday" buying. I studied what customers held in their hands as they waited in long lines at the cash wrap. How much of their Black Friday haul was based on need, how much on want? Scolds say it's overwhelmingly the latter, but I was resolved to keep an open mind.

What I observed was that most customers appeared more weary than needy or wanty. Feeling a touch woozy myself, I opted to head home to poke around online and leaf through books in my growing Buy library. Following right behind me on the Magnificent Mile were two women in town for the weekend. I knew they were tourists because they debated whether to check out "a few more stores before heading back to the hotel." One asked the other if she had any interest in returning to the store where earlier in the day she had tried on a fur coat. "That was the single most expensive thing I have ever had on my back," the woman answered. "So, absolutely not. I do *not* want to go back there. You know me. *I* know me. If I try that coat on again I'll start rationalizing all the reasons I need it."

For the remainder of Black Friday, through the weekend and into Cyber Monday (the online equivalent to Black Friday), I burrowed into the distinction between wants and needs. This is far from a simple question. No, I take that back. For those who write marketing textbooks, it isn't all that complicated. One of the most widely used college marketing texts puts it this way: "An American *needs* food but *wants* a Big Mac, French fries, and a soft drink. . . . Wants are shaped by . . . one's society and are described in terms of objects that will satisfy needs." The textbook doesn't begin to address how tricky the needs-versus-wants issue can be. In his book on advertising, Michael Schudson devotes a chapter to what he calls "The Anthropology of Goods." He points out what's obvious to most people other than Buy Scolds: that human "needs" are both biological and social, and that even Karl Marx understood that life's "necessities" transcend what is required simply to survive. Food, shelter, and clothing are needs—no one would argue—but Marx kept an open mind about what modern Buy Scolds usually write off as marketing-induced indulgences. He believed the things we buy fall into two categories: material necessities and material luxuries. And he concurred with Adam Smith (no Marxist, he) in the view that frippery has its place, that without certain adornments a man risks disgrace and life as a social outcast, which in turn causes him to "fall into extreme bad conduct." Marx—I'm still talking Karl, not Hart Schaffner—would likely accept Adam Smith's contention that even a linen shirt was a necessity, at least back in Smith's day. Absent a linen shirt, Smith said, a member of the working class would rightly be "ashamed to appear in public." As for material luxuries, well, Marx and the Scolds line up nicely on the issue. Luxuries are proof of capitalist exploitation and thus a Marxist/Scoldist no-no. It's extremely unlikely that Marx would have issued a need pass to my friend with the Lionel collection, especially given that some of his layout's plastic people live high on papier-mâchè hills in plastic houses much larger than those of the poor plastic people who toil on the edges of the train board.

What's a want? What's a need? Philosophers, and later psychologists, have mulled over the question for a long time. We saw earlier how Maslow's pyramid of needs gave rise to lifestyle bucketing. Another influential psychologist, Henry Murray, whose work preceded Maslow's, identified nearly as many human needs as Baskin-Robbins has flavors. We have *primary* needs—food, water, oxygen—and a couple of dozen *psychogenic* needs, i.e., needs rooted in the mind. These include our need for affiliation, dominance, order, exhibition, play, sex, and avoidance of harm. Here's a quick exercise designed to take inventory of your own psychogenic-need fulfillment. Walk around the house and identify those material objects you didn't really *need* need but bought because you talked yourself into *thinking* you needed them. A new Armani power tie that hangs in the closet amid three dozen other power ties, some of them not even spotted? Perhaps your psychogenic need to make a dominatingly good impression? That shiny Ibex Apogee mountain bike in the garage, right next to your still highly functional former mountain bike of choice? Perhaps your psychogenic need to broadcast proficiency of performance?

A "Need": Just a "Want" in Need of a Cheap Excuse?

Closeted in my office, I found evidence that yesterday's wants have a way of turning into things we just have to have. In the ten years from 1996 to 2006, the number of people who concluded that they needed a microwave jumped by over a third, the Pew Research Center reports. In fact, the study shows that there are now more microwave needers among us (68 percent of those asked) than there are television needers (64 percent). An even higher percentage of us profess a need for a clothes washer (90 percent) and a dryer to go with it (83 percent). This raises the tantalizing possibility that clean clothes are deemed more integral to the American Dream than microwavable snacks and televised sports. The Pew Study indicates that our professed need for a computer zoomed from virtually zero in 1983 to about one in two of us in 2006, the sharpest of all I-need-it trajectories and one not likely to diminish. A person's age, Pew says, plays a major role in determining what we believe we need versus what we only want. Staying with computers, one of every two of us between eighteen and sixty-four say we need a computer at home, while only 38 percent over sixty-five say so. On the other hand, 73 percent of us over sixty-five demand a TV, while just over half of those eighteen to twenty-nine say they need one (a number likely to decline significantly as more and more video—plus social networking, porn, and of course, shopping—is delivered via the Internet).

Surely, it occurred to me, government bean counters ought to have a good handle on the distinction between wants and needs. Much depends on it, especially in times when unemployment is high, wages are stagnant, homes go unsold, and millions and more millions of us are trying to scrape by. How else can policymakers assess the economic health of the society as a whole or subgroups within it? How else can bureaucrats fix the poverty line and determine eligibility for food stamps or housing assistance? In other words, we *need* "objective" benchmarks in order to judge whether citizens' basic needs are being met, and to make necessary adjustments to entitlement programs and tax laws. A few mouse clicks put me up to my eyeballs in U.S. government data. I discovered that for the feds there are but three fundamental needs, and they're the obvious ones: food, shelter (including utilities), and clothing.* Everything else, by default, falls into the want category. But even here the difference between needs and wants gets loopy. Over time, changing lifestyles throw official need indexes out of whack—our reliance on e-mail, for instance, makes it harder to live without a computer. The same goes for dining habits. When the government calculates what the average consumer unit (household) spends on food annually, it breaks down expenditures into what we spend to eat "at home" and what we spend to eat "away from home." The average of those categories (annually, over $6,000 per household) represents one of the benchmarks agencies use to establish eligibility for food stamps and other forms of assistance. Yet people, affluent and not so, have over the years grown accustomed to eating out more. We eat out not out of *need* to eat but out of *want* to eat out. Back in the days of the Ladies' Mile, our grandparents spent barely three cents out of every food dollar at restaurants and greasy spoons. By the late 1980s, Americans spent twenty-nine cents out of every food dollar at fine-dining establishments, bistros, food courts, and drive-thrus. Today it's forty-three cents.

Government agencies don't provide an especially enlightening picture of the difference between wants and needs, but their reports contain a boundless supply of arresting factoids, a sampling of which I pass along:

- If we're empty nesters, we're likely to spend more on food now than when our kids were at home. We eat out more often, and at pricier joints. Linda and I fit this profile. A Buy Scold would argue that eating out is an extravagance best reserved for special occasions. Part of me agrees, especially the part of me that shows up at the table the moment the waiter delivers the credit card chit. That part of me likes to point out to the rest of me that I have just consumed a few good books, a couple of haircuts, or an unexpected gift now and then for Linda or the kids.

- The percentage of income we spend on clothes does not, on average, correlate with income. It's constant across the board.

---

*Notice that medical care, for the moment, isn't one of them.

- The percentage we spend on housing (including utilities), however, dramatically varies with income, even though there's really no *need* for this. Greater wealth triggers a perceived need for additional square footage.

- Needwise, the most challenged household unit of all is the single parent, who spends a higher percentage of his/her income on the three officially sanctioned needs—housing, clothing, food—than do all other household configurations, rich or poor.

The tussle over what's a need and what's a want can become exceedingly messy. Does the following exchange ring a bell?

"I need it!"

"Like hell you need it!"

Exchanges like this can doom a marriage. State by state, grounds for divorce range from just two or three biggies (California: irreconcilable differences and incurable insanity, that's it), to a dozen or more (Tennessee: separation for two years, no children; natural continuous impotency; bigamy; adultery; willful or malicious desertion or absence; conviction of an infamous crime; attempts on life of other by means showing malice; wife was pregnant at time of marriage by another without husband's knowledge; habitual drunkenness or abuse of narcotic drugs contracted after marriage; inappropriate marital conduct; abandonment by husband; husband's refusal or neglect to provide for wife). Notably, there's not a state in the union where grounds for divorce specifically include what is—by far, I venture—the leading cause of household and marital discord: the failure between parties to agree on what's a need and what's a want.

I don't know about your household, but mine, thankfully, is relatively need-versus-want harmonious, though we do have our moments. Detente stems from a strictly enforced understanding arrived at after years of unpleasant exchanges like the one above. The policy now is that any two of the four of us can shop together without fear of shattering a relationship, but experience has taught us that when we add a third or fourth party, all hell breaks loose.

Linda to Lee, glancing at Ned: "Tell me that you honestly believe he really *needs* that."

Lee to Linda, glancing at Katherine: "Doesn't she already *have* that?"

Lee to Linda, or Linda to Lee, glancing at Ned and/or Katherine: "I don't give a damn that he/she *wants* it. What I'm saying is that he/she doesn't *need* it!"

Ned or Katherine, glaring at Linda and/or Lee: "Why is he/she always getting what *he/she* wants and I never get a thing!"

In our family, when irritation flares over buying practices it's often on account of me, a master of mixed want-need messaging. Generally impatient in a store, I'm also a wildly inconsistent and impulsive spender. This mirrors nearly word for word what many men, including my friend Dan Okrent, say about themselves. Okrent confesses that the Internet has made him "ridiculously penny-wise, pound-foolish. I'll spend an hour comparing prices on a fifty-dollar computer gizmo, then go out and blow three hundred on dinner without a second thought. Once I start thinking hard about something I might want to buy, I'm on a speedy and slippery slope downhill. If I think I might want it, I must have it."

Similarly, I'll go to some lengths to save pennies on flashlight batteries but think nothing of booking ridiculously expensive family vacations, often with minimal due diligence. Several years ago, while eating lunch alone, I paged mindlessly through a travel magazine and I spied an ad for what looked like an idyllic resort in Mexico. Within five minutes I'd booked a week's stay over Christmas break, my lunchtime appetite curbed by the exorbitant rack rate we'd be paying. Then, fighting off cognitive dissonance, I congratulated myself on how lucky we were to get into an in-demand place so late in the season. I assumed I'd pounced on a last-minute cancellation; it turned out that we were almost the only guests there.

Linda—well, you already know quite a bit about her based on the little black dress excursion. A high self-monitor, her perception of wants-versus-needs is influenced by the degree to which a want aligns with what she thinks she needs to fit into a given setting. The greatest Buy difference between us is that (like many men) I worship at the altar of instant gratification, while Linda insists on a solid, enduring fit between purchase and purpose.

"Why should I rush into buying something I don't love, or something I know I'll almost never use or wear?" she says, which usually prompts me to suggest that she quit dithering.

Ned and Katherine are substantially different from their parents and from each other: same gene pool, different want-need MO. Ned tends not to want all that much, but what he wants he wants fanatically. Last year he was stalking the streets of Chicago armed with a small-caliber debit card.* He surely had little or no awareness of how much money was in that account, yet he was content to know that if he elected to use it, a card reader would either accept payment or not, *c'est la vie*. This is not to say that Ned is ambivalent about what he wants when he wants it. A hunter not a gatherer, on that day last year he was intent on bagging a specific pair of wants: Onitsuka Tigers. Neither an extinct species of great cat nor a Japanese baseball franchise, they are $85 athletic shoes named for Kihachiro Onitsuka, who fifty years ago founded the Asics footwear company—Japan's answer to Nike, Adidas, and Puma. Each of those megabrands maintains trendy stores of their own within easy walking distance of where we live, but Ned trucks right past those outlets.

Though not an outright rebel—no tattoos or Mohawk—Ned shops to his own drum. He wraps his everyday self (*today's* everyday self, for his everyday self is likely to be different tomorrow) in a wardrobe that's hard to classify: neither preppy nor grunge, nor nerdy by default. On the day he went Tiger hunting, for example, he wore Diesel jeans, scuffed pointy shoes his friends call his "witch shoes," a T-shirt with an Asian rock band silk-screened on the front, a beat-up, monogrammed Tiffany belt buckle he once received as a birthday present from generous friends of ours, and lime-colored socks filched from my dresser drawer. Only a specific pair of Onitsuka Tigers would complement that particular look. Why Tigers, and only Tigers? Because, he said, Tigers are "cool." "Cool" is what drives a lot of boys (men, too) to want what they want, whether they need it or not. "Cool" also drives girls and women to want many of the things they want, whether they need them or not. But girls and women more often tell you they want things because they're "cute," a quality most boys and men rarely give two cents for. Others, of course, don't give a damn about cool *or* cute; they demand common sense and value. Before buying anything, they do their homework. They live by the gospel of *Consumer Reports* and Epinions .com. They subscribe to Angie's List. As for Ned, he does none of that. He hunts without a map, plan, or strategy. On that afternoon last year, he left

---

*We decided to give our kids debit cards to teach them how to live within their means. We deposit their allowance, and that's it for the month. In theory, a good idea. It caps their income, they can't spend more than they have, and it provides a good early indicator of how a kid will manage spending when he or she grows up—not that you can do anything to change it.

the apartment having made no effort to determine where, or even whether, his prized Onitsuka Tigers with the red and blue stripes were to be found in Chicago. He didn't go online, he didn't phone around to stores. He simply tucked his debit card into the back pocket of his jeans, jammed in a pair of earbuds, and went forth on foot. And by the way, if and when Ned does find what he's looking for, he'll never return it, even if when he gets it home he discovers that it doesn't fit, or it's broken, ripped, or missized.

Katherine, in contrast, is a person who, were you to awaken her in the middle of the night and inquire after her debit card balance, will report the exact amount—though she'll be pissed off that you roused her. Katherine is a self-monitor, but less so than her mother. Yes, she endeavors to match her needs and wants to given situations, but not if it means buying something she deems to be over-the-line trendy: she wants/needs a cool cell phone but not a model too many others have; she wants/needs big furry boots but not the ubiquitous Ugg boots (at least not until last winter, when she relented and bought a pair). When shopping, Katherine pursues her calibrated wants or needs through gathering, not hunting. She moves through a store (Urban Outfitters, Zara) at a deliberate pace, slow-mo actually, with an air of faint detachment. With Katherine, many things she momentarily "really wants" have a way of reconstituting themselves into things that she "kinda wants." This explains why, even as she's paying for something, she's more certain than not that she'll return it unworn within a few days.

What I mainly took away from my Black Friday–to–Cyber Monday lost weekend was this: beyond basic food, clothing, health care, and shelter needs, what's a need and what's a want is inescapably subjective. I also came away with a few other conclusions about the need-want tussle:

1. If Buy Scolds have a beef with how much we spend on what *they* deem to be trivial wants, let them come right out and say it to our faces and quit blaming it on the Sell Side. After all, we're not sheep, and no one can turn us into sheep unless we give thumbs up to the regression.

2. Economists, who once believed that they knew the difference between wants and needs, are of little help. Why? There are many reasons, not least the fact that economists don't get out of the office enough to observe firsthand how we live and buy: the inconsistent father, the self-monitoring

mom, the college kid who hunts morning to night for a pair of Japanese athletic shoes, the high school coed with a love/hate relationship with trend-right furry boots. Life on the Buy Side is best observed by those willing to watch and ask questions. *That dress you wore to the fund-raiser—how did it make you feel? Do all salespeople creep you out, or just the pushy ones? If those Onitsuka Tigers could talk, what would they say about you?*

3. Finally, little kids—*for sure*—can't tell the difference between needs and wants. Here the Buy Scolds are dead-on. Expose our kids to ingenious packaging (try me!) or too many commercials (buy me!), give them a long leash in supermarket aisles, and they're on their way to full citizenship in a want-want-want-want world.

Just one caveat: it's tempting to decry our kids' lust for the right pair of Nikes—*environmentally toxic, expensive!*—but it's hardheaded to ignore the fact that a kid can pay a high tariff if he doesn't get those shoes. The price, says David Wooten, a marketing professor at the University of Michigan, comes in the form of other "adolescents [who] use ridicule to ostracize, haze, or admonish peers who violate consumption norms." That doesn't mean we *should* buy him those Nikes—it means we need to strike a sensible balance.

10

You Are What You Buy

In search of a Unified Theory

Is it bad that I make snap judgments about girls based on what jeans they wear? When I see a girl in Sevens, I dismiss her. If she's wearing Citizens, I'm skeptical. . . . If she's in Diesels, that's legit, as that's an enduring brand. But right now, I'm looking for girls in Hudsons.
—Posting on Slate.com

WHY WE BUY WHAT WE BUY IS NO EASY puzzle, that much has been established. Some say we buy because the planet is under the control of nefarious beings: corporate fat cats, ravenous retailers, brand managers wielding marketing gimmicks. Others aren't so lathered. How, where, what, and why we buy, some say with academic reserve, derives from a maelstrom of economic, geographic, cultural, and social factors, many of which are beyond our control: the overall supply of goods and services; the degree of wealth in the society and how it's distributed; whether we live in a densely populated trading area where shopping has melted into everything or a place where it hasn't—though with the coming of the Internet there's effectively no such place.

This high-altitude view doesn't do it for me. It doesn't capture what happened the day Katherine and I encountered the big man in shorts and flip-flops who was so eager to get his hands on Tom Ford's new fragrance. After we left the grooming counter, we took the escalator up to the top floor of the mall. Over lunch I decided to interview Katherine about her personal Buy profile, as good a way as any to gain further traction on this second half of my expedition. I was curious about why some of us shop responsibly while others are reckless; why some enjoy shopping while others despise it. Drawing two axes on a paper napkin, I asked Katherine to mark where she thought she fell on a scattergram. Her placement (marked by the X) surprised me:

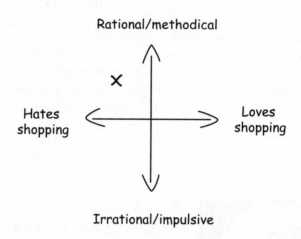

"Hey, you have a closetful of clothes," I said. "You're up on the latest, you read fashion magazines, you spend time in malls with friends. Admit it, you like shopping."

"Uh-uh," she replied. "I don't like trying clothes on. I'm usually not sure about whether something's worth the money. Salespeople creep me out. I like the idea of buying, but I don't like *shopping* at all."

Back home, Katherine retreated to her bedroom, where she shopped the iTunes Store for—what?—love in a download? I retreated to my office and pulled the paper napkin from my pocket. The lunchtime buy-o-gram was hopelessly incomplete. It didn't begin to get at why Katherine—you, me, the guy at the grooming counter—do what we do when we shop. I scribbled more dimensions on the napkin:

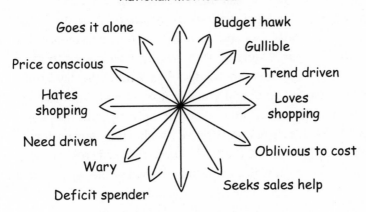

Rational/methodical

Goes it alone

Budget hawk

Gullible

Price conscious

Trend driven

Hates
shopping

Loves
shopping

Need driven

Wary

Oblivious to cost

Deficit spender

Seeks sales help

Irrational/impulsive

The more variables I added, the more glaring the omissions. I had noth-ing to signify whether our amygdalas are working or on the fritz; nothing to take into account whether we live in a high- or low-density population zone; no reference to our cognitive ability to keep numbers straight in our heads (i.e., how price retentive we might be). Me, I wouldn't know the price of a dozen eggs if you tried to beat it out of me with a rubber pullet. Surely there must be a more elegant way to capture the forces in play when we buy. You'd think that with so much shopping going on, so much surveillance, so much data, we'd by now have a clearer understanding of why we buy what we buy. Really, think about it: physicists pursue "unified field theories" to connect divergent particles and waves. If we can presume to do this with the universe, why not with what happens in a store?

Why not a Unified *Buy* Theory?

Casting Around

In fact, my search for an all-inclusive Unified Buy Theory has been going on for some time now. I've accumulated books full of postulations relating to what makes shoppers tick. Many of the titles dangle the promise that a UBT might be here and now: *How Customers Think*, for instance. The author is Gerald Zaltman, a professor at the Harvard Business School and a partner in a consulting firm that deploys "patented scientific processes" to delve into "the hidden meanings that drive human behavior." Zaltman's notions are post-Freudian, with an emphasis on how the brain traffics in images, not words. His approach is based on the premise that only a small portion of our "thoughts"—5 percent, but who's counting?—are conscious; the rest is "hidden knowledge." I remember the day I spied a copy of *How Customers Think* and cracked it open with high expectations—definitive title, respected author—only to have my optimism dashed early on. Yes, the book delivers provocative insights into how customers think, but we'll likely have found a cure for cancer, reversed greenhouse gas emissions, and figured out which came first, the hen or the egg, before Zaltman or anyone can say with certainty how mental metaphor-making determines what we buy. In Zaltman's view we'll need to have untangled the mechanics of brain-mind-body-social interaction. No, this is not a simple puzzle, the riddle of why a man in flip-flops wants to be the first on his block to dab on Tobacco Vanille. To solve the riddle, says Zaltman, researchers will need to escape the narrow conceptual and intellectual alleyways that constrict the study of consumer behavior.

I try not to think about the money I've spent on books less worthy than Zaltman's. I'm staring at the tottering pile now: a couple of dozen aimed at midlevel marketing and sales managers, titles I've picked up at airport bookstores that are littered with drive-by swipes at Unified Buy Theories. Most revolve around the notion that "we are what we buy," that cliché with the ring of natural law, an echo of the "you are what you eat" mantra invoked by the counterculture decades ago to extol the benefits of macrobiotic food.*

Most of these books, having posited the notion that you are what you buy, expand on it by noting how our adoration of specific brands bonds us to others with the same preferences. We share loyalty (bordering on obsession) to VW Beetles or Vermont Castings woodstoves. These allegiances herd us into "brand tribes," a fashionable Sell Side term these days. Brands, these books further observe, have personalities—they're human, sort of, with distinct personality traits to which we buddy up. My trusty marketing text cites a study listing five traits exhibited by brands and, by extension, us: sincerity (Hallmark), excitement (BMW), competence (Amazon), sophisti-

---

*Actually, it's been kicking around much longer than that. A version of it was first dished up in 1826 by gastronome Brillat-Savarin. .

cation (Tiffany), ruggedness (Ford Bronco). The list is woefully incomplete, of course. It leaves out brands with less savory qualities: overbearing (Microsoft), rapacious (Google), scheming (Fox News).

Those who contend that we *are* the brands we buy, and that those brands are us, began to beat that drum at a time (the sixties) when social institutions and traditions were coming unglued—"the Age of Discontinuity," as management guru Peter Drucker called it. The ties that had bound us one to the next—neighborhood, town, family, faith—were sundering. About the only things with centers that held, champions of brand power maintained, were the products and services with which we strongly connected: Johnson & Johnson, Disney, Marlboro, Maytag, and later Nike, Apple, Starbucks, Jet-Blue, Nintendo.

That we buy because our personalities are reflected in brands, and that brand loyalty extends membership in a tribe, are propositions now firmly fixed in the Buy zeitgeist. In 2001 two social scientists, Thomas O'Guinn and Albert Muniz, published a paper titled "Brand Community." The premise was that we and fellow admirers of a brand share a "consciousness"—a "we-ness"—that encourages collective fealty to a set of established rituals and even shared moral responsibility for how our brands choose to behave. Back when we still bought SUVs, Ford Bronco drivers expressed their "we-ness" by reminding fellow tribe members that to trade in a Bronco for a lightweight Japanese SUV was tantamount to mortal sin. Mac users exhibit "the characteristics of a threatened community," say O'Guinn and Muniz—namely, cohesion, trepidation, and outright contempt directed at those who fall outside their "we-ness." They write: "While enjoying, even reveling in their underdog status . . . [Mac users] cannot understand why the rest of the world does not appreciate what they have known for so long: the superiority of the Mac way of doing things." Apple fans (myself included) can be insufferably self-satisfied, a smugness tempered only by what O'Guinn and Muniz say is a constant fear of "abandonment" by Apple and by Steve Jobs in particular. This anxiety flared in 2007 when Jobs notoriously dropped the price of the iPhone not long after early adopters had braved endless lines to pay through the nose for it. Jobs stuck it to the tribe again the following year, when Apple released a second-generation phone that was, in the company's words, "Twice as fast. Half the price."

In making the case that we seek out brands that complement our temperaments and aspirations, O'Guinn and Muniz downplay the Buy Scold charge that brands have the resources and smarts to conscript us into their tribes. No, all that brand marketers can do, according to their paper, is sketch out a *hoped-for* brand personality. It's you, me, and others, in aggregate, who get to decide whether a brand has a winning personality or not. The Internet, as O'Guinn later explained to me, is the "backyard fence" across which we and fellow tribe members toast the brands we like and roast the ones we don't.* I asked O'Guinn if he could think of instances in which a shrewd marketer had been able manipulate an aggregation of ewes into a bona fide brand herd. Not really, he shrugged, recalling how GM's Saturn division had tried to create a brand community but never fully pulled it off. When I asked Al Muniz the same question—can brand communities be manufactured?—he came up with but one example: Jones Soda, the quirky Seattle-based bottler whose products are sold at Starbucks, Panera Bread, Barnes & Noble, and other specialty outlets. It wasn't the company's energy drink, WhoopAss, that glued Jones fans together; it was the opportunity the brand gave them to upload photos of themselves, their kids, or their pet goats, so that just possibly they might wind up on the label of a bottle of Jones Blue Bubble Gum or Fufu Berry soda.

Social critics such as James Twitchell suggest that some of us maintain closer relations with brand avatars (Ronald McDonald, the Ti-D-Bowl man, back when Twitchell was writing) than with our own relatives. "Brands," Twitchell says in *Branded Nation*, "are the new lingua franca . . . ligatures that hold experience together." If you're a computer geek you find your community in compatriots who are fluent in Linux code. Complete strangers, walking the same breed of dog, cross busy streets to exchange intimacies about Fido and Spot's respective toilet habits. If you're a college, a church, a museum, a charity, or a monkfish, to be unbranded or misbranded is to be nowhere and no one.†

---

*Al Muniz, coauthor of the brand community paper, uses an in-class exercise to illustrate the ubiquity of antibrand communities. He asks undergraduates to call out brand names at random, then Googles each of them, adding "+ sucks" to the search box. Rarely does a search fail to turn up scores of sites dedicated to trashing a product or store.

†During the 2008 presidential campaign, political blogs were consumed by how the race played out brandwise. The Republican party brand was universally judged to be "broken." BrandObama, effectively built on the brand values of Hope and Change, came under fire when Obama began his move to the center on foreign policy, government wiretapping, and gun control issues, causing consternation among members of the Obama brand tribe. "Obama Undercuts His Brand" was a lead headline on the Huffington Post.

* * *

Buy Scolds are of course horrified by the notion that you may be on more intimate terms with the Ti-D-Bowl man than with your own hubby; that you spend more quality time with Aunt Jemima than with your dear Aunt Bertha. How pathetic, Scolds lament, that Ralph Lauren or Rachael Ray or the Pillsbury Dough Boy have become, as psychologist put it, "congruent with self-concept"? The Scolds decry how our infatuation with brand-name motorcycles, computers, dolls, and boxes of interlocking plastic bricks fill those parts of our souls previously occupied by social, moral, and civic ideals. Don't you see, they sputter, that brands are little more than slick lies—slick lies, says Benjamin Barber, professor of civil society, to which "professional market doctors [surgically attach] generic sentiment"?

Those who promote the potency of brands turn their backs on the Scolds' disdain. Generic sentiments? Brands are anything *but*, they counter. Brands, great ones anyway, make our hearts flutter, says Marc Gobé, a global brand-image consultant. Gobé says that "the *emotional* aspect of products" is a key determinant of why we choose specific offerings and the price we're willing to pay for them. "By emotional," Gobé says, "I mean how a brand engages consumers on the level of the senses [and] how a brand comes to life for people and forges a deeper, lasting connection."

Strong brands are *lovemarks*, says Kevin Roberts, CEO Worldwide of Saatchi & Saatchi, the advertising mega-agency. Roberts, speaking at a university lecture series, described the circumstances behind his branding thunderbolt: "I live in Tribeca and my wife is in New Zealand. . . . So, I was there unloved [one night when I] opened up a couple of bottles of red wine and was doodling around at 2:30 in the morning. . . . I started to draw a little heart, okay? And then I saw heart marks and then love marks. . . . I thought, I've got it, this is so simple. What's the deepest emotion of all?" Well, love, of course. A lovemark, then, at least as I understand it, is kind of *like* a brand, but more powerful and affecting than a mere brand because lovemarks, says Roberts, have what it takes to pierce the "heart as well as your mind, creating an intimate, emotional connection that you can't live without. Ever." Turn your back on a mere brand, Roberts claims, and you'll replace it with another. (Nice knowing you, Ban Powder Fresh Roll-on!) Lose a lovemark, though, and you'll mourn its passing, because lovemarks have three powerful qualities: "Mystery, sensuality, and intimacy," says Roberts.

Brands, when they're working right, aren't mere love vessels, they're "valuable resources for identity construction"—ours, that is—according to Douglas B. Holt, an American social scientist now teaching at Oxford.* Brands mediate the culture, and certain ones tap into what Holt calls "myth markets," and thus become "iconic" and highly profitable. Over its brand life, Mountain Dew, for example, is notable for having tapped into three distinct myth markets, growing more successful each time. In the fifties and sixties Mountain Dew played to the "hillbilly" myth market; in the seventies and eighties, the "redneck" myth market; beginning in the nineties, the "slacker" myth market, wherein one finds surfboarders, skateboarders, X-gamers, Xbox gamers, fans of *Beavis and Butt-head* and all things *Jackass.*

When they're working right, brands are also reflections of national identity, according to Clotaire Rapaille, a French-born anthropologist *cum* psychoanalyst *cum* marketing consultant who lives and works in a Tudor mansion in Tuxedo Park, just north of Manhattan (shades of Ernest Dichter). Renowned for his élan, Rapaille is partial to velvet frock coats and starched collars. In the portrait on his Web site he stands surrounded by a collection of superbly branded cars that includes a Rolls, a Porsche, and a PT Cruiser, among others. Rapaille's signature theory—an intriguing one—is that we unconsciously view the world, and thus the things we buy, through national "Culture Codes." For example, the French Code for "cheese" is ALIVE, says Rapaille in a best-selling book published in 2006. This explains why the French handle cheese as if it were a baby and store cheese at room temperature, in a cloche that allows air in but keeps bugs out, an environment indeed fit for an infant. The American Code for "cheese," on the other hand, is DEAD, which is why we pasteurize the living life out of it, and keep it refrigerated in Saran Wrap as if in a morgue. The German Culture Code for cars, Rapaille says, is ENGINEERING, while in America it's IDENTITY. The Germans want cars that *function*; we want cars, he says, that evoke "the freedom of getting behind the wheel for the first time, and the excitement of youthful passion." Brands such as Jeep—or at least Jeep a decade ago—and the PT Cruiser are each expressions of a distinctive identity, in contrast to the cookie-cutter sedans for which Detroit has been infamous.

*   *   *

---

*His chair is endowed by L'Oréal—a fragrant chair, if ever there was.

Having sampled a decent number of branding disquisitions, I'm left with little energy to delve much further. I can, however, offer three extended insights into how we relate to brands, and how brands relate to us.

Brands Connect Us to Others

I can personally testify here, so indulge me for a moment. In the late sixties my mother rewarded my more or less acceptable college career with a generous offer: she'd top off the money I'd been saving to buy the car of my postpubescent dreams: an MGB—steel gray, red leather interior—not hugely expensive but intoxicatingly cool. After a ridiculously long wait—foreign cars, still a tiny portion of the market, took forever to cross the Atlantic—I learned that the car had arrived. I rushed over to the dealership. Sunny day, birds singing, roads dry, ideal motoring conditions. The salesman handed over the keys. I clicked on the ignition, slipped into first, and off I went in search of any curve worth a downshift. Stopped at a red light, I drew in deep drafts of New Car Smell, genuine English leather commingled with the not unpleasant odor of plastics and assorted toxic materials used in the manufacture of dashboards. I glanced into the tiny rearview mirror and saw—in one of those slow-motion takes—an outsized American car, a Pontiac, bearing down on me. The driver's mind, if he had one, was evidently elsewhere. The Pontiac slammed into the MG's tiny trunk. I was shaken *and* stirred, maybe dead for all I knew, though my instinct for irony was apparently intact. I opened my eyes. Before I checked for protruding bones or blood splatters, I looked at the odometer. Man (me) and machine (MG) had managed to travel all of 4.7 miles before fate had put a sizable dent in what should have been one of the most cherished Buy days of my life.

Mangled though it was, the MG was still drivable, so I tooled around in my wounded sports car for five or six months, until replacement parts arrived from England. If I had any solace it was this: I'd become a key-carrying member of a community. I was connected to kindred souls hitherto unknown to me. You know what I'm talking about if you drove a foreign car back then: MG, Triumph TR-4, Austin-Healey Sprite, Volvo P1800, Jaguar XKE, VW Beetle. To drive one was to keep your eye peeled for cars of your own kind. When you spotted one (a chap in a tweed cap invariably behind the wheel), you flashed your headlamps, the way a ship uses a signal light to transmit Morse. The meaning of the flash was clear to both parties: you drive an MG, I drive an MG. Our bond is the signet attached to the grille just beneath the hood (or "bonnet" as the collective "we-ness" knowingly referred to it):

Flashing at strangers in broad daylight was about as far as I went to acknowledge membership in the royal order of the leaking ragtop. Others of you carried your car keys on a fob with the car's logo stamped on it. You subscribed to magazines devoted to your beloved brand. You sent photos and letters back and forth, trading customization ideas, comparing tire performance. You joined local and national clubs that sponsored weekend picnics and road rallies. Me, I just flashed my headlamps at every oncoming MG, and oncoming drivers flashed back. Whenever I caught a flash too late to reciprocate, I felt truly crummy, as if I'd let someone down.

Brands Express Our Values

Brand central in Chicago is located in a seven-block stretch of the Magnificent Mile, where tribe members come to hunt, gather, or just shoot the breeze at their community centers of choice. A multigenerational female tribe, for instance, crowds into American Girl Place, which recently expanded into a vast space at the Water Tower mall. If you're the mom or the grandmother of a young girl, you likely know all too well the passionate and expensive attachment your girl has formed with one of the historical dolls that are the mainstay of the AG product line. An American Girl doll, among her other virtues, is the anti-Barbie (who, by the way, is as bootylicious as ever at age fifty). There's Addy Walker, newly escaped from slavery but separated from her father and brother, who've been sold off; there's Josefina Montoya, growing up in New Mexico in the 1820s, mourning the death of her mother while coming to terms with the newfangled ideas of her recently arrived aunt; there's Kirsten Larson, blue-eyed and blond under a gingham bonnet, fresh from Scandinavia, now settled on the Minnesota frontier; there's Molly McIntire, in oval specs and pigtails, longing for the end of World War II, dreaming of the day her daddy will—with luck—return from a distant battlefront. Each is wholesome, heroic in the face of hardship, and not exactly bereft of things to own: party dresses, feast day finery, pinafores, snoods, head warmers, slippers, dance outfits, knitted woolens, St. Lucia outfits. Nor are they bereft of cabin, farmhouse, or lean-to furnishings: beds, tufted comforters, commodes, lazy Susans, storage trunks, washstands, mirrored chifforobes, rolltop desks. They have a menagerie of bunnies, horses, dogs, and cats. And each has a six-volume set of books—available in a protective slipcase—that chronicles her ups and downs, smiles and frowns.

Only the sourest Buy Scold would fail to acknowledge at least some redeeming value in the American Girl product line, notwithstanding the marketing testosterone that courses through this $500-million-a-year brand. Yes, there's a lot to buy, and everything's dear: dolls that cost $100, whose life challenges and exemplary characters all but demand that a mom or grandmother shell out for dresses (starting at $22), a cozy nightshift ($52), a stenciled storage trunk ($159). Only the crustiest Buy Scold would deny that the American Girl brand offers collateral value: each doll includes, at no extra cost, a trace of a history lesson with a nod to multicultural understanding and compassion. Even a Buy Scold should acknowledge that to buy your daughter some interactive playtime with an American Girl doll is preferable to putting a TV in her room and injecting her with Hannah Montana disease.

Brand theorists take quite an expansive view of what's really on sale here at American Girl Place. I've got study in hand, a work in progress by a cross-disciplinary team of researchers who spent considerable time hanging out at American Girl Place, photographing customers and staff, interviewing them about the merchandise on display: the dolls, the American Girl magazine, American Girl movies, and American Girl outfits for real girls that match their dolls'. The observers saw something close to brand quintessence here. There's *interaction*: an environment charged with energy and activity, a destination that exemplifies a successful "brandscape," as it's called in the trade. There's a photo studio where you can pose for pictures with your dolls; a café where you can partake of brunch with your dolls; a salon where you can indulge your dolls with a new 'do or trade up to the full Pampering Plus package—a facial to remove greasy fingerprints and ketchup stains, a manicure in the form of a fresh set of nail decals. There's *learning and enlightenment*: this is not ordinary "shopping." Sure, American Girl Place reverberates with the familiar whining and crying, but it's not over spangled hairclips or peekaboo tank tops. The products here have redeeming qualities: historical narratives, social/ethical take-aways, however melodramatic. Finally, as the research team noted, here is where *memories* are made. Not just the cornball, ghost-written "memories" in the books about what "real life" was like for a black girl running from slavery or a fair-skinned girl huddled against the cold prairie wind. No, the memories in question bind one generation to the next. Said a grandmother interviewed by the research team: "Well, I think grandparents . . . parents, too, but especially grandparents . . . like to create memories for the children and for the family, you know? And I just thought that this could be one of those memories for her. . . . That she'd say, 'I remember my grandmother, my Nanna'—she calls me Nanna—'my Nanna and my mom and I went to American Girl . . . '"

A few blocks to the south of American Girl Place, I met up with Albert Muniz, coauthor of the brand-community paper and a marketing prof at DePaul University. I thought it would be good to have an expert guide me through Chicago's principal brand district. It was a dreary, soggy afternoon, but Muniz was buoyant. He and his girlfriend had just returned from a pleasant vacation, which explained his nut-brown suntan at the tail end of a Chicago winter. Moreover, Muniz had just learned that newly published rankings continued to list "Brand Community" as one of the ten most cited papers in the field of social science. Muniz is a genial, short fellow with a buzz cut—fitting, perhaps, given that much of his academic career has been devoted to why we buzz about certain brands, even dead or dying ones.

Back in 2005, Muniz and another social scientist (Hope Jensen Schau of Temple University) infiltrated the hardy community that continues to bond around the Apple Newton. The Newton, you'll recall, was the first personal digital assistant to hit the market (1993). Newton was riddled with technical bugs, widely derided by the press, and effectively driven from the marketplace when the PalmPilot came along three years later. Undaunted, a few thousand Newton worshippers remain in this PDA's bug-infested thrall—a community, Muniz contends, that displays many of the classic signs of a religious order or an embattled cult. Newtonians are *fatalistic*. They know their days are numbered but they're determined to hang on in the name of their holy motherboard ("Would the last person to leave the platform please turn off the backlight?" reads one online post). Newtonians feel *persecuted*: Newton didn't fail them, Apple failed Newton by not having the faith to support the device through its initial shortcomings. Newtonians display signs of *marginalization*: they lash back by demonstrating the minor miracles a Newton can perform when confronted by nonbelievers who remark, "I can't believe you're still screwing around with that." For the faithful, Muniz says, the Newton is thus akin to a religious totem.

Having chatted about the Newton, Muniz and I took the escalator up to the LEGO store. At the entrance we gaped at several awesome LEGO constructions, our wonder only slightly undercut by the knowledge that they owe their grand-scale existence to sophisticated CAD software. The displays are amazing nonetheless: a gigantic LEGO spider about twelve feet long, big enough to cause havoc were it to attack the construction that sits just a few feet away—a mammoth LEGO Chicago Marriott with a million tiny LEGO windows, LEGO-paved driveway, LEGO landscaping, even LEGO hotel guests and pedestrians walking around at the base.

At the time we visited the LEGO center, a dark cloud hung over this Denmark-based brand as it gamely celebrated its fiftieth anniversary. For decades, Muniz told me, LEGO had fought a losing battle to prevent makers of cheaper plastic bricks from violating its trademark protections. It also, needless to say, faced pitiless competition from electronic toys and video games that, well, if you were a ten-year-old boy, what would you rather do on Christmas morning: fire up Halo 4 on your new Xbox and hunt for exploding skulls or lie quietly on the rug snapping tiny colored bricks together? In quasi-desperation, some years ago LEGO began to attach itself to newer, flashier brands. As Muniz and I strolled through the store, we were struck by the degree to which LEGO had become a licensing platform for the advancement of other brands with their own communities: Star Wars, Harry Potter, and Nickelodeon, among others.

No question: LEGO faces vexing community issues, the greatest being that kids grow up. By far the largest segment of the LEGO brand flock—boys mostly—say farewell to the community around the time hair begins to sprout anywhere below the scalp. And yet, Muniz explained as we headed back to the escalator, some of them, when they reach their twenties or thirties, hit the bricks again to become part of a tribe known as AFOL (adult fans of LEGO). Collectively, they buy about 10 percent of the bricks LEGO sells a year. AFOLs meet annually at BrickFest, where they build

Gothic cathedrals and fearsome plastic reptiles, and screen stop-action animation videos starring their favorite "minifigs" (miniature figures). The rest of the year they spend thousands of dollars on new bricks, mechanical pulleys, motors, and lighting systems. AFOLs refer to themselves as survivors of what they call the Dark Ages: the years between the time a kid puts away childish things and the time he might feel a stirring to once more lay plastic bricks.

Exiting the mall, Muniz and I dashed around the corner to a shrine operated by one of America's top three or four most "iconic brands." If you're a Harley-Davidson devotee, you're assumed to be the sine qua non brand communitarian. James Twitchell, author of *Branded Nation*, on the Harley community: you're "clustered like pilgrims around an icon of worshipful concentration"; you're part of a community "so deep in pretend lore that . . . both the machine and owner share the same name: 'Hog.'"*

Harley-Davidson provides an object lesson in how a company can torque loyalists' brand perceptions in new directions when necessary. Back in the 1970s stories appeared that augured trouble in Harley-brand paradise: Harley bikers were all bandana, no bite. While a few hogs got their rocks off beating up hippies with pool cues at music festivals, that glowering sociopath who passed you on the highway was now unmasked as a doctor, dentist, or accountant who on weekends swaddled his balding noggin in a rag and slipped a Harley-branded wife-beater around his paunch. The chick riding on the bitch seat was probably the renegade's never-beaten wife, a junior high math teacher maybe, trying gamely to wrap her arms around her outlaw's jelly belly.

In his book *How Brands Become Icons*, Douglas Holt describes how Harley saw the writing on the men's room wall, the disconnect between its mean-assed imagery—Dean, Brando, Fonda the Younger, Hell's Angels—and the milquetoast buyers who were, in fact, the brand's bread and butter: "politically conservative, white, middle-aged, middle-class men" (up to and including Malcolm Forbes). And so Harley brilliantly revised its tribal image: it took the proto-outlaw hog rider and morphed him into a

---

*Etymologically, "hog" is the acronym of the Harley Owners Group, which has over a million members worldwide. HOG is also the stock symbol for Harley-Davidson, Inc. (In 2005 the company's ticker ID was the more sober HDI.) In any event, out on the street (*not* Wall Street), "hog" is commonly pronounced *hawg* by those in the know, regardless of education level or professional status.

libertarian fond of the open road. It was a picture-perfect brand position-ing set against the sunrise of Ronald Reagan's new American morning.

The change in Harley brand personality brought tremendous sales growth over the decades that followed, but it didn't prevent hard-core Har-ley nuts from aging, which poses a problem for the company, Muniz ex-plained. The median age of a Harley rider, midthirties in the Reagan years, is today fifty-plus. This means that a sizable chunk of Harley's weekend-warrior community will soon be driving your hogs to a urologist's office or dismounting permanently thanks to creaky joints. Muniz told me he'd heard rumblings that Harley was aggressively courting African Ameri-can and Hispanic customers, groups whose participation in the Harley brand mythology traditionally languishes in the single digits. And, on the premise that women can be hogs too, Harley is actively "wooing fe-males," in the words of a *New York Times* headline. Harley a *"wooer"*? The *Times* piece describes a dealers' convention in Nashville where a market-ing consultant gave Harley salespeople lessons on how best to woo the ladies: keep your hair neatly groomed, offer a firm but not too firm hand-shake, clean the restrooms, set aside space for a children's play area, and put a plant outside "to say you are female-friendly." The strategy seems viable: women now account for some 12 percent of Harleys sold annually (up from 4 percent in 1990). There's a for-women-only section on the Har-ley Web site. Click on MOVE UP TO THE FRONT SEAT and you're instantly vaulted from the bitch seat to a page inviting you to attend a Harley-Davidson "Garage Party" specifically for women who are "non-riders [with] little—or even no—prior knowledge of motorcycles." The *Times* reporter attended one of these parties and chatted with a forty-something woman wearing a Harley T-shirt adorned with neither a skull nor BORN DEAD but with roses and a butterfly.

Muniz and I browsed the Harley community clubhouse collection, mar-veling over how respectable Harley membership had become. You can still buy Harley die-cast hog replicas, key chains, bandanas, T-shirts, leather vests, studded dog collars, but you can also pick up Harley greeting cards (Muniz sprang for one, a get well card for an ailing uncle), poker chips, a wall clock, and tins of Harley-Davidson coffee.* Will all this tinkering re-

---

*Perfect for the morning after an evening of too much Tommy Bahama Ultra-Premium Rum, or Jimi Hendrix Electric Vodka, or Martha Stewart Cabernet.

duce Harley's fervent brand community to a bland community—and if so, does it matter? Yes, for some anyway. If you're an ancien régime hawg, you're uneasy about Harley wooing recruits with whom you have little in common. You understand that the company has good reason to crack these new customer segments—nobody wants to wind up in LEGO's brick shoes. You also understand that Harley must do what it can to replace you and your pals, given that you're off replacing your hips. But Harley-Davidson *Garage Parties*? You see dispiriting headlines: HARLEY FACES ROUGH RIDE DESPITE RECORD PROFITS. Others of your ilk echo what's been running through your mind:

> I ride with old, traditional guys, and we don't like what's happened with Harley. [It was] like in being an exclusive club. . . . Now it's kind of a broken group with doctors, lawyers and Wall Street yuppies.
>
> —Hog rider for twenty years, an investment adviser
> who was never a wild one to begin with

Brands Keep Their Promises—or Else

I said good-bye to Muniz and trudged home along the Magnificent Mile. A blast of arctic air heaved me into a Starbucks, where I ordered a "small" coffee. (I belong to that tribe of curmudgeons who eschew the company's "tall," "grande," and "venti.") Starbucks' desire to promote community was explicit in its original business model. As a student of the company told the *New York Times* in 2004, Starbucks represents "the corner bar of the 21st century. It symbolizes the hunger for community in today's atomized world . . . a public space where people can go to be with other people."

My seat by the window gave me a straight shot at the Apple Store across the street. On this bone-chilling weekday, Apple's silvery Chicago flagship offered refuge to an unending stream of brand acolytes and assorted e-freeloaders who came in from the cold to check their mail. Apple remains brand-community viable, not brand-community iffy, as Harley and LEGO are, and certainly not brand-community endangered, as Starbucks is. The Starbucks tribe, if there truly ever was such a thing, had grown restless. So restless that founder Howard Schultz felt he needed to take hyper-caffeinated action to prevent more of us from disclaiming membership in his tribe. In early 2007, Schultz sent around a frank, two-page "internal" memo to senior execs, a document so widely publicized that it was reasonable to assume that the entire nation had been blind-copied. The memo's subject line: "The Commoditization of the Starbucks Experience," though it could as easily have been titled "The McDonaldization of the Starbucks Experience." The memo told Starbucks execs that they had to urgently address a slew of self-inflicted brand wounds mostly attributable to the company's rapid expansion. There were now over sixteen thousand Starbucks outposts worldwide, approaching half as many as McDonald's. So many new Starbucks stores, so little time to have gotten them right. Real estate leases had been negotiated on the fly. Newly opened stores cannibalized recently opened stores just around the corner. The result, Schultz opined, was the "watering down of the Starbucks experience." In its quest for speed and efficiency, Starbucks had installed automatic espresso machines that, compared with the old La Marzocca machines, removed "the romance and theatre" associated with all that hissing and banging that happened when a barista whipped up your latte by hand, a ritual you enjoyed watching. There was the changeover to "flavor lock packaging"—another efficiency move—which effectively rid the air of the aroma of freshly ground beans, the brand's "most powerful non-verbal signal," in Schultz's words. And there was—again in the name of global expansion—the implementation of "streamline store design," which Schultz said ignored "the soul of the past" and compromised "the warm feeling of a neighborhood store." The changes turned Starbucks into what, from the beginning, it swore it would never be: just another chain in what the Sell Side refers to as the "limited service restaurant" category.

Starbucks, in other words, had broken promises it had made to its tribe. Revisit Schultz's decade-old history of the rise of Starbucks ("printed on totally chlorine free paper") and the chapter titles reveal the disconnect between what Starbucks promised and how things turned out: "A Strong Legacy Makes You Sustainable for the Future"; "People Are Not a Line Item"; "The Best Way to Build a Brand is One Person at a Time"; "You Can Grow Big and Stay Small"; "How Not to Be a Cookie-Cutter Chain." And then there's chapter 21: "How Socially Responsible Can a Company Be?" That doesn't gibe with National Labor Relations Board allegations (denied by Starbucks) that the company used illegal tactics to stave off baristas' attempts to unionize. Then there were the news stories about how the National Coffee Association of the USA—the trade lobby of which Starbucks is the eight-hundred-pound gorilla member—tried to prevent Ethiopian coffee growers from winning American trademark protection for two of their prized varietals (Sidamo and Harrar). Starbucks had long ago demonstrated the value of turning native coffee beans into intellectual property, locking up trademarks on a wide range of brews sold in its stores: Komodo Dragon Blend, Café Estima Blend, Africa Kitamu. It wasn't in Big Coffee's interest to allow a faraway country to stamp ® on its beans. The dispute might have remained at a low PR simmer except that Oxfam, the global relief and development organization, jumped into the thick of it, charging that if these efforts succeeded, the coffee establishment would effectively prevent $88 million a year in incremental profits from flowing into one of the most destitute countries in the world.*

Finally, as if all that weren't enough, one other small problem emerged: brand loyalty has its price limits. An okay if not great cup of coffee *definitely* has its price limits, regardless of whether the joint smells like fresh coffee or showcases a barista's bravura performance. Even before the current economic swoon, customers had become sensitive to the costs of repeated visits to Starbucks. Four years ago I overheard a woman in an affluent Chicago suburb, the wife of a CEO, tell friends how proud she was of her college freshman son, who'd announced plans to become more financially responsible by eliminating all visits to his campus Starbucks. And, more recently, it became common to hear others refer to Schultz's company as "Fourbucks."

Had Starbucks been better attuned to these and other tribal tom-toms, the company might have avoided, or at least lessened, its current headaches. I say this based on a recent trip to Madison, Wisconsin, where I had coffee with Craig Thompson, a marketing professor at UW. Thompson had pointedly suggested that we *not* meet at Starbucks but rendezvous instead at a shop called Steep & Brew, an independent outfit that operates a couple of stores in Madison and happens to sit directly across from a Starbucks on

---

* An overwhelming amount of this would wind up in the pockets of the major growers and distributors, not the workers, but that's another story.

State Street. I sat waiting for him under a giant banner with a deliriously happy cow on it. The banner promoted the fact that only politically correct java was poured on the premises.

In the name of local color, I should point out that State Street, if you've never had the pleasure, serves as the university's high street (in more ways than one), a shopping drag that time might like to forget but can't, not in a liberal college town where the sixties keep on keeping on. State Street is home to head shops, New Age bookstores, homeopathic drugstores, vintage clothing joints, and a couple of independent cafés such as the one Thompson had suggested. Inexorably, Gap, Jamba Juice, Starbucks, and other chains have muscled into the neighborhood, despite efforts to keep the environs safe from "mallification" and the accompanying cultural oppression that gives Buy Scolds plenty to chew on. A few years ago I was walking down State Street, minding my own business, when a shaggy-haired guy looked me up and down and snarled, "You and your fucking Banana Republics."

Craig Thompson, a tall, slender man, delivered his thoughts at a decibel level that challenged the quietude at Steep & Brew, where every table and all nooks and crannies were occupied by students bent over textbooks and laptops. Faithful communitarians, they had come to draw succor from the caffeinated, the organic, the shade grown, and the fairly traded, qualities people found wanting in the Starbucks experience. As far back as 2004, Thompson had published a paper built around interviews with a few dozen declared conscientious objectors:

> Patrick, thirty-one, a small-business owner, some college, married with kids: Starbucks is "so calculated as to be unappealing. . . . Punch in the numbers and get curvy furniture and a broad palette of pleasing pastels. . . . I'm sorry, that just doesn't work for me. I'd rather have tradition, you know."

> Sandra, thirty-three, a graduate student working on a PhD, single, said she bought her coffee at Starbucks but did so furtively: "In my circle of friends it's not socially acceptable to go to Starbucks because [it] destroys all the local coffee shops." She'd reached the point "that if I want to go to Starbucks and carry something out, I will bring my own cup so I can walk around . . . in public."

Debbie, twenty-six, a market researcher, college degree, single, objected to the fact that in Chicago there's a Starbucks "on almost every corner. . . . There's even a *Simpsons* episode where Bart Simpson walks into the mall, and then you see a Starbucks and you see next door: 'Coming Soon—Starbucks.' Then he leaves and you see the whole mall from the inside, and it's wall-to-wall Starbucks."

What comments like these signify, Thompson told me, is "brand inversion." It's a situation whereby you, your boyfriend, Bart Simpson, and the media coalesce to "rework" a brand, unbrand it and then rebrand it—"uncool" it, in the words of Douglas Holt, who has collaborated with Thompson on branding studies. Uncooling brands is a favored tactic among antibranding guerrilla fighters such as Kalle Lasn of *Adbusters*. Holt points out that it's the very companies marketing experts laud for their innovation and marketing proficiency—Nike, Coke, McDonald's, Microsoft, Starbucks—that often find themselves the most relentlessly attacked. The underlying point here is that a brand is not what its parent company says it is or wants it to be, it's what we and the culture choose to make of it. Our loyalty, you see, is highly conditional. We promise to love, cherish, honor, and remain faithful only so long as the brand doesn't do thoughtless or stupid things and in so doing wreck our trust. We'll desert them if they change their ingredients or formula (as Coke did), spread themselves thin (as Halston did decades ago), or fail to uphold humanitarian principles (as Kathie Lee Gifford and Nike did, though Nike recovered nicely). JetBlue was beloved by its tribe members until a) in 2007 it left passengers stranded on a JFK runway for ten hours; and b) barely a year later announced it would sell, no longer supply, blankets and pillows on its flights, straining credulity by calling the cheapskate move an "eco-conscious, health-conscious and customer-conscious decision."

When brands aren't straight with us, they're toast. The other night a writer named Lucas Conley, a self-appointed but genial Brand Scold, turned up on the *Colbert Report*. Conley's new book, *OBD: Obsessive Branding Disorder*, argues that brands can stretch only so far before they become a joke. Conley and Colbert chortled over how there are now Vatican-branded credit cards and NASCAR-branded romance novels. If you were a faithful member of those flocks, your heart might never forgive, for these are no longer the brands you married. Brands know this and often take preventive steps. In 2007, Burger King, bowing to the animal rights movement, announced it would seek not to buy its eggs and pork from suppliers that raised animals in cages, the *New York Times* reported. The company further promised to give preference to suppliers that favored gassing or "controlled atmospheric stunning" as opposed to electric shocks, prior to slaughter. A nice gesture, but I'm still not chowing down there anytime soon.

11

You Are *Why* You Buy

*You buy for a) status, b) therapy, and/or
c) it's complicated*

As much as any other social group, national advertisers helped to popularize a pseudo-religion of health and all anxious self-absorption.
—Historian T. J. Jackson Lears

THE ALLURE OF "YOU ARE WHAT YOU BUY" lies in how simplistic it is. Advangelists tap it to inform the selling of everything: cars, grooming products and cosmetics, electronics, home furnishings. Buy this lipstick and your lips will be as plump, luscious, and bursting with flavor as Angelina's. Buy this laptop and you'll go from square to hip, from PC Guy to Mac Dude. Mac Dude wears standard-issue jeans and a collarless pullover. He's unpretentious, creative, likable, mildly droll, youthful but not so cutting-edge as to be flaky. Want to be someone like that? Switch operating systems, bro. PC Guy, Mac Dude's dorky foil, is—until Microsoft decided to spend hundreds of millions to try to counter the image with Jerry Seinfeld—a cube in nerdy eyeglasses, boxy suits, and clunky Florsheims, a genial dolt, someone you'd rather not be.*

---

*Indeed, mere *exposure* to the Apple brand may get our creative juices flowing. A recent controlled experiment found subjects who'd been "cued" by references to Apple products performed better on a creativity test than those who'd been cued by references to IBM products.

But "you are what you buy," when all's said and done, is a poor excuse for a Unified Buy Theory. What a product signals about you isn't always so clear. Or if it is to you, it isn't to another. Consider Rolex Man: silver haired and middle-aged, with an $8,000 Oyster Perpetual Yachtmaster on his wrist. What does this watch make of the man? Discerning gentleman? Weekend commodore? Corporate mucky-muck? Vegas high roller? Russian oligarch? Long Island Mafioso? It depends on your worldview, your values. Rolex would have you see Rolex Man as a silver fox who wins trophies in the board room and at his yacht club's weekly regattas. To further the image, Rolex plays up the Yachtmaster's performance capabilities, the fact that it's equipped with a countdown function that allows Rolex Man to program in the exact start time of a race. It has a ring command bezel that rotates ninety degrees. But these features may not impress you if, considering the watch's price tag, your values tell you that anyone who wears such a watch must have a moral compass on the fritz. Is Rolex Man even remotely aware of what time it is? Forty million Americans live below the poverty line. The small fortune Rolex Man spent on his Yachtmaster is more than enough—USDA data confirm it—to put food on the table of an American family of four for an entire year or more. And there's another problem with "you are what you buy": it doesn't address motivation, the *why* behind a Buy, what drives us to turn certain material possessions into objects of lust. Why is Rolex Man so bedazzled by a timekeeping *want* that, in your view anyway, he loses his bearings?

Tricky questions. But now and then someone comes along who can take us to the brink of answers, and thus to the doorstep of a Unified Buy Theory. Herewith my three fearless nominations for best attempt at a modern-day Unified Buy Theory, from the glory days on the Ladies' Mile to the present:

1. We buy because buying confers status. Thorstein Veblen stands as the granddaddy of modern Unified Buy Theorists, an unkempt academic from the heartland whose ideas still influence the Buy Scolds who contend that we buy too much, too mindlessly. Veblen famously proposed that buying tastes and standards rain down from above: that is, from the rich folks whose carriages splattered mud on the teeming masses along the Ladies' Mile.

Veblen was forty-two when *The Theory of the Leisure Class* hit the bookstalls in 1899. The work was a dissection, a spoof some say, that addressed upper-crust pomposity on the one hand and on the other how the rest of us sought to emulate that pomposity. Nothing new about that, even in Veblen's time. For centuries society's haves did what they could to fend off have-nots looking to trade up. In her splendid history of Renaissance shopping, Evelyn Welch tells of a Florentine law that forbade peasants to wear silk, velvet, belts adorned with silver, gold, gems, or pearls, even if the riffraff *could* afford them. But the issue was effectively a nonstarter until the early 1900s. Then mass production kicked in around the globe, yielding a torrent of affordable goods. Working stiffs enjoyed steady employment and weekly paychecks. The servant class shrank, an emulation class rose from its lint. Everyday folk now had the means to buy goods previously reserved for the social tippy top. The merchant princes accordingly piled such goods high in their palazzos, within grasp of the lower classes: notch-collared waistcoats, fine millinery, and silk undergarments handsomely displayed for streams of factory hands and shopgirls with money in their pockets. *Leisure Class's* chapter IV, "Conspicuous Consumption," introduced the term that would come to characterize this drive to trade ever upward while proving useful to Buy Scolds as a lasting indictment of the wastefulness of the American buyer.

Born in 1857 in Cato, Wisconsin, Veblen was the son of Norwegian immigrants. According to the Modern Library's edition of *Leisure Class*, he was so precocious his parents excused him from chores so that he might cultivate his bountiful mind. He studied at Carleton College, then at Johns Hopkins, Yale, and the University of Chicago. He was a man of few airs: bushy browed, hair parted down the middle, a bristly intellectual who had a tough time holding a teaching job. Ill groomed and ill mannered, he might have done better had he himself picked up a few cravats and emollients (though he was known for comporting with colleagues' wives, who found him "irresistible," according to Louis Menand's *The Metaphysical Club*). Veblen died in 1929, but *Leisure Class* lived on. The book, especially chapter IV, secured him a place on the Great Books list, sandwiched between Twain and Virgil. John Kenneth Galbraith said of him: "No man of his time, or since, looked with such a . . . penetrating eye not so much at pecuniary gain as the way its pursuit makes men and women behave."

Galbraith, it would seem, spoke too soon. For beginning in the sixties, it became apparent that tastes no longer just trickled *down,* they trickled every which way. They trickled in from the bohemian and hippie outer fringes, up from the ghetto and the grunge. While it remains swell to be, or pretend to be, rich and classy, it became even sweller for many of us to be, or pretend to be, hip and cool, a lively accounting of which Joseph Heath and Andrew Potter provide in their social history *Nation of Rebels*. One of the authors of the book cites not only patrician objects of status, but such trendy, personal acquisitions as a pair of Ray-Bans, a Solomon snowboard, and a Mini Cooper. If you don't bother to read the book, just look around. Straight guys opt to be made over by queer eyes. Suburban kids wear ghetto-baggy shorts, their lids turned backward. And does anyone in America—including those who go by Muffy, Bunky, or the Chipster—*not* have a tattoo?

None of this means that Veblen wound up on the wrong side of Buy history. The point isn't that we are no longer conspicuous consumers, it's just that the culture has shuffled who we choose to emulate and what we conspicuously consume. I just ran across a chart, the work of two professors in India, that chronicles the ongoing reordering. Once upon a time—we're talking *long* before the Ladies' Mile—slaves, women, and food served as the ultimate status symbols. By the time Veblen came along, and for nearly a century thereafter, our objects of hot pursuit consisted of finely wrought, manmade stuff. Status symbols, in other words, come and they go. The list below is drawn from *Lifestyle Marketing: Reaching the New American Consumer*:

- 1900s: Model T Fords, pianos, radios, hand-cranked victrolas
- 1910–1919: fur hats, electric clocks, fountain pens, Kodak cameras
- 1920s: gin, vacuum cleaners, electric washing machines
- 1930s: baseball tickets, canned food, indoor plumbing
- 1940s: television, air travel, electric refrigerators
- 1950s and 1960s: color televisions, credit cards, convertibles, stereo sound systems, 35mm cameras, Andy Warhol lithographs
- 1970s to the present: solar-heated vacation homes, BMWs— no need to keep going; this is where we all came in.

2. We buy because buying is good *for us.* The next nominee for viable Unified Buy Theory—consumption is therapeutic—comes attached to a juicy conspiracy theory. The idea that we buy because buying is curative also dates from around the time of the Ladies' Mile. In the midst of growing abundance, Americans discovered that shopping in a well-stocked palazzo felt good. It was more emotionally uplifting than buying carpet scraps or day-old carrots from a pushcart. There was a problem, though. Yankee character didn't cotton to the notion that money existed to be spent, or that spending freely was much cause to rejoice. On the contrary, the American ethos was tethered to the idea that self-sacrifice was virtuous and scarcity a fixture of the human condition. Ned and Katherine's great-grandparents, much as they might have been tempted to masquerade as Carnegies and Vanderbilts, were not altogether comfortable racing home from the factory floor, jumping into a quick bath, running pomade through their hair, and hopping a trolley down to the Ladies' Mile, there to drop a week's wages on high-button kicks. Would high-button shoes and silk scarves make them feel richer and more self-satisfied? Sure—were it not for the guilt attached. Sell Side solution: get rid of that nagging guilt and convince working folk that buying was not only morally acceptable, not just a ticket to higher social status, but in fact was healthy for body and soul. Buying had to be positioned as a tonic, a pick-me-up.

With characteristic fervor, the Sell Side set out to rewire the national character by forming a coalition of the willing, able, and avaricious: those who sold goods (merchants), those who lent money to those who sold goods (bankers), those who created ads for those who sold goods (the adman in the gray-flannel waistcoat), those who transported the goods to those who sold them (railroad barons), and those who sold goods to those who sold them to upwardly mobile working stiffs (manufacturers and importers).

No one has written more incisively about this seismic cultural shift than Rutgers historian T. J. Jackson Lears. In 1983, Lears published a provocative twenty-thousand-word essay in *Advertising & Society Review*, "From Salvation to Self-Realization: Advertising and the Therapeutic Roots of the Consumer Culture, 1880–1930." He argued that beginning at the turn of the last century, the Sell Side, its advertising arm in particular, took cues from others who had perfected feel-good messaging: psychologists, quacks (spiritual and medical), liberal ministers, and other apostles of self-empowerment. The Sell Side discovered that it could now move boxcars of goods by trumpeting the physical and emotional healing power of such consumer products as soap, corsets, breakfast cereal, and tobacco products. American advertising fell under the sway of what Lears calls a "therapeutic ethos." Shopping, no less than the amusement parks popping up all over the country, offered *relief*. Buying, lots of buying, was the antidote for what plagued modern existence: the anonymity of city life, the tedium of the workplace, the loss of individuality brought on by the growth of impersonal corporations. Newspaper ads waxed eloquent about the *sensual* experience inherent in material goods: how a piano sounds, how an undergarment feels, how food tastes. Beginning in 1910, doctors in starched white coats started turning up in all kinds of ads, notably for cigarettes, where they would remain until the Surgeon General clamped down in the mid-1960s: "Not a cough in a carload" (Old Gold); "Inhale to your heart's content" (Embassy); "It's a psychological fact: Pleasure helps your disposition" (Camel). And while egregious false smoking claims would be reined in, today we need only flip open a magazine or turn on the television to be soothed by ads for all manner of "enhancement technologies": clothes that make you pretty, face cream that makes you young, pills and cars that make you erect, beer that makes you sociable, electronic gadgets and computers that keep you plugged in.

3. We buy because buying is an expression of our tastes, and our tastes . . . well, it gets complicated. It's a challenge to distill this final Unified Buy Theory into a digestible one-liner, so I'll go at it this way: at the end of August 2005, Hurricane Katrina made apocalyptic landfall on Louisiana's Gulf Coast, a storm that claimed nearly two thousand lives, displaced hundreds of thousands, and washed away a great American city, destroying or severely damaging $100 billion worth of property. Concurrent with the havoc, Secretary of State Condoleezza Rice was enjoying a few days of rest and rejuvenation in New York City. There she volleyed with Monica Seles, who was in town for the US Open. She scored good seats for a sold-out performance of *Spamalot*. And she was spotted, on the second day of the greatest natural disaster in U.S. history, trying on shoes at the Ferragamo boutique on Fifth Avenue.

Questions arose over executive competency, national preparedness, and effective leadership during a humanitarian crisis of unparalleled scale here in the United States. Recriminations flew. How could this happen in the richest country in the world? These were, and remain, questions deserving of historians' attention. But they're not the point of this case study. The point turns on a subquestion: How does it happen that an African American woman, born and raised in the segregated South, with parents of modest means, metamorphoses into a woman of high intelligence and professional accomplishment who, in her severely limited spare time, dazzles as a masterful interpreter of Brahms, fine-tunes her body with determined vigor, and—to cut to the chase—possesses a cultivated taste for expensive shoes, granted that her timing leaves something to be desired?

Possible answers are to be found in one or both of the foregoing putative Unified Buy Theories. According to Veblen's status-emulation theory and the buy-as-therapy theory, Condi was a) engaging in conspicuous consumption, unremarkable save for the fact that New Orleans was dissolving at that exact moment; and/or b) Condi was simply doing what we all do now and then—seeking relief from the stresses of workaday life via the therapy of self-gifting.

But there's another way to look at Condi's proficiency at the keyboard, her disciplined quest for superior physical conditioning, and her shoe buying behavior, and that's through the lens of French sociologist Pierre Bourdieu. His take involves the complex interweaving of social class and cultural tastes (including our preferences for music, art, literature, home furnishings, food, and footwear) and stems from his own upbringing. The son of a farmer turned postman, Bourdieu grew up in a small village in southwestern France. He spent his early academic career in Algeria, where he observed colonialism's impact on a fragile, indigenous culture. Eventually he settled in Paris and became nationally known for his outspoken opposition to globalism's cold heart, at one point providing intellectual air cover for a group of French farmers who defended their cultural and economic turf by laying siege to a McDonald's. When Bourdieu died in 2002 he was eulogized as one of France's leading public intellectuals.

Bourdieu's masterwork was a book called *Distinction: A Social Critique of the Judgment of Taste*, published in 1983, which the International Sociological Association cites as one of the most influential works of the last century. In the introduction to the English edition, Bourdieu assured his Anglo-American audience that even though *Distinction* focused on the French social order, he wasn't just whistling Paris. "I have every reason to fear that this book will strike the reader as 'very French,'" he wrote, "which I know is not always a compliment." Bourdieu argued that we in the States should not dismiss his thesis, that the "curiosities and frivolities" of Parisian art and culture bear more relevance to American life than appears at first blush. The American social psychologist Erving Goffman assured Bourdieu that the Parisian "art of living" holds enduring "fascination" for many on this side of the Atlantic and not just "snobs and socialites" either. Goffman's endorsement carried weight. His own masterwork, *The Presentation of Self in Everyday Life*, greatly influenced a generation of Sell Side academics and civilians, not least Paco Underhill, who refers to the book as one of the inspirations that led to his forays into the world of retail anthropology. Goffman's thesis: the world—including the stores that clutter it—is very much a stage, and you and I are actors on that stage. Playing our respective roles, we emit signals, mostly unconscious, through what we buy, wear, and use—they're props. We take on our self-assigned character roles in the hope that we can induce others to see us in a desired way.

Distinction turned out to be a smash hit with American social scientists, who to this day regard Bourdieu's work with a reverence matching or exceeding their esteem for Veblen. Bourdieu's view of consumption is more nuanced than Veblen's. According to Veblen, those who have it, or wish to have it, flaunt it. For Bourdieu, this is little more than a starting point. It wasn't conspicuous consumption that drew Condi to Ferragamo, nor was she on a feel-good therapy run. As Bourdieau would see it, Rice's taste in shoes, no less than her love of Brahms, derives from cultural capital she had acquired over the years. And where do you get cultural capital? You get it from the socioeconomic hand you're dealt—the class you're born into, *plus* the level and quality of the education you receive. If you're raised in a household that places a premium on learning, social skills, and critical thinking, you'll bank a higher amount of cultural capital, which in turn shapes your tastes and buying preferences. Condi wound up at Ferragamo not because she was to the manor born, but because her solidly middle-class, professional parents gave her piano lessons, celebrated great music and art, stressed the importance of academic success, and set high expectations for career and creative accomplishment. Says Condi biographer Elisabeth Bumiller, Condi's parents "poured their hearts into the project of their lives: the teaching, molding and polishing of Condoleezza." These cultural investments have appreciated over time, enabling Condi to draw on them when she sits down at the piano or decides she needs, or wants, a new pair of pumps.*

Based on interviews with some twelve hundred French men and women about their social backgrounds and consumption choices, Bourdieu's explication of how individual taste is formed runs deeper than I can, or should, try to explain here. *Distinction* contains dozens of charts, a lengthy exploration into Kant's view of aesthetics, and ruminations on French movies and art as reflections of social stratification. Anyone wishing further details is invited to settle down with a Kir Royale or pop a can of Pabst Blue Ribbon (depending on your parents' social class and your level of education) and have a go at it. For the less intrepid, a few items from the tasting menu should suffice. They provide a sense of how wealth, social status, and acquired tastes, when thoroughly blended, help explain why some of us drive past Piggly Wiggly to shop at Whole Foods, or vice versa, plus a broad range of other cultural, social, and consumer preferences:

- If your father, say, was a manual worker or craftsman of some sort, and if you listen to any classical music, you're likely to prefer "Blue Danube" to *The Well-Tempered Clavier*. If your father was a doctor or teacher, you prefer the latter to the former.

- If your level of schooling ended with technical college and your family is working class, there's scant chance you make your furniture purchases on Antiques Row. However, if all you have is a technical degree but your family is upper class, there's a good chance that you *will* shop there, as opposed to at Aaron Rents.

- If you're a junior executive or a secretary, you're most likely to buy things to make your home "comfortable" and care less about whether it's "practical" or "easy to maintain." If you're a manual

---

*Sarah Palin's cultural capital, on the other foot, led her not to Ferragamo but to a brand called Naughty Monkey: specifically, that notorious pair of red peep-toe pumps with three-and-a-half-inch heels ($89). Palin set off a customer run on the Naughty Monkey brand after she wore the shoes the day John McCain introduced her as his running mate. Naughty Monkey, according to its marketing director, targets twenty-something women who go clubbing (referring to nightclubbing, not dispatching baby seals). Within three months Palin had traded her Naughty Monkeys for Cole Haan boots, part of the infamous $150,000 wardrobe the Republican National Committee spent to outfit the candidate at Neiman Marcus and Saks Fifth Avenue, among other stores Joe the Plumber presumably doesn't frequent.

worker, you also want it to be "comfortable" (everybody puts the highest premium on "comfortable"), but "practical" and "easy to maintain" are close seconds.

- Women who work in offices are considerably more likely to wish they had "different faces" than do women who live on farms, and also—by a margin of almost two to one—believe that beauty depends on "the care you take" in pursuit of a better face.

Bourdieu's view of consumption fills certain glaring holes in Veblen's theory, which leans heavily on the straightforward connection between your economic capital and your consumer choices. But wealth alone doesn't address why, for example, someone like Condi, when picking a restaurant, might well pass on an expensive steakhouse—slabs of aged beef, gigantic iceberg wedges—in favor of one with a *nouvelle* menu—Asian fusion, say. Daniel Miller, who teaches at University College London, points out in his book *Material Culture and Mass Consumption* that the greater your cultural capital, the likelier it is you'll turn to cuisine that "refuses any suggestion that food might be for sustenance [and] which emphasizes the aesthetic of presentation." Cultural capital explains the difference between Condi Rice and someone who grew up on Park Avenue, whose father made a fortune in scrap metal yet rarely opens a real book, holds his fork in his fist, someone for whom a museum shop is the logo concession at Giants Stadium.

Having done my best to grapple with Bourdieu's thicket of numbers and social insights, I took it to the streets. One balmy Chicago evening Linda and I attended an outdoor music concert. The woman seated behind us was well into her seventies and had clearly, painfully clearly, spent thousands on nose and face work, plus a thousand or two on what she was wearing that night: an expensive hooded sweatshirt adorned with sequins, designer cargoes garlanded with drawstrings, white leather Pumas. What on earth had induced her to buy and wear these things? Conspicuous consumption? Conspicuous she was, though in a fringe-y way, not in a leisure-class way: no diamonds or fancy watch, but clothes designed and marketed with her teenage grandchildren in mind. Therapeutic benefit? She did seem quite happy. She was garrulous and vivacious, sitting with a group of friends who, though the same age, were more wrinkled and frumpy. The orchestra reached the finale of its rousing seventeen-minute performance of Ravel's *Bolero*—

a piece favored, presumably, by those whose cultural capital stretches about as far as "Blue Danube." Mindful of Bourdieu's *Distinction,* I tried to connect all the disparate dots, particles, and waves that defined the woman behind me. Face lift. Sequined sweatshirt. *Bolero*—later the theme song from *10.* Dudley Moore. Bo Derrick. Midbrow. Eternal youth. Puma. Randomly colliding particles—or the beginning of a revealing portrait of this woman: how she looks, the music she listens to, the things she buys?

In the aftermath of that evening I called a halt to the search for a Unified Buy Theory and decided to set social philosophers aside for a while to open a new line of inquiry. What about novelists? Novelists are in the business of assaying greed and longing, vanity and pride. So I began to explore how twentieth-century fiction writers variously take up the matter of shopping and buying. This foray led me to a couple of books by a British-born literary critic named Rachel Bowlby. The more recent of the two, published in 2001, was *Carried Away: The Invention of Modern Shopping.* In a series of essays Bowlby connects literary references to shopping with personal observations of how shoppers behave in stores. The common thread is desire. Bowlby devotes a chapter to Theodore Dreiser's *Sister Carrie,* in which she cites Carrie's "great awakening" (*Carried Away*, get it?) as Dreiser's heroine strolls the Ladies' Mile in the late nineteenth century: "Women were spending money like water. She [Carrie] could see that in every elegant shop she passed. Flowers, candy, jewelry seemed the principal things in which the elegant dames were interested. And she—she had scarcely enough pin money to indulge in such outings as this a few times a month." Dreiser, Bowlby says, here offers a startling insight into the essence of modern American life (well, startling in 1900, maybe not so not today) and that is this: "To have lived is to have spent."

Compared with what I'd been feeding on, not just Veblen and Bourdieu but an ongoing diet of How-to-Ambush-the-Customer blueprints and Repent-Ye-Sinner sermons, Bowlby's *Carried Away* is, while not exactly a beach book, refreshing. It offers a lively account of how the supermarket emerged as the "great retailing change of the twentieth century." There's a nice section on a phenomenon we encounter when we shop for nearly everything now, not just groceries at Ralph's, but desks and beds at Ikea, lawn mowers and PVC piping at Home Depot, laptops and GPS devices at

Best Buy, any of the 150,000 items available at an average-size Wal-Mart. It's called self-service, the ultimate death of the salesman in this our modern Buy culture. Now that the world's gone self-service, nothing and no one stands between us and all there is for us to buy, nothing except—I love Bowlby's phrase for it—"an endless 'perhaps.'"

Bowlby's other book on consumption culture, *Shopping with Freud*, was published in the early 1990s. I'd put off opening it out of fear that it would turn out to be yet another exegesis on how psychosexual embers are ignited by Oscar Mayer wieners. False alarm. In *Shopping with Freud*, Bowlby reflects on how writers as diverse as Oscar Wilde (in *The Picture of Dorian Gray*), Mary Shelley (in *Frankenstein*), Aldous Huxley (in *Brave New World*), and D. H. Lawrence (in *Lady Chatterley's Lover*) variously work the seam between consumption and gender identity, consumption and lust. In *Lolita*, for instance, Humbert Humbert leverages a bagful of gifties to work his wiles on his material girl, using the Buy to narrow the age/temperament gap between the two: "I bought her four books of comics, a box of candy, a box of sanitary pads, two cokes, a manicure set, a travel clock with a luminous dial, a ring with a real topaz, a tennis racket, roller skates with high white shoes, field glasses, a portable radio set, chewing gum, a transparent raincoat, sunglasses, some more garments—swooners, shorts, all kinds of summer frocks. At the hotel we had separate rooms, but in the middle of the night she came sobbing into mine, and we made it up very gently."

Bowlby's linkages betwixt life, lust, and spending are provocative. But in the end it was her discovery of a long-lost book that grabbed my full attention. In the concluding essay in *Shopping with Freud*, Bowlby refers to a work called *The Consumer: His Nature and His Changing Habits*, by one Walter B. Pitkin. While hardly of Wildean or Nabokovian literary caliber, Pitkin was popular in his time, the author of self-help books back in the 1930s. His other books include—great title—*A Short Introduction to the History of Human Stupidity*, and the one he's best known for, *Life Begins at 40*, which was made into the movie starring Will Rogers. But it was something Bowlby had spotted in *The Consumer* that led me to track down a tattered copy that languished in the library stacks at St. Mary's of the Springs College, East Columbus, Ohio. It was immediately clear that *The Consumer* is not the sort of self-help mush we're used to today: it isn't slapdash, isn't set in the type size a seven-year-old can deal with. Nor does it promise to cure the shopping disease and save your marriage in the thirty minutes it takes to read. *The*

Consumer is packed with charts and comprehensive reporting about household debt levels, consumers' "empty motions" (e.g., buying soft drinks when you're not thirsty), comparisons of salaries and spending patterns across various professions, and a breakdown of who in the Great Depression was in a position to buy refrigerators, ranges, and fashionable clothing. But what intrigued me most was the observation Rachel Bowlby had alerted me to, although she thought the distinction a bit simplistic. Maybe it is, but I found it useful for purposes here. Pitkin divides buyers into two types of people, a distinction that allows us to distill this . . .

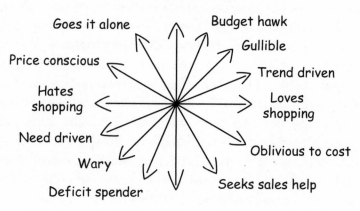

. . . into this:

What Walter B. Pitkin was getting at is that each of us tilts in one or the other of these Buy directions. If we're Classic buyers, we gravitate toward Buys with utilitarian value—generic products, stuff that fills a specific need. A Classic buyer would, for example, agree with Veblen's take on spoons: "A hand-wrought silver spoon . . . is not ordinarily more serviceable . . . than a machine-made spoon of the same material." Classic buyers are those who favor the "clean-cut." "Clean-cut," says Pitkin, is precisely the quality Henry

Ford delivered with the Model T: "a single, sharp, and well-defined idea." There was, wrote Pitkin, "nothing of beauty in [the Model T's] line, still less in its color; it contained no cigar lighter, no mirror, no powder puff, no clock, no compass, no barometer, and no radio." In today's terms, the Classic buyer might go for a Volvo station wagon, affectionately referred to as a "brick." This term of endearment signifies that the vehicle is sturdy and unburdened by flashy design features. The Classic buyer vows to maintain his brick conscientiously for 150,000-plus miles.

The Romantic buyer, in contrast, favors qualities that lie beyond the necessary or practical. A Romantic—be he/she a poet, composer, or buyer—lets loose the imagination and embraces extravagance. The Romantic buyer revels in color choices and optional equipment, bells and whistles he/she may never use, because they're novel, diverting, and might come in handy someday. A Romantic might likewise buy a bricklike Volvo wagon—utility and safety *do* count—but a Romantic's brick would be equipped with DVD monitors mounted in the backrests, a blow-your-head-off sound system, and a shockproof, weatherproof, reverse-image backup video camera to keep an eye on one's Romantic rear end. Or, take cell phones. While the crusty Classic buyer sees no need for a crappy camera crammed into a cell phone, the Romantic demands a camera, a calculator, a calendar, and a Web browser packed inside. Oh, and maybe a $75 Juicy Couture case, or a $1,000 snap-on Swarovski crystal faceplate.

Walter Pitkin's Classic-Romantic paradigm is a trifle simple, yes, but the more I thought it about it, the more potential use I found for it. It neatly addresses a number of questions about why some of us move in one Buy direction and others go the opposite way:

- You shop around. I don't.
- You know what things cost, or *should* cost. I don't.
- You read the fine print on warranties and disclaimers. I don't.
- You return mail-in rebates. I don't.
- You see through a store's pricing tricks. I don't.
- You're a prisoner of value. I'm a prisoner of desire.

12

The Classic Buyer

Price and value: your head wants to do the right thing

One Midwest [supermarket] chain [sold] nine cans of sauerkraut a week at a dime apiece, but 441 cans priced at ten cans for $1.
—*Time* magazine, 1958

INFATUATED WITH PITKIN'S CLASSIC-Romantic paradigm, I began to put it to the test when interviewing shoppers, friends and strangers alike. I explained to them that Classic buyers are price conscious, practical, methodical, rational, and that Romantic buyers are more open to taking fliers on things they buy. I'd whip out my notebook and draw a self-styled Classic-Romantic Buy-O-Gram, then ask people to put a mark where they thought they fell along the spectrum:

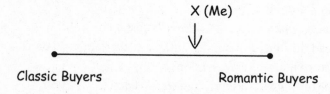

X (Me)

Classic Buyers   Romantic Buyers

Just for the fun of it, take out a pencil and mark where you think you net out. (Don't get hung up on the fact that you may be Classic when it comes to certain Buys, Romantic about others.) Once you've designated your own spot, mark where you think your spouse and kids fall, and then throw some friends and neighbors onto the scale. Now that I've given this simple test to men, women, and teens, my sense is that those who cluster toward the Classic end of the spectrum are typically thriftier and more ambivalent (sometimes hostile) about the act of shopping than those who whoop it up near the Romantic end. Classics' basements, closets, and attics are better organized, less cluttered. And Classics seem to have a firmer grasp of how much they spend on what. As for whether Classics of your acquaintance are more interesting, surprising, more fun to be with than Romantics, I leave that up to you.

When not shoving pad and pencil across the table, I also sent out questionnaires asking people of all ages and income levels about their buying tastes and preferences. I didn't ask outright whether respondents think they are Classics or Romantics, but I could detect Classic or Romantic tendencies in how people answered my questions. Consider the contrasting testimony from the following two women:

The first—I'd deem her a Classic buyer—is in her midtwenties, a self-described "vegetarian-feminist," "very patient and planned" whenever she buys. "I do Internet research because it's important to know where and how things are grown or made, especially food and beauty products. I want to know what's going into my body. I guess this is somewhat atypical. Most people just want the cheapest thing possible—which is why Sprawl-Mart is so popular."

The second—I'd judge her a Romantic shopper—is a midforties graphic designer who wears glasses with bright green frames and whose behavior in and out of stores ranges from quirky to flamboyant. By her own admission she flirts with shopaholism but holds on by the tips of her brightly lacquered fingernails: "There are times I think that buying something will improve my life in some lasting way, but mostly I just enjoy the mindless excitement of the moment. There are times when I'm shopping that I feel physically energized, happier. Pure self-indulgence."

Eager to burrow further into the underlying differences between Classic and Romantic buying behavior—why some of us are devotees of the tried and true, others reach for the new and different—I set Pitkin's simple dichotomy against heavier-duty consumption theories. Academics who finely sift the whys of consumption contend that a number of prestige-related motivations are in play. These include:

1. Status: We buy because many Buys exude a strong aroma of higher social standing. Thorstein Veblen wrote the book on this one.

2. A fondness for the unique: We buy to stand apart from the crowd. This is a plausible explanation for why my son turns Chicago inside out looking for a pair of Onitsuka Tigers.

3. Social benefit: We buy to fit in. Nyah, nyah, I've got Ugg boots, too!

4. Emotional benefit: We buy because many Buys provide "hedonic value"—i.e., they elicit pleasure. Hey, dig my train layout!

5. An appreciation of quality: We buy because certain Buys are reputed to be technically superior and well crafted. See Rolex Man.

6. An appreciation of value: We buy because we place a premium on getting good bang for the buck.

Romantic buyers—lovers of choice, suckers for extra features—buy for any and all six of those reasons. But Romantics are especially susceptible to reasons 1 through 4: *status, uniqueness, social benefit,* and *emotional benefit.* The Classic buyer, on the other hand, clings principally to reasons 5 and 6: an appetite for *quality* and *value.* Classics are generally thrifty, yes, but not necessarily skinflints. They buy deliberately, and find comfort in list making. Classic buyers are do's-and-don'ts kind of folks.

Do	Don't
Shop around.	Shop around so much that you spend on gas what you saved shopping around.
Buy in bulk.	Buy in such bulk that you blow off the "sell by/use by" date.
Go food shopping with a detailed list.	Go food shopping when you're hungry as a horse, even *with* a detailed list.

Do	Don't
Choose items—golf balls, say—that match your level of competence. Why pay more for "accuracy," "bite," or "distance" when your shots don't demonstrate accuracy, bite, or distance?	Choose items—golf balls, especially—thinking that they'll "elevate" your level of competence. Just as clothes don't make the man, neither do his balls.
Accept researchers' findings that unintended purchases often result in happiness, yes, but happiness tempered by guilt.	Forget the same researchers' findings that *not* making an unintended purchase often results in a strong feeling of *pride*.

Pricing Games

Classic buyers, as noted, put a premium on benefit per dollar spent. They train their antennae on what things *ought* to cost, then buy or don't buy accordingly. You'll rarely hear a Classic buyer say that she "treated herself" to this or that because "Dunno, I was just in the mood." Consciously or otherwise, there's a sliding scale embedded in the Classic buyer's skull:

For its part, the Sell Side considers numerous variables when it sets its prices: profit and market-share goals, the target customer and what he's willing to pay, where a product sits relative to given product category, the current state of the economy, whether the product is newly launched or an established brand. Classic buyers don't give a fig about much of that. Sell Side retailers, faced with the challenge of overcoming the Classic buyer's cost-benefit computational instincts, juggle pricing schemes to fake Classics out of their sensible shoes. They know that brilliant pricing strategies can befuddle even those who maintain a sure grasp of what a "typical" or "fair" or "reasonable" price should be.

My stints at Lands' End and Sears advanced my awareness of the pricing tricks the Sell Side uses to break down a Classic buyer's resistance. Among the reasons Lands' End and Sears made fractious bedfellows is that their pricing philosophies were dramatically opposed, each based on how the company regarded its customers. Sears, while it sometimes talked up the quality and benefits of certain product lines—Craftsman, Die-Hard, Kenmore—generally used its advertising money on hard-sell tactics like holiday sales blowouts and bargain days. At Lands' End, we assumed that our customers were Classically inclined, and that they therefore appreciated knowing as much as possible about how we arrived at our prices and what features were built into every product we sold. We believed it crucial to maintain a civilized discourse with these customers—they were, after all, smart and inquiring, eager to know why goats in Inner Mongolia yield higher quality cashmere than their long-lost goat cousins in Australia or Texas. Our catalogs used long-copy entries to tell customers about what goes into the making of a well-made dress shirt (a mitered yoke), and how many belt loops (eight) a customer should expect on a good pair of pants. And we made a solemn promise never to play the Hi-Lo pricing game, never to mark prices up so we could then mark them down in phony "sales." We went to some lengths to explain why the prices we asked were reasonable—it was because we controlled the manufacturing process and could thus sell finished goods at more or less wholesale prices. No middleman was involved. The only time we reduced our fair and generally transparent prices was when we found ourselves with unplanned excess inventory, whereupon we sent out Overstocks catalogs that fessed up: "Oops, our dumb move is your good fortune!" Sears never communicated this way with its customers. At Sears it was Sale! Sale! Sale!

Knowing that there was more to pricing than the approaches used by Lands' End and Sears, I hit the road again, this time to the Wharton School at the University of Pennsylvania, where I sat in a sun-drenched lounge chatting with Steve Hoch, an engaging and respected professor. I'd first met Hoch while wandering about the National Retail Federation's BIG Show. He and a couple of colleagues were manning a table with a Wharton School banner stretched across the front, their purpose being to give the Sell Side an appreciation of the breadth and quality of Wharton's retailing research. Back in the 1970s, before moving to academia, Hoch spent some time at Disney, a stint that gives him bragging rights about how the "real world" works. There's still a touch of Southern California about him—on the day I called on him he was sporting a Tommy Bahama–ish short-sleeved shirt, jeans, and hiking boots. We shot the breeze about the Sell Side landscape, how different kinds of stores serve or fail the expectations of buyers whether Classic or Romantic. Think about what matters to you. Lack of clutter? A feeling of control over the environment? "Stickiness," as the trade calls it— the contentment that comes from knowing the things you want will be in stock and in their appointed places?

Hoch told me he evaluates stores across three dimensions and that in his opinion there's not a store on earth that excels at all three. Two of the dimensions struck me as particularly appealing to those of you who placed yourselves on the Classic end of the Classic–Romantic continuum. The first dimension, Hoch said, was indeed *value*: how well does a store deliver its goods to you, and at what price? Costco excels at delivering value, Hoch told me. He was impressed with how the company does business generally, its pricing "transparency" specifically. Costco sells everything more or less at cost, sucking the bulk of its profit out of the annual dues you pay, which is an effective business model, Hoch pointed out. The second dimension—also important to Classic buyers—is how *accessible* a store is. By this Hoch meant a couple of things: not only how convenient it is to get to the store, but how easy it is to get in and out of the place. On this dimension, he said, Costco merits no more than a so-so. Hoch's third dimension, *discovery*, is a quality Romantic buyers prize highly. Discovery, Hoch explained, refers to how certain stores provide novelty and surprise, encourage you to interact with merchandise, and provide easy access to friendly sales assistance. The Apple Store is discovery-rich. A Build-A-Bear Workshop, where Katherine and I once father-daughter bonded, is discovery-rich. Costco? Not really.

Hoch sometimes consults on behalf of Sell Side firms that want to re-search and test various pricing "tricks," as he referred to them. These tricks, Hoch said, are made possible by "information asymmetry," i.e., when one party to a prospective Buy (the retailer) holds more information than the other party (the customer). With information vested in their favor, stores roll out myriad pricing schemes, settling on those that ring your Buy bells.

The Sell Side knows that our reaction to an asking price, and thus our decision to buy, is based on perceptions of price and value that we've acquired over time or are planted on the spot by a promotion or discount. Think about it. You see something. You gauge its features. You weigh what the store thinks you ought to pay for it. What's going on in your head? Well, if you're a Classic buyer, your mental hard drive whirs into action, tries to calculate whether the asking price is good, bad, or just about right. But good, bad, or just about right *relative to what?*

Here's where it gets interesting. Hoch and like-minded researchers run experiments aimed at what they refer to as "anchors" in our heads, especially in the heads of Classic buyers. An anchor, which often comes in the form of a "reference price," is what your internal hard drive searches for, then gloms on to, when asked to make a judgment about whether a price is good, bad, or just about right. Researchers debate whether the brain uses a rolling average or a weighted average of price tags past. Leaving such technicalities aside, if your reference price for an acceptable little black dress, say, or for a navy blazer, is $300, you'll be comfortable buying one for $300 ("seems fair!"). Find a dress or blazer that costs less or is on sale, and you'll be more than comfortable taking it home ("great deal!"). But if you have no good sense of a reference price for an acceptable little black dress or navy blazer, there may be second thoughts or buyer's remorse in store for you.

Reference prices become anchored in our heads chiefly because we shop a great deal and over time learn what things are generally worth. But what if you have no prior knowledge? Say you don't shop a lot or find yourself shopping for something entirely new and different? In *The Art of Pricing*, Raji Mohammed refers to studies that indicate that if we're unfamiliar with a given product category—high-definition video monitors, say—we're likely to anchor our decision making to the price of the most expensive, multifeatured model. This high-priced model, with its panoply of features, becomes the anchor, the reference price, by which we try to decide which cheaper model is the best alternative. After all, Classic buyer that you are, you're willing to make trade-offs when it comes to mysterious switches and buttons you'll never in a lifetime know what to do with. Mohammed also refers to studies that show how we tend to anchor our perception of private-label prices to what famous labels charge for comparable items. These studies suggest that that our magic number is at least 15 percent—any savings short of that leads us back to more widely recognized brands.

Retailers know how to *implant* reference prices. Dan Ariely, the behavioral economics professor who wrote *Predictably Irrational*, notes that shrewd restaurateurs understand why it pays to include high-priced entrées and superexpensive vintages on their menus and wine lists: not because they expect us to order them, but because we have a tendency to order the *next* most expensive selection. Why? Because even though the highest-priced items are out of the question, we don't want to be taken for total pikers. The Sell Side deploys a cruder version of this trick. It's called bait and switch. As Sarah Maxwell describes in her pricing book, *The Price Is Wrong*, retailers bait us in all manner of ways, taking advantage of the fact that, according to supermarket studies, barely one in two of us know the going price of an item we're about to buy. No wonder, then, that retailers lure us in with a low reference price only to be out of stock of the item when we show up. Similarly, as Maxwell points out, stores "reduce" a deliberately high reference price to a price too desirable to turn down: "WAS $200, NOW just $59."

The continuous sabotaging of our reference-price machinery isn't necessarily shady; indeed, it's often self-inflicted. Brian Wansink, in his book *Mindless Eating*, points out that many of us are tempted to recoup our annual warehouse-club membership fee by bulk-buying items we don't really need in the first place. Save $5 on ten gargantuan forty-eight-packs of effervescent sugar water, and wow, we congratulate ourselves, we're dollars ahead of the game. The problem is that those bottles take up a lot of space at home, so we start guzzling away to free up space in the cupboard or fridge. Then we go back to the warehouse for more soda, thus perpetuating a vicious cycle of mindless buying (and chronic eructation).

When we're not undermining our own reference-price machinery, the Sell Side manipulates it in ways that are perfectly aboveboard. Consider a practice that Land's End uses with Classic buyers, those who like to think they make buying decisions based on rational comparison.* Say that you, a Classic buyer, are in the market for a down jacket but have little sense of what a "fair" price is. Knowing that Lands' End is likely to have a generous selection of down jackets, you open the new fall catalog and there it is: a colorful

---

*This particular strategy is known in the trade as "good, better, best," and was hardly original to Lands' End. Company lore has it that Stanley Marcus, the merchant prince who built Neiman Marcus, drilled the value of GBB into Lands' End corporate consciousness while serving as a consultant back in the 1980s.

two-page spread featuring down jackets in a range of colors—just what you're looking for! Zippered pockets, weather resistant, lightweight but certain to keep you toasty on cold winter mornings when you're out with Fido. Scanning the page, you see that there are various versions of these down jackets. The least expensive one—fewer zippered pockets, comes in just three colors, carries a lower "temperature rating"—is shown in a small-ish photograph down at the lower left-hand corner of the spread. It costs, say, $69.95. The highest-priced version ($175.95) is filled with premium goose down, has a "fur"-lined hood, and is pictured in a smallish photograph in the upper right-hand corner of the spread. The bulk of the lay-out—the vast portion of graphic real estate—is devoted to the midpriced version ($89.95): no fur-lined hood, a temperature rating higher than the low-priced jackets, more than enough zippered pockets. At Lands' End, we referred to this prominently featured item as the *hero*. The hero might be pictured in a single giant photo or fanned out in a series of pictures show-casing the many colors the hero comes in.

The down jacket spread had been carefully crafted to accomplish several goals. The main one, of course, was to sell you a down jacket, and the Lands' End merchants were pleased if you bought any one of the three versions of-fered. But the version they most wanted to sell you was the midpriced hero, on which they'd made the biggest inventory bet. Here the plot thickens. The other two jackets served as anchor manipulators (though we never called them that), their role being to point you to the hero product. Pricing experts refer to this as the "decoy effect":

The Hero

Decoy 2

Decoy 1

$69.95

$89.95

$175.95

Decoy 1, the cheapest jacket, delivers the message that Lands' End knows from *value*, that its product line includes items at prices low enough to give, say, Target a run for its money.

Decoy 2, the most expensive jacket, signals that Lands' End knows from *quality*, that the company is more than just a midpriced, midlevel clothing label for customers of middling taste.

The hero thus draws benefit from its positioning vis-à-vis its neighboring downy pals; it embodies both quality *and* value, and in so doing implants a comforting reference price in your brain.

The Sell Side has countless other ways to manipulate our anchor points. Back in the late 1990s, Stephen Hoch, along with Brian Wansink and Robert Kent, published an oft-cited study that shows how grocery stores try to fiddle with the Classic buyer's anchors. The paper examines four kinds of anchor-based promotions that supermarkets fire our way, all of which have been proven effective in grabbing our attention and increasing spend. The promotions begin with the assumption that we have a reasonably good idea of what a given item should cost, even though we often don't. Now the fun begins as stores set about trying to manipulate us into unplanned Buys:

Weird-price anchor manipulation: A box of baby wipes, $1.09! Two-pack of rechargeable batteries, $4.78! Like a lot of people, when I see a price that doesn't end in 0, 5, or 9, I take it as a signal of a good deal, that the retailer has worked to cut the cost of a product to the bone, and that chances are good I'm not likely to find a much better price were I to drive all over town comparison shopping for baby wipes or AAA batteries.

Multiple-unit anchor manipulation: 3 for $1.97! 12 for the price of 10! A baker's dozen for $2.99! Most of us are strongly attracted to this sort of offer. Many of us *will* buy, say, three candy bars when the price is "3 for $3!" even though we may only want one, and one that can be had for a buck. Other multiple-unit price studies show that a discounted price on a single item (a bottle of Pepsi, say, priced at $1.49, 17 percent off the regular price) will sell more units than bottles of regular-price Pepsi. But a sign that offers a *two-for* deal (*two* bottles of Pepsi for $3.00) was found to be more effective than a straight cents-off discount.

Quantity-limit anchor manipulation: Limit of 12 per person! Limit of 1 per visit! 4 per person per day! A sense of scarcity exerts a magnetic pull on many shoppers. The very existence of a limit pushes us in the direction of that limit.

Suggestive selling anchor manipulation: Grab 6 for study night! Buy 8 and save a trip! Buy 12 for your freezer! These kinds of "suggested use" come-ons work because they provide us with a rationale to buy. And they drive up profit margins because they enable the store to sell more units without lowering unit prices.

Expansion anchor manipulation: 101 uses! Buy a month's worth! Buy for all your friends! These tugs work because they stimulate fresh thinking on our part. They also keep profit margins healthy because they, too, require no discounting on the part of the store.

Sellers of luxury goods in particular have much to gain by understanding anchor pricing. Say you're a Classic buyer with a weakness for designer labels. Remember all those cubbies at the Chanel boutique, each one containing a pair of sunglasses costing $350? Peanuts—if you're anchored to what a *dress* costs at Chanel. And what's a few hundred dineros for a sweater at Ralph Lauren's stately emporium when Ralph is displaying a $14,000 alligator "Ricky" bag just a few feet away from that sweater? A *Wall Street Journal* story quotes a Sell Side consultant who defines a smart retailer as one who, after rubbing your nose in prices you can't afford, "moves you right along to where you can salvage your pride." Thus it's *anchors aweigh!* at Coach stores, where one or two very expensive bags are bathed in high-wattage white light. Yet there are also, as the *Journal* reporter observed, "scores of similar, smaller, less-elaborate bags . . . nearby, primed to walk out the door. And if you can't even go that far, try the wallet or the keychain." Call it psychological bait and switch, a ploy Coach has mastered as well as any retailer on the Sell Side. In 2008, *BusinessWeek* named Coach the "best performing" company in America, noting the company's shrewd decision to add superexpensive bags to its line to keep the brand "aspirational" (a quarter of Coach's sales come from bags costing over $400), then cranking out more and more lower-priced bags when the economy turns to mush, as the economy most assuredly did the year *BusinessWeek* handed out its commendation.

Whether our put-upon brains are aware of it or not, our anchors are continuously yanked by a host of price manipulations that Classic and Romantic buyers find alluring if not irresistible. When Linda and I undertook a kitchen renovation in our apartment, we went to a big Chicago-area appliance store and picked out a refrigerator, oven, cooktop, microwave, dishwasher, clothes washer and dryer—the whole works, and far from cheap. We figured we had more than enough leverage to negotiate a generous discount—20 percent, 30 percent, maybe more, we told ourselves. When we proposed same to the salesman, he declined, then "thought" for a moment. "Tell you what I'll do," he finally said. "I'm already as low as I can go on all these things, but I'll throw in the washer and dryer for nothing." Though tempted, we didn't bite. Instead, we went home and did the math: at dealer cost, the washer and dryer knocked—at most—a single-digit percentage off the overall package. We resolved to find a better deal elsewhere.*

The salesman's offer was yet one more of the trade's innumerable tricks. Below you'll find a flurry of others drawn from books and articles about pricing, some written to sharpen the wits and practices of Sell Side salespeople, others aimed at shoppers who should turn to them in self-defense:

- There's "segment-based" pricing, most commonly known as "package deals" (airfare + hotel + rental car). Segment-based pricing also includes, among other machinations, "bundling" (local calling + long distance calling + cell service + Internet access + cable or DSL); "interval pricing" (vacation clubs, fractional jet rental); "payment pricing" (PAY NO INTEREST FOR FIVE YEARS!!); "all-you-can-eat" pricing (or "all-you-can-drink" at Club Med, "all-you-can-text" at Sprint, Verizon, or AT&T).

- There's "nine-and-zero effect" pricing, which, though no one seems to understand precisely why, signals that prices ending with a nine ($19.99) offer "value," while prices ending in zero ($20.00) hold out the promise of "quality." This is why, as pricing expert Mohammed says, there's a nine at the end of prices on McDonald's menu, goose eggs at the end of prices at upscale restaurants or restaurants trying to fake it.

- There's "prestige" pricing, which has proved highly effective in post-yuppie America: build up the price of an existing commodity to an unheard-of level, make sure it comes in an elegant/hip/expensive label, bottle, box, jar, or tube, and more than a few of you (Romantics especially) will bite. We're all familiar with this: it's how Perrier (now Voss and others) turned the trick with water. It's how

---

* And failed miserably.

Absolut turned it with vodka. The steadfast Classic buyer, though, remains unfazed. Novelty? Discovery? Fancy bottles? Balderdash! The Classic buyer steps through the revolving door focused and prepared. He's got his list, the inviolable list, in his pocket. A woman in black approaches, brandishing an atomizer. The Classic responds, in so many words, *Don't aim that thing at me, spritz somebody else with Tom Ford!* The last thing a Classic buyer wants is to become distracted, lest he take his eye off the Buy he walked in for.

• There's "penetration pricing," whereby a new store in the neighborhood, say, lures you away from established competitors with eye-popping values, then ratchets those prices upward over time.

• There's penetration pricing's evil twin, "skim pricing," which is the two-step Steve Jobs performed when launching the iPhone: a seller sets a high initial price, grabbing those who haven't the willpower to wait for the price to come down (Apple users are Romantic to the core), then later lowers (skims) the price to suck up greater market share. Jobs's introductory iPhone, priced at $499, set the anchor. When, after several months, Jobs lowered the price by a hundred dollars, the phone seemed like an even better deal. Then, the next year, Apple added features and lowered the cost further still, to $299. For Apple, the pricing strategy paid dividends coming and going: Romantics had to have the phone, so to hell with the high price, thus giving Apple high profit margin. Classics waited a while and got a much sweeter deal, thus extending Apple's market share.

• And then there's what *Consumer Reports* calls "shrinking package pricing": the price doesn't change at all, but the price per ounce does. In 2008, *CR* revealed how the Sell Side had effectively raised the price of canned tuna, coffee, paper towels, candy bars, and many other items by giving us a lot less at the same price. Unless we're anchored to existing can and bottle capacities—personally, not my strong suit—we walk blindly into a higher cost of living.

Confronted with all these pricing tricks, what is the poor put-upon Classic brain to do? Answer: the best it can. It does what it can to assess what something ought to cost, what something costs here versus what it costs there, what the true cost is after we factor in gas mileage and sales tax as against shipping and handling. In the end, well, the brain is only human—it works the way it works, and in mysterious ways. Why, for example, do we stand a better chance of remembering a price of $9.12 than a price of $8.57? The answer surprised me—$9.12 has *fewer syllables.* According to a 2006 paper in the *Journal of Consumer Research,* every extra syllable in a product's price decreases our ability to remember that price by some 20 percent. Why? Because the brain's "phonological loop"—an important regulator of memory—can hold only 1.5 to 2 seconds of spoken information. If there's good news in that, it's for people—customers, not salespeople—who talk fast. Those who talk fast—such as Hungarians, apparently—are better at price recall because they can fit more syllables into their phonological loops.

Something for Nothing

If you're a Classic buyer, or a Romantic buyer for that matter, nothing intoxicates the spirit like getting something, or the delusion that you're getting something, for no cost at all: "$0" trumps all other reference prices implanted in our brain, a fact so obvious you'd assume researchers would have better things to do than run experiments on why this is so. But they do run those experiments. In *Predictably Irrational,* Dan Ariely summarizes his findings and offers a theory on the irresistibility of $0. The reason we like FREE!, he says, is not because we're necessarily cheapskates but because most of us are "intrinsically afraid of loss." With FREE! there's no apparent downside, zero likelihood that we're making a mistake. Except, of course, there is that likelihood, as Ariely explains. We wind up with no-fee checking accounts minus certain services that, when we need them, wind up costing us more than if we'd opted for an account that carried a nominal fee. Or we go to museums on no-entry-fee days, only to wade into mobbed galleries that prevent us from experiencing any communion with the art we came to see. Or we buy a car that costs more than another car because we're offered free oil changes for three years—even though, as Ariely learned from personal experience, those free oil changes saved him all of $150. I succumb routinely to the siren call of FREE. To obtain free shipping from an online bookseller, I frequently add a title or two to my shopping cart even though I have no great desire to read those books. There they sit, in reproachful silence, on my night table for months on end. FREE! turns out to be pretty pricey.

In addition to FREE!, all of us—Classics and Romantics—are similarly vulnerable to a little something extra, a throw-in. Such marketing efforts begin the moment an American is sprung from the womb. As *Business Week* once reported: "At 1:58 P.M. on Wednesday, May 5, in Houston's St. Luke's Episcopal Hospital, a consumer was born. Her name was Alyssa J. Nedell, and by the time she went home three days later, some of America's biggest marketers were pursuing her with samples, coupons, and assorted freebies. Procter & Gamble hoped its Pampers brand would win the battle for Alyssa's bottom. Johnson & Johnson offered up a tiny sample of its baby soap. Bristol-Myers Squibb Co. sent along some of its Enfamil baby formula."

Thus were Alyssa and her proud parents bushwhacked by multiple acts of "sales promotion," which exerts a "push-pull" effect on customers or customers-to-be. Coupons, premiums, free samples, rebates, loyalty programs, cash-back offers, contests, sweepstakes, all these promotions "pull" you into making a Buy. Coupons in particular provide a big tug, particularly if you're a practical-minded, utility-above-all-else Classic buyer—which is why nearly *300 billion* coupons are issued every year, about a thousand per person in the United States. You need detergent. Detergent is detergent, even for a fervent Romantic. You have a coupon for Tide. You redeem the coupon. But watch out: there are those behind you in the checkout line who, studies have found, "stigmatize" people who use coupons as cheapskates, even "stigmatize by association" others in the same line even if they don't redeem coupons.

Anyway, redeeming coupons is an example of the "pull" side of sales promotion. The "push" side has to do with the fact that those who sell you the detergent, or a car, or a DVD player, are also open to a bonus, a commission of some sort. In other words, there are sales promotions that push *them* into pulling *you*. It's greasing the wheel—not a trade term, just a fact of everyday Buy life. This, too, is taught at our finest business schools. A suggested topic for a term project in the Sales Promotion course at Dartmouth's Tuck School of Business: "Evaluate the current and future success of online couponing. What types of firms are using this form of promotion? What are the various ways it can be implemented? What factors contribute to its success?"

The ubiquity of wheel greasing didn't hit home until the day I took the Red Line downtown, then walked over to Chicago's McCormick Place Convention Center. Assembled there was by far the largest production of *Grease* ever staged—the annual Motivation Show: 250,000 square feet devoted to giving us a gentle pull or those who sell you things an extra push. A survey commissioned by the Motivation Show reports that the Sell Side spends $46 billion a year on motivational giveaways. About a quarter of that comes in the form of token items (aka *tchotchkes*)—gift cards, tote bags, books, silverware, you name it—stuff that's thrown into the fray to induce purchase or reward those who induce us to make a purchase.

The full scope of Motivation World wasn't immediately apparent as you entered. In fact, the first booth I came to—it had attracted a nice little crowd—belonged to a small firm that manufactures temporary (FDA approved!) tattoos. Anyone can order custom-made stick-ons consisting of a logo or other graphic so long as the order is "in increments of thousands," which means companies large and small, fund-raising organizations, even you, if you're planning a big birthday party. They are, in effect, stick-to-the skin equivalents of online widgets, retailer-circulated mini-applications that friends send to each other on Facebook or MySpace. Victoria's Secret, for example, has a widget, "Which Victoria's Secret Angel Are You?" that includes a personal-style quiz. Widgets are easily downloaded; tattoos need to be handed out. The booth had a huge pile of free samples, so I helped myself to a few packs, knowing that my daughter and her dorm mates would get their kicks one evening pasting Home Depot, Google, and other logos to their foreheads or God knows where else.

Before heading deeper into the hall I pondered whether I was sufficiently motivated to attend any of the scheduled presentations at the Motivation Show. Workshops included "Promoting at the Edges: How to Reach the Growing Group of Boomers, Tweens, and Teens with Effective Promotions"; "The Rise of the Geek: How Rapid Technological Changes Are Impacting the Way We Promote to Consumers"; and "Metric Matters: How to Use Cutting-Edge Measures to Ensure That You Are Getting the Full Impact of Your Promotion Dollars." Concluding that I was *not* sufficiently motivated, I decided instead to wander aimlessly through promotionland.

The world of sales motivation is wildly, bizarrely diverse. The next time you walk out of a store and wonder why a salesman worked so feverishly to nail down a deal, don't just think "commission." He or his entire sales team could be *this close* to winning an all-expense-paid, hair-raising ride at the Richard Petty Driving Experience. In fact, the King, Petty in the flesh, was signing autographs at the Motivation Show. He wasn't especially regal in his trademark wraparounds and feathered cowboy hat, standing there beside a spit-polished red-white-and-blue Dodge Charger. The Australian tourist bureau was nearby, complete with baby kangaroos, attracting a large crowd who wanted their photos taken with the animals. A trip Down Under— who wouldn't twist your arm hard for a chance to cop it? The Vegas tourist board was in the hall as well. And a contingent from Brazil, lorded over by a twelve-foot cardboard cutout of the Christ the Redeemer statue that stands atop Corcovado Mountain, plus three *dançarinos da samba*—two guys and a sexpot in a slinky dress—who every so often writhed sensually to the beat of a boom box. The principality of Monaco was there, so was the Dubai tourist board, not to mention a couple of weathered but amiable folks from Lecuyer's Tru-Tale Lodge, Canada's "premier Fish & Vacation Lodge" on the eastern shore of Lake of the Woods, just 712 miles northwest of where I was standing at the Motivation Show. Who wouldn't work to get you to buy if your signature on the receipt transported them to a place where a muskie under fifty-four inches isn't a legal catch?

And, of course, spread out across the convention floor were a multitude of companies offering gift cards (MACY'S GIFT CARDS MEAN BUSINESS), phone cards, golf balls, food (GODIVA: "Call us today and discover the many ways you can share a world of indulgence with your clients and customers"), coffee mugs, athletic gear (NIKE: "Reward YOUR champion"), mouse pads, mini-penlights, shot glasses, pens, notepads, T-shirts, most of which can easily be stamped with the logo of a store, bank, insurance firm, credit card company, any brand, any product, then distributed to sales associates, buyers, or buyers-in-waiting. Over 70 percent of surveyed consumers say they receive at least one such item a year. And apparently it works, at least in the short term. Over three-quarters of those who receive a promotional item in the course of a year—especially flinty Classic buyers, I imagine—can recall the brand stamped on the mug or the ball or the mouse pad, a significantly higher percentage than those who saw an ad just last week for the same brand in a publication.

But there's a downside to sales promotion, to the giveaways, the coupons, the rebates and kickbacks, the sales that happen because someone desperately wanted us to set them on the road to Rio where they would gaze up at Jesus the Redeemer and samba the night away. Studies show that over the long term, sales promotion often erodes our loyalty to brands, a case of *what have you greased me with lately?* Hooked on fixes, it's the fix that matters to us, not who the beneficent greaser was. Madison Avenue thus takes a snooty view of sales promotion—sure, a giveaway can grease a one-time sale but won't forge a "lifetime customer" (as if many of us ever are). The advangelist tries to persuade clients that they're shooting themselves in the foot by allocating such a large share of their marketing spend (75 percent isn't uncommon) to point-of-sale promotions. Much of that money, they say, would be better spent on good old advertising, which reinforces—cue the fanfare—*brand equity*.

Greased out, I left the Motivation Show and met my family for dinner. I handed over the packets of temporary tattoos to Katherine. That weekend she and her girlfriends back at the dorm attended a school Halloween dance, where they boogied with Google and ▨ pasted on their foreheads. For whatever lasting good that did the Sell Side.

13

The Romantic Buyer

Novelty and desire: your heart just wants to have fun

There is no pleasure like the spending of money.
—Gertrude Stein

THE CLASSIC BUYER BUYS, OR TRIES TO buy, from the head down: relies on reason, compares prices, weighs benefits, all in search of good value. For Romantics the heart, not the head, is the lonely hunter (or gatherer). A middle-aged woman who lives in New York City confesses to a frisson whenever she enters—of all places—Bed Bath & Beyond. She says she likes to shop there for practical reasons but for fanciful ones, too. Bed Bath & Beyond is stacked floor to ceiling with pots and pans and toasters and toilet seats, items that we all need to buy now and then but not necessarily until the old ones give way. This woman says what she likes best about the store isn't that it stocks 300,000 items, most of them strictly utilitarian. What she likes is the "surprise element." She takes what is akin to a child's delight in the mundane items that call out, "*You don't* need *me but take me, take me anyway.*" She explains that she's drawn to the design of products that strike her eye as "new" and "different"—OXO kitchen gadgets, for example. To a Buy Scold, this woman's weakness for reimagined can openers and basting brushes makes her a victim of slick product design. I think Buy Scolds are too hard on this shopper. What's going on here is fundamentally human. We are, as Peter

Whybrow maintains, "instinctively drawn to the unexpected." Whybrow isn't a marketing consultant, he's a psychiatrist who teaches Bio-behavioral Science and directs the Neuropsychiatric Institute at UCLA. His provocative *American Mania: When More Is Not Enough* explains how, beginning 200,000 years ago, the human brain embarked on an evolutionary path that evolved into the forty-five-ounce bean (mostly water) that we now lug into Bed Bath & Beyond, the one that's annually subjected to fMRI scans during Super Bowl commercial breaks. Specifically, Whybrow cites what he calls the "dopamine superhighway" that zips through our cranial cavity and stokes interest in the new and different.

"Cool!" is the approbation of choice for Romantic customers (five years old and up) when encountering any item that's even minimally ingenious or novel. In this context, the first recorded use of the word occurred in the 1880s, when the interjection "Dat's cool!" turned up in a guide to "Negro English." "Cool" went mainstream in the fifties and sixties, when mass culture co-opted it from beboppers, beatniks, rock-and-rollers, and hippies—Romantics all. Now, of course, it's applied so indiscriminately as to be meaningless, except as evidence that we live in an age far more romantically indulgent than classically restrained. In 2008 the CEO of J. Crew—J. Crew!—was crowned by *Fortune* the "King of Cool." Hmm. "Coolest Products of the Year" lists, issued by trade associations, consumer magazines, and business schools outnumber even Best Dressed and Sexiest Men or Women rankings. Stanford hosts the annual Cool Products Expo. In 2008, PCBC (née Pacific Coast Builders Conference) bestowed its *palm d'or* on the "cool" QuickDrain USA Shower Wall Drain. Sites all over the Internet are scouting for cool, throwing anything new and vaguely different at the cool wall, betting that some will stick. Our mass obsession with cool sends Buy Scolds around the bend. To them, "cool" is contemptible, a "selling point" manufactured by conniving marketers who seek to confer cool on their products via advertising, event sponsorship, online chatter, and old-fashioned word of mouth. Our unceasing quest to wear cool, drive cool, drink cool, eat cool, and behave cool is a sign, says Naomi Klein in *No Logo*, that we are a society "riddled with self-doubt." Our collective weakness for "cool," Klein says, is indicative of why marketing studies calculate our "aspirational age"—yours and mine—to be seventeen years old.

Sociologist Colin Campbell and others suggest that consumption and the romantic impulse, with its relentless fondness for cool, are entwined.

But it's best not to follow Campbell too deeply into these woods, for they're dense and it's hard to find a way out. Let's leave it at this: romance, as Campbell says in *The Romantic Ethic and the Spirit of Modern Consumerism*, isn't just schmaltz the Sell Side slathers on when it markets automobiles, underwear, and fragrances. Our romantic longings, our "apparently endless pursuit of wants," our love of the new and different, are the fuel that powered the rise of capitalism itself, in Campbell's view.

The Buy world today reeks with romanticism. Just turn on the television. Ever since I discovered Pitkin's Classic–Romantic paradigm I've been keeping a scorecard. I watch TV with a yellow pad by the bed. I tally commercials: "Classic" commercial appeals ("Buy me—I'm simple, useful, long lasting!") versus "Romantic" ones ("Buy me—I'm packed with options, I'm trendy, I'm hot, I'm the latest and the greatest!"). So far my Classic list is pathetically short: a few ads for long-lasting batteries and some other boring things. The Romantic list runs on and on. Watching NFL games, I'm floored by how *romantic* car and truck advertising is. A Ford commercial comes to mind: a huge Ford pickup is lowered off the rear ramp of a cargo plane that has just touched down. The driver of the truck, which remains chained to the plane, applies his Ford-tough brakes and brings 30,000 tons of cargo plane to an effortless stop. A wry and manly voiceover says something to the effect that "Chances are you'll never have to stop a thirty-thousand-ton plane with your pickup"—a guy can dream, can't he?—"but isn't it nice to know the stopping power is there in case you do?" Another car ad boasts of not one but *two* sunroofs. How romantic can you get?

In the absence of an elegant über-theory that explains a woman's weakness for Bed Bath & Beyond, I revert to the why-we-buy list I drew up back at the BIG Show in New York City. The first item had to do with how the lion's share of in-store Buy decisions are made more or less spontaneously, infatuation at first sight: "Whoa, what an incredibly cool basting brush!" Since the BIG Show I've heard much testimony from normal, everyday people who associate the Buy with this sort of rush—a tickle of delight, a jolt of pleasure. They are, to varying degrees, prisoners of desire:

> Shopping is pleasurable, a rare treat. It feels satisfying to fulfill a nonnecessary desire—to indulge, even if it's just once in a while.
>
> —College student, female, twenty-two

I like buying booze because I love bars. I like buying clothes because I enjoy playing around with image. I buy books because I like to read them.

—Administrative assistant, male, midtwenties

There is a thrill to leisurely browse a flea market, because there is never any particular must-have item. It's joyous then to discover a desirable object. And then there is great satisfaction after having brought it home and integrated its beauty into the other everyday items of one's surroundings (peace-inducing).

—Artist, female, fifty

Not exactly portraits of the buyer as rational chooser. No wonder traditional economists threw up their hands and surrendered the study of consumer behavior to those with the curiosity and patience to be still, to watch, and to ask why we select specific booze brands and basting brushes.

Please Don't Eat the Dog Food

A milestone in the legitimization of the Romantic Buy impulse occurred at the annual meeting of the Association for Consumer Research in Cambridge, Massachusetts, in 1986. A scholar named Russell Belk rose and walked to the lectern to face a couple of hundred association members who spent their days brooding over what he referred to as "micro issues." These academics carried out narrow, tightly controlled experiments usually involving volunteer students who were rewarded with coffee mugs or dollar bills for their participation. Belk, a freethinking and at the time romantically disposed professor at the University of Utah, was serving a term as the association's president. A slight man in his early forties, his hair was pulled back in a ponytail and he wore an earring in one lobe. The 'tail and the stud had been recent additions, he explained when I called to ask about that day in Cambridge. "I guess I was going through a midlife crisis," he said.

At the time of the conference Belk was engaged in the Odyssey Project, in which he and other researchers roamed the country in a van. Their mission was to record not the self-serving half-truths and faulty recollections of why we say we buy—"I gave it a lot of thought," "I weighed and compared," and so on—but to collect raw evidence of what we actually *do* when we're at swap meets, art fairs, and in supermarkets. The crew stopped for a time in a New York suburb, where they observed the everyday shopping behavior of middle-aged housewives. They hung around a farmers' market, taking notes, asking questions.

Belk called his talk "Happy Thought," after a two-line poem by Robert Louis Stevenson. You might remember it hazily from *A Child's Garden of Verses*. Belk began his address with a recitation: "The world is so full of a number of things, / I'm sure we should all be as happy as kings." (The poetry poses no threat to Pound or Eliot or even Allen Ginsberg's elegiac howl about Walt Whitman in a California supermarket: "What peaches and what penumbras! Whole families shopping at night! Aisles full of husbands! Wives in the avocados, babies in the tomatoes!")

But the Stevenson poem captured precisely the main points Belk wanted to drive home that day: how "childlike wonder"—romance at its most innocent—plays a guiding role in why we buy, and to stress how our Buy world is indeed filled with wondrous things, diverse and abundant, which we everyday folk, hardly kings or queens, take pleasure in acquiring. In so doing, Belk said, we make ourselves "royally happy." Instead of pursuing this fruitful link between pleasure and purchase, Belk told his audience, they were squandering their time on what Saul Bellow referred to as "the dog-food level of things": the "petty, stupid, and dull rather than profound, insightful and interesting." The researchers didn't take kindly to the charge that they'd been barking up the wrong tree. Belk sensed their hostility yet kept going. He said the time had come for researchers to learn new tricks, to turn from their fixation on profit and loss—the dog-food level stuff—and feast on the wondrousness of the "macro." He offered a welter of research questions waiting to be explored: What is the relationship between what we buy and inner satisfaction? How do we decide—when we resolve to clean out the attic and garage—that certain items are "junk" and others are "collectibles" to be preserved and cherished? What *emotional* impact will burgeoning consumer cultures have on billions of people in places where consumption is surging, such as India and China?

Belk's dog-food address represented a fresh way to think about how and why we buy, one that refuted the long-standing assumption that we operate dispassionately and in accordance with the laws of supply and demand, i.e., that we are, in the main, Classic buyers. It challenged the Buy Scolds' charge that you, poor ewe, are a barnyard creature branded and prodded by Sell Side herders. In truth, Belk stressed, invoking Stevenson's lines, we're more like grown-up kids who happen to be living at a time when—every day!—a touch of Christmas is in the air. Witness the Romantic who rambles expectantly through Bed Bath & Beyond. "For such a child," Belk writes, "desire is palpable, and hope hangs as heavily as stuffed stockings on the fireplace mantel."

The Romantic you no doubt knows this feeling of excitement. Maybe you felt this excitement the day your Prince came: that supersized tennis racquet, clad in titanium, engineered to yield sweeter ball contact, enhanced power, maximum spin, pinpoint precision. Maybe you felt it that day in the fitting room, when you sucked in your belly and slithered into a Spanx bodysuit you'd just read about online. Kids, as Belk told his erudite audience that day, feel this sort of romantic rush all the time. They go mental in toy stores, where everything is new and different, their spirits soaring—at least for the brief time it takes to rip the package apart in the backseat of the car, or break it into bits, or lose it at the playground.

The premise that the Buy is shot through with pleasure and wonder took hold in the years following Belk's recommendation that researchers turn their attention to how consumption soothes the savage heart. Some overreached in making the case: a paper in the early 1990s looked to the American songbook for evidence of the link between consumption and romance. It cited the lyrics of "These Foolish Things (Remind Me of You)," the thirties ballad with lilting references to cigarettes, airline tickets, silk stockings, perfume, and a piano, consumables that are "props [used] to enhance the romance in a relationship." For his part, Belk kept at it, devoting years of research to the theme he'd sounded in Cambridge. A decade after his dog-food address, he and a couple of coauthors published a paper devoted to the metaphors associated with the wonderment inherent in the Buy:

Metaphors for *lust*—the word "luxury," Belk reminds, derives from the Latin *luxuria*. Nothing closeted about our lust for luxuria. Luxury apparel and accessories are a $270 billion industry.

Metaphors for *getting high*—rug collectors in Turkey, Belk reports, refer to themselves as "addicts." Compulsive buyers say that buying makes them "drunk," gives them "a rush."

Metaphors for *gluttony*—Danes, Belk reports, commonly refer to good-looking blouses, cars, or sofas as "delicious." Belk writes that we are "transfixed with an overwhelming and urgent appetite [for them]." Buying *is* like eating. We eat when we're not hungry; we buy when we don't need. A helpful source, the behavioral economist Dan Ariely, suggested that I peruse *Mindless Eating* by Brian Wansink, who directs the Food and Brand Lab at Cornell. I leafed through it, mentally crossing out references to "eating" and "food" and substituting words that relate to "buying." Thus re-edited, *Mindless Eating* turns out to be one of the more astute Buy guides on my shelf:

- "Increasing the variety of . . . ~~food~~ goods increases how much everyone ~~eats~~ buys."

- "[The] longer you stay at the ~~table~~ store, the more you tend to ~~eat~~ buy."

- "Birds of a feather ~~eat~~ shop together. . . . If there's a majority of ~~overweight people~~ spendthrifts in the family, the frequency, quantity, and time spent ~~eating~~ buying puts pressure on a person who's trying to ~~lose weight~~ reduce spending."

Temperatures Rising

After Belk described his dog-food speech to me, we talked about how the Buy is now routinely associated not just with junior-grade yearnings for things—desire, pleasure, thrills—but with all-consuming love. We talked about fetishes. My hard drive groans with fetish references. Many of us throw "fetish" around when we talk about things we love to buy: women's shoes, for sure, but also neckties, wine, vintage posters, golf clubs. We don't just shop for these things, we crave them, as many people tell me. We stroke the fabric of dresses on a rack; we gaze dewy-eyed at the sleek lines of a laptop; we inhale the sweet scent of leather-trimmed captain's chairs in a new F-150 pickup. We have a fetish for manly. We have a fetish for frilly. Belk and I chatted about how the concept of fetishistic Buys stems from primitive society, and how it was adopted by Karl Marx, later Sigmund Freud, and eventually our affluent society. The *Oxford English Dictionary* tells us that the term "fetish" long predates the whoop-de-doo over the contents of Imelda Marcos's closet. It derives from the French word *fétiche*, meaning "charm," that's applied to any object—a pebble, a shell—that natives on the Guinea coast believed exerted some sort of power or enchantment over their daily lives. Karl Marx famously incorporated the idea of material fetishes into his political philosophy. With the coming of the industrial revolution, as hands-on craftsmanship gave way to mass production, workers became alienated from the goods they produced. Material goods were thus stripped of any "objective value." To restore value and "meaning" to goods, capitalist tools and their advangelist propagandists realized the need to invest those goods with artificial qualities. The result? "Commodity fetishes," as Marx called them. Marx would surely take issue with how interlocking C's on a pair of sunglasses increase four-, five-, or sixfold the actual material value of those goods. A half century later Freud weighed in with his notion that for proletarians and bourgeoisie alike there are inanimate objects to which we form no small measure of attachment, often psychopathic.

Cut now to my hard drive, which is stuffed with historical and modern references to how we turn goods, even stores, into fetishistic objects:

- A cultural historian tells of how, in the Napoleonic era, the cashmere shawl represented a "fetish evoking sensual fantasies of the Orient."

- *Artforum* reviewed the newly opened Prada store in SoHo: "In the name of 'individualized service,' the customer is tracked and controlled by gizmos like a super-Hi-end lab rat—not least impressively, turning blah stuff like RFID (Radio Frequency ID tags) into fashion fetishes that recall Courreges' wacky love affair with the Space Age."

- The *New York Times* reported that Home Depot has finally opened an outpost in Manhattan. The reporter described the new store in terms of matrimony and bondage: "a giant three-floor wedding cake of a space," crammed with items "seductive to someone like me," enough to keep him "enslaved for ten years."

- The *Times* again, on one of the least fetishy stores I can think of, Brooks Brothers, which had just hired Thom Browne, "the men's designer with the serious dapper fetish, to create a line of suits that will be unveiled in September."

Browse the online shopping blogs, and you'll hear direct echoes of Sade and *The Story of O* on sites that all but moan, squeal, and throb with fetishistic ecstasy. A site devoted to my erstwhile employer, SlaveToTarget. com, features a set of handcuffs adorned with the red Target bull's-eye. The site's motto: "a little red cart romance never hurt anybody." The site's raison d'être: "WE LOVE TARGET. CAN'T GET ENOUGH OF IT. WANT TO MARRY IT." The anonymous editor of SlaveToTarget.com describes herself as an "Internet dork and Target lover, end cap whore and $1 section addict." One day I gave her a call. It turns out that Target's love slave is a respectable thirty-one-year-old mom named Liz Sorensen, who has a couple of pre-K kids and lives in upstate New York. Sorensen said she started SlaveToTarget. com just for kicks. She's never taken a penny from Target, though the company did call to congratulate her when, in 2005, *Forbes* named SlaveTo-Target.com one of its favorite blogs. I asked Sorensen how she came to be enslaved by Target. Not a week goes by, she told me, that she doesn't drop a hundred bucks at the store, scooping up "trendy but affordable" clothes for herself and diapers for her kids. She claimed that her kids are happy only when swathed in Target-brand diapers. Such a testimonial is sweet music to Sell Sider ears: swaddle 'em, romance 'em when they're young, and they're yours for life.

Stores of Our Dreams

Many people I've interviewed have confessed that certain stores turn them on. And that's no accident: stores go to considerable expense to set the trap for seduction. The trade term for this is "atmospherics." What I once tried to orchestrate with a flickering candle stuck into a Chianti bottle, a splash of Canoe, and a Johnny Mathis record, retailers achieve with carefully planned lighting design, music playlists, artificial aromas, and fetching graphics. Some of us, Romantic buyers, anyway, fall heart over head for these atmospherics. When I talked with Paco Underhill, he pointed out the effective sensory allure of stores such as Crate & Barrel and Williams-Sonoma, how their "stage-set lighting"—consistent in both their stores and catalog photography—created an aura of, if not a love nest, then a "dream home."*

On the down-and-dirtier side, there's Abercrombie & Fitch, both the old (as in my day) A&F, where the atmospherics were intense, and the cur-

---

* Mary Ann McGrath, a marketing professor at Loyola University in Chicago, told me that an uncommon number of women she has interviewed confess to deep specific longing for a "Crate & Barrel home," meaning one that is well lighted, uncluttered, and clean.

rent iteration, where the stores are configured to activate nineteen-year-old pheromones while holding fogies like me at arm's length. For me, the old A&F was Desire Central. Located at Forty-fifth and Madison in Manhattan, the store was a short walk from my office. A few times a month I'd duck in there at lunchtime, sometimes to buy, usually just to hang out. Back then there were no babes on the sales floor wearing tights tucked into calf-length boots—no babes at all, in fact. The salespeople were mostly beefy bald guys, chunky, not hunky the way they are now at A&F. But man, that place was *hot*. I remember a six-foot, reared-up grizzly with four-inch claws ready to rip customers a new one. Sweet. I remember a buffalo head, actually quite a few dead heads on the walls, with eyeballs nastier than Dick Butkus's. Two-hundred-pound tarpons hung from the rafters. The store was crammed with manly attractions: twelve floors of same, if I remember correctly, four or five devoted to sturdy jackets, vests, gloves, hats, parkas, belts, socks, and boots—all primo—clothing guaranteed to keep your tool cool in the summer, warm and cozy when the air was arctic frigid.

I'm getting warm now just thinking about that place: House of Hardy fly rods, Randall hunting knives, gorgeous Old Town canoes, tents that ranged from lightweight and snug to multichambered palaces for moguls who, at the end of a hard quarter-day's trudge through the bush, laid on cocktails and a sit-down dinner for a safari of twelve. There were handmade gun cabinets, shooting prints, vintage wilderness maps all over the place; these weren't ersatz, decorative touches, the vintage (or pseudo-vintage) objects Ralph uses to dress his stores. You could take golf lessons at A&F, and hang out on the roof where world-class fly casters double-hauled two hundred yards of shooting line with a flick of the wrist. Then, your pulse still racing over the image of a steelhead stripping line down to the backing, you could stop off at the fishing department and choose among tens of thousands of finely tied flies. No visit to *my* A&F was complete without punching 7, where you stepped out of the elevator into an armory fit for a royal shooting party, where hundreds of rifles and shotguns were lovingly displayed, and where in 1968 a thirty-four-year-old immigrant from Queens bought a box of shells, loaded one of the shotguns, put the barrel to his head, and fired.

Today, of course, A&F also stirs the flesh, but in a wholly different way. When A&F opened its new flagship on Fifth Avenue in 2005, *New York Times* reporter Alex Kuczynski felt the full force of retail body heat: "a sprawling nightclub of a place with muscled young men standing guard at the front entrance, their smiles entreating passers-by to look. At their backs, the front windows are mysteriously shuttered. Inside, the lighting is a moody chiaroscuro, and the music thumps." These atmospherics were there for a reason: A&F, Kuczynski noted, had figured out that "the most efficient way to move tons of jeans and T-shirts is not to sparkle with antiseptic, anodyne cleanliness like Gap, but to sell these relatively generic pieces of clothing using the sexual ideology of the new millennium, an era informed by readily available pornography, the strip-club aesthetic and a post-AIDS abandon. The nightclub setting and the racy marketing campaigns make the clothes more appealing."

Feeling a little frisky after I came across that *Times* piece, I dropped in on our local A&F, in the Water Tower mall on the Magnificent Mile, where the scene seemed decidedly less lascivious than the one Kuczynski had described. (This is, after all, Chicago.) Yes, there were the usual huge black-and-white photos of shirtless hunks with six-pack abs, and the place reeked of "8," A&F's dreadful answer to Chanel No. 5. I saw but two vestiges of the testosterone-rich days of yore, of *my* A&F: a solitary moose head on a wall and a canoe that dangled listlessly from the ceiling. No matter: the store was jammed with customers for whom the atmospherics were appropriate. As for me, I felt nothing but melancholy. To cheer myself up, I walked a couple of blocks south and bought a new iPod.

Atmospheric Pressure

Romantic buyers, always open to seduction, suck stores in through their eyes, nose, and ears, which in turn influences their shopping moods and behavior. (If there's anything wrong with shopping online, it's the dearth of atmospherics—though at least one e-commerce site, CaféScribe, which sells textbooks, has tried to stir up some by mailing users scratch-and-sniff stickers that emit a bookish smell.) Atmospherics work on us the way conditioning does. If the store is Pav★Mart, we're the pooches. Pav★Mart stimulates, we respond. Teenage Romantics have been observed to spend more time shopping—and they buy more—when a store pulses with music. Older Romantics respond similarly when Vivaldi washes over the sales floor. Store illumination is an atmospheric that either lights our fire or douses it. Sell Side jewelers have found that customers tend to reject diamonds if the light on the gems is overly green or yellow, so they fire 4,700°K halogen lamps at the ice, which produces a cast that's slightly blue. Lighting really matters, no less in a store or restaurant than onstage or on the screen. It isn't "just illumination," cultural critic Virginia Postrel notes, "it's identity, emotion, drama." Good lighting excites, bad lighting brings us down. An industry survey reports that 70 percent of us said we shop in stores where the lights are either too bright (21 percent) or inadequate in some other way (48 percent). "Overhead fluorescent lighting, still all too common in fitting rooms, is harsh and unflattering," the trade pub *Chain Store Age* chided in a story that urged retailers to brighten up their lighting act. "Adding . . . lighting directly to the mirror to reduce the shadows cast by overhead lamps can do wonders," the story advised.*

Whether we're aware of it or not, we're creatures who respond to store atmospherics across a series of what specialists refer to as "nonverbal dimensions." Since the mid-1970s, environmental psychologists have used box-and-arrow diagrams—what they call "PAD models"—to illustrate the cause-and-effect relationship between atmospherics and our nonverbal response to them. PAD denotes Pleasure, Arousal, and Dominance (which sounds more than a little fetishy to me). A straightforward PAD model looks like this:

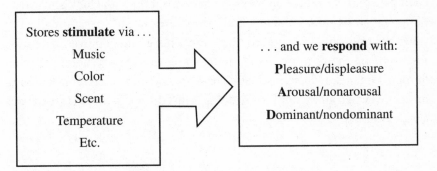

Stores **stimulate** via . . .

Music
Color
Scent
Temperature
Etc.

. . . and we **respond** with:

Pleasure/displeasure
Arousal/nonarousal
Dominant/nondominant

Adapted from Richard F. Yalch and Eric R. Spangenberg, "The Effects of Music in a Retail Setting on Real and Perceived Shopping Times," *Journal of Business Research* 49, no. 2 (2000), pp. 139–147, with permission from Elsevier.

**Chain Store Age is chockablock with tidbits for retailers looking to improve their atmospherics: e.g., stores ought to pay more heed to their bathrooms, right down to their stainless-steel toilet partitions, which should have a "patterned finish for added texture and durability."

The "pleasure" and "arousal" dimensions in the right-hand box refer, respectively, to a) whether a store emits positive or negative vibes, and b) whether it excites or dulls the senses. The "D" in the equation, "Dominance," refers to whether we feel *in charge* when we work the aisles at Pav★Mart—are we in control, do the salespeople work at our behest? Or does the noise, clutter, lousy lighting, and bad service put us out of sorts and so reduce us to blobs of confusion that we can't wait to flee, perhaps without buying? Studies show that when we feel in control, we give higher marks to salespeople and rate stores favorably even when they're hectic and crowded. In other words, if the overall PAD atmospherics are positive, we'll shop Pav★Mart with the acuity of a hungry fox. If the atmospherics are wanting, we lumber around till it's finally time to meet our buds at Panda Express.

The Pleasure-Arousal-Dominance model above is an abbreviated depiction of the many atmospheric conditions that can affect our mood and behavior while shopping. Musical genre, lighting, and smell are only starters. In a study that reviews several decades' worth of atmospheric studies, researchers L. W. Turley and Ronald E. Milliman identify *dozens* of variables that may please or annoy us, or may cause us to feel juiced or wasted, in control or submissive. These include traffic congestion outside the store, ceiling height, placement and length of checkout lines, the look and clarity of signage and displays, and how salespeople are dressed. To capture the full range of atmospherics, we need many more boxes and a quiver of arrows. Just compare the primitive PAD model above to what psychologists call a Stimuli-Organisms-Response (SOR) framework, and you'll see what we're up against when all we think we're doing is just dropping into a store to have a look around:

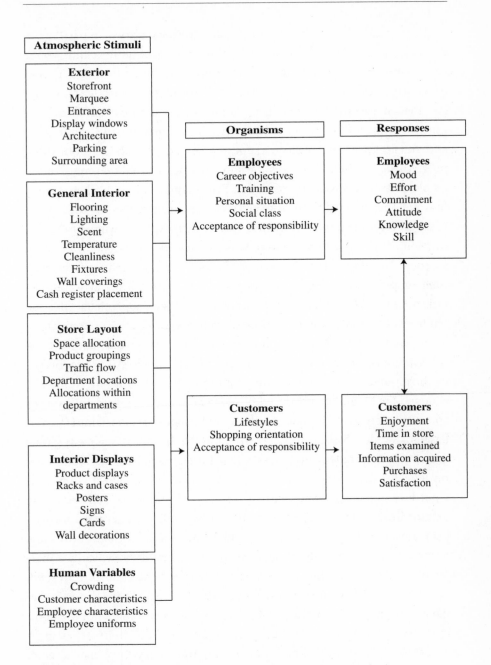

Adapted from Richard F. Yalch and Eric R. Spangenberg, "The Effects of Music in a Retail Setting on Real and Perceived Shopping Times," *Journal of Business Research* 49, no. 2 (2000), pp. 139–147, with permission from Elsevier.

Some findings described by Turley and Milliman are worth passing on, if only to give wait-and-whiners something to reflect on next time you're staring into space while your Romantic spouse is killing the better part of a beautiful Saturday afternoon. Take store music. There's evidence to suggest that, at least in a supermarket, loud music doesn't adversely affect how much we buy. It does, however, influence how much time we can tolerate such music; the wrong music in a supermarket tends to accelerate our shopping. Music soothes or enrages the shopping beast in subtle ways. For example, researchers Richard Yalch and Eric Spangenberg published a study in which they divided music into genres—"foreground" music (vocals) and "background" music (instrumental only)—then explored whether the distinction made any difference to how we *perceive* the passage of time when we shop. They found that younger shoppers perceive that they spend more time shopping when instrumental tracks are played. They also found—returning to PAD model—that in-store music has an appreciable effect on our level of *arousal* but not on our perceived level of *pleasure* or *dominance*.

As far as I can tell, though, there are few universal truths about atmospheric impact. Romantics are, after all, a fickle bunch. All of the foregoing boxes and arrows were rattling around in my head one afternoon as I shopped the Magnificent Mile with Ned, who is about as Romantic as they come. We were in H&M, one of a cluster of European retail chains (H&M is based in Sweden, Mango and Zara in Spain) that have enjoyed heady global growth. These retailers hold mass appeal for teens, young adults, and even my wife, because a) their prices range from highly reasonable to how-can-I-not-buy-it-even-if-I-only-wear-it-once, and b) because such chains are extraordinarily adept at jumping on fashion trends. Their speed to market is notoriously quick—from runway to, er, in-house design reworking, to manufacturing and shipping, to in-store availability is typically a matter of weeks, not months. Merchandise is thus continuously refreshed, which means that your son or daughter, or you or your wife, drops in frequently to snap up something before it disappears. But that's not the point of the story. The point is that as Ned and I entered the men's department at H&M, there was—techno? trance?—anyway, *really loud* instrumental music, heavy on the bass, blasting through H&M's audio system. You don't need a postgraduate degree in Retail Atmospherics to know that the music was meant to put customers, in H&M's case mostly young and hormonal, in the mood for Buy love. I asked Ned, who's a musician and unusually attuned, to tell me what he thought of the music and whether it made him want to buy more.

"What music?" he answered, not looking up from a stack of dress shirts.

Nose Job

A woman I know, a novelist, in her fifties, who disdains ostentation, who lives comfortably but isn't an over-the-top spender, tells me that "smell is an important factor" when she shops. Some smells turn her off—"anything with too much fragrance, particularly in the patchouli family, sends me screaming out the door." But other aromas, pulpy aromas, unleash a flood of desire. "I love the smell of fresh lumber," she says. "But what I like best of all is the smell of stationery supplies. I cannot pass a Kate's Paperie [a small chain selling expensive paper products in Manhattan] without going inside." She's not the only woman—and they've all been women—who has told me that there's something decidedly arousing about the smell of paper. The owners of Kate's Paperie are aware of this; their Web site promises an in-store shopping experience that will "awaken your senses!" They launched Kate's "to convey the sensuous and touchable nature" of paper products. As far as I know, Kate's Paperie doesn't manipulate the aroma of its stores. Nor, apparently, does Cinnabon, the single most recognizable nasal call of the mall. In *Mindless Eating*, Brian Wansink tells us that the company insists that franchises be placed apart from any other mall stores that sell food so as to preserve the chain's deadliest marketing weapon: the waft of its cinnamon rolls. The aroma sets off a metabolic chain reaction: once the sticky sweet smell leaves Cinnabon, it enters our nasal passages and cues our brains to release dopamine, thus kicking our pleasure system into higher gear. And not for a minute or two, either. In 2006 scientists found evidence that neurotransmitter dopamine continues to be released for up to *an hour* after initial inhale, which leads to speculation that we may remain in a happy (buying) mood for a good sixty minutes after something like a Cinnabon cue enters our system.

Given the apparent selling power of aroma, there are plenty of Sell Side "scent marketing" specialists who try to exploit the fact that one of the quickest ways to a Romantic's heart is through the nose. Scent marketers claim that aromas seduce us by playing on memories and emotions that shunt aside rational decision making. In 2008, according to *The Economist*,

Harrod's in London pumped a dozen different aromas into various departments, including the scent of chocolate in the women's shoe section and cut grass in outdoor furniture. They even provided lime- and basil-scented register receipts. In the United States, scent marketers are especially active in the hospitality business, at hotels, spas, and casinos, where Romantics are inclined to gather. I received a nice briefing on all this one humid, Lake Michigan–smelling August afternoon, when I had a drink with Mark Peltier, who was in Chicago on a sales trip. Nearly twenty years ago Peltier started a company called Environmental Aroma Systems—AromaSys—in Lake Elmo, Minnesota. AromaSys sells smells that it claims are "site-specific, fine-tuned . . . for the customer." His clients are mainly hotels and casinos that want to infuse what Peltier calls "nature's most appreciated scents" into their establishments' public spaces. Intense and loquacious, Peltier told me he got the idea when he was in the air force back in the midseventies, stationed near smoggy San Jose. Day-tripping among the thousand-year-old redwoods of Muir Woods, he was struck by an idea—"it blew the molecules of my mind," as he put it. The notion was to "capture nature, then figure out how to pump it into a building." After all, he reasoned, ancient temples and Roman baths were enhanced by spice and flower fragrances.

The question was how to weaponize such smells for commercial gain. Sometime after his Muir epiphany came another aha moment: Peltier would ionize scented liquids into diffusible form, then pump products calibrated to precisely the right aroma level into rooms. A precise level is crucial, he explained. Crank the aroma up too high and all you've done is create noxious, olfactory Muzak—or, worse yet, CNN Airport that you *breathe*. No, atmospheric aromatics need to be subtle enough that the patron hardly knows the smell has been pumped in, subtle enough that you'll say the air smells "fresh" or "appealing"—but not "scented." Peltier's initial plan was to inject his tailored scents into office buildings, where a whiff of ionized nature should reliably "enhance worker performance and productivity." But employers weren't interested. A few retailers, however, were intrigued. Victoria's Secret, the LVMH Fashion Group, Thomas Pink, and a few others sniffed around the idea to varying degrees. For Peltier, though, the big win, the big *Wynn*, turned out to be the hospitality industry—notably Steve Wynn, who remains an enthusiastic client and who has used AromaSys in public spaces throughout the Bellagio and his other properties. So have other top-tier Vegas casinos, as well as Marriott, Four Seasons, and Ritz-

Carlton Hotels & Spas. They commission Peltier to mix up a custom aroma, or they choose from dozens of existing AromaSys scents, among them Woodlands ("enriches a woodland-themed property or initiates the senses to the holiday season"), Seduction ("a hypnotic array of beautiful flowers, exotic woods, and rich spices . . . appropriate for either high-end retail extravaganzas or resorts promoting romantic atmospheres"), and my favorite, Pump'd ("young and buff, this scent kicks it up a notch and gets your energy flowing!").

I asked Peltier how he would scent the hotel bar we were sitting in. The room was darkly lit, a highly polished place with sleek black chairs and blood red velvet draperies. Tiny lights sparkled in the ceiling. "Maybe 'Black Cashmere,'" he responded. "Oak moss, with a blend of citrus aromas. Or better still, 'Seduction,' which has a hint of patchouli."

Thingness

While they may influence Romantic buyers' moods and behavior, ear- and nose-based atmospherics pale in comparison to visual stimulation—that is, the way a product is designed and packaged. Remember that all-important first "moment of truth"? How a Buy needs to catch our eye? In today's marketplace, things need "thingness," as students of material culture have been known to call it, "thingness" being that quality or qualities that gives an item "attitude." Today, if something ain't got "thingness," it ain't got a thing.

Our thing for "thingness" is why Ford Motor's chief paint designer attends Fashion Week in New York: to seek design inspiration and color cues.

Our thing for "thingness" is why, in 2006, Home Depot (not to be confused with Apple) announced the launch of "Orange Works," a partnership project with the Arnell Group, a top design/branding firm. What came of it was the HomeHero line of fire extinguishers and smoke alarms: elegant, sleek, snow white, "products designed to complement any home décor." Apparently kids' nursery furniture also needs "thingness." There's a store in Brooklyn called Mini Jake, "a modern children's store" whose owner told an interviewer, "Everyone who was buying *Dwell* and Eames chairs suddenly had kids. There was a void to fill."

Our thing for "thingness" extends to lowly cleaning supplies. Procter & Gamble's admired CEO, A. G. Lafley, tells interviewers, "I want P&G to become the number one consumer-design company in the world." His epiphany, his collision with "thingness," occurred when Lafley was posted in Asia and observed how in Japan "the department-store beauty sections are as good as it gets in the world." When he returned in the late 1990s to eventually run P&G, "it became quite clear to me that design was not only important in beauty, it was even more important in household care and consumer care." So it came to pass that P&G bottles Fabreze fabric softener in a "Décor Collection," packaging so elegant you'll not only be drawn to it at the supermarket, but once at home—or so the Sell Side would like to believe—you'll display the spritzer as a decorative element. Why hide such refinement behind a cupboard door? Design and packaging, "thingness," make the Romantic think "I want it, I need it. It's fresh, it's new, it's distinctive, it's me, or the me I want to be."

How did eye appeal, how did "thingness," become so crucial to Romantic buyers and all but the crustiest Classic buyer? The reasons are many:

- *Our attention spans are shorter, our loyalty spans, too. They need to be continuously revivified.* Through the early nineties, when I worked in magazines, it used to be that to redesign a publication was to risk widespread disaffection, if not outright defection, by readers and advertisers alike. One fiddled with the layout, the typeface, and the magazine's logo at great peril. Readers complained about even tiny graphic changes, and advertisers placed you on probation: *You took away my magazine! It was better before! Now I can't find anything!* Today magazines undergo frequent facelifts so as not to look prematurely aged. The same goes for product packaging. A story in the *New York Times* reports that over the course of a century, Pepsi changed the look of its bottles and cans all of ten times. Now it changes them every few weeks. "Customers are looking for what's new," says the packaging head at Unilever, explaining why the company decided to reshape its Suave shampoo bottle for the first time in a quarter century, and why Axe shower gel now comes in a container that resembles a video-game joystick.

- *We're willing to pay more for thingness:* The technical term is "hedonic pricing." I need a new toothbrush. I go to the drugstore. I don't look at the price. I don't notice whether the bristles are soft or hard. I choose on the basis of color and shape (as if my teeth care about "thingness").

- *We live in the era of the "aesthetic imperative":* That's cultural critic Virginia Postrel's explanation for why I scrub my teeth with a thick-handled, raspberry-colored toothbrush. Postrel reflects insightfully about our weakness for eye candy, for thingness, be it in the form of toothbrushes or toilet brushes. She says there are several factors at work here. Good design at cheapo prices. The demise of Puritanism. The feminization of men. The acceptance of formerly outside-the-mainstream style influences: gay, ghetto, and Asian. The world, in other words, is phat.

- *We need thingness; it's an anthropological given:* "Aesthetics is not a luxury, but a universal human desire," Postrel maintains. Look at how aboriginal peoples adorn themselves. Look at the soaring cathedrals in Europe, built by poor but romantically inclined workers. Buy Scolds take issue with this sort of argument. Enough legitimizing the idea that eye-pleasing scarves and bracelets are higher-order-need satisfiers! Break loose the handcuffs that enslave you to Target's thingness! For Buy Scolds, these marketer-created consumer "fetishes" are tantamount to blindfolds, nipple clamps, and spreader bars. Naomi Klein, in *No Logo*, details the global branding movement's corrosive impact on labor practices, freedom of speech, and consumer choice, and describes how in the early 1990s Nike and Reebok battled each other in a ferocious game of "advertising chicken." Each dramatically increased its respective marketing budget in what Klein calls a "fetish strategy." By the end of the six-year chicken war, the fetish strategy enabled Nike to swoosh from $750 million in annual revenue to $4 billion, as a purveyor of fetishes so irresistible that kids sometimes robbed, even killed, to get their hands on the right pair. Today Nike is a $16 billion company, though like most of the athletic shoe category it's running into an economic headwind at the moment. Nevertheless, its 2008 product line featured a $175 pair of sneakers called Jordan Spiz'ikes, shoes with ultrahigh thingness described by Nike as "a mix-mash shoe touting the great Spike Lee and Mike Jordan . . . with design inspiration from MJ's image/sophistication and Spike's film-making savvy . . . to create a fresh, functional sneaker for the hardwoods." Foul! cry critics of hyperconsumption. Spiz'ikes are likely just one more big leap toward ecological disaster, since many athletic shoes are a mishmash of ethylene vinyl acetate, polyurethane, rubber, artificial leather, plastic, and liquid silicone, glued and stitched by third world workers.

So goes the gloom-and-doom side of the Romantic buyer's descent into the decadence of thingness. Buy Boosters, though, say we have every right to turn those high-priced Nikes into whatever magic charm our hearts desire. They maintain that arguments like Klein's amount to little more than "Marx lite," as cultural critic James W. Twitchell has scoffed. If the fetish fits, if you believe $175 athletic shoes will somehow make you run faster, leap higher, hang in the air, even *fly*, all the while *looking* fly, well, *just do it, dammit.*

14

The Stop-Me-Before-I-Buy-Again Buyer

Where self-indulgence ends and self-destruction begins

> Oh God, yes. I remember this one. It's made of silky velvet, over-printed in a paler blue and dotted with iridescent beads. As I stare at it, I can feel little invisible strings, silently tugging me toward it. I have to touch it. I have to wear it.
>
> —Sophie Kinsella, *Confessions of a Shopaholic*

 MORE LIKELY A ROMANTIC THAN A Classic buyer, you walk into a store and spy something of interest—blame it on the thing's thingness, or the music in the store, or the ionized aroma pumped in from a small tank mounted in the stockroom. You don't really need the thingy thing that catches your eye but you buy it anyway. As happened the other day when Linda and I were strolling down the Magnificent Mile. We decided to take a quick pass through the ground floor at Bloomingdale's. Out of the corner of her eye Linda spotted a necklace. Forty bucks. We stopped at the counter and the salesperson—Janie on the spot—handed the piece to Linda, who held it up to her neck.

"What do you think?"

"Nice, really nice," I replied, reflexively patting my pockets to see whether I'd brought along a credit card. Regrettably, I had, and I immediately placed it on the glass counter. "From me to you," I said to Linda, and in the same breath to the salesperson, "We'll take it." Then, to Linda: "Looks great. Let's scram."

Nice gesture, faulty delivery—not uncommon when a person, even one generous of spirit and wallet like me, is firmly in grab-and-go mode. I'm not passing along this incident to puff myself up or to illustrate what an impetuous spender I can be. I mention it only to make the obvious point that a vast number of our buys are simply the result of random collision and snap decision making. Most impulse buys are inconsequential. Some, of course, bring disappointment and regret. That wireless home-entertainment system you pounced on, that drove you nuts when you tried to set it up? Those seersucker cargoes you thought were spiffy? What were you *thinking?* Those salt and pepper shakers shaped like lightbulbs? They were cute, they made you smile, but now they're gathering dust on the windowsill beside your cactus collection, which also seemed cute at the time. We're all guilty of impulsive Buy behavior. For some of us, though, impulse buys occur with such startling frequency that a line is crossed. On this side of the line we live a normal, if now and then profligate, Buy life. Cross the line and we spiral into Buy hell.

Where exactly is that line, anyway? And how do we know we've crossed over?

In Harm's Way

Wanting to find out whether everyday shoppers know the difference between impulsive and compulsive buying, I posted a survey online and invited many of those in my e-mail address book to fill it out. One question asked whether respondents thought they bought on the safe side of the line—i.e., they were run-of-the-mill impulsive buyers—or whether they thought they sometimes ventured across the divide. More than a few said they crossed the line with disturbing regularity and labeled themselves compulsives. A woman in her twenties who works for a nonprofit said she considered herself a compulsive buyer because she goes without buying for a while but then breaks down, at which point she "binge buys everything in sight." A man, also in his twenties, said he likewise lives on the brink: "I love to acquire random things, then work hard to pay off a credit card, but in no time max it out again."

Many people who were seemingly normal, at least to my eye, told me they thought of themselves as potentially out of control. A couple of teenage girls admitted that they strongly identified with Becky Bloomwood, the wastrel heroine of Sophie Kinsella's bottomless pit of an oeuvre (*Confessions of a Shopaholic, Shopaholic and Sister, Shopaholic Takes Manhattan, The Dreamworld of a Shopaholic, Shopaholic & Baby*). Others, men and women both, recalled domestic smackdowns ignited by the alleged out-of-control spending habits of one party or the other. Two women said that if forced to choose, they'd take shopping over sex any day of the week. Many self-selected over-the-liners confessed to credit card balances with trajectories that paralleled that of the national debt. Still, as far as I could tell, nearly all of these self-described shopaholics lead reasonably well managed lives.

Until the latter part of the past century, not much attention was given to defining what separates normal spending from compulsion. A 1915 textbook proposed a term for the latter: "oniomania"—*onio* deriving from the Greek word "to buy." Later on, psychoanalysts conjectured that there must be some sort of link between out-of-control spending and other forms of aberrant behavior: kleptomania and pyromania, to name two. It wasn't until the 1980s that researchers seriously began to probe for the seam that separates buying like crazy from buying that is certifiably so. Yuppies had come along. If not compulsive buyers, they were certainly ebullient ones: free-spending early adopters of handhelds, CDs, portable computers, early nibblers of artisanal cheeses and sushi (though not in combination), early tipplers of designer vodka and wine from obscure vineyards in Chile and New Zealand. Slumbering scholars sat up and took a closer look at the social, cultural, and economic implications of what was now seen as shop-till-you-drop spending.

Journalists also stepped into the breach. In 1984 the *Washington Post's* Style section reported that Buckingham Palace flacks were trying to douse rumors about the fragile state of Charles and Diana's marriage, notably the persistent whisper that Diana was practically living in Sloane Square, spending $4,000 *a week* on clothes. The *Post* passed along the palace's denial that Diana was a "shopaholic," thus assuring her immortality, etymologically at least, in the *Oxford English Dictionary*. In no time the widespread incidence of "shopaholism" was being bandied about on TV chat shows and in magazines and newspapers: tearful stories of wrecked lives, news of neighborhood support groups such as Shopaholics Limited in Brooklyn, an early pioneer in the treatment of Buy overdose. A headline in the *New York Times* on June 16, 1986: SHOPPING ADDICTION: ABUSED SUBSTANCE IS MONEY. The story described a forty-eight-year-old mother of two whose "addiction is not drugs, gambling or alcohol but spending." She had just served a year in a California prison for embezzling money from an employer to feed her habit. The piece noted that psychiatrists and financial counselors believed that she was just "one of millions . . . who shop obsessively out of boredom, anxiety, anger, joy or fear of being hurt." One psychiatrist offered a money quote: "They feel compelled to go shopping [because it elicits] a euphoria. . . . Afterward they feel anxiety, guilt, shame and self-recrimination because they were out of control, and it becomes a cycle."

By the late eighties researchers were earnestly addressing the cause of and the potential cure for—uh, what do we call this scourge? "Shopaholism" grated on the scholarly ear. The coinage trivialized the problem and signaled all-out *addiction*, which maybe it was, maybe it wasn't. Some academics preferred the term "pathological buying," which gets at the maladaptive, disease-y aspect of the affliction. In the end, everyone more or less settled on "compulsive buying," defined as follows: *"Chronic, repetitive purchasing [that is] a response to negative feelings and that provides immediate short-term gratification, but ultimately causes harm to the individual and/or others."*

The key word is *harm*.

To qualify as compulsive, buying must lead to a condition more serious than stuffed closets. To be judged aberrant, chronic buying must bring on shame, alienate friends and family, wreck a job, or precipitate a combination of these calamities. Compulsive buying usually involves heavy credit card debt, and concomitant lying about the debt to family, friends, and colleagues. True shopaholics raid kids' college funds to pay off creditors. When the truth is revealed, many declare personal bankruptcy in an effort to call off the dogs.

Today there remains a fair degree of debate over compulsive buying. Not about its dire consequences—deceit, despair, humiliation, wrecked careers and families—but about what it really is:

1. Some say it's an *addiction*—a credible supposition given the likelihood that if you binge buy you're likely to compulsively drink, gamble, and/

or abuse drugs. But unlike those other high-profile addictions, compulsive buying remains short on fear factor: no public service spots ("This Is Your Brain on Credit Cards"), no mention of it on the school calendar's Healthy Choices Day. Indeed, one self-help book refers to compulsive shopping as the "smiled-upon addiction." After all, it's only *shopping*: it poses no immediate danger to bodily organs, and those in its grip have a genuinely pleasurable time while roaming the mall.

2. Others say compulsive shopping is an *impulse control disorder* akin to the inability to control anger. Or the inability to resist the urge to swipe something that doesn't belong to you. Or the inability to walk away from the craps table when you reach a preset loss limit.

3. Others say compulsive shopping is addiction-*like*, but it's more precisely a form of *obsessive-compulsive behavior*. There's a counterargument to this. True compulsive behavior is defined as an attempt to erase, avoid, or counteract a perceived negative, usually a *specific* one: germs, clutter, anxiety-inducing cracks in the pavement. With compulsive buying, what's to counteract?

4. Others say compulsive buying qualifies as an *affective-spectrum disorder*. ASDs include a broad range of psychiatric and medical conditions routinely treated with antidepressants and other drugs: bulimia nervosa, panic attacks, attention-deficit/hyperactivity, irritable bowel syndrome, the list goes on.

5. Still others say compulsive buying is neither a true addiction nor a form of obsessive-compulsive behavior. These holdouts (inside and outside the medical establishment) contend that compulsive buying is little more than "normal" buying carried to an extreme. Bingeing is made possible by easy access to credit cards (more on which later). Given that there's little financial incentive to propagate this relatively benign view of Compulsive Buying Disorder—no hours to be billed, no pharmaceutical profits to be made—those who advance this interpretation are, lobbyingwise, whistling in the wind.

6. Finally, some say that whatever compulsive buying is, there may be a genetic basis for it. "Close relatives of compulsive shoppers are more likely to be compulsive shoppers themselves, or experience mood disorders or substance abuse problems, than the relatives of noncompulsive shoppers, but how and why is not clear," Donald Black told me. Black, a psychiatrist and leading authority, added that it likely isn't *compulsive buy-*

ing that's genetically passed on, but rather a predisposition for "impulse control disorders."

Compulsive Buying Disorder is currently under consideration for inclusion in the 2011 edition of the American Psychiatric Association's *Diagnostic and Statistical Manual of Mental Disorders (DSM-V)*. This would be a big deal. New editions of the *DSM* come along but once every several decades. The *DSM* is the Bible—critics call it the psychiatric *billing* Bible—of mental disorders, with sales of over 800,000 copies. *DSM-IV*, the current edition, runs to nearly a thousand pages and contains three times the number of qualifying disorders than did the first edition, published in the early fifties. The *DSM* lists accepted diagnoses and treatment criteria for, among other afflictions, Substance-Induced Psychotic Disorder, Transient Tic Disorder, Male Erectile Disorder, Antisocial Personality Disorder, multiple variants of Bipolar Disorder, to name a few. When and if Compulsive Buying Disorder makes its debut, at least three significant developments will occur: a) Compulsive Buying Disorder will be taken more seriously by the worldwide psychiatric and medical establishment, b) it will be easier for doctors and binge buyers to bill insurance companies for medical treatment, and c) drug makers will have greater incentive to promote pharmacological treatment with existing antidepressants or to sink R&D money into developing new medicines. With "medicalization," though, comes the concern that we'll discount the social causes at work: namely, careless use of credit cards and lousy personal money management.

Through the early 1990s, argument over diagnoses aside, an important question remained unaddressed. By now we'd agreed on a name for superheated buying, and we recognized the havoc it caused, but no accepted litmus test existed to distinguish the "normal" heavy buyer from the true compulsive. In other words, where is that line? In 1992 social scientists Thomas O'Guinn and Ronald J. Faber stepped up and published a landmark paper that proposed a screening device. O'Guinn and Faber had been thinking about compulsive buying for a few years, exploring the notion that it's the buying process itself, not what is bought, that drives the compulsive to the mall. Like most of their peers, they acceded to the notion that compulsive shoppers bought as a way to alleviate tension and anxiety. They saw a solid connection between compulsive buying and low self-esteem, though which was the cause and which the result was a matter of debate.

Either way, *where's the damn line?* Faber and O'Guinn's Compulsive Buying Scale (CBS) drew that line. The screener consisted of a set of behavioral and economic conditions that, when present, effectively distinguished the *true* compulsive buyer from the garden-variety profligate spender. O'Guinn and Faber devised the test after they had circulated a questionnaire to a randomly selected sample of the general population and also to members of a compulsive-buyers' support group in the San Francisco Bay Area. The survey consisted of twenty-nine statements that addressed buyers' state of mind and spending behavior. Respondents were asked to assess where they fell using a five-point scale that ranged from "very often" to "never." After running the usual statistical analyses of the responses, O'Guinn and Faber concluded that there are seven conditions that, when they occur at least "very often," point to the true compulsive buyer. If you're sitting here wondering whether you are, in fact, out of control, grab one of your four thousand mindlessly acquired fountain pens and rank yourself on the salient seven below, keeping in mind that most of us are guilty of some of these transgressions now and then. A bona fide compulsive is one who falls toward the extreme on pretty much *all* of them. You know you've crossed the line when:

1. You buy things even though you can't afford them.
2. You believe others would be horrified if they found out about your spending habits.
3. You write checks even though you know there's not enough in the bank to cover them.
4. If you have any money left at the end of a pay period, you are compelled to spend it.
5. You make only the minimum payments on your credit card statements (if you make any at all).
6. You feel anxious or nervous on days you *don't* go shopping.
7. You buy things to make yourself feel better.

One frigid winter morning I left Chicago and drove west across the tundra to meet up with Tom O'Guinn at the University of Wisconsin. It was now fifteen years since he'd coauthored the landmark paper that laid out the Compulsive Buying screener, more than a couple of decades since he and Albert Muniz had proposed the idea that we belong to "brand communities." In the interim, O'Guinn had moved on. Sporting a vivid yellow dress shirt, he greeted me cheerfully in his office in Grainger Hall, home of the UW business school. He was now executive director of the brand-management center at UW, which struck me as a pretty sweet deal. He teaches but one course sixteen weeks a year, which leaves plenty of time to attend conferences and hobnob with CEOs on the school's advisory board. On matters of consumer behavior and the role of advertising and branding, O'Guinn is an inveterate inquirer into nearly everything that orbits around the Buy. Expounding in his office, he often turned his face to the window, as if glancing at sticky notes posted on the bare tree limbs. Plenty of ideas posted out there: O'Guinn was among the first to look into how race and ethnicity shape buying patterns, how television programming influences one's self-perception as a consumer, how the history of advertising reflects—sometimes ignites—broad cultural change. As we chatted about all this research, O'Guinn moved easily from topics as abstruse as the Rolling Stones as a totemic global brand to the ubiquity of North Face outerwear, standard-issue clothing for college students at UW and elsewhere.

But what I'd come for was some background on how O'Guinn and his colleague Faber had come up with what O'Guinn refers to as "the gold standard" tool that's now widely deployed to identify compulsive buyers. The idea for the screener, he told me, was hatched in Las Vegas, while he and Faber were taking a break from a scholarly conference there.

"Ron and I were just sitting around watching people at the tables," O'Guinn recalled, peering out his office window. "Then I turned to Ron, or maybe he turned to me, and said, 'You know, I know people who shop the way these people gamble.' The term 'compulsive buying' was floating around by then but wasn't used all that much. So we spent a couple of years doing groundwork. As things turned out, the scale proved to have surprisingly good psychometric properties. Right away, clinicians started using it. And Ron and I began getting calls from various companies which wanted to know more about certain customers who were over the edge." O'Guinn chuckled. "One of the first companies to call was a credit card company. The guy wanted to talk about whether he could use the screener as a way to filter customers. 'Until certain [overextended] customers get into trouble,' he said, 'they're *fabulous* customers. They pay high APRs, buy a ton of stuff. It's only after they fall off the edge that there are problems all around, for them and for us, of course. So we're wondering if there might be a way for us to use your scale to figure out whether somebody is here'"—O'Guinn motions with an outspread arm— 'and not here.'"

"Then what happened?"

"Nothing came of it," O'Guinn said mirthfully.

O'Guinn takes justifiable pride in the Compulsive Buying Scale. "You know," he said, gazing at the illusory Stickies, "a lot of what we academics do is sit around and try to figure out how to sell people stuff. But partly due to the scale, compulsive buying has gone from a derisive topic of humor— usually at the expense of women—to a tool that has been used for all sorts of valuable things, even to prove mitigating circumstances in criminal trials. I am happy to say that this is the one thing I've done in my career that has actually helped people."

Not long after that visit, there was big news on the compulsive buying front: the most ambitious survey yet of how the universe of compulsive buyers breaks down. Underwritten by a pharmaceutical grant, and published in the *American Journal of Psychiatry*, the survey found that about 6 percent of American adults qualify as compulsive buyers, a figure consistent with most previous studies, though some have indicated a percentage twice that. The new study reported that half of all compulsive shoppers are married (many more *may* have been married before the shit hit the fan). It found that racial distribution among compulsive buyers roughly parallels that of the overall population, with Hispanics proportionately somewhat less at risk. It noted that compulsives tend to cluster in lower-income brackets and reaffirmed previous research suggesting that the onset of compulsive buying typically occurs in the late teens or twenties.

One further finding generated a good deal of discussion in the media. The survey found that men are just about as likely to be compulsive buyers as women, even though women have generally had to take the rap. Intrigued, I phoned Lorrin Koran, the study's lead author and a professor of psychiatry and director of the Obsessive-Compulsive Disorder Clinic at Stanford. I asked Koran why he thought the media give male compulsives a pass. He said that it's partly due to the fact that men are less disposed to come forward and talk about behavioral problems in general, and less likely to fill out surveys about their shopping proclivities. He said men who buy compulsively also have a sneaky way of positioning themselves not as out-of-control shoppers so much as *collectors*. "Collecting" provides a man with a neat cover for extreme Buy behavior, an "intellectual rationalization," as Koran put it. He told me about one male patient with a stash of over fifty cameras, even though the man never takes pictures. Another had squirreled away two thousand wrenches, a "collection" easily concealable in a basement corner or garage. On the other hand, Koran pointed out, the things that women hoard—clothes, usually—are more conspicuous: drawers and closets packed with items, many with price tags still attached, clothing that has never been, and never will be, worn.

Splurchases

A few weeks after visiting O'Guinn, I found myself thinking about that forty-dollar necklace Linda and I impulsively bought at Bloomingdale's that day. Here was a case of pure "splurchase"—a term that pops up in Packard's *The Hidden Persuaders* and is now bandied about on shopping blogs. There was nothing *compulsive* about that Buy, it was just a textbook example of impulsivity, defined by the American Marketing Association as "a purchase . . . made without prior planning or thought [that usually] involves an emotional reaction to the stimulus object." Linda and I may have frittered away forty bucks, but self-immolating buyers we are not, certainly not according to the O'Guinn-Faber screener:

1. You buy things even though you can't afford them.

   Me: Never.
   She: Never.

2. You believe others would be horrified if they found out about your spending habits.

   Me: Never.
   She: Never.*

---

*If you don't count shoes.

3. You write checks even though you know there's not enough in the bank to cover them.

    Me: Never.
    She: Rarely.*

4. If you have any money left at the end of a pay period, you are compelled to spend it.

    Me: Never.
    She: Never

5. You make only the minimum payments on your credit card statements (if you make any at all).

    Me: Never. Always pay entire balance.
    She: Rarely.

6. You feel anxious or nervous on days you *don't* go shopping.

    Me: Never.
    She: Never.

7. You buy things to make yourself feel better.

    Me. Sometimes.
    She: Sometimes.

No, that necklace was impulse pure and simple, a transaction lacking forethought. We chose to be "myopic," as researchers say, to the fact that the necklace would eventually have to be paid for, but the purchase was symptomatic of no chronic behavior on our part, at least none that might cause harm. Still, what made us do it? Why did we, why do we all, succumb—as one study puts it—to "spontaneous and unreflective desires to buy, without thoughtful consideration of why"?

---

*Just had a tiff over this. Linda says "never" but, trust me, it's "rarely." I know because I access our respective checkbook balances online (not snooping, just keeping financial affairs in order) and I know that there have been occasions—maybe three or four in the 20-plus years we've been married—when her checkbook ink ran red.

*   *   *

Having been thwarted in my quest for an overarching Unified Buy Theory, I had no illusion that I'd find anyone who could stuff impulsive buying into a tidy syndrome. Researchers don't seem all that interested in the question. Why isn't there an *Impulsive* Buying Screener? I'd asked Tom O'Guinn when I met with him in Madison. He shrugged and said that years ago he'd thought about trying to come up with such a test but had moved on to other interests. Impulsive buying doesn't pack as much punch as compulsive buying. "We tend to trivialize it," O'Guinn said. "You know, it's just a lot of small stuff at the checkout counter. We see it as 'unidimensional'—an act that results from lack of planning, lack of cognition, you know, just unreflected behavior."

Absent a cogent Unified Impulsive Buy Theory, I can at least offer some generalizations about splurchasing. There's some correlation with age: impulse buying slopes upward from our teenage years through our thirties, at which point it abates somewhat. And there is consensus that impulsive buying is on the rise, thanks to e-commerce and TV home-shopping, neither of which requires us to change out of our sweatpants and leave the house to make a splurchase. And, as we've seen, a vast number of impulse triggers are planted by retailers, what I call Improvised Buy Devices: three-for-the-price-of-one signs, flashy displays, salespeople motivated by a free trip to the Richard Petty driving school.

Impulsive and compulsive buyers are similar in certain ways. Helga Dittmar, a British sociologist, is a Buy scholar who has run countless experiments demonstrating how—for both impulsive and compulsive buyers—short-term gratification ("I want that little black dress *now!*") trumps long-term consequences. And, thanks to ATMs, debit and credit cards, and online shopping, we can almost always have it now. Dittmar and others contend that the rush to buy is tied to bolstered self-image. Hold a necklace to your neck, for instance, and suddenly, in Dittmar's words, "psychological buying motivations become more powerful than price and usefulness." Nearly any item can do the trick—a comely tank top, a manly Titleist 907D1 driver. Dittmar points to "high-impulse" and "low-impulse" goods. A $500 golf club with a gigantic head is a low-impulse good, while clothing and jewelry are definitely "high impulse." High-impulse goods are those that prompt you to say, "They put me in a better mood" or "They make me feel more like the person I want to be" or "They express what's unique about me." Lower-impulse goods, body care products, for example, don't promise quite the same benefit as clothing or jewelry, but you still buy them impulsively, though with a nod to value for money.

So next time you're in a store and conditions are ripe—synthesized cover arrangements of Abba played at optimum decibel level, earth-tone-colored walls, xenon puck lights bathing the contents of a display case—you might want to keep the following in mind:

- Impulsive buying is largely about *affect*, i.e., we tend to use the impulsive buy as a "mood management tool." If we're in a lousy mood, we'll use it to summon a bit of cheer. ("Go mental in the shoe department!" Simon Doonan, creative director at Barneys New York, exhorted on his store's Web site during the 2008 holiday season.)

- Impulsive buying is about the collapse of willpower, the failure of self-regulation. Those who study the brain generally agree that self-regulation is a "limited resource"—each of us has a finite supply. Sandra Aamodt and Sam Wang, who've written about the brain for general-interest readers, say that given our limited capacity for self-regulation, to exert "willpower in one area often leads to backsliding in others." If we give in to impulsive urges to buy gadgets or clothes, there's a better chance we'll give in to eating more ice cream or drinking more booze. Our reservoir of willpower rises and falls according to how often we expose ourselves to temptation. The more we shop, the lower our reservoir of self-regulation.

- Impulsive buying isn't just about emotions and moods. We're influenced by the presence of others—"group-level consideration" it's called. If you're a woman (more likely than a man to shop with friends or in the company of multigenerational family members), you're probably familiar with group-level consideration. Group values establish "norms." Roam the Magnificent Mile with a pack of impulsive, free-spending pals and it's pretty easy to join in, even though impulsive buying is otherwise out of sync with your "normative" buying behavior. Conversely, take your tightfisted mom, in from Grover's Corners, out for lunch and a stroll down the Mile, and it's unlikely you'll return home with anything more than the headache that hit when she told you, *again*, how you were spoiling your kids or how a dollar doesn't buy what it used to. In fact, your mother needn't actually be *in* from Grover's Corners to put a damper on your impulsive buying. She could merely be a distant voice whispering *no*, even as your pals egg you on with how *cute* you look in that faux-fur hat with the goofy-but-adorable earflaps. Not that you need another hat, not that you don't already have a great many hats, but what the hey, your mother's not around, so you go for it.

Impulsifiers: A Brief History of Credit Cards

And, of course, it's *easy* to go for it. It's especially easy because we have a pocket or purse full of little plastic cards, each with a magnetic strip on the back, produced in universal format ID-1, measuring 3.370 x 2.125 inches— a proportion mathematicians refer to as the golden ratio. For Sell Siders, this card represents the golden goose. Nothing can top the ease with which credit cards activate the unpremeditated decision to buy right here, right now, as in the case of the forty-dollar necklace. Studies show that credit cards not only facilitate spending, they decrease the amount of time we take to decide on one product over another. They're also why we leave higher tips when signing a bill charged on a card than when we pay with cash.

The credit card as we have come to know it, love it, hate it, use and abuse it, was born, fittingly, along with the baby boom. Boomers are the first generation to live from cradle to grave with plastic in its pocket:

1949. A watershed year in impulsive Buy history. A little piece of cardboard, the Diners Club card, entered circulation. It was the brainchild of Frank X. McNamara, who as the story goes reached into his pocket at Major's Cabin Grill in New York City only to discover that he'd left his billfold in another suit. Embarrassment! Shame! Apologies all around! McNamara's wife dipped into her pocketbook for a fistful of lettuce and saved the day, but McNamara resolved that no man or woman need ever again bear the psychic scars of such a contretemps. By the end of the following year, four hundred restaurants, thirty hotels, a slew of car rental agencies, and five florists were accepting McNamara's little piece of cardboard.

1958. Another watershed: the Great Fresno Drop. The Bank of America mailed sixty thousand credit card solicitations to well-heeled California consumers who, according to *Fortune*, "suddenly [find] that thousands of dollars in credit [have] literally dropped into their laps."

1973. *Another* watershed: Dee Hock, a visionary at BankAmericard (which later evolved into the Visa network) anticipated William Daniels's immortal advice to Dustin Hoffman in *The Graduate*. There was one word, and only one word, to describe the future: *plastic*. Hock opted to invest millions in electronic processing systems, better to speed and record the growing number of credit transactions taking place across the country. Most major retailers, however, remained chary about accepting payments from card customers other than those who carried store-issued Charga-Plates.

1979. The big breakthrough: JCPenney agreed to accept bank-issued credit cards, the first big retailer to do so. My former Sell Side employer, Lands' End, was among the first direct-to-consumer retailers to accept cards—and *over the phone*, no less. By now we had traveled so far down Plastic Boulevard that *Time* magazine marveled at how prevalent cards had become: a California civil servant used a credit card to buy a Maxfield Parrish work priced at $14,000, an amount equal to his annual salary. Emory University allowed students to use credit cards to pay for evening courses in belly dancing. At the Cottontail Ranch, the whorehouse between Reno and Vegas, signs posted above the beds told johns that plastic was a welcome form of exchange for pleasures obtained. Said Roger Martin, PR manager of the Windows on the World restaurant atop the World Trade Center, "If a person with a card sees a thirty-five-dollar bottle of wine on the list, after one drink he'll decide to buy it. Shoot the works, baby! It's funny money, not green hard cash."

"Evil!"

American consumers now pack an average of four cards apiece, safeties off. We make about a third of our purchases with credit cards, which helps explain why there's currently a trillion dollars in outstanding revolving debt—around $3,000 for every man, woman, and child in the country. The average household stares at a monthly balance of $9,000. These averages are misleading. Big spenders, not necessarily one and the same with big debtors, carry huge monthly balances but pay them on, or close to on, time. And a fair number of us are plastiopaths—we don't use credit cards at all. Nearly a third of us who do use them pay our monthly balances in full. One researcher who has spent years studying the effects of credit card spending told me, "What's amazing is not that people abuse credit cards, it's that more people don't."

There's irrefutable evidence that packing a card, or four, or a dozen or more, increases personal spending. And there's no question that credit cards have the capacity to muddle one's buy/don't-buy decision-making process. I think back to my visit to Carnegie Mellon, when George Loewenstein chatted amiably about the difference between spendthrifts and tightwads. The morning after our dinner, I headed over to his house for coffee and freshly baked bran muffins. The professor lives in a comfortable Victorian house with his wife, who teaches history at Carnegie Mellon, two kids, and a gentle, lumbering dog. Loewenstein was characteristically laid back as we talked in the living room while the kids got themselves ready for school and the dog dozed in a sunny corner. He described the conclusions he'd reached about how we variously cope with the "pain of paying," the games we play with ourselves. Paying in advance, for instance, affords a kind of get-it-over-with comfort. To pay upfront for an annual health club membership is easier on the insula than writing a check every month. Loewenstein described experiments that revealed that we recall vacations more positively if we paid beforehand rather than shelling out as we went along. I asked Loewenstein what he thought about credit cards. I could almost *see* anger flashing in his brain, no fMRI scanner necessary.

"There's just one word for credit cards, and that's *evil*," Loewenstein declared. "Credit cards ease—they *anesthetize*—the pain of paying."

Extraordinary, no, what a little plastic card can do? Set it down it on a counter, give it a quick swipe, and—as if by magic—it erases the barriers that separate self-regulation from self-indulgence. The reasons to revile credit cards are many: Over a million declared personal bankruptcies a year, a number that has been increasing steadily. APRs that range from the usurious to the rapacious. Relentless spending-is-cool marketing campaigns directed at eighteen-year-olds, advertising that rests on the good old "hook 'em when they're young" strategy that worked wonders for the tobacco industry. Now that home prices have tanked and home equity loans are difficult to obtain, credit cards are the first and last resort for anyone in search of extra bucks to spend on discretionary Buys. These are reasons enough that social critics and the likes of George Loewenstein get agitated when credit cards come up for discussion. The link between plastic and overspending is, to Buy Scold Juliet Schor, nothing short of "Pavlovian." In *The Overspent American*, Schor relates that the mere existence of MasterCard signs in a psychology lab induced subjects to spend more money in a controlled experiment—notwithstanding the fact that subjects had been explicitly told to ignore the logos, that they were part of an unrelated project.

What can be done to lessen the evil? I asked Loewenstein that morning. He wasn't in favor of direct regulation of credit card companies; instead, he advocates a "libertarian paternalistic" approach. Require credit card companies to put a boldface notice at the top of our statements: "At your current rate of X, your total balance and minimum monthly payment at year's end will be Y and Z." In other words, give cardholders an unobstructed view of the abyss. If debtors choose not to apply the brakes, at least they'll crash with eyes wide open.

Those who defend credit cards cite the giant boost they give the economy. Plastic provides the jet fuel for consumer spending; it's the engine that powers the Consumers' Republic. Pay your balance in full every month and you make money on the float. Plastic is convenient—you rent a car, buy groceries, and don't have to fill out a snoopy credit application. Cards level the playing field, sort of, between haves and have-nots. They give the have-nots a taste of the *have*—even if it takes over twenty years and $2,300 in interest to pay off a $1,000 *had-to-have*, which assumes that the have-not works off the debt with minimum monthly payments. Champions of revolving credit follow the same logic as law-abiding members of the NRA—credit cards don't break people, people break people.

E-pulsive

I mentioned earlier that impulsive buying is on the rise. Credit cards are not the only culprit. The World Wide Web offers us unparalleled opportunity to window-shop from home or work—it's impossible to imagine a channel better suited to round-the-clock splurchasing. Estimates are that half of all online purchases are unplanned, which is not remotely surprising given that everything under the sun is for sale on the Web, and we can shop virtually anywhere in the world. From Chicago I just impulsively sent Ned, who's in Philadelphia, a CARE package of bagels and smoked salmon from Zabar's in New York. What's not to like about how the Internet offers abundant choice and a reliable way to secure a good price? In fact, the only reasons *not* to make a splurchase online are a) you may worry about your credit card info falling into the wrong hands, b) your inability to self-regulate demands immediate gratification—i.e., instant possession is ten-tenths of the fun of shopping, c) you cling to the quaint notion that it helps to see, touch, try on, and try out what you're buying, and d) you think a trip to the post office to mail something back is a huge hassle.

The Internet shopping window, it's said, opens onto two horizons. As one researcher puts it, there's an "immediate purchasing horizon"—*I want it now!*—and a "future purchasing horizon"—*I want it but maybe not now, maybe a little later.* If we want something now, we go online and proceed in what's called "directed" Buy mode. Google "Onitsuka Tigers," then search for a pair with red and blue stripes. Otherwise, we can proceed in "exploratory" mode. We click this, we click that, the way kids frenetically push buttons in a science museum. For the impulsive buyer, shopping online is both like and unlike shopping in a store. One thing they have in common is that what we *say* we do when shopping isn't necessarily what we *do* when shopping. Many of us say, for example, that we buy online impulsively when a site offers some sort of come-on: a price that's "Internet-only!" or includes "Free shipping!" Chances are, we're kidding ourselves, or we're kidding whoever's conducting the survey. User Interface Engineering, an online consulting firm, suggests that many of our impulsive online buys have little or nothing to do with price breaks or free shipping. More than we realize, our impulsive online Buys have to do with how we choose to navigate the Web. Say you're looking for a new pair of earbuds. There are a couple of ways to click your way to them. You can use a site's search box: type in the brand or model, and the site takes you there. Or, you can use the site's category links: Shop All Departments > Electronics > Headphones > Earbuds and Earphones, at which point you can page through until you find the earbuds you're looking for. According to an online consulting company, shoppers who use the latter method, link-to-link, are allegedly three times more likely to continue browsing after they found the earbuds they came looking for, and they make three times as many impulse buys as those who cut to the quick via the search box.

In a real store the same situation obtains: the more we eyeball, the greater the chance our eyeballs will land on an appealing impulse purchase—up to a point, anyway. Too much clutter, too many varieties of the same thing, can be paralyzing, prompting us to flee a Web site or a store, the so-called paradox of choice. Excessive choice induces brain freeze. Optimally, says one report, we want maximum flexibility of choice and "minimal decision complexity." That's not likely to happen in a typical supermarket, where we spend, on average, twenty-two minutes and in that time are confronted with fifty thousand choices.

It's a given that areas in a store that draw the heaviest traffic—checkout lanes and cash-wraps—are chockablock with inexpensive and easy-to-justify, buy-now items: gift cards, candy, gum, magazines, key chains, penlights, multihead screwdriver sets. But a store has many other ways, more artful ones, to tickle one's impulse bone. When I visited the National Retail Federation's BIG Show at the Javits Center, I sat in on a presentation by Andrew McQuilkin, a VP at FRCH Design Worldwide, an architectural and brand communications shop. McQuilkin, a stocky, earnest chap with a goatee, harbors what he calls a "big passion" for fixtures. A good store fixture is one that beckons us by displaying merchandise in a fetching way, one that puts us in direct touch with what we had no intention of buying when we walked in. The highlight of the presentation was McQuilkin's list of effective store fixtures, splurchasewise:

- *Open-sell cosmetic displays.* McQuilkin talked about how much he admired Sephora's brightly lit shelves. To the impulsive buyer they're what a bare bulb is to a moth. Open-sell *anything* improves the chance that we'll buy. Years ago I realized that I avoided clothing stores that kept neckties in cases behind the counter. I felt stupid trying to remote-control the salesman's hand: "No, sorry. Not that one. *That* one. The one just below the first one, no, *next* to that one, the chartreuse, or whatever that's called—puce?—no, not the one with the little unicorns, the one with the—what are they, tiny pigs?—I can't make them out from here . . ." Not a winning formula if a store wishes to encourage impulsive behavior.

- *The "puck" wall:* I'd never heard the term but we're all familiar with it. A puck wall—especially the sort favored by The Limited, according to McQuilkin—is basically an upgraded take on the cheaper and ubiquitous slat wall. It's a wall studded with nicely finished, usually chrome, "pucks" or pegs. Shrewd retailers use these pucks to show how "separates" might be coordinated to achieve a variety of completed "looks." You may have been after a skirt, but wow, that top displayed on the puck wall looked *really cute* with the skirt below it. Next thing you know both are nestled in your shopping bag. The puck wall is an example of what the Sell Side calls "integrated merchandising."

In Praise of Serendipity

It's Sunday afternoon backyard barbecue time. You drive to the supermarket. All you need is a chicken. Across from the poultry counter there's a display of iron cookware in the shape of—what?—kind of like a coffee-cake pan with a perforated base and a cylinder in the middle that resembles a cooling tower at a nuclear power plant. The display identifies the cylinder as an "infusion tower" that you fill with beer or other liquid, and that the cookware is designed to roast a chicken in an upright position. You just insert the tower into the chicken's, um, "cavity." When heated on the grill, the liquid in the tower infuses the chicken with flavor. The bird's upright position assures that it will remain moist and tender. This strikes you as a novel idea, so you place one of the pans (twenty bucks) in your shopping basket, along with the plump fryer you originally came in for. A few hours later you and your family are raving about the most succulent chicken ever consumed in your subdivision, perhaps anywhere on the planet. It's called "beer-can chicken," and it's reason enough to wonder whether Buy Scolds, your mother, and your own guilty conscience are too quick to condemn impulse buying. As for the Buy Scolds' commandments:

Never shop without a list!

Keep asking yourself: Do I *need* this? Will I *use* this?

Don't shop when you're tired! You can't think straight when you're tired, can't focus on fairness of price or actual need!

And never, ever, go food shopping on an empty stomach!

Follow such advice to the letter and you'll likely never experience the indescribable pleasure of beer-can chicken. You'll miss out on other things, too. Researchers Dennis Rook and Robert Fisher remind us that indiscriminate buying has been associated not just with kleptomania and pyromania but with emotional immaturity, primitivism, low intelligence, even social deviance. And yet, they also point out, there are salutary unplanned purchases, too: a spontaneous gift for a pal who's been under the weather; your impulsive decision to pick up a dinner tab for family or friends; and, yes, taking home an extra bottle of ketchup when there's a twofer to be had, especially if the product has the half-life of plutonium.

15

Martians Buy, Venusians Shop

Old myths die hard

One of the most uncomfortable times I felt shopping, it was our
fifth anniversary, and I wanted to get her some lingerie. . . . I was
very uncomfortable there. . . . I just had [salespeople] pick stuff out
and I paid for it and left.
—"Darren," a thirty-two-year-old Chicago shopper

"MEN BUY, WOMEN SHOP," A COMMON
refrain, suggests that men and women
are opposing life forms when they enter a
store. Women, shoppers from Venus, are
said to be "communal," meaning they take
the needs and wants of others into account
when making Buy decisions. Men, shoppers from Mars, are said to be "agentic,"
that is, goal directed, when they stride into
stores, and are typically in a "work frame," says sociologist Colin Campbell.
Men approach the Buy as a problem in need of a solution, requiring time
and energy that can be more productively invested elsewhere, as in cheering
on the Bears. In work frame, the male shopper's nervous system experiences
stress, which gives way to such symptoms as dyspepsia and impatience.
Martians invariably shop solo, not in packs. Unencumbered by companions,
they whirl dervishly through revolving doors. Women, says Campbell, are
typically in a "leisure frame." Shopping is recreational, social, a sport unto
itself—or, more charitably, an act of love since women generally serve as the
family's chief purchasing officer. Martians, so goes conventional wisdom,

shop not to spread love; they shop to win. For all these reasons, Venusians are widely assumed to be well adapted to life on Planet Retail, physically and emotionally. Unhurried and unruffled—or so convention would have it—Venusians squeeze for ripeness, sniff for freshness, and pay heed to sell-by dates.

How much of this actually holds in today's Buy world? There have been no end of cockamamie theories about what men and women are really after when they go shopping. In *The Hidden Persuaders*, Vance Packard told of research linking women's menstrual cycles with their buying decisions, positing that when women are feeling cyclically "high"—meaning "creative," "sexually excitable," "narcissistic," "outgoing"—they're tempted to try a new brand of cake mix. When they're feeling cyclically "low"—"in need of attention," "want everything done" for them—they'll scan the supermarket shelf for a cake mix that promises "no work, no fuss, no bother."

Unaware of any recent studies that delve into the relationship of menstrual cycles to shopping behavior, I'll take a straighter and narrower path through the minefield of how women and men are alleged to do their respective buying. Here's a summary of fresh, less incendiary findings:

- *Who enjoys shopping more?* More Venusians (67 percent) say they enjoy shopping, while only about one in three Martians is manly enough to say anything vaguely positive about the activity.

- *Who checks price tags?* Nearly everybody checks price tags, though women (87 percent) check them a tad more often than men (72 percent).

- *Who buys more gifts at the mall?* Women. Duh.

- *Who's more likely to be packing an actual shopping list when out shopping?* Women, and by a large margin.

- *Who's more likely to shop via catalog or online?* Men go online, women prefer catalogs.

- *Who, among single men and women (unmarried, without children at home), spends more money on what?* Single men spend more of their income on food—they eat more, and they eat out more. Single women—this goes without saying—spend more on apparel. The single Martian owns an average of 1.4 vehicles, the average Venusian, just under 1.

- *Who, when it comes to elderly shoppers (over sixty-five), shops more frequently?* This one's interesting. Senior Venusians shop *less often* than the average Venusian, but wizened Martians shop *more often* than the average Martian. Go figure.

- *Who (over fifty) puts a high premium on what?* This one's interesting, too. Women fifty and over place a high premium on a) discounts, b) getting good value for money, and c) quality of goods. Men over fifty also put a high premium on getting stuff on sale, but opt strongly for other qualities when shopping: a) breadth of selection, and b) convenient location. (Rank speculation on my part, but perhaps the latter correlates with senior Martian bladder control issues.)

Improve Your Shopping Skills: Buy More!

A few years ago *Women's Wear Daily* published a survey about differences between men and women who go shopping for apparel and home furnishings. The survey indicated that a sizable majority of women (67 percent) report that they "don't mind," or "like," or "love" shopping for clothes, while the remaining third said they shopped as little as possible—"to get what I need," or because "I don't like shopping at all." Men, once again, are just the opposite: two-thirds told the surveyors that they shop for clothes strictly to "get what I need" or because they "don't like" shopping, nohow, no way. In an effort to explain the male-female buying dichotomy, the *WWD* piece suggested that women are more avid clothes shoppers because they have more to avidly shop *for*. I recently confirmed this by analyzing the mall directory at Water Tower Place on the Magnificent Mile. It listed twenty-nine stores that sold women's apparel, eleven that sold men's (women's, too, by the way, and in greater quantity than their men's lines). In a minor but intriguing development, today's limp economy has sent sales of women's apparel down (no surprise), but the sale of men's clothing is reportedly *up*. *Retailer Daily* takes a stab at an explanation: "Men buy formal, fashionable clothes during times of economic stress as a way to appear more serious about their job amid the threat of layoffs". I suppose this is plausible, but women work, too.

Good times or bad times, women enjoy, and are also challenged by, far greater choice in the marketplace. Consider the need for a pair of every-day pants. When a Martian, or more likely his wife, decides he is is over-due for a new pair of chinos that might actually fit and flatter, there are but two key decisions to be made: pleats/no pleats? cuffs/no cuffs? As *Women's Wear Daily* attests, life is far more complicated for the Venusian who, having taken stock of her closet, decides she needs or wants the distaff equivalent of those chinos. She faces a bewildering set of options:

Wide leg?
Boot cut?
Capri?
Low rise?
Peg?
Gaucho?
Cigarette?

At the department store, the Venusian thus undertakes an arduous and time-consuming exercise: sorting through the above variables, followed by a protracted trial-and-error session in the changing room. She pulls pants on, pulls pants off, checks the front, checks the butt. (With pants you don't worry about messing up your hair.) Meanwhile, outside, the impatient Martian slouches on a bench (if there is bench) without a backrest. *Women's Wear Daily* reports that Venusians spend roughly twice as much time shopping for clothes as Martians do, which strikes me as a laughable underesti-mation.

Colloquies on the theme of "Men buy, women shop" produce a torrent of conjectures. A joint survey by the Wharton School's Jay H. Baker Re-tail Initiative and a Toronto-based consulting firm solicited the views of a top marketing exec at CVS, the big pharmacy chain. He opined that there are "many dimensions" to why women are more "invested" in shopping and buying. Their role as caregivers has much to do with it: women bear greater shopping responsibility for kids, for aging parents, and often for their spousal Martians, which includes dragging recalcitrant hubbies over to the chinos rack at Big 'N Tall, or hauling the pants back home to their lazy other halves. Buying for these multiple constituencies builds "acute shopping awareness," according to the CVS exec. In accordance with the use-it-or-lose-it principle, Martians who rarely shop, or rely on Venusians to shop for them, grow less attuned to the task. A man's interest in shopping, perhaps his adeptness, too, atrophies over time.

The Wharton survey also addressed issues relating to customer dissatisfaction: namely, are Martians and Venusians aggrieved by the same things when in a store? A qualified yes on this one. Because women are more invested in the shopping experience, they can be understandably annoyed when salespeople fail to acknowledge their existence, as when a cluster of sales associates are so caught up in their own conversation they fail to render assistance. One fed-up Venusian told the researchers, it's as if "you [are] intruding on their time." Martians, for their part, have a separate beef with salespeople. In the main they don't give a rat's ass about service with a smile. They neither expect nor *want* to engage in chitchat with a clerk. What drives the Martian up the wall are "lazy" salespeople who don't bother "to check for additional stock or take you to the item [you're] looking for." What a Martian wants—pretty much all he wants—is for someone to tell with him whether a) the damn thing's in stock, and b) if the damn thing *is* in stock, where the hell is it?

Oh, and another thing that makes Martians miserable, according to the Wharton survey: *distance*. The checkout line needs to be short, and the walking distance to the Martian's parked car should be well within the comfort zone of, say, a garden slug.

Despite these observations, it's dicey to conclude that men and women are as distinct as conventional wisdom makes them out to be. Moreover, there are subspecies within the Venusian and Martian classifications themselves, which further muddies the water. Perhaps a field guide is in order:

Buy Polars

This subspecies cuts across the Martian–Venusian divide and encompasses a shopping behavior that by now we're sick and tired of hearing about—"cross-shopping." Buy Polars are male *and* female buyers who can blissfully shop at both the top and the low ends of the market, moving comfortably through expensive specialty stores, designer boutiques, and big-box discounters. Up through 2006, Buy Polar behavior was held to be so remarkable that it inspired relentless media attention and such serious scrutiny as *Treasure Hunt: Inside the Mind of the New Consumer,* by

Michael J. Silverstein, a senior VP at the Boston Consulting Group. Just a few years earlier, Silverstein and a colleague had written what turned out to be *Treasure Hunt*'s unpremeditated prequel, a best seller devoted to the new American consumer's mind (a mind that has apparently devolved since then, given the economic downturn). *Trading Up: Why Consumers Want New Luxury Goods . . . and How Companies Create Them*—heralded our obsession with fancy labels and hoity-toity stores. Conventional wisdom held that products that had fallen behind the luxury curve had to hustle to catch up to the luxury-bedazzled American customer: Payless shoes, Samsonite luggage, LensCrafters had come to the conclusion that their merchandise would be best marketed as fashion accessories, not utilitarian objects.

In the more recent book *Treasure Hunt*, Silverstein drew in his sails a bit. While he acknowledges we still cruise into Williams-Sonoma for expensive coffee grinders or Neiman Marcus for sunglasses with eye-popping prices, we also go "treasure hunting" at Wal-Mart, T.J. Maxx, Costco, and the Dollar Stores. The *affluent* Martian or Venusian, see, is equally at ease when trading up *or* trading down.

Silverstein spends considerably more time profiling the Treasure Huntress, which is understandable in light of the fact that 90 percent of married women identify themselves as the principal shopper in the house, "influence" 80 percent of car-buying decisions, and head up 40 percent of all households with at least $600,000 in assets. Silverstein is squeamish about "dealing in [gender] stereotypes or archetypes," but he can't help but stress that the Venusian runs the Buy show: 1) most prominently, a woman takes the role of "purchasing agent, casting an eagle eye on price and value"; 2) she and sister Venusians often assume the role of "martyrs"—his word, not mine—by scrimping and putting the needs of family members ahead of their own; but 3) women also behave as "consuming hedonists [especially] when the pressure of playing the purchasing agent becomes just too great or the martyrdom becomes just too great to bear." This conflict explains why, according to Silverstein's thesis, we see so many purchasing agents at the spa, getting massages and buying luxury face creams, and observe so many martyrs laying down credit cards for expensive shoes and jewelry, all the while exulting in their treasured finds: a $2.29 jar of honey at Aldi, a "steal" of an Hermès scarf (real or fake) on eBay.

Venusian Subspecies

Bring-Back Queens

Martians and Venusians collectively return tens of billions of dollars' worth of merchandise a year, though the rate of returns varies wildly depending on product category. Electronics stores such as Best Buy experience extremely high return rates, the result being a mountain of computers, peripherals, and other items we bring back not because this or that feature doesn't work but because we chose products with so many superfluous features that we never figure out what to do with them. "Features creep" it's called, and it accounts for at least 50 percent of returns in the consumer electronics field. Home appliances, too, are vexing. The *Harvard Business Review* issued a report on "features fatigue." Exhibit A: the Bosch Benvenuto B30 espresso and coffee machine, with a "digital screen [that] asks the user to select from 12 drink options and to make myriad decisions about energy-saving modes, timer programming, and water hardness settings." Who needs the aggravation? So we box it up and take it back.

Not everyone succumbs to features creep. Classic buyers—men and women—try to keep things in perspective. The other night I was hanging out at a big electronics store, listening in on a conversation between a customer and a sales associate. The customer, a strapping guy in a leather jacket, was looking to buy a Webcam for his daughter. He scrutinized two models, poring over the features listed on the boxes. Both were made by LogiTech. One cost $27.88, the other $37.98. Befuddled, he asked the salesperson to explain the difference between the two. "This one has more features," the clerk said (apparently he'd had as much product training as I'd received at Target). The customer stood there speechless for a while. "Well, we're talking about a thirteen-year-old," the dad said finally, "and she don't need a lot of features." He walked off with the cheaper model and presumably never returned it.

The clothing business deals with a return rate nearly three times greater than the national average for all returns. A typical clothing store can expect that 20 percent of what it sells will boomerang back, while the online return rate for apparel is nearly twice that. A Venusian subclass is responsible for an enormous chunk of this: Bring-Back Queens, they've been called, women imprisoned in an endless cycle of buy and return. Some BBQs are more regal than others. *Marie Claire* magazine quoted a twenty-seven-year-old Venusian who's right up there in the BBQ purple:

Call me on a Saturday afternoon, and I'm likely to be returning something. . . . Being a serial returner requires effort. It's imperative to remember each store's return policy and the date that you bought something. I have a little accordion file that I keep all my receipts in, separated by cash and credit-card purchases. I also like using store cards because I don't have to worry about charging up my other credit cards, plus I get incentives, coupons, and gift certificates. At the end of each month, the receipts go into a separate monthly envelope and are filed into a bigger one for the year. It's a lot of work, but because I return so much stuff, it's the only way!

A woman in her midforties, with four young kids, confessed to me: "I leave the tags on everything, because I'm so indecisive I know I can change my mind when I get home. I give a purchase the chance to hold its own in the closet. If, after a week or two, it looks weak, or I come to my senses, back it goes. I *love* any store with a lenient return policy." A friend of hers admitted that she would be a Bring-Back Queen if she could only get her act together: "I have a closetful of things that don't fit but I was too lazy to return them. I just took two pairs of ski pants (mine) and a pair of madras shorts (my son's) to Goodwill, all with the tags still on." I suggested warily to Linda that she might qualify as a Bring-Back Queen, citing her frequent shuttles to the Magnificent Mile. While I've met many Bring-Back Queens who revel in this indictment—they *enjoy* the life of a Bring-Back Queen—Linda took umbrage, admitting that, yes, she buys and returns "a fair amount of stuff, but not *that* much. "At worst," she conceded, "I'm a Bring-Back Princess."

The Bring-Back Queen subspecies dates back to the Ladies' Mile era, when the big department stores extended hitherto unimaginable return privileges to their customers. Your own great-grandmother may have been a Bring-Back Queen. But while the palazzos on the old Mile may have accepted your great-grandmother's returns, they didn't give her points for high character. A retail merchant complained to the *New York Times* in 1916, as debate raged over whether customers should receive full, partial, or zero credit for merchandise returned to a store: "There are certain kinds of women . . . who are selfish, those who are very careless, and those who have too much time and money for their own good."

That Venusians make returns with far greater frequency than Martians is undisputed. Women *buy* a great deal more, so of course they return more. But on a percentage basis they return more, too. A survey of online buyers indicates that women return at twice the rate of men. Martians, it is said, are more likely to be satisfied when something is, if not particularly good, then "good enough," according to an e-commerce analyst who has run return-rate numbers. And there's another reason men are chary about returning: the wimp factor. Several years ago focus group sessions elicited testimony that a typical Martian, having cranked up sufficient metabolic output to drag himself to a store in the first place, finds it insurmountably challenging to make a trip back. Many in the discussion groups allowed as to how they, or Martians they knew, wished to avoid any "conflict" at the returns desk. Thus do those Martians take the path of least resistance: they throw what should be returned into the recesses of a closet and turn the page.* If you happen to be such a man, bear in mind that retailers view returns as a necessary and ultimately *profitable* evil of doing business. A professor at the Texas Tech business school says that the grace with which a store handles returns "can be the difference between turning a profit and losing money," since "it takes five times as much investment to bring a new customer into the store than it does to deal with an unhappy customer." Given that only a fraction of returns are fraudulent, he says, "[a retailer] has to think, 'Do I want to damage this relationship or not?'"

Solid evidence points to stay-at-home moms as the most hyperactive BBQs, no doubt owing to the fact that they continuously commute between home and mall. The more trips, the more Buys. The more Buys, the more regretted or ill-advised Buys. But how to explain why so many older, post-child-raising Venusians buy if only to return? An aversion to changing rooms, many women tell me. Why suffer the claustrophobia of an airless cube, why mess up your hair, when in the comfort of your own home you can discover that something doesn't fit, doesn't look good, you really don't need it, really can't afford it, or that the buttons are already hanging by gossamer threads?

Bring-Back Queens for a Day

Bring-Back Queens for a Day are customers who buy something *knowing* they'll return it in a day or two. Strictly speaking, this isn't "returning" at

---

*College students in general, male and female, are also extremely wimpy about returning stuff, and for essentially the same reasons as the mature Martian: timidity and slothfulness.

all, it's "borrowing," and the cynic might see it as little more than short-term shoplifting. A Chanel bag for a big night out. A designer dress for an evening fête. (And to think, we paid *good money* for that little black dress.) Venusians, far more often than Martians, use retail stores as lending libraries, but Martians are guilty, too: a business suit for a job interview, a vest for the old tuxedo, easy come, easy go back, especially if a Martian can con his wife into returning it. Just make sure you haven't let out the waist or given the item the Jackson Pollock treatment with red wine and salad dressing. Although I can't find a great deal of statistical evidence about the male-female return-it-in-a-day split, a British study did find that the Venusian overnight borrowing rate is some four times greater than Martians'.

Gamers

For this principally but not exclusively Venusian subspecies, shopping is a sport that calls for stamina and an exuberant sense of shopping as recreation. Gamers buy into the ethos that outfoxing retailers isn't everything, it's the only thing. For the seasoned gamer, shopping is akin to Dungeons and Dragons, or chess, or bridge, but better than all those games put together: the winning player scores lots of really good stuff on the cheap, then gets to boast about how clever she is.

Like fantasy sports, Buy gaming exists on a mass scale because the Internet came along to provide a playing field big enough to accommodate millions of obsessive enthusiasts. There are thousands of shopping blogs, most of them with low or no traffic, maintained by Buy gamers with an irrepressible need to pass along tips about where to get slam-dunk deals, conduct buzzer-shot negotiations, and score free throw-ins. A handful of these blogs attain critical mass, drawing in hundreds of thousands, even millions, of like-minded gamers who check in and out throughout the day. If you're a Venusian gamer whose sport is clothes shopping (by far the most popular form), you may have already bookmarked numerous "social-shopping" Internet sites. This represents more bad news for Starbucks, because this way you don't have to meet friends for coffee if you want to shoot the breeze about recent acquisitions or talk about what's hot, what's not. Retailers themselves—from Nordstrom, Sears, Gap, right down to the hippest, minimalist boutiques—are leasing space on networking destinations devoted strictly to the sport of shopping, each with a distinct personality and target customer. If you're a woman of a certain age and with rather mainstream tastes, perhaps you log on to Stylehive.com. If you're a bit younger and hipper, you go to StyleFeeder.com ("The Personal Shopping Engine"). Here you'll be introduced to a photo gallery of celebrities (on the order of Mary-Kate and Ashley) and everyday Stylefeeders, whose miniprofiles include plugs for their own blogs or employers, complete with embedded links to product pages. Here gamers' curriculum vitae read like sanitized versions of the standard Playmate of the Month bio: "Annette, a video producer in Los Angeles, CA . . . uses StyleFeeder to shop for travel gear, motorcycle clothes, and work costumes. Right now, she's picking out pretty dresses for an elegant voyage around the world, and also motorcycle gear for a trip to Vegas with her newly acquired motorcycle license. She's not sure which she'll do first, but is pretty certain she'll get around to both within the year."

Gamers live exciting lives. The stands are always full, the crowd is on its feet, and it's *always* a beautiful day to go shopping.

Homettes

If there's anything unequivocal to report about the shopping differences between Martians and Venusians, it's that Venusians have a lock on throwing home shopping parties and a near-lock on buying goods from the TV shopping networks, principally QVC and the Home Shopping Network (the latter once derided as "junk for jerks"—an unkind assessment, yes, but one passed along to me by a former exec of that network). TV shopping and in-home party selling each hauls in about $10 billion a year in sales, nearly all it of from Venusians.

As a Martian, I feel little desire to participate in either of these Buy arenas, though I confess to some curiosity about the inner workings of home shopping parties: Do partygoers buy because they really want to, or because they feel obligated to the host? Offer me fly-on-the-wall press credentials and I'd probably drop in on a shopping party or two, nibble on the cheese and crackers, and observe the social interplay. But which product party, ideally? Tupperware (plastic storage bins)? Mary Kay (cosmetics)? Million Wishes (women's apparel from the company that owns Anne Klein and Jones New York)? Southern Living at Home (pottery, decorative accessories)? Pampered Chef (bakeware, cutlery)? Temptations (Vibro Pod digital music stimulators, doggie-position support straps)?

Until such an invitation arrives, and I'm not holding my breath, all I can do is gather intelligence from a distance, my opera glasses trained on the living room bay window. From what I can tell from reading about shopping parties and asking around—Linda has attended three and bought nothing—gatherings range from a lot of fun, to incredibly depressing, to occasions that leave Venusians wrestling with issues of etiquette that strain the bonds of friendship. One day a letter turned up in Miss Manners' mailbox at the *Washington Post*:

Dear Miss Manners:

I hosted one of those home shopping parties for a group of friends and had a very good turnout. However, one thing I noticed was that a close relative of mine didn't purchase anything. Now, I know that you shouldn't feel obligated to buy anything at these functions. However, I have attended several home parties for her in the past, and I felt that it was discourteous not to support your host. Later on, a few of my girlfriends and I had a separate discussion on whether you should have to buy something at these types of parties. One girlfriend's response was that no, you shouldn't, while the other friend's reply was that you should buy at least something since the host is supplying food and drinks. With these two quite different responses, I have become confused. . . . What do you think should be the correct courtesy . . . ?

Miss Manners' trenchant reply:

Miss Manners asks you to bear in mind that when you give such a gathering, you should be acting as a saleswoman who incidentally serves refreshments, not a social hostess who incidentally embarrasses her guests into spending money they would not otherwise spend. A respectable salesperson . . . does not bludgeon potential customers into paying for things they do not want. A reason not to invite this relative to a shopping party would be that she is not interested in the kind of merchandise you are selling. For the same reason, and not to punish her, you needn't attend hers. . . . Wouldn't you both come out just as far ahead, and not have your houses full of unwanted clutter, if you saw each other over a (freely offered) cup of tea?

Given the apparent risk to long-standing friendship and the thorny ethical conundrums shopping parties elicit, why do Venusians, in growing numbers, host or attend these events? Well, as far as the hostess is concerned, party-giving is an opportunity to be in business for herself. She sets her own hours and invests little more capital than it takes to buy munchies at Sam's Club. Hosting a party, whatever the risks to friendship, beats schlepping one's wares door to door: the seller gets to stay home, while the customers come knocking on hers.

Friends of Faux

In 2007 a conflicted home partygoer e-mailed an editor at *Kiplinger's*: "I attended a home-shopping party recently where the hostess was selling fashion accessories that were knockoffs of designs by Tiffany and Gucci (she boasted of it). I was apparently the only guest who felt uneasy about this. I didn't say anything, but I didn't buy. The hostess, a friend, seemed slightly miffed. Should I tell her of my qualms?"

The editor's advice was light on empathy, heavy on geopolitical import: "Consider sending a tactful note that seeks to educate rather than scold. Tell her how lovely the goods were, but say that you're troubled by the damage done to the U.S. and other developed nations by the global epidemic of intellectual-property theft, including patents and copyrighted designs, books, music, movies and the like."

The selling and buying of counterfeit goods is, as everyone knows by now, a colossal business perhaps amounting to $600 billion in sales worldwide. No reliable figures exist as to how much of the stuff is bought by women (heavy buyers of pirated handbags, sunglasses, and perfumes), how much by men (electronic gadgets, video games, and software). But for reasons not entirely fair, there's more heated discussion about Venusians who purchase fake goods than Martians.

One afternoon I survived a vivid crash course in counterfeit buying courtesy of Susan Scafidi, a law professor who lives in New York City. Scafidi specializes in intellectual property issues, with a particular interest in fashion and design. We met for lunch in SoHo, where Scafidi straightaway pulled a copy of *Women's Wear Daily* from her authentic designer handbag and held up an ad for a Skecher shoe that looked every bit like a Croc. She then briefed me on a) how wide the world of piracy stretches, b) why copycatting is not only wrong on its face, it really *does* line the pockets of no-goodniks—mobsters, terrorists, and other miscreants, c) how it encourages child labor, and d) how it causes harm not only to big-name designers, who have the means to defend themselves, but more damagingly to up-and-coming designers who are routinely ripped off by big-name designers—who themselves cry foul over the global counterfeit racket.

After lunch Scafidi and I walked a few blocks over to Canal Street, which is to New York's illicit marketplace what Madison Avenue is to the city's legitimate, superpremium market. Dante would have had a field day shopping on Canal Street. After snaking through throngs gathered around street sellers and storefronts stocked with counterfeit everything, Scafidi and I entered an unmarked door and climbed the stairs of a creepy building to a floor of locked, makeshift rooms whose plywood walls were festooned with ersatz designer bags: Chanel, Prada, Coach, nothing but the best. Even an untrained eye like mine could tell that some of these bags were comically fake: crappy plastic, not even crappy leather, with misspelled logos glued on with mucus. Other bags were passable fakes. A "Chanel" bag, for example, looked, felt, and smelled real, to me anyway, but Scafidi pointed out that the authentic version sports a vivid pink lining, not a black one, a detail likely lost on nearly everyone except, paradoxically, the most *inconspicuous* consumers: those who "take inner pride in the fact that their bag is the real thing, even if only a few cognoscenti know [it]," in the words of journalist John Seabrook. Some of the bags, though, were truly masterful counterfeits, right down to the microscopic details engraved on the hardware.

Anyway, calamity struck right then and there. In a move that ranks among the dumbest in a lifetime of klutzy moves, I made the mistake of pulling out a small notebook to record what Scafidi was telling me about the nuances of faked goods. In an instant we were confronted by a diminutive Asian woman, who reached for her cell phone and ordered us back down the darkened stairs. By the time Scafidi and I hit the street, vendors and what I presumed to be lookouts were all snapping open *their* cell phones, in the kind of synchronicity of a wave fans execute at a football game. The word was out: keep your eye on these two. Maybe we were cops—New York City police claim to issue thousands of summonses during crackdowns and mount the occasional, highly publicized raid (not that it makes a dent). Or maybe we were undercover Vuitton dicks. Whatever we were, we weren't part of the familiar swarm off the tour buses that stop at Canal Street so that tourists from Dubuque, Dublin, Barcelona, Hamburg, or wherever can make frenzied ten-minute sweeps of the stalls and plywood showrooms.

My time with Scafidi was memorable and instructive. In addition to that firsthand look, I came away with a typology of those who patronize the murky world of the counterfeit Buy:

- **The Unrepentant:** You know who you are—a counterfeit maven and proud of it. You buy fake, you boast that you buy fake, you make a day of it shopping for fake.

- **Hapless Dupes:** You're not complicit, you're merely innocent victims of faux. Linda, for instance, recently spotted a pair of sunglasses—a fancy brand called Blinde—at a store here in Chicago. The eyewear was ridiculously expensive ($250), so Linda passed, admirably but regretfully. Later that day, however, she found what looked to be the very same pair on eBay, offered by a seller with a reassuringly high shooting-star rating. Price: $60. So she bought the sunglasses, which arrived promptly and as promised: squeaky clean, new, and nestled in an embossed Blinde eyeglass case. The only thing fishy was the price. So, who knows? The sunglasses might be genuine: overstocks, maybe, or goods that fell off the back of a truck. Or, sure, they might be fake, right down to the tiny brand markings on the frames. Linda, who disdains buying counterfeit stuff in the belief that a) it's unethical and b) it benefits the no-goodniks, remains mildly troubled yet pleased that she copped a great deal.

- **Aiders-and-Abettors:** You take comfort that you're not buying *counterfeits* exactly, you're buying aboveboard goods that are virtually identical to the real thing. For designers and retailers, knockoffs are routine business. A women's clothing designer told the *New York Times*: "If I see something on Style.com, all I have to do is e-mail the picture to my factory and say, 'I want something similar, or a silhouette made just like this.'" A factory in India will have this designer's knockoffs in stores way before the products that inspired them make it to the shelves. Now and then there are dustups. Coach sued Target several years ago for selling alleged facsimiles of Coach bags or what might have been "gray goods": legitimate brand-name products that flow freely through beyond-the-mainstream distribution channels and wind up on retailers' shelves, then on yours.

The buyer who aids and abets by buying close facsimiles generally buys without a guilty conscience. It's plain those aren't *VLs* scattered all over that

Vuittonesque bag selling for $29.95, they're *ULs*. And so what if that wrap dress is Diane von Furstenberg–*ish*? It's one-fifth the price! While some countries, France in particular, have stringent trademark laws that protect product design, we in the United States are lax about such issues.* We're mainly concerned about protecting registered logos. Something called the Design Piracy Prohibition Act has been languishing in Congress for a few years. If enacted, it would rein in some of the more blatant instances of knocking off but would do little to eradicate it. Nor would it protect you when you go looking online for a deal. In the meantime, online sellers—eBay in particular—are fending off lawsuits filed by luxury brands that demand that sellers do a better job of policing the bad guys. In 2008 the global docket sagged under such cases. Although eBay generally prevailed, it didn't always. A U.S. court ruled against Tiffany's claim; a Belgian court dismissed one brought by L'Oréal. In France, though, a French court ordered eBay to pay $61 million to luxury goods company LVMH Moët Hennessy Louis Vuitton, which claimed that 90 percent of Vuitton bags and Dior fragrances sold on eBay were phony. Whatever the legal outcome of these ongoing skirmishes, the brands score winning points in the court of public awareness. Purists now think twice about where to buy. The Aiders-and-Abettors don't care.

Martian Subspecies

Bulk Heads and Repeat Offenders

Beyond the basic male shopping types described early on—grab-and-goers and wait-and-whiners—there are additional male subspecies on my homegrown list. The first two, Bulk Heads and Repeat Offenders, close cousins, came to my attention shortly after I'd started work at Lands' End. When we analyzed past-purchase history, we saw that a significant number of Martian buyers fell into these two related categories. Bulk Heads are Martians who, when they do buy something, buy multiples of it so they won't have to shop again anytime soon. Daniel Gilbert, who wrote the best-selling *Stumbling on Happiness,* is a confessed Bulk Head, though

---

*A French court found against Ralph Lauren some years ago, after Yves Saint Laurent accused him of taking liberties with a Saint Laurent black tuxedo dress. Lauren, in turn, was awarded damages against Yves Saint Laurent's chairman, who'd made disparaging comments about him in *Women's Wear Daily.* It's a jungle out there.

he bulks up at Costco, not Lands' End. There, Gilbert says, he buys five to ten pairs of cargo pants at a time, in different colors. "My life is full of decisions, and any time I can eliminate one, I feel that I have scored a victory," he notes.

At Lands' End, we saw a great deal of evidence that Martians are recidivistic, i.e., Repeat Offenders. These male buyers order the same thing(s) over and over. They're "replacement," not venturesome, buyers, which explains why so many Martians look the same day after day, year after year: button-down dress shirts for work (blue or white); polo shirts for the weekend (various colors—here Repeat Offenders can let 'er rip); too-big-in-the-seat khakis for work that, when hopelessly frayed or spotted, are gradually relegated to the weekend wardrobe.

Martians have their reasons for buying the same things ad nauseum. The obvious one is that buying the same thing time and again is fast and easy, leaving the Repeat Offender more time to nap. Another reason, noted earlier, is that opting for the known quantity minimizes the chance that a purchase may have to be returned to the store. A third reason—which I'm sure has been tested extensively but I'll go with my gut here—is that Martians repeatedly buy the same things to avoid an anguishing bout of buyer's regret or "post-purchase dissonance," to use the technical term. Martians, their egos on the line, do not like to be wrong. The phrases "I told you so" and "You paid *what*?" do not sweet music make in a Martian's ear.

Collectors

Absent any hard data that pin down the degree to which Martians and Venusians collect stuff, I'm nonetheless putting this subspecies in the male column. Women, too, amass collectibles, though they don't make nearly the same public display men do. This might have something to do (again) with the fragile Martian ego—in this case the need for "self-enhancement," which Russell Belk and others contend is one of the principal reasons people collect in the first place. Belk writes: "Many . . . who are inhibited and uncomfortable in social interaction, surround themselves with favored objects upon which they project humanlike qualities. [They] find comfort in being with them and regard them as friends." Boy, do they. As we all know, grown men find comfort in collecting and displaying baseball cards, cigar labels, stamp albums, scorecards, Martini shakers, logo'd golf balls. Robert Gottlieb, the renowned book publisher who went on to edit *The New Yorker*, famously collects women's purses, unabashedly so. In the late 1980s, Gottlieb featured part of his collection in a sumptuous coffee-table book, *A Certain Style: The Art of the Plastic Handbag, 1949–59*. Carolyn See reviewed the book in the *Washington Post*, calling it "a solemn, serious gift book . . . that [takes] the concept of 'silly' way on out to the cosmic level." That's hitting below the belt, in my view. So what if a man amasses five hundred plastic purses? To each his own favored object of projection.

A brief, graceful rumination on why we collect stuff is William Davies King's *Collections of Nothing*. By "nothing," King means nothing particularly exotic or valuable. He collects labels of tuna fish cans, boasting nearly fifty, from Albertson's Solid White to Von's Chunk Light, with Bumble Bee Prime Fillet Solid White Albacore in Water and Trader Joe's Chunk Light in Water, Salt Added, in between. King also collects soup cans and water bottles. He collects empty Cheez-It boxes and old dictionaries. His reflections on *why* he collects these things are wry and moving. "The widely shared impulse to collect," he says, "comes partly from a wound we feel deep inside this richest, most materialistic of all societies, and partly from a wound that many of us feel in our personal histories. Collecting may not be the most direct means of healing those wounds, but it serves well enough."

Action Figures

Even though men may stand tall when unveiling their collections of purses or tuna labels, when actually shopping they usually wear a mask of indifference or feign childish ineptitude, appealing to mommy-wives to step in and bail them out. What gives with Martians, anyway? Craig Thompson has proposed that myth-making is at work here, which was another reason—the uncooling of Starbucks was the first—I met with him at that Madison coffee shop. Back in 2004, Thompson and Douglas B. Holt published an article called "Man-of-Action Heroes: The Pursuit of Masculinity in Everyday Consumption." They had spent a couple of years interviewing men of varying ages, and their paper focuses on two particular men who use consumption in different ways but for similar ends. Each reflects the tension Thompson and Holt say exists in the male culture—the need to cultivate the image of breadwinner versus the image of rebel.

Robert is a middle-aged, successful dentist—competitive, macho, athletic, politically conservative, a Martian who devotes a huge amount of time and money to auto racing and collecting hockey cards. The other study subject, Donny, is also middle-aged, but working class, semiskilled, and overweight. Given Donny's blue-collar background, the paper proposes, it would be reasonable to assume that he bowls or hunts or fishes and that the things he buys would likely be gear appropriate to those pastimes. But Donny's key material possession is a sewing machine. He buys fabric and spends his free time making or altering clothing for his ex-wife and his girlfriend. He prides himself on the ability to walk into a women's clothing shop and know how this top will look with that skirt—"not that I'm gay or anything," he makes sure to add.

Thompson and Holt argue that Robert and Donny represent two sides of the Martian coin. The consumption choices they make are rooted not in any desire to "prove" their masculinity, nor to "compensate" for male insecurity. (You know the rap, that a man in a red Corvette has some pathetic need to signal that he's really *not* hung like a hamster, or that dudes hang out at ESPN Zone because it's a refuge where they can escape their otherwise neutered workaday lives.) Thompson argues that it's not that simple. A man's consumption impulses are not as compensatory as we like to think. What many men are trying to do, he asserts, is balance their role as respectable breadwinner with a form of expressed "rebellion" that comes in many forms: they race cars, sew women's pants suits, or collect plastic women's purses, for that matter. Rebellion is rebellion. In these ways, Martians cultivate what Thompson and Holt refer to as a "man-of-action" image. They want to be seen as responsible and rational, yes, but at the same time strive to be creative, potent, youthful, unconventional, danger-defying. So they buy time at baseball fantasy camps, day-trade the market, spend small fortunes on rare trading cards, scout for the new Tom Ford fragrance, help their women shop for skirts—all in an effort to avoid giving the impression they're conformist, ineffectual, or dull.

Metrosexuals

Back in 2003 a "new" man—not really new, just newly named—burst onto the scene, his arrival announced in the pages of a slender blue book titled *The Metrosexual Guide to Style: A Handbook for the Modern Man.* Author Michael Flocker enjoyed a rush of attention, no matter that he coined neither the metrosexual term nor the concept. A Brit named Mark

Simpson came up with the idea a decade before. *The Metrosexual* provided consumption and etiquette tips for a male subspecies Flocker defined in four-part harmony: he was "a twenty-first century trendsetter"; he was "a straight, urban man with heightened aesthetic sense"; he was "a man who spends time and money on appearance and shopping"; and he was "a man willing to embrace his feminine side." The book made for a swell gift item. Some people gave it to guys who displayed discomfiting signs of sartorial and epicurean vanity, that is, men who shopped too much. Others gave it as a none-too-subtle hint to uncouth grab-and-goers or wait-and-whiners who'd rather doze off to ESPN than sweat over the right wine for a dinner party.

Frankly, I never understood why the metrosexual generated so much interest. Call them what you will, men with "metrosexual" leanings had been doing the wine, cooking, and fashion thing for decades by the time the book came out. I knew a lot of them. Today they're paunchy, bald, and so creaky with age they have trouble reaching down to slide a shoehorn into their Italian loafers (which, if you saw *Frost/Nixon*, you know the disgraced president regarded as "effeminate"). The middle-aged Martians I'm talking about are veterans of the "Peacock Revolution" of the sixties. They made peace with their inner "Sensitive Man" in the seventies. They curled up with Robert Bly and Robert Parker in the eighties and nineties. And today they have no trouble buying into the idea that it's entirely hairy-chested to have facials, pedicures, and their backs waxed once a month.

But just as they're not particularly "new," they're also not entirely comfortable veering too close to Venusian consumption patterns. In 2008, researchers Linda Tuncay and Cele Otnes went shopping with over a dozen heterosexual men in their twenties and thirties and found that their informants (all from New York or Chicago) were to varying degrees "identity vulnerable." That is, they clung to the view that shopping is culturally "perceived as a 'feminine' activity," and that a heterosexual-homosexual "boundary" exists. Fearing they would be looked on as "too gay" were they to take an avowed interest in fashion and grooming products, they used an assortment of strategies to find the right clothes and hair gels. When asking for help, their instinct was to ask women or gay men, whom they regard as more expert, and avoided seeking guidance from other straight men, not an especially "guy thing" to do.

When deciding what to purchase, some straight guys rely on "cues"—if they see lighter colored clothes in the women's department, they'll seek out dark colors in menswear. Another strategy is to hand the steering wheel over to a pro, a custom shirtmaker, for example, or a personal shopper, whose intervention takes the male shopper off the gender-vulnerability hook. And then there's the old standby strategy: surrender. Just do what your wife or girlfriend tells you to do. Surrendering keeps the peace. *Okay, okay, I'll buy teeth whitener if it'll make you happy.* Surrendering is also a sure way for a man to get out of a store in a flash. If, with Valentine's Day coming up, a saleswoman at Victoria's Secret tells a guy, "Trust me, she'll *love* this pink Flyaway babydoll, it's a hot seller," most men won't be inclined to stand there reflecting, or to reach out to feel whether the teddy has a better hand than the babydoll. They assent to the babydoll with a grunt, whip out their credit cards, then beat it.

Transgenderfication

The arrival of the metrosexual underscored acceptance of the idea that there's a trace of Venusian in every Martian buyer, and a touch of Martian in every Venusian. Or, to put it in graphic form, each of us falls somewhere on a continuum:

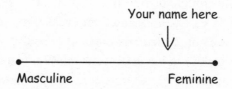

This continuum marks a change of climate. In the fifties, the difference between "gender" and "sex" was quite clear: there was no difference, at least no difference we could comfortably talk about in public. A *man* shopper (thump! thump!) was one who exhibited a set of universally accepted traits such as, you know, the manly ones: "aggressive," "competitive," "willing to take a stand." A *woman* shopper (chirp! chirp!) was "gentle," "childlike," "warm," and, you know, "likes to shop." Today, while many use the terms "gender" and "sex" interchangeably, political correctness dictate that "sex" refers to what we are biologically and "gender" refers to "norms" and social roles associated with being male or female. These days a good way to start a bar fight, especially in a college town, is to propose that *gender* ID and *genital* ID are, or worse yet *should be*, one and the same. And there's wisdom in that. To varying degrees every man/woman shops/buys with head/heart, not simply his/her sex organ. If a straight guy can learn a few tricks from a queer eye (especially if that's what it takes to score), hey, he's all ears.

The "modern woman," well, she too is now more commonly accepted as a mixed-gender breed, not a robotic shopping machine, the way we regarded her in the fifties. In a half century, say Rutgers business school professors Elizabeth C. Hirschman and Barbara B. Stern, she has gone from being a "Passive Princess" to something approaching a "Great Goddess"— willful, intelligent, and passionate, and not just about shopping. Marshal Cohen, an oft-quoted analyst at the NPD Group, a consumer research firm, sees her in a somewhat less epic but still favorable light:

- Adventurous yet Cautious
- Practical yet Indulgent
- Confident yet Seeking Acceptance
- Mature yet Youthful
- Single yet Maternal
- Educated yet Thirsty for Knowledge
- Feminine yet Corporate
- Career-Oriented yet Domesticated

Just How Male-Female Are *You*?

Having moved on from the Gender ID Stone Age, researchers set about developing simple, easy-to-administer tests to quantify just how much each of us tilts in one or the other gender direction—to what measurable degree are we feminine or masculine? Curious to determine where I personally net out, I took one of the more widely used of these instruments: namely, the Bem Sex Role Inventory (BSRI), developed thirty years ago by psychologist Sandra Bem, now at Cornell. The BSRI, according to the official test booklet, "treats femininity and masculinity as two independent dimensions rather than as two ends of a single dimension, thereby enabling a person to indicate whether she or he is *high* on both dimensions ('androgynous'), *low* on both dimensions ('undifferentiated'), or high on one dimension but low on the other (either 'feminine' or 'masculine')." So, here, give it a go yourself:

The Bem Sex-Role Inventory Test*

Following are thirty personality characteristics. Rate yourself on each, using a seven-point scale: 1 = never or almost never true; 2 = usually not true; 3 = sometimes but infrequently true; 4 = occasionally true; 5 = often true; 6 = usually true; 7 = always or almost always true.

1. Defend my own beliefs____
2. Affectionate____
3. Conscientious____
4. Independent____
5. Sympathetic____
6. Moody____
7. Assertive____
8. Sensitive to needs of others____
9. Reliable____
10. Strong personality____
11. Understanding____
12. Jealous____
13. Forceful____
14. Compassionate____
15. Truthful____
16. Have leadership abilities____
17. Eager to soothe hurt feelings____
18. Secretive____
19. Willing to take risks____
20. Warm____
21. Adaptable____
22. Dominant____
23. Tender____
24. Conceited____
25. Willing to take a stand____
26. Love children____
27. Tactful____
28. Aggressive____
29. Gentle____
30. Conventional____

Now, tote up the scores you assigned to items 1, 4, 7, 10, 13, 16, 19, 22, 25, and 28. Divide the total by 10 and you'll arrive at your raw masculinity score.

Tote up the scores you assigned to items 2, 5, 8, 11, 14, 17, 20, 23, 26, and 29. Divide by 10 and you'll have your raw femininity score.

Based on norms established by controlled testing, the median masculine score turns out to be 4.8, the median feminine score, 5.5. If your score exceeds both of those norms, consider yourself, at least as defined by this test, to be "androgynous." If your score is lower than both norms, consider your-

*Reproduced by special permission of the Publisher, Mind Garden, Inc., www.mindgarden .com, from the *Bem Sex-Role Inventory*, by Sandra Bem. Copyright 1978, 1981 by Consulting Psychologists Press, Inc. Further reproduction is prohibited without the Publisher's written consent.

self "undifferentiated"—which is not a bad thing, though it doesn't sound very interesting.

Consumer behavior researchers have conducted lots of studies to find a relationship between your BSRI score and personal shopping behavior—a tempting proposition, though conclusions reached fall way short of the sensational, witness these observations drawn from a scholarly journal:

- "High feminine" males have more unfavorable attitudes toward feminine hair spray products than do "low-or-medium" feminine males, however counterintuitive that might seem.

- Feminine gender identity correlates positively with heavy involvement in Christmas gift shopping—no reason to issue a press release on that. More interestingly, gender identity seems to be a more significant attitude shaper about Christmas shopping than is actual biological sex. For example, a "feminine" male may hit the stores on Black Friday with more gusto than, well, your run-of-the-mall, somewhat less "feminine" woman.

- Masculine males are more likely than feminine males to remember specifics of past gift giving—somewhat surprisingly, in my view. And masculine males were found to be more "object-" than "person-focused," meaning, I think, that they tend to spend more effort working through the "what" of a gift than reflecting on the "for whom" it's intended.

Gender ID tests enliven boring dinner parties when administered over dessert. But knowing that a person's masculine/feminine BSRI raw score is 6.1/3.1* neither predicts nor exposes a person's actual shopping behavior. The only way to know how someone shops is to go shopping with him or her. Lately I've been out on buying trips with men and women I'd not met before, matchmaking courtesy of a third party with a broad network of Chicago friends. I don't ask my subjects to take the BSRI, I just accompany them into stores they like to visit and beseech them not to be on their best

---

*The author's.

Buy behavior on my account. These entirely unscientific field trips tell me that men and women don't altogether conform to the "Martians buy, Venusians shop" canard. Here are two dossiers, each a profile in normal if blended Martian–Venusian behavior patterns.

John Greene: Martian with Venus Rising

I met up with Greene on the Magnificent Mile. He's African American, grew up in a middle-class household, and enjoyed an expensive education at a private high school. He's now a financial planner for a big insurance firm, clearly an up-and-comer there.

Greene had on a lavender, western-style shirt. He told me he reads *GQ* regularly and keeps up with the latest style trends. He was metrosexually well groomed and told me he visits his barber every two weeks. He knows precisely what he's after when he goes shopping. He's a hunter and not a gatherer. He explained in detail how he operates on a superstrict budget and keeps a spreadsheet with twenty-some categories on it, including food, rent, insurance, car, entertainment, and shopping. By "shopping" he really means clothing, a category to which he allocates precisely 7 percent of his disposable income. While he keeps a cap on overall spending, he imposes no limits on given items, meaning he sees nothing wrong with buying a pair of sweatpants for $400 or sunglasses for $300 if his monthly category balance permits. Unmarried though "open to it," Greene said he foresees no potential spending conflicts with his future wife, despite his spreadsheet discipline. "She'll get onboard," he said, looking me squarely in the eye.

Greene shops almost exclusively at the big department stores—Nordstrom, Macy's—where he spends more money on casual clothes than on dress shirts and suits. He's a click-on-the-calculator, cost-per-wear kind of guy. He figures the sort of shirt he's wearing today will give him good cost-per-wear. He'll wear it on weekends over the course of several years. Dress shirts last only a year or so, he says, and therefore he won't spend big bucks on them.

The reason for his department-store excursion that day was that Greene and a pal were scheduled to go on a cruise to Cozumel and he needed some "specific things." We walked over to Water Tower Place, where longtime tenant Lord & Taylor was shutting down for good. The ground floor was

283 / Martians Buy, Venusians Shop

bedecked with red CLOSE OUT! signs offering 70 percent or more off on the dribs and drabs that remained. Greene checked things out. He looked at ties—Tommy, DKNY, Kenneth Cole—noting, "Paisley is in, according to *GQ*." He especially liked one of the paisley ties reduced to just $16, but said he didn't really need it, so he didn't bite. He then stopped at the men's grooming counter, where everything was dirt cheap. He passed. "They don't have what I like—D&G cologne."

Leaving Lord & Taylor empty-handed, we walked over to the Macy's men's department, where Greene closed in on what he'd come for: a few casual shirts. He said he wanted to look "crisp" on the cruise. He stopped momentarily to look at a pair of Ralph Lauren swim trunks, blue with a white drawstring. He liked the bathing suits but again didn't bite, noting that he already had two nice pairs of trunks.

I asked him how he felt about paying a higher price for well-known brands. "Labels matter," he replied. He said he trusted the fact that brand and price are generally indicative of a product's quality. Considering a stack of Polo polo shirts in a rainbow of colors, he eventually selected a white polo with a black logo, but a few minutes later he returned it to the shelf, substituting two RL T-shirts, one white, one black. He already owned enough polo shirts, he explained, and he figured he'd be more comfortable on the cruise—and would look crisper—in T-shirts. Then, a spontaneous, unpremeditated Buy! A package of Calvin Klein boxer briefs, mixed colors, including red plaid. *Fini*. Throughout the excursion he requested no sales assistance, explaining that he prefers to do his own shopping and seeks help only when matching shirts and ties.*

Anyway, there you have him: Martian with Venus rising. He follows the trends and enjoys the act of shopping—but only for what he needs, when he needs it, never spending more than 7 percent a month on clothes.

Blagica Stefanovski: Venusian with Mars Rising

Blagica (Blah-*gee*-tsa) is in her early thirties, a self-employed entrepreneur rolling out an online marketing business. We introduced ourselves and chatted at the espresso bar outside the Nordstrom store on the Magnificent

---

*Social scientists would say Greene's service preferences comprise his system of "persuasion management."

Mile. Blagica told me that she grew up in the Detroit suburbs, where her Macedonia-born parents worked in the auto industry. Her father was "a saver" who never used credit cards and allowed his daughter only the rare indulgence. This wasn't an issue until fourth or fifth grade, she explained, at which point she developed her first brand crush. She craved a sweatshirt with "I.O.U." on the front, the 1980s teenage fad brand.*

Dad: You want I.O.U.? *You* pay for I.O.U.

So be it. Beginning in high school, Blagica worked part time in women's clothing stores, including Nine West, the shoes and handbag chain. There, she said, she developed a sharp eye for how women shop. "Basically, there are three kinds of women shoppers, and a good salesperson can tell the difference in one second," she said. "You have the woman who's not really in the store to buy—actually, she's there just to buy time. Maybe she's waiting to join up with a friend, meeting somebody for lunch, whatever. This kind of woman will do a sweep around the store, not really focusing on much, just taking things in—bored, tuned out.

"Then you have the woman who *is* searching for something specific—a pair of everyday flats, maybe. This shopper *only* focuses on flats. A good salesperson needs to zero in on this kind of customer and not be distracted by the one who's killing time [read: *sales commission*].

"Finally, you have the woman who shops in a gaggle. Gaggles come in two varieties," Blagica explained. "Some gaggles are on a mission—one gaggler needs something specific for a specific occasion. Other gaggles are just making a day of it. A good salesperson needs to focus on gaggle number one" [read: *sales commission*].

I asked to hear more about gagglenomics.

"Well, there's usually one person in the gaggle who takes the lead," Blagica said. "It's not always based on her personality or temperament, it just happens that way. Often she's an instigator who'll say something like, 'These are *so* cute,' wagging a pair of shoes in the direction of the gaggle. The others will then offer opinions. It isn't unusual for one girl to say that *she'll* buy them if the instigator passes. Or, one or several of them may trash the shoes, which generally puts an end to the discussion. Sometimes an instigator has a wingman: a member of the group whose views carry more weight than

---

*Not to be confused with another I.O.U, a contemporary brand of evangelically inspired lines of clothes whose initials stand for "Inward. Outward. Upward."—references to passages in Jeremiah, Corinthians, and John.

the others'. The instigator will look to the wingman for a thumbs-up, or the wingman will throw out pros and cons—'The heel's too high, the color's wrong.'" Blagica paused here. "This is really bad customer strategy," she said. I asked her why. "Customers should *always* discuss a purchase out of the salesperson's earshot, because a good salesperson knows how to influence the debate: 'Yes, it's a higher heel but the platform sole makes them really comfortable to walk in.'"

As for her own buying habits, Blagica struck me as a tad more Martian than Venusian. In fact, she reminded me a bit of John Greene. While she employs no spreadsheet to guide her monthly spending, she does hew to a disciplined MO. There's a reason for this. Postcollege, she said, she let her credit card balances get "out of hand." Now she was debt-free, aside from the mortgage on her condo. With a slight smile, she said that she'd become more and more like her father. Her ATM, she said, "is a secret place in my apartment" where she parks spending money.

But *unlike* John Greene, Blagica is firm about what she'll pay for what.

Everyday shoes? "A hundred dollars max."

Evening shoes? "Sixty-five dollars—don't wear them much."

Athletic shoes? "A hundred dollars—I have three or four pairs of Pumas. I *love* Pumas. On a trip to Europe I saw that everyone was wearing Pumas with everything: jeans, slacks, even with what I consider 'glamorous' outfits."

Jeans? "Today I'm wearing a pair from Gap. Cheap. For a while, I bought 7 For All Mankind jeans because they were distinctive. One hundred and thirty a pair. Now everybody seems to have knocked them off, so I don't buy them anymore."

Finally, off we went to buy. It was clear that Blagica upends the old Martian–Venusian cliché. She *doesn't* shop to shop—she shops to buy. On this day she said she needed undereye concealer, so we headed directly to Sephora, not just because the selection is bountiful or because of flashy store design and shelf lighting, but because of a little card Blagica carried in her purse. Not a credit card, it was a Sephora loyalty card, then available in certain cities and likely a test prior to a national rollout. Blagica brightened when she told me about the benefits this little card carried—free samples on her birthday and loyalty points toward free samples with every purchase.

At the makeup counter, a saleswoman extolled the benefits of a brand Blagica had never heard of. Blagica's style of persuasion management prompted her *not* to take the saleswoman's word for it. She politely asked to sample the unknown brand, but "not from a test jar already opened," she said firmly. She tried it. She liked it. She was happy with what she saw in the mirror. She bought it. The experience left her feeling good, not least because the tiny $16 jar turned out to be four bucks less than the price she'd assumed she'd have to pay when we entered the store.

Anyway, there she is: Venusian with Mars rising. She follows the trends, sort of. She likes to shop—but only for what she needs, when she needs it. She speaks up. She asks questions. She pays cash. She tests before buying, but never from an opened jar.

16

Shoptimism

Final closeout: four ways to say Good Buy

And this brings us to the unique paradox of the human condition: that man wants to persevere as does any animal or primitive organism: he is driven to the same craving to consume . . . and to enjoy continued experience.

—Ernest Becker, *Escape from Evil*

 I CHECK THE CALENDAR. SIXTY-TWO days between now and yet another Black Friday, sixty-five to Cyber Monday, ninety-six shopping days till Christmas. We're heading into what Sell Siders call the "Hard Eight," the eight most critical weeks of the year—make-or-break time. This morning Santa, undaunted by the Great Recession, sent an advance team to scope out the Magnificent Mile, where his workers will wrap strands of white lights around the trees that line the avenue. Across the country, faux villages and long-in-the-tooth suburban malls are also preparing to spruce themselves up for the holidays. Everybody's nervous-plus: customers, giant sponges, swarming algae, all braced for what forecasters say will be the least merry retail season in memory. But the show will go on as scheduled. Selling seasons wait for no Martian or Venusian to give a thumbs-up or thumbs-down, nor for any uptick in consumer confidence. Buying seasons just come and go, even in times like these.

And more than a few have come and gone since the evening I helped a

Target customer track down that Jack LaLanne power juicer with whisper-quiet motor. Or that afternoon when we watched as Linda turned left and right, trying to decide which little black dress was most age- and occasion-appropriate. Over the course of those selling and buying seasons, strangers, friends, and family members acquired an assortment of things they thought they needed or wanted and many things they neither needed *nor* wanted but bought anyway. A three-pack of men's boxers, bound for Cozumel. A jar of reasonably priced undereye concealer, plus rewards points. An elusive pair of Onitsuka Tigers, white with red and blue stripes. Ugg boots, sworn never to be acquired, then acquired anyway. An OXO turkey baster, ergonomically designed to fit the hand and pleasure the eye. Was it the in-store music that sold us on those things? A beam of halogen light precisely aimed? Were we grabbing at romance? Fending off boredom? Or did some Sell Side Svengali make us do it?

Over the course of buying seasons past, we roamed the Magnificent Mile and traveled to sundry corners of the Sell Side: a huge showcase for advanced technology systems that keep track of trillions of *ka-chings;* a campus lab where a computer monitor revealed the region of the brain that glows when threatened by a disturbing commercial; a dank hallway on Canal Street from whence we were chased back to the land of the above-board. Along the way a motley band of shoppers, snoops, merchants, marketing gurus, scholars, and scolds had their say. Many claimed insight into the why, how, what, where, and when we buy, yet none could connect all the dots. As the celebrated anthropologist Mary Douglas declared in her classic *The World of Goods:* "It is extraordinary to discover that no one knows why people want goods."

Why, then, even go to the trouble of trying?

Well, like it or not, whether you're a classic tightwad or a romantic spendthrift, shopping and buying are central to the well-being and destiny of the Consumers' Republic. Our economy, our culture, and our social order are built around the Buy. For better and worse, America *is*, on balance, what it buys: until now, gas guzzlers and McMansions and $350 sunglasses that too often we couldn't afford, and now no-name diapers and plain-vanilla gadgets that do only what they're supposed to, and at nominal cost. Our values are also reflected in *how* we choose to purchase things—as a nation we can elect to pay as we go, or play kick-the-bills-down-the-road, sometimes for months and years, sometimes for a generation or two. What's unconscionable about the latter course is that our grandchildren will be the ones to pay for our splurchases.

Mary Douglas, while stressing how important it is to understand our relationship to the material culture, resisted the conclusions of behaviorists who conclude that you and I are necessarily irrational and feckless. She held firm against puritans who deride shopping as frivolous and brushed aside the argument that we're hapless ewes herded by Sell Side shepherds. In rejecting the all-too-familiar take on the modern buyer—we're robotic, out of control, harrumph, harrumph—she argued that buying choices might be better viewed as *assertive* acts, not knee-jerk responses to advertising. Douglas proposed that the things we *don't* buy might say more about who we are, or would like to be, than the things we *do* buy. In her view the brands and products we reject are themselves declarations of self. Pink? Gag me. Tom Ford? Lah-dee-dah. Reading Douglas, I remembered something a Buy scholar had pointed out one afternoon: that when we walk down the Magnificent Mile, or amble through a lifestyle center or suburban mall, we can't help but notice the many people carrying shopping bags. So we leap to the conclusion that *everyone, everywhere, all the time*, must be shopping and buying as if there's no tomorrow. Those without shopping bags simply don't register. I sometimes think about that now as I stroll along the Magnificent Mile. I look at those who aren't carrying shopping bags (most aren't). They're consumed with other matters. They're running to and from work or en route to their dentists, accountants, marriage counselors, shrinks, many of whom maintain offices in the Loop, where Marshall Field is now Macy's (oh, bitter day!), where the Sears flagship store has no shortage of Lands' End merchandise to unload, and where there are plenty of empty storefronts.

Though I like it very much, the notion that we are what we *don't* buy doesn't cut it as a Unified Buy Theory. Over and over, as these past selling seasons attest, we violate our own resolve. Our closets, basements, and attics are crammed with things we didn't especially want in the first place. We bought them for dumb, half-baked reasons. That gray suit I bought last year: Linda has long told me that I look lousy in gray, that gray makes me even grayer than I am. Gray simply doesn't suit. But I bought the gray suit anyway. *Why?* Because a new suit, even a gray one, dressed up a blue mood one day? Or because a barbershop copy of *GQ* had planted a seed that gray was In? Or because Moe the haberdasher, having cornered me in the three-way mirror, assured me that I looked richer, thinner, younger, smarter in that *particular* shade of gray—not gray, "*slate*"—even though I knew, at some level, that Moe was just blowing smoke, that he was probably stuck with a rack of gray suits he needed to move to make room for a bright new season of merchandise.

You are what you buy, you are what you *don't* buy—enough already! There *are* no airtight Unified Buy Theories. There are, though, some final takeaways, and now that we've arrived at the closeout, it's time to lay them out. Throughout this shopping trip I've been hoarding certain receipts: memorable moments, snatches of testimony by those who altered the way I thought about the Buy going in. As I rummage through these mementos, I find yet more evidence that Buy Scolds fire without aiming. Sure, we make countless Buys deserving of scorn—impulsive, compulsive, irrational, just plain stupid and wasteful. But we also make *good* Buys that deserve to be celebrated. Memo to Buy Scolds: it isn't *that* we buy, it's *what* we buy that matters in the end. Here, then, are four categories of Buys worth making, weatherproof Buys no matter the economic climate:

Good Buy 1: Happiness
The Who-Says-You-Can't-Buy-It Buy

My hoarded receipts document back-and-forth debate over whether material goods carry any intrinsic meaning, let alone whether they can bring us happiness. The other day I found myself wandering around Filene's Basement on the Mile, surveilling shoppers who cut across social and economic lines. They rooted through racks of overstocks and tons of marked-down merchandise with big-name designer labels. I observed no enthusiasm or joy. It occurred to me that in the Age of Cheap we might be suffering from a collective affliction: Satisfaction Appreciation Deficit (SAD).

This should come as heartening news to Buy Scolds, who have long held the view that material stuff is just that: stuff. Various studies show that we're happier when, instead of loading up on trinkets and superfluous clothing, we spend our money on social interaction and life experience, both of which can deliver lasting bang for the buck. One such paper is titled "To Do or to Have? That Is the Question," by Leaf van Boven and Thomas Gilovich, of the University of Colorado and Cornell, respectively. The study weighs the value of the *experiential*—Buys "made with the primary intention of acquiring a life experience"—against the value of the *material*—Buys "made with the primary intention of acquiring . . . a tangible object." Experiential trumps material on several counts, the paper tells us:

- Experience, relative to stuff, allows for greater "positive reinterpretation." That is, we think back on the experiential more fondly.

- Experience is "more central" to one's identity.

- Experience provides greater "social value."

Here's an example: Say you finally managed to take that trip to Paris, maybe your first and last. What wound up as the most meaningful part of that trip, what made you happiest? Well, maybe those evening strolls along the Seine. Your photos show how relaxed and contented you were at the time, nestled in the warm embrace of the city. Those riverside walks were certainly more expressive of you than, say, the little black chemise you picked up on the Left Bank and which, upon your return, you discovered had a nearly identical twin hanging at H&M. And then there was that serendipitous encounter in the café, where you chatted with an amusing, outrageous couple from Sweden, she a harpist with the Gothenburg Symphony, he a photographer with a new coffee-table book, *Nous Sommes Tous Transvestites. Mon dieu!* you remember thinking as you toasted one another with a glass of sublime (if soon to be piddled out of your system) Bordeaux. You were certainly not in Paris, Texas, anymore! As for the little black chemise that's barely a year old, it's missing a button, frayed at the neckline, and you've just issued it a ticket to Goodwill.

Those who believe that it's better to buy experience and lay off stuff cite evidence generated by the new "science of happiness," as *Time* called it on a 2005 cover that featured a big yellow smiley face—not, one assumes, a Wal-Mart product placement. The *Time* story brought attention to psychologist Martin Seligman, who in his book *Authentic Happiness* warns us to think twice about taking "short cuts" on the bumpy road to bliss by ignoring social relationships in favor of overreliance on drugs, chocolate, television, spectator sports, and, yes, shopping.

So, now that we've reached the final closeout, think about it: what purchasable things or experiences make you happy? One of my saved receipts is an exercise borrowed from a paper written by Nobel Prize–winner Daniel Kahneman and four colleagues. For the next three or four weekends, keep a list of everything you do—how you spend your time and money. Your list, say the authors, might look something like this:

Attended a movie, play, concert, sporting event

Went out to eat or drink

Read a book/listened to music

Performed household chore(s)

Shopped for things I wanted (e.g., clothes, gadgets, DVDs, video games)

Shopped for things I really needed (e.g., groceries, gas, cleaning supplies)

Engaged in intimate relations (from child care to making whoopee)

Surfed the Web

Watched TV

Attended church

Exercised

Visited friends

Visited relatives

Now, using Kahneman's survey questions, rate how you felt immediately after you engaged in each of those activities, using a scale ranging from 0 ("Not at All") to 6 ("Very Much"). In other words, "I came away feeling...":

Happy (0–6)

Frustrated/annoyed (0–6)

Depressed/blue (0–6)

Hassled/pushed around (0–6)

Warm/friendly (0–6)

Angry/hostile (0–6)

Worried/anxious (0–6)

Enjoyed myself (0–6)

Tired (0–6)

After the three or four weekends, add up, then average, the "happiness/unhappiness" scores you assigned to each activity. Thenceforth, plan your weekends accordingly. If your scores indicate that you didn't particularly enjoy shopping for things you sort of wanted, well, shift your time and spending to a higher-rated activity—maybe it's playing Lexulous with Facebook friends. Never mind that some Buy Scold will see it as another step on the road to infantilization. Live a little. Play on. Upgrade your broadband if need be.

Good Buy 2: Transformation
The Further-Enhancement-of-You Buy

This next Good Buy came into focus in a roundabout way. Several selling seasons ago, when I was casting around for people to educate me about various aspects of the Buy, I asked Wharton School professor Stephen Hoch to suggest names of people who might further enlighten me. He recommended that I get in touch with John Deighton, a Harvard scholar and currently editor of the *Journal of Consumer Research*. Deighton in turn gave me a short list of additional folks to talk to, one of them anthropologist Grant McCracken, described by Deighton as something of a freethinker with a broad range of opinions on the connections between consumption and culture. Deighton chuckled when I asked him to tell me a little bit more about McCracken. "He's done a lot of teaching, but not at the moment," Deighton said. "Not enough oxygen for him." Nor enough water, I gathered. "McCracken," Deighton said, "likes to drink from a fire hose."

A conventional résumé captures the background but not the essence of Grant McCracken: PhD, University of Chicago; Visiting Scholar, Cambridge University; Senior Lecturer, Harvard Business School; Research Affiliate, MIT; author of dozens of scholarly papers and seven textbooks. What McCracken does these days is take his fire hose on the road as a consultant to corporations and think tanks. His mission, he says, "is to turn thousands of people into anthropologists"—or, to be more precise, ethnographers, cultural anthropologists who, like Margaret Mead, rely on fieldwork, not controlled experiments, to analyze beliefs and customs, not least of these how and why we consume.

A theme runs through McCracken's work: consumption is *transformative*. Consumer goods build "bridges" to our hopes and ideals. Consumer goods drive an ever-renewing western culture. Consumer goods are "instruments of change." When we buy consumer goods, McCracken asserts, we are buying "templates for the self." Sounds ponderous, but it isn't really. One of his books is titled *Big Hair: A Journey into the Transformation of Self.* The premise: "Hair matters in our culture . . . because it is a way, perhaps the most important way, women transform themselves."

How does the transformative power of hair relate to the things we buy? Venusians and Martians alike spend billons a year on shampoos, conditioners, mousses, gels, sprays, tints, teasing combs, home permanent kits, and dubious hair growth products. Buying a new 'do or going from color-me-gray to Champagne Dreams ("medium iridescent blonde" from Herbal Essences Color Me Vibrant collection) are transformation-of-self opportunities readily available at any CVS or Walgreen's. McCracken sees little wrong with availing ourselves of these products. However mundane, they are change agents. This is a decidedly upbeat view compared to what Buy Scolds see when they walk through the hair care aisle: a sea of items barely distinguishable from one another, with ungodly profit-margins built in, manufactured and marketed by male-dominated companies and their lackey ad agencies, whose mission is to spread insecurity and pit us against each other on the basis of whose hair is richer, fuller, softer, straighter, curlier, bouncier, or least likely to fly away.

On one of his visits to Chicago, McCracken joined Linda and me for dinner, a satisfyingly experiential evening of social interaction. He told us of a prior trip to town when he appeared on *Oprah* to talk about an essay he'd written. The essence of it—based on in-home, ethnographic forays—was that American families transform their living spaces through a quality McCracken calls *homeyness:* rooms that are "unpretentious," "comfortable," "welcoming," "relaxed"; warm colors on furniture, cozy fabrics, displays of family heirlooms, gifts, and crafts; "memory walls" of family photographs. Such things transform houses into homes that express the values of those who live therein. "Anyone who wants to know what's important about the things people buy shouldn't just *ask* them about it," McCracken said over dinner. "They should invite themselves into other people's homes and ask about the things best loved, the things people keep on their walls and on the mantel. Ask where those things came from, how folks came to own them, and what meaning they hold in their lives."

While McCracken twits more sober academic colleagues by proclaiming the transformative power of Big Hair and the importance of family photos on the wall, he's most often cited for introducing the so-called Diderot Effect, a key insight into the Buy's transformative power. As McCracken relates in *Culture and Consumption* (1988), the Diderot Effect derives from a famous essay by Denis Diderot, the eighteenth-century French philosopher. Titled "Regrets on Parting with My Old Dressing Gown," it tells the story of a dressing gown that had been given to Diderot. The gown set offs a chain reaction that, quicker than you can say "*Trading Spaces*," wholly transforms the philosopher's immediate surroundings, floor to ceiling. Lolling about in his elegant new threads, Diderot frets that his desk is out of sync with this finery, so he goes out and acquires a new desk. In short order, *everything* in Diderot's once comfy/shabby study is new and different: the chairs, wall hangings, bookshelf, clock.

Now, if you're a fan of *Trading Spaces* or *Extreme Makeover: Home Edition,* you may think that anybody in his right mind, even an eighteenth-century philosopher, would be ecstatic about kicking back in a spanking new, spiffed-up crib. Diderot, though, feels anything but elation. Gone is the Bohemian Philosopher Formerly Known as Diderot.

Buy Scolds, always on the lookout for a party to poop, see a dark lesson in Diderot's tale. They say Diderot preferred the *old* Diderot, and felt melancholy at his passing. Maybe he did. But what if Diderot was bloody sick and tired of the Bohemian Philosopher Formerly Known as Diderot? A new cloak could just as easily have added a bounce to his step. And the chain reaction that ensued—a vase of fresh flowers on the desk, a couple of new prints on the wall, a fresh coat of homey color on the wall—well, where's the crime in that? If a new pair of jeans begets a new pair of Onitsuka Tigers and you *like* the new you in the mirror, then I say go with it. Just make sure there's a sufficient balance on your debit card to pay for those shoes and pants, plus enough left over to get you through the month.

Good Buy 3: Self-Extension
Or, the You = You + Your Things Buy

Having granted that certain Buys can transform us—refashion our image, add homeyness to our home—it's reasonable to wonder what exactly lures us to the specific qualities projected by those transformative Buys. What attracts us, say, to a particular ivory hair clip or to a certain old photo, one that so radiates family closeness that we choose just the right frame for it, then position it prominently on the mantel? Conspicuous consumption? Hardly. Neither the inexpensive hair clip nor the framed photo is pretentious. Neither was acquired with the thought—certainly not conscious—that the hair clip was so very, oh, Ivanka Tramp, or that the framed photo evokes the Vanderbilts posed on the lawn one lazy afternoon at Newport. Fact is, that photo may well have been snapped outside a cheesy restaurant in the Wisconsin Dells.

There are those who regard the hair clip and the framed photo as *component parts of one's self-identity*. Psychologist William James was onto this back in 1890, and for all we know the insight came as he strolled the Ladies' Mile, feeling natty as hell in his favorite wool waistcoat and floppy silk bowtie. James wrote:

> a man's self is the sum total of all that he can call his, not only his body and his psychic powers, but his clothes and his house, his wife and children, his ancestors and friends, his reputation and works, his lands, and yacht and bank-account. All these things give him the same emotions. If they wax and prosper, he feels triumphant; if they dwindle and die away, he feels cast down,—not necessarily in the same degree for each thing, but in much the same way for all.

That passage was resurrected by Russell Belk in a seminal essay entitled "Possessions and the Extended Self." The article explores the intimate relationship between *having* and *being*, a conundrum that has been batted back and forth by philosophers throughout the past century, not least by Jean-Paul Sartre. Sartre, in Belk's words, maintained that "the only reason we want to have something is to enlarge our sense of self and that the only way we can know who we are is by observing what we have. In other words, having and being are distinct but inseparable."

Ergo the hair clip, the framed photograph, are extensions of we who possess them. I know, it's easy to poke fun at this idea—God help me if the sum total of *moi* is a bit of blood and flesh rounded out by an iPhone, an Audi station wagon, a bottle of Heinz ketchup, and a box of Cheerios, all of which I personally lay claim to. We've all seen "Me and My Stuff" magazine features that take a celebrity or fashion designer, or just someone famous for being famous, and profile those human beings solely on the basis of what they wear or rub into their skin:

Shampoo: Phyto
Toothpaste: Colgate Total
Sneakers: Nike Air Max
Watch: Rolex GMT-Master II
Day bag: L. L. Bean tote
Evening bag: Chanel
Underwear: Hanky Panky

Vacuous? Of course. But Belk makes a compelling case about the interdependence of having and being. In fact, he even proposes four stages of human development based on the connection between having and being: 1) as *infants* we seek to distinguish ourselves from our environment; 2) as *children* we seek to distinguish ourselves from others; 3) as *adolescents* and *adults*, we use our possessions to help "manage" our identities; and 4) as *old folks* we rely on certain possessions to maintain a sense of continuity and prepare for the end. Nearing that end, we cherish not only letters and photographs but also things we purchased over the years, thoughtfully or impulsively: jewelry, china, mementos of various kinds, even, perhaps, an old dressing gown. "Our accumulation of possessions," says Belk, thus "provides a sense of past and tells us who we are, where we have come from, and perhaps where we are going." Something to think about next time you lose a possession that had come to mean something important to you. A break-in, a house fire, your own carelessness, it doesn't matter how it occurred. The response is the same: a part of you has gone missing.

Good Buy 4: Everlastingness
The By-This-We-Shall-Be-Remembered Buy

That a Buy has the power to transform, that a Buy is a means to happiness, that a Buy becomes an extension of self, all these propositions were rattling around when, in March 2007, I came across a *New York Times* story about a multimedia artist named Rosemary Williams. A recent transplant from Brooklyn to St. Paul, Minnesota, Williams had created a sculpture she called "Wall of the Mall." The construction consisted entirely of shopping bags from each of the five hundred-plus stores at Mall of America, which still stands as the Mt. Rushmore of America's consumer culture. The *Times* piece noted that Williams didn't think of herself "as much of a shopper." Before spending months at MoA she was actually a little afraid of shopping, and her first trip to the mall had induced something akin to nausea. As for the bag sculpture, the project had run into a Sell Side obstacle: while some MoA stores were willing to hand over a free shopping bag, more than a few told Williams that store policy dictated that they could provide one only if she bought something. So Williams started buying. The mother of two young kids, she found that there were everyday things she could pick up at MoA—toothpaste, shampoo, socks. If she needed to buy other stuff to get shopping bags—jewelry, home furnishings, silk-screened T-shirts, nose rings—she decided that she would de-bag them at home, then return the goods to the stores. Thus Williams transformed herself into a Bring-Back Queen for the sake of her art.

Having never visited the Mall of America, and intrigued by the news that Williams had become so caught up in her project that she was narrating a twenty-seven-part series of podcasts ("Rosemary Goes to the Mall: One Woman's Lonely Journey Around the Mall of America"), I decided to fly to the Twin Cities and spend a day walking the corridors with her. I was curious to find out to what degree Williams might have been Diderot Effected. Did all that buying transform her in some meaningful way? And I was curious to know whether anything she'd bought at the Mall of America had become a lasting extension of her self.

Williams and I caught up with each other in front of Urban Outfitters, near the west entrance, then sat down to chat at one of the mall's three Caribou coffee shops. We could just as easily have communed at one of the two Starbucks or Gloria Jean's, at any of the three pretzel stands, five ice cream emporiums, four chocolatiers, three baked-goods shops, thirty fast-food restaurants, or, had we the stomach for it, the twenty eateries the mall directory classifies as "sit-down" or "quick serve" restaurants (from Bubba Gump Shrimp Company to Hooters to Wolfgang Puck Express). At MoA, there's no fuel shortage for local shoppers once they've parked their cars in one of the mall's 12,550 garage spaces.

Williams was in her thirties and entirely unpretentious. Also articulate and charming. Before she began her lonely journey through the Mall of

America she was, like many of us, leery about life in the Consumers' Republic but far from an anticonsumerist. While the scale of the place and the gross food choices put her off, she conceded that the sprawling mall served a few legitimate purposes. In Brooklyn there were crowded parks and busy shopping streets where families found a sense of community. It wasn't like that in and around Bloomington, Minnesota. Whatever its excesses, MoA truly served as a community gathering place. Schools take end-of-year class trips there: amusement rides, a miniature golf course, NASCAR and space simulators, easy access to Dippin' Dots and French fries, what's not to love? Companies arrange outings at MoA, where they honor long-time service and express appreciation for jobs well done. There's a wedding chapel, an aquarium, a fourteen-screen movie theater, musical performances and magic shows, and lots of places for birthday parties. On that happy front there was Club Libby Lu, a retailer whose mission was "to create a spontaneous environment that encourages girls to express their imagination and individuality." Nice thought, but on the day Williams and I wandered past Libby Lu, what imagination and individuality we observed came in the persons of two eight-year-olds who emerged from the store's Sparkle Spa crowned with identical Hannah Montana hair extensions and coated in lip gloss and body shimmer. You couldn't help but think of JonBenet. (Founded in 2000, bought by Saks, Libby Lu grew to ninety-eight stores, then went out of business in the retail whiteout of 2008.)

Williams told me that she'd grown up near Washington, D.C., solidly middle class, academically and artistically gifted. She bought her clothes at Value Village, where for cents on the dollar she thriftily pulled together "a vintage bohemian look." "I wasn't much of a shopper," she reiterated as we window-shopped MoA's twenty-eight beauty and health stores, seventeen electronics stores, thirty-seven gift stores (including three devoted to mall brand-wear such as the "Mall of America Survivor" baseball cap); seventeen jewelry stores; thirty-eight men's and women's apparel stores; twenty teen-fashion stores; and sixteen sporting goods stores. Over the course of her lonely two-and-a-half-month journey through the mall Williams had dragged her part-horrified, part-fascinated Buy self into all of them, buying when she needed to, returning items for the most part, but now and then keeping things that surprised her.

"I found myself giving in to, well, stuff that was weird, or weird-cool, to be more precise, at least for me," she said, as we maneuvered through hundreds of moms and their kids; seniors doing their daily walking thing; local high school kids on spring break; a large group of Asian teens on an international school trip and the most fashionably dressed shoppers we'd seen all day. Her eye peeled for the weird and cool, Williams bought and kept a pair of Pumas because, even when worn with an old T-shirt and jeans, they "expressed something about me." (See "Good Buy: Self-Expression.") She bought and kept a pair of Gravis sneakers—Gravis being a surfer-skateboarder-snowboarder brand marketed to buyers half her age. (See "Good Buy: Transformation.") "Even now," she said, "those shoes are fun to wear." (See "Good Buy: Happiness.") In time, rather than just grab any old item, knowing full well she'd return it, she found herself looking for the "right thing." And it was generally fun, Williams said, trying on clothes she "would never think of actually wearing." A $100 Stella McCartney yoga mat beckoned to her one day. "It was really beautiful," she remembered. "Yet, really, hundred-dollar yoga mats run counter to yoga, unless I'm mistaken." There was a gold lamé gym bag that, for an instant anyway, caught her attention, "not that I would ever wear gold lamé, and not that I even belong to a gym."

"So these things you didn't buy but were attracted to, or the things you bought and didn't return—they offered what, exactly?" I asked Williams.

She thought about that for a second. "I'd say they offered a sort of hopefulness." Aha, shoptimism! "However momentarily," she added, "the things I bought and kept turned out to be somehow enhancing."

In the final episode of her twenty-seven-part marathon podcast, Rosemary Williams wrestles with what it all meant—those months of trips to the mall, the Buys, the returned Buys, the values on display at the Mall of America. Williams concludes there are lessons good and not-so-good to be drawn from her experience. On the one hand, yes, she was "sucked in." She found herself attracted to a great many things that she never thought she needed or wanted prior to embarking on her project. She confesses that she came away feeling that she had gained a certain "permission to shop," though she doesn't say who or what had denied her such permission to begin with. She says she "became better as a shopper." She came away with a sharper eye, a greater willingness to branch out. Those months at MoA had to a degree liberated her. Even so, she lamented that many of her originally "enhancing" Buys had lost their luster over time. Having gained a few pounds, she no longer wore the $20 Dubble Bubble T-shirt, a sentimental favorite. ("As a kid I always liked Dubble Bubble because of those little cartoons inside the wrapper. The shirt was 'identity through a brand moment,' I guess you could say.") A belt loop on a briefly beloved pair of jeans ripped its stitching. Other Buys more or less dissolved after a few washings.

Near the end of the final podcast, Williams recounts a story she'd told me at Caribou Coffee. I don't exactly remember how the subject came up that day—I may have wondered whether anything she bought at the mall had wound up on her walls or mantel. Whatever the prompt, she recalls the day she and her brother traveled back east to clear out their father's home after he'd died. He had long been retired, and in his later years, after he and Williams's mother divorced, he'd become avidly interested in cooking. He loved giving dinner parties and drank a lot of wine, Williams said. Food and entertaining became the center of his life. During a renovation—Diderot Effected, quite possibly—he carved a large kitchen out of his very small house. About two-thirds of the downstairs was suddenly a kitchen, a comfortable space dominated by a marble-topped island that become a showroom for his enormous collection of equipment and gadgets, many of which, Williams said, nobody really "needs." But her father felt he *did* need them, she said.

He needed a wall-mounted rack of stainless-steel Rösle kitchen tools fit for a surgeon. He needed an asparagus cooker, "even though any fool with a pot or frying pan can do a great job with asparagus," Williams said. He needed a garlic-shaped garlic roaster, "even though anyone with a cookie sheet can roast cloves of garlic." These Buys represented, she said, "his own little world." Williams moved some of her father's world back to her own house in Minnesota—a few pieces of furniture, a clutch of kitchen gadgets. Some never quite felt at home there, she told me, but others became enmeshed in Williams's own day-to-day world. Material things have a way of doing that: they're ours, but conjoin us with those who are gone. As historian Leora Auslander has written, "The rings I never take off that belonged to my dead grandmothers provide a daily connection, as if our fingers could still touch." The saddest part of closing down her father's world, Williams said, was that her father's iPod had been stolen at the hotel he was staying in the day he died. That iPod—an everyday thing that's advertised on television and on bus shelters, fondled by hordes in gleaming stores, gifted and self-gifted by the millions—was "personalized with the music he was listening to at the time," Williams said. "It would have been a wonderful thing to have taken away."

I go back and pull out our family photo albums. Not the earliest ones that capture, in faded Kodacolor, the hula-hoopla and gigantic tailfins of the fifties, but the more recent albums, crammed with images taken over the past twenty years. Here, in as-yet unfaded print after print, is a vivid record of having *and* being, a testament to the relationship of what we buy to who we were and are: there's Ned and Katherine, grinning and wobbling on cross-country skis, parentally bestowed on a Christmas morning. There's Woody at eight weeks, a wrinkled, yelpy, uncontrollable puppy—little did we know that for $900 we'd gotten an incredible bargain. There's Ned and Katherine again, now teenagers, Ned outfitted in an existential Look of the Moment, Ray-Bans and Onitsuka Tigers, Katherine in the Ugg boots she swore she'd never buy because everybody else had them. And finally there's Linda, looking like neither a flapper nor a dominatrix, smiling brightly, dressed in one hell of a smashing little black dress.

AFTERWORD

The perfect gift

THIS SHOPPING JOURNEY IS OVER. BUT NOT SO MY HOLIDAY GIFT buying. Too many choices, too little time. I can brave the crowds on the Magnificent Mile, grabbing and going. Or, as is more likely, retreat to the blissful quietude of online picking and clicking. That will take care of the how. Now it's a matter of what and for whom.

The way we set about gifting others, and how and when we gift ourselves, has received its share of attention over the past decades. In the midnineties Cele Otnes and Richard F. Beltramini pulled together an anthology of gifting studies that provides a sampler of insights—data-rich, of course—into the American way of giving and getting:

- The reasons we bestow gifts, according to respondents: they enable us to express pleasure or show friendship (42 percent); they are means by which we obtain or bestow pleasure (27 percent); because we feel obligated to (15 percent).

- Money—not china or kitchen appliances—has become the wedding gift of choice, a development that the Romantic buyer in me takes as unwelcome news.

- We give gifts "coded" to express "positive emotions," depending on the occasion. For birthdays, housewarmings, at the end-of-year holidays, we give gifts coded "Joy." For graduations and retirements, we give gifts coded "Pride." For hospitalizations and going-away parties, we give gifts coded "Hope." And on Valentine's Day, Mother's and Father's Day—also at funerals—we give gifts coded "Affection." And, yes, on all of the above as well as other occassions, we give gifts coded (you can always tell) "Obligation."

The gifting anthology devotes a chapter to "self-gifting"—as in, *"Here, from me to me, with love and kisses!"* A box of chocolates, a dozen roses, a pair of platform pumps, a new putter. The technical term for self-gifting is "monadic gifting"—i.e., relating to "one," as opposed to "dyadic gifting," wherein two "agents" are at play. For Classic buyers, the kind who cling to the virtue of self-denial, a monadic gift not infrequently comes with strings attached: anxiety and guilt. David Glen Mick, a former marketing executive and now a consumption don at the University of Virginia, has examined the occasions and excuses that characterize monadic gifting, or "special in-dulgences," he calls them. There are "romantic" self-gifts that express how peachy we feel about ourselves at any given moment. And there are "thera-peutic" self-gifts that jack up our spirits when we're low. But some self-gifts, in my experience at least, defy explanation. Last week I gave myself a silky black turtleneck. All I can say about the circumstances surrounding this monadic gesture was this: I was hanging around a store, keeping warm as I waited for Katherine to meet up with me. I was not, as far I know, feeling blue, nor had I done anything that day or even month that begged for self-reward. Here's why I think I gave myself that shirt: It was on sale. It had a satisfying, smooth feel. I had nothing better to do at the time. And I had my credit cards with me.

The gifts we give, to others or to ourselves, add up to one enormous gift to the Sell Side. Each of us, on average, spends of a couple of thousand dol-lars a year on gifts, roughly half of it during the "Hard Eight," that is, the eight-week holiday shopping season. Many economists aren't crazy about our lumping so much spending into this short burst of buying. Doing so results in what they call "deadweight loss," a term I gleaned from the *Wall Street Journal*, which posits that the economy, you and me, too, would ben-efit if our Hard Eight spending were spread out over the year, if our buying decisions were made in a less manic way over the course of twelve months. Who needs so many superfluous picture frames, or DVDs of movies we never bothered to see when they were in theaters, or three pairs of extra socks? A business school professor told the *Journal*, "We'd be able to eke out more satisfaction from the same amount of spending." Deadweight loss notwithstanding, our Hard Eight gifting favors categories such as consumer electronics and clothing, and increasingly, gift *cards*—yet more pieces of plastic. Once considered "cold," "unimaginative," and "impersonal" expressions of affection, cards are now "super acceptable," as an American Express exec told a reporter. In our mature Consumers' Republic, it's the convenience, not the thought that counts.

The Best Gift Giver I Know

With the Hard Eight just ahead and Linda's birthday a few weeks after that, I've resolved not to give gift cards to anyone in the family. Otherwise, I'm stuck for inspiration, which is where Lisa Grunwald comes in. Lisa is a friend who lives in New York City, a talented novelist, a huge-hearted wife and mom, smart, funny, sardonic, immensely kind. As a shopper, she is deeply ambivalent. The anthropologist Mary Douglas might see Lisa as an exemplar of the consumer who is resolutely, if quietly, hostile to the need to buy the latest this or that. To a large degree, Lisa is what she *doesn't* buy. Everyday shopping leaves her cold. "This week's apples and shampoo are just going to have to be replaced by next week's apples and shampoo, and where's the fun in that?" she tells me. But there's one kind of Buy at which Lisa excels, and that's gifting.

I ask Lisa whether she gives gift cards. Yes, turns out she does, but only as birthday presents her kids give to their friends, cards exchangeable for music and books. Otherwise, when Lisa shops for gifts she says she looks for "the unexpected." Stalking the unexpected requires a lively imagination and a grasp of the quirks of one's circle of gift getters. It's "an all-year-round, any-kind-of-weather sport," she reports. "Because the interests and tastes of my friends and family vary, the hunt for great gifts takes me from clothing boutiques to electronics stores, crafts fairs to eBay." But *where* she buys takes a backseat to *what* she buys. "I would like to think that if the presents I purchase are all laid out on a table, unwrapped, the people for whom they were intended would know instantly which presents were theirs."

Lisa uncannily reflects what experts say are the keys to gift-giving prowess. Russell Belk, the professor who urged his colleagues to give up their dog-food research, says that a quintessential gift satisfies six criteria, which together confirm that Lisa doesn't just give *good* gift, she gives perfect gift:

1. *The perfect gift requires us to make an "extraordinary sacrifice."* By "sacrifice," Belk doesn't mean that we need to pawn our departed mother's

handmade quilts to help pay for the $7,000 doghouse with an Italian leather armchair (Neiman Marcus offered one in a recent Christmas gift catalog). "Sacrifice" needn't call for *financial* sacrifice. In Lisa's case, sacrifice comes when she puts aside a challenging section of the novel she's writing to make time to explore an antiques barn, where she once found a 1940s telephone for her daughter, a thoroughly modern adolescent who finds movies and Broadway musicals of that period irresistible.

2. *The giver of a perfect gift wishes "solely to please the recipient."* The perfect gift isn't one that begs for reciprocation or proclaims that you're one hell of a big-time spender. The perfect gift, Belk says, is about the recipient, not about you. Lisa gets that. One year she came upon a mourning locket offered on eBay. There was an "H" engraved on it. Lisa's stepmother's late beloved dog was named Harry. Lisa bought the piece, placed a picture of Harry inside, and gave it to her stepmother on Christmas morning.

3. *The perfect gift is "a luxury."* By "luxury," Belk doesn't mean that the perfect gift need be spattered with VLs or interlocking Cs. In this context a luxury is anything that isn't strictly a necessity. To buy and give someone a pair of underwear or a mop and a bucket is thoughtful if the recipient's in need of them. But gifts such as these don't exactly communicate that the recipient is in some way extraordinary. Lisa needs no remedial training on this point. When her husband, Stephen, was a kid, he loved a book called *Little Lefty*. Its author was Matt Christopher, and it was one of those corny, Horatio-Alger-in-spikes tales that boys love—or used to, before PlayStations came along. Lisa says that Stephen would often reminisce about *Little Lefty*, "the way an immigrant talks about the Old Country." One year she hunted down a copy of the book (I just saw one online for $1.99) and gave it to Stephen on his birthday. "He not only wept when he opened the package," Lisa tells me, "but he reread it right away, and somehow didn't find it lacking."

4. *The perfect gift is appropriate to the recipient.* All of Lisa's above-cited gifts qualify as appropriate and then some. As was the canvas tote she once bought for her friend Cathy. On the side were the words "It Is What It Is," a phrase that Cathy happens to use inveterately. What can be more appropriate than letting someone know you actually listen to what they say, right down to their asides and throwaway lines?

5. *The perfect gift is "surprising."* If surprise weren't universally appreciated, Belk says, gift wrap would never have come into being. Surprise is why we why love getting presents on days that aren't birthdays, anniversaries,

Christmas, Mother's or Father's Day, Valentine's Day, Grandparents' Day, or any of the other Sell Side–manufactured giving days. Last year Lisa's daughter Elizabeth performed in a school production of *The Sound of Music*. While such an occasion doesn't require a gift, many of us buy unsurprising bouquets for our pint-sized leading ladies and would-be prima ballerinas. Lisa didn't spring for a bunch of carnations; she bought Elizabeth a pair of glove forms. Why? "So I could give her a big hand."

6. *The perfect gift is one that the recipient desires.* Belk says that we don't have to jump through hoops to give a perfect gift. Santa didn't get to be Santa by ripping children's wish lists into shreds. The words "It's just what I always wanted!" are confirmation that you've bagged a perfect gift. For Lisa's thirteen-year-old son, Jonny, for whom "it's all technology, all the time," Lisa says, a trip to the Apple Store or Best Buy involves a double-barreled reward. "Virtually any object or piece of software we take home will delight him, and since I share his addiction to all that stuff, we can browse together, while saying, sometimes in the same breath: 'Like, how cool is *that?*' "

NOTES

Mainly to avoid the distraction of formal footnotes, I've tried to incorporate as many sources as possible—books, publications, Web sites, and the rest—into the main text. Below are additional references that relate to academic studies cited throughout the book, as well as some suggestions for further reading or Web browsing. See Selected Bibliography for full book citations.

Foreword and Prologue

On the effect artificial fragrance has on men's confidence, see S. Craig Roberts et al., "Manipulation of Body Odour Alters Men's Self-confidence and Judgments of Their Visual Attractiveness by Women," *International Journal of Cosmetic Science* 31, no. 1 (2009): 47–54.

Among the more useful standard marketing textbooks consulted: *Principles of Marketing* by Philip Kotler and Gary Armstrong; *Kellogg on Marketing*, edited by Dawn Iacobucci; and *Consumer Behavior*, by Del I. Hawkins, Roger J. Best, and Kenneth A. Coney.

References to how long customers are willing to wait at checkout lines are taken from a story in *Chain Store Age*, August 2008. (*Chain Store Age* and *Shopping Centers Today* are two of many retail trade publications that offer useful news and trend reports on the current state of the Sell Side.) Hospital emergency-room wait times reported in the *Wall Street Journal*, October 30, 2008.

For details on the customer-satisfaction study concerning changing rooms, see *Chain Store Age*, March 2007.

The Spanish government's action to fatten up store dummies was reported in *The Guardian*, January 25, 2007.

1: A View from Within

Details concerning Chicago's place in American advertising history can be found online at the Web site of the Chicago Advertising Federation: chicagoadfed.org.

Danielle Crittenden Frum's Huffington Post rant against Ikea appeared February 4, 2007. Guy Crittenden's tribute to Ikea ran as an editorial in *Solid Waste & Recycling*, February 2007.

The story about Gap's ongoing challenges appeared in the *New York Times* on January 9, 2007. The same paper had an account of the company's new design efforts on October 14, 2008.

2: Lost in Retail Space

The U. S. Bureau of Labor Statistics—bls.gov—provides a boundless supply of industry-by-industry tables that detail consumer and retail spending, including comprehensive demographic breakdowns.

3: How We Got Here

Todd Gitlin offers a superb social and cultural profile of the 1950s in his book about the tumultuous decade that followed—*The Sixties: Years of Hope, Days of Rage*. Lizabeth Cohen's *A Consumers' Republic: The Politics of Mass Consumption in Postwar America* is likewise an engagingly written history of the time, focusing on how citizenship gave way to consumership.

For a detailed study of sexual advertising content aimed at young adults, see Tom Reichert, "The Prevalence of Sexual Imagery in Ads Targeted to Young Adults," *Journal of Consumer Affairs* 37, no. 2 (2003): 403–412.

Theodore Levitt's classic *Harvard Business Review* article, "Marketing Myopia," was first published in 1960. It can be Googled and downloaded from a variety of sources. Over the years this work has been widely anthologized and praised for its articulation of how companies misjudge selling opportunities by defining themselves too narrowly and for not adjusting strategic visions when new technologies reshape the marketplace.

For recent assessments of Ernest Dichter's influence on motivation research, see Katherine Parkin, "The Sex of Food and Ernest Dichter: The Illusion of Inevitability," *Advertising & Society Review* 5 no. 2 (2004); and David Bennett, "Getting the Id to Go Shopping: Psychoanalysis, Advertising, Barbie

Dolls, and the Invention of the Consumer Unconscious," *Public Culture* 17, no. 1 (2005): 1–25.

4: Downtown

The epigraph for this chapter is from Elaine S. Abelson's *When Ladies Go A-Thieving: Middle-Class Shoplifters in the Victorian Department Store.*

James Woods's references to stream of consciousness are drawn from his collection *The Irresponsible Self: On Laughter and the Novel.*

Statistics relating to U.S. shoplifting and Organized Retail Crime were drawn from *Chain Store Age*, December 2007, and from annual FBI data.

Additional information on the history of the Ladies' Mile can be found at Tom Fletcher's New York architecture Web site: nyc-architecture.com.

5: Midtown

The epigraph concerning the demographic marketing goals of Nair was quoted in the *New York Times*, September 14, 2004.

For more insight into the relationship between marketing and ethnic identity, see Mark S. Rosenbaum and Detra Y. Montoya, "Am I Welcome Here? Exploring How Ethnic Consumers Assess Their Place Identity," *Journal of Business Research* 60, no. 3 (2007): 206–214.

For details concerning current gay and lesbian brand preferences, see "Highlights from 2008 Prime Access/PlanetOut Gay and Lesbian Consumer Study," available at primeaccess.net/c2_gpr.php.

Abraham Maslow's thoughts on the relationship between the pyramid of needs and the American Dream can be found in *The Maslow Business Reader*, edited by Maslow and Deborah C. Stephens.

For details on the study linking thin fashion models to one's perception of self-esteem, see Dirk Smeesters and Naomi Mandel, "Positive and Negative Media Image Effects on the Self," *Journal of Consumer Research* 32, no. 4 (2006): 576–582.

6: Brain Wave

For the full findings of the shopping-bag study, see Gerard Prendergast et al., "Consumer Perceptions of Shopping Bags," *Marketing Intelligence & Planning* 19, no. 7 (2001): 475–482.

For insights into the methodology of qualitative research—specifically the "shopping with customers" approach—see Tina M. Lowrey, Cele C. Otnes, and Mary Ann McGrath, "Shopping with Consumers: Reflections and Innovations," *Qualitative Market Research* 8, no. 2 (2005): 176–188.

For a psychological overview of consumer research, see Itamar Simonson et al., "Consumer Research: In Search of Identity," *Annual Review of Psychology* 52 (2001): 249–275.

Advances in Behavioral Economics, an anthology edited by Colin F. Camerer, George Loewenstein, and Matthew Rabin, is a valuable academic resource. For general readers, the first chapter, "Behavioral Economics: Past, Present, and Future," by Camerer and Loewenstein, is of particular interest. So, too, chapter 3, "Mental Accounting Matters" by Richard H. Thaler.

The *Forbes* cover story "In Search of the Buy Button," which exemplifies the gee-whiz interest we take in the potentials and perils of neuromarketing, was published September 1, 2003, and is available on the magazine's online archives.

For the fascinating and widely cited study that explores the compelling attraction of neuroscience and why so many of us defer to its purported findings, see Deena Skolnick Weisberg et al., "The Seductive Allure of Neuroscience Explanations," *Journal of Cognitive Neuroscience* 20, no. 3 (2008): 470–477.

7: Bombarded

Survey results relating to customer perceptions of pharmaceutical advertising were drawn from a 2003 presentation prepared by Linda F. Golodner, president of the National Consumers League.

For a study on how negative attitudes toward advertising take root, see Peter R. Darke and Robin J. B. Ritchie, "The Defensive Consumer: Advertising Deception, Defensive Processing, and Distrust," *Journal of Marketing Research* 44, no. 1 (2007): 114–127.

Adbusters.org is an unusually lively, well-designed Web site that offers access to the eponymous magazine, features videos and anticonsumer blogs, and hosts an online shop where culture-jammers can "unswoosh" via the cathartic purchase of Adbusters' proprietary Black Spot sneakers.

For comprehensive details concerning Trix the Rabbit's mythological lineage, see Thomas Green, "Tricksters and the Marketing of Breakfast Cereals," *The Journal of Popular Culture* 40, no. 1 (2007): 49–68.

For the study on the questionable appeal of one's own morphed facial features, see "Can You See Yourself Using This Brand?" The work was conducted by Ronald J. Faber, Brittany Duff, and Yulia Lutchyn. References in the text were taken from a draft version the authors had prepared for a 2003 conference at the University of Minnesota.

8: You

The epigraph is a quote that appeared in a *New York Times* article: "Brands for the Chattering Masses," December 17, 2006.

Randall Rothenberg's astute essay on the course of twentieth-century advertising was part of *Advertising Age's* multiedition commemoration of what it aptly called "The Advertising Century." An online version of the 1999 project, including lists of influential ad campaigns, jingles, slogans, along with other Madison Avenue nostalgia, is available at adage.com/century.

For more on the "creepiness factor" and thoroughgoing discussion of a full range of online privacy issues, visit truste.org.

9: Poor Ewe

For further insights into aspects of antibranding ideology, see Douglas B. Holt, "Why Do Brands Cause Trouble? A Dialectical Theory of Consumer Culture and Branding," *Journal of Consumer Research* 29, no. 1 (2002): 70–90.

James Twitchell's oft-cited essay "Two Cheers for Materialism" was originally published in *The Wilson Quarterly* 23, no. 2 (1999): 16–26.

For a fuller discussion on consumption norms and their impact on teenage self-esteem, see David B. Wooten, "Ridicule and Consumer Socialization among Adolescents," *Journal of Consumer Research* 33, no. 2 (2006): 188–198.

10: You Are What You Buy

"Brand Community," the pioneering paper by Albert Muniz Jr. and Thomas C. O'Guinn, was originally published in the *Journal of Consumer Research* 27, no. 4 (2001): 412–432.

Saatchi & Saatchi's Kevin Roberts's disquisition on "lovemarks" were offered at a Leadership Lecture he presented at the University of Pennsylvania's Wharton School of Business in spring 2008.

The American Girl study—as yet unpublished—was conducted by Nina Diamond, Robert Kozinets, John Sherry, Albert Muniz, Stefania Borghini, and Mary Ann McGrath. It was presented at the Society for Applied Anthropology conference in Dallas in 2004.

For more on Craig Thompson's interviews with disenchanted Starbucks customers, see Craig J. Thompson and Zeynep Arsel, "The Starbucks Brandscape and Consumers' (Anticorporate) Experiences of Globalization," *Journal of Consumer Research* 31, no. 3 (2004): 631–642.

For further details on how consumers redefine and uncool brands, see Douglas B. Holt, "Why Do Brands Cause Trouble?," *Journal of Consumer Research* 29, no. 1 (2002): 70–90.

11: You Are *Why* You Buy

The epigraph is drawn from the work discussed later in this chapter: T. J. Jackson Lears, "From Salvation To Self-Realization: Advertising and the Therapeutic Roots of the Consumer Culture, 1880–1930," *Advertising & Society Review* 1, no. 1 (2000). It originally appeared in Richard Wrightman Fox and T.J. Jackson Lears, eds., *In the Culture of Consumption: Critical Essays in American History, 1880–1980* (New York: Pantheon, 1983), 6–17.

The footnote (page 184) about how exposure to the Apple brand breeds a sense of creativity is from a study by Gráinne M. Fitzsimons, Tanya L. Chartrand, and Gavan J. Fitzsimons, "Automatic Effects of Brand Exposure on Motivated Behavior: How Apple Makes You 'Think Different'," *Journal of Consumer Research* 35, no. 1 (2008): 21–35.

For a discussion of status symbols through the ages, see Himadri Roy Chaudhuri and Sitanath Majumdar, "Of Diamonds and Desires: Understanding Conspicuous Consumption from a Contemporary Marketing Perspective," *Academy of Marketing Science Review* no. 11 (2006): 1.

12: The Classic Buyer

For reflections on prestige-related reasons for why we buy (page 200), see Franck Vigneron and Lester W. Johnson, "A Review and a Conceptual Framework of Prestige-Seeking Consumer," *Academy of Marketing Science Review* 9, no. 1 (1999): 1–15.

For more on how supermarkets deploy anchor-based promotions, see Brian Wansink, Robert J. Kent, and Stephen J. Hoch, "An Anchoring and Adjustment Model for Purchase Quantity Decisions," *Journal of Marketing Research* 35 (1998): 71–81.

For details on the relationship between syllable count and our ability to recall prices, see Marc Vanhuele, Gilles Laurent, and Xavier Dreze, "Consumers' Immediate Memory for Prices," *Journal of Consumer Research* 33, no. 2 (2006): 163–172.

The *Business Week* article that described promotional giveaways in the pediatric ward, titled "Hey Kid, Buy This," was reported by David Leonhardt and Kathleen Kerwin and published in the magazine's June 30, 1997, issue.

For more on how coupons can stigmatize, see Jennifer J. Argo and Kelley J. Main, "Stigma by Association in Coupon Redemption: Looking Cheap Because of Others," *Journal of Consumer Research* 35, no. 4 (2008): 559–571.

13: The Romantic Buyer

The epigraph, Gertrude Stein's quote, was taken from Ann Douglas's *Terrible Honesty: Mongrel Manhattan in the 1920s* (New York: Farrar Straus & Giroux, 1995).

For more on consumption as an expression of desire, see Russell W. Belk, Güliz Ger, and Søren Askegaard, "Metaphors of Consumer Desire," *Advances in Consumer Research* 23 (1996): 368–373.

The full text of Russell Belk's "dog-food address" to the Association for Consumer Research was published in *Advances in Consumer Research* 14, no. 1 (1987): 1–4.

Belk's comparison of consumption to the excitement felt on Christmas morning is taken from Russell W. Belk, Güliz Ger, and Søren Askegaard, "The Fire of Desire: A Multisited Inquiry into Consumer Passion," *Journal of Consumer Research* 30, no. 3 (2004): 326–351.

For more on how piped-in music may influence the time we spend in stores, see Robert F. Yalch and Eric R. Spangenberg, "The Effects of Music in a Retail Setting on Real and Perceived Shopping Times," *Journal of Business Research* 49, no. 2 (2000): 139–147.

14: The Stop-Me-Before-I-Buy-Again Buyer

For the landmark paper that established the gold-standard screener for compulsive shopping, see Ronald J. Faber and Thomas C. O'Guinn, "A Clinical

Screener for Compulsive Buying," *The Journal of Consumer Research* 19, no. 3 (1992): 459–469.

For more details about how impulsive buying correlates with age and other variables, see Jacqueline J. Kacen and Julie Anne Lee, "The Influence of Culture on Consumer Impulsive Buying Behavior," *Journal of Consumer Psychology* 12, no. 2 (2002): 163–176.

For further reflections on high-impulsive versus low-impulse goods, see Helga Dittmar's "Symbolic Meanings of Goods as Determinants of Impulse Buying Behaviour," available online at kent.ac.uk/ESRC/dittrep.htm.

Sandra Aamodt and Sam Wang's thoughts about self-regulation were reported in the *New York Times*, April 1, 2008.

For an early but still valid discussion of credit cards and spending levels, see Richard Feinberg, "Credit Cards as Spending Facilitating Stimuli: A Conditioning Interpretation," *Journal of Consumer Research* 13, no. 3 (1986): 348–356.

The source for how navigational links influence our impulsive online purchases is a white paper titled "What Causes Customers to Buy on Impulse?" It was distributed by User Interface Engineering, Bradford, Massachusetts.

For more on both the pathology and salutatory benefits of impulsive buying, see Dennis Rook and Robert Fisher, "Normative Influences on Impulsive Buying," *Journal of Consumer Research* 22, no. 3 (1995): 305–313.

15: Martians Buy, Venusians Shop

The epigraph was drawn from an interview published in a study by Linda Tuncay and Cele C. Otnes: "The Use of Persuasion Management Strategies by Identity-Vulnerable Consumers: The Case of Urban Heterosexual Male Shoppers," *Journal of Retailing* 84, no. 4 (2008): 487–499.

For additional details on the differences between how men and women behave in shopping centers, see Nusser A. Raajpoot, Arun Sharma, and Jean-Charles Chebat, "The Role of Gender and Work Status in Shopping Center Patronage," *Journal of Business Research* 61, no. 8 (2008): 825–833.

"Features fatigue"—buying off more than we can chew—is examined in greater length in "Defeating Features Fatigue," an article published in the *Harvard Business Review*, February 2006, pp. 98–107.

The subject of the "overnight borrowing" of merchandise has not been studied extensively, but further details can be found in Francis Piron and

Murray Young, "Retail Borrowing: Insights and Implications on Returning Used Merchandise," *International Journal of Retail & Distribution Management* 28, no. 1 (2000): 27–36.

Douglas B. Holt and Craig J. Thompson's "Man-of-Action Heroes" theory is more fully explicated in "Man-of-Action Heroes: The Pursuit of Masculinity in Everyday Consumption," *Journal of Consumer Research* 31, no. 2 (2004): 425–440.

For more on "Passive Princesses," "Great Goddesses," and other contemporary female archetypes, see the excellent anthology *The Why of Consumption*, chapter 9: "Representations of Women's Identities and Goals," by Elizabeth C. Hirschman and Barbara B. Stern.

The masculine-feminine behavioral traits cited on page 281 were culled from a study by Kay M. Palan: "Gender Identity in Consumer Behavior Research: A Literature Review and Research Agenda," *Academy of Marketing Science Review* [online] (2001).

16: Shoptimism

Mary Douglas's contention that we are what we *don't* buy is argued in an anthology entitled *The Shopping Experience*, edited by Pasi Falk and Colin Campbell. See "In Defence of Shopping" (chapter 1).

Leaf van Boven and Thomas Gilovich's "To Do or to Have? That Is the Question," about the relative benefits of the material and the experiential, was published in the *Journal of Personality and Social Psychology* 85, no. 6 (2003): 1193–1202.

The "happiness-unhappiness" weekend exercise is adapted from Daniel Kahneman et al., "Toward National Well-Being Accounts," *American Economic Review* 94, no. 2 (2004): 429–434.

Russell Belk's classic "Possessions and the Extended Self" first appeared in the *Journal of Consumer Research* 15, no. 2 (1988): 139–168.

For a moving account of the emotional power inherent in possessions that once belonged to loved ones, see Leora Auslander's "Beyond Words," an essay published in the *American Historical Review* 110, no. 4 (2005): 1015–1045.

SELECTED BIBLIOGRAPHY

Abelson, Elaine S. *When Ladies Go A-Thieving: Middle-Class Shoplifters in the Victorian Department Store.* New York: Oxford University Press, 1992.

Anderson, Chris. *The Long Tail: Why the Future of Business Is Selling Less of More.* New York: Hyperion, 2006.

Ariely, Dan. *Predictably Irrational: The Hidden Forces That Shape Our Decisions.* New York: HarperCollins, 2008.

Barber, Benjamin R. *Consumed: How Markets Corrupt Children, Infantilize Adults, and Swallow Citizens Whole.* New York: W. W. Norton, 2007.

Becker, Ernest. *The Denial of Death.* New York: Free Press, 1973.

———. *Escape from Evil.* New York: Free Press, 1975.

Bell, Daniel. *The Cultural Contradictions of Capitalism.* New York: Basic Books, 1976.

Bosshart, David. *Cheap: The Real Cost of the Global Trend for Bargains, Discounts and Customer Choice.* London: Kogan Page, 2005.

Bourdieu, Pierre. *Distinction: A Social Critique of the Judgement of Taste.* Cambridge, MA: Harvard University Press, 1984.

Bowlby, Rachel. *Shopping with Freud.* London: Routledge, 1993.

———. *Carried Away: The Invention of Modern Shopping.* New York: Columbia University Press, 2001.

Camerer, Colin F., George Loewenstein, and Matthew Rabin. *Advances in Behavioral Economics.* Princeton, NJ: Princeton University Press, 2004.

Campbell, Colin. *The Romantic Ethic and the Spirit of Modern Capitalism.* London: Wiley-Blackwell, 1987.

Carey, John. *The Intellectuals and the Masses: Pride and Prejudice among the Literary Intelligentsia, 1880–1939.* Chicago: Academy Chicago Publishers, 2002.

Cohen, Lizabeth. *A Consumers' Republic: The Politics of Mass Consumption in Postwar America.* New York: Vintage, 2003.

Cohen, Marshal. *Why Customers Do What They Do.* New York: McGraw-Hill, 2006.

Conley, Lucas. *Obsessive Branding Disorder: The Illusion of Business and the Business of Illusion.* New York: Public Affairs, 2008.

Dichter, Ernest. *Motivating Human Behavior.* New York: McGraw-Hill, 1971.

———. *Getting Motivated: The Secret Behind Individual Motivations by the Man Who Was Not Afraid to Ask "Why?"* New York: Pergamon Press, 1979.

Donaton, Scott. *Madison & Vine: Why the Entertainment and Advertising Industries Must Converge to Survive*. New York: McGraw-Hill, 2004.

Douglas, Mary, and Baron Isherwood. *The World of Goods: Towards an Anthropology of Consumption*. New York: Basic Books, 1979.

Elias, Stephen N. *Alexander T. Stewart: The Forgotten Merchant Prince*. Westport, CT: Praeger, 1992.

Elliott, Carl. *Better Than Well: American Medicine Meets the American Dream*. New York: W. W. Norton, 2003.

Falk, Pasi, and Colin Campbell. *The Shopping Experience*. London: Sage, 1997.

Fishman, Charles. *The Wal-Mart Effect: How the World's Most Powerful Company Really Works—and How It's Transforming the American Economy*. New York: Penguin, 2006.

Flocker, Michael. *The Metrosexual Guide to Style: A Handbook for the Modern Man*. Cambridge, MA: Da Capo Press, 2003.

Frank, Thomas. *The Conquest of Cool: Business Culture, Counterculture, and the Rise of Hip Consumerism*. Chicago: University of Chicago Press, 1997.

Gitlin, Todd. *The Sixties: Years of Hope, Days of Rage*. New York: Bantam, 1993.

Gladwell, Malcolm. *The Tipping Point: How Little Things Can Make a Big Difference*. New York: Little, Brown, 2000.

Gobé, Marc. *Emotional Branding: The New Paradigm for Connecting Brands to People*. New York: Allworth Press, 2001.

Goffman, Erving. *The Presentation of Self in Everyday Life*. New York: Doubleday, 1959.

Hawkins, Del I., Roger J. Best, and Kenneth A. Coney. *Consumer Behavior: Building Marketing Strategy*. Boston: Irwin McGraw-Hill, 1998.

Heath, Joseph, and Andrew Potter. *Nation of Rebels: Why Counterculture Became Consumer Culture*. New York: Collins Business, 2004.

Hine, Thomas. *Populuxe*. New York: Alfred A. Knopf, 1986.

Holt, Douglas B. *How Brands Become Icons: The Principles of Cultural Branding*. Boston: Harvard Business School Press, 2004.

Horowitz, Daniel. *Vance Packard and American Social Criticism*. Chapel Hill: University of North Carolina Press, 1994.

———. *The Anxieties of Affluence: Critiques of American Consumer Culture, 1939–1979*. Boston: University of Massachusetts Press, 2004.

Iacobucci, Dawn. *Kellogg on Marketing*. New York: Wiley, 2001.

James, Clive. *Cultural Amnesia: Necessary Memories from History and the Arts*. New York: W. W. Norton, 2007.

King, William Davies. *Collections of Nothing*. Chicago: University of Chicago Press, 2008.

Klein, Naomi. *No Logo: No Space, No Choice, No Jobs*. New York: Picador, 2000.

Koolhaas, Rem, et al. *Harvard Design School Guide to Shopping*. Cologne: Taschen, 2001.

Kotler, Philip, and Gary Armstrong. *Principles of Marketing*. Upper Saddle River, NJ: Prentice-Hall, 2008.

Lasn, Kalle. *Culture Jam: How to Reverse America's Suicidal Consumer Binge—And Why We Must*. New York: William Morrow, 1999.

Li, Charline, and Josh Bernoff. *Groundswell: Winning in a World Transformed by Social Technologies*. Boston: Harvard Business Press, 2008.

Lindstrom, Martin. *Buyology: Truth and Lies About Why We Buy.* New York: Doubleday, 2008.

Marcus, Stanley. *Minding the Store: A Memoir.* Denton, TX: University of North Texas Press, 1974.

———. *Quest for the Best.* New York: Viking, 1979.

Maslow, Abraham H., and Dorothy C. Stephens. *The Maslow Business Reader.* New York: Wiley, 2000.

Maxwell, Sarah. *The Price is Wrong: Understanding What Makes a Price Seem Fair and the True Cost of Unfair Pricing.* New York: Wiley, 2008.

McCracken, Grant. *Culture and Consumption: New Approaches to the Symbolic Character of Consumer Goods and Activities.* Bloomington: Indiana University Press, 1988.

———. *Big Hair: A Journey into the Transformation of Self.* Woodstock, NY: Overlook Press, 1995.

———. *Culture and Consumption II: Markets, Meaning, and Brand Management.* Bloomington: Indiana University Press, 2005.

Michman, Ronald D., Edward M. Mazze, and Alan J. Greco. *Lifestyle Marketing: Reaching the New American Consumer.* Westport, CT: Praeger, 2003.

Miller, Daniel. *Material Culture and Mass Consumption.* London: Basil Blackwell, 1987.

Mitchell, Arnold. *The Nine American Lifestyles: Who We Are and Where We're Going.* New York: Warner Books, 1984.

Mohammed, Rafi. *The Art of Pricing: How to Find the Hidden Profits to Grow Your Business.* New York: Crown Business, 2005.

Nocera, Joseph. *A Piece of the Action: How the Middle Class Joined the Money Class.* New York: Simon & Schuster, 1994.

Otnes, Cele C., and Richard F. Beltramini. *Gift Giving: A Research Anthology.* Bowling Green, OH: Bowling Green State University Popular Press, 1996.

Otnes, Cele C., and Elizabeth H. Pleck. *Cinderella Dreams: The Allure of the Lavish Wedding.* Berkeley: University of California Press, 2003.

Packard, Vance. *The Hidden Persuaders.* New York: David McKay, 1957.

Pitkin, Walter B. *The Consumer: His Nature and His Changing Habits.* New York: McGraw-Hill, 1932.

Postrel, Virginia. *The Substance of Style: How the Rise of Aesthetic Value Is Remaking Commerce, Culture, and Consciousness.* New York: HarperCollins, 2003.

Rapaille, Clotaire. *The Culture Code: An Ingenious Way to Understand Why People Around the World Live and Buy as They Do.* New York: Broadway, 2007.

Ratneshwar, S., David Glen Mick, and Cynthia Huffman. *The Why of Consumption: Contemporary Perspectives on Consumer Motives, Goals, and Desires.* New York: Routledge, 2000.

Ries, Al, and Laura Ries. *The Fall of Advertising and the Rise of PR.* New York: HarperCollins, 2002.

Ritzer George. *The McDonalization of Society.* Thousand Oaks, CA: Pine Forge Press, 1995.

Scafidi, Susan. *Who Owns Culture?: Appropriation and Authenticity in American Law.* New Brunswick, NJ: Rutgers University Press, 2005.

Schor, Juliet B. *The Overspent American: Why We Want What We Don't Need.* New York: Basic Books, 1998.

———. *Born to Buy: The Commercialized Child and the New Consumer Culture.* New York: Scribner, 2004.

Schudson, Michael. *Advertising, The Uneasy Persuasion.* New York: Basic Books, 1984.

Schultz, Howard. *Pour Your Heart into It: How Starbucks Built a Company One Cup at a Time.* New York: Hyperion, 1997.

Seabrook, John. *Nobrow: The Culture of Marketing, the Marketing of Culture.* New York: Alfred A. Knopf, 2000.

Seligman, Martin. *Authentic Happiness: Using the New Positive Psychology to Realize Your Potential for Lasting Fulfillment.* New York: Free Press, 2002.

Silverstein, Michael J., with John Butman. *Treasure Hunt: Inside the Mind of the New Consumer.* New York: Portfolio, 2006.

Soto, Terry J. *Marketing to Hispanics: A Strategic Approach to Assessing and Planning Your Initiative.* Chicago: Kaplan, 2006.

Surowiecki, James. *The Wisdom of Crowds.* New York: Doubleday, 2004.

Thaler, Richard H., and Cass R. Sunstein. *Nudge: Improving Decisions About Health, Wealth, and Happiness.* New Haven, CT: Yale University Press, 2008.

Thomas, Dana. *Deluxe: How Luxury Lost Its Luster.* New York: Penguin, 2007.

Twitchell, James B. *Lead Us into Temptation.* New York: Columbia University Press, 1999.

———. *Branded Nation: The Marketing of Megachurch, College Inc., and Museumworld.* New York: Simon & Schuster, 2004.

Underhill, Paco. *Why We Buy: The Science of Shopping.* New York: Simon & Schuster, 1999.

———. *Call of the Mall: The Geography of Shopping.* New York: Simon & Schuster, 2004.

Veblen, Thorstein. *The Theory of the Leisure Class.* New York: Modern Library, 2001.

Wansink, Brian. *Mindless Eating: Why We Eat More Than We Think.* New York: Bantam, 2006.

Welch, Evelyn. *Shopping in the Renaissance.* New Haven, CT: Yale University Press, 2005.

Whyebrow, Peter C. *American Mania: When More Is Not Enough.* New York: W. W. Norton, 2005.

Wood, James. *The Irresponsible Self: On Laughter and the Novel.* New York: Picador, 2006.

Zaltman, Gerald. *How Customers Think: Essential Insights into the Mind of the Market.* Boston: Harvard Business School Press, 2003.

ACKNOWLEDGMENTS

G aining access to a store or e-commerce site requires no official letter of introduction or special favor. But here's a nod anyway to Steve Jobs (Apple Store), Howard Schultz (Starbucks), Terry Lundgren (Macy's), Michael Duke (Wal-Mart), Leslie Wexner (Limited Brands), Jeff Bezos (Amazon), Mickey Drexler (J. Crew), and especially Bob Ulrich (former CEO of Target), not to mention hundreds of other major and minor merchant princes, for their unwitting hospitality these past three years. Not once—save for that hair-raising episode on Canal Street—was I challenged to explain why I was lurking in their stores, peeping at customers and sales associates, while not (aside from the occasional burst of impulse) stooping to buy all that much.

Gaining access to research papers and out-of-print books, well, that was another story. Here I needed as many friendly introductions and favors as I could haggle. Harvard's John Deighton, the editor of the *Journal of Consumer Research*, kindly issued me a passkey to the archives of that publication and pointed me in the direction of contributors whose work he deemed most appropriate to the task at hand. He and numerous other academics responded graciously and promptly to e-mails, phone calls, and the occasional request for a face-to-face meeting. I thank them all for their unstinting time and patience, particularly Grant McCracken, Russell Belk, Stephen Hoch, Thomas O'Guinn, Al Muniz, George Loewenstein, Americus Reed, Daniel Horowitz, Craig Thompson, Mary Ann McGrath, Linda Tuncay, Dan Ariely, Ronald Faber, Lorrin Koran, Cele Otnes, and Lisa Penaloza. A special thanks goes to Brittany Duff and Dan Duff for the morphing of Sam Waterston and the stand-in "subject," page 120. Donald Black and Scott Rick not only enlightened me on the mysteries of compulsive buying and brain science, they were also kind enough to review portions of the manuscript. Needless to say, any misinterpretations of studies in those or any other specialized fields rest with me.

Al Filreis, who directs the Center for Programs in Contemporary Writing at the University of Pennsylvania, deserves great thanks for the many favors he bestowed: an ongoing opportunity to exchange ideas with the talented undergrads who find inspiration and refuge at the beloved Kelly Writers House at Penn, and also for swinging open the door to the online resources and stacks at the Van Pelt Library. Thanks, too, to Mingo Reynolds and John Carroll for helping me make the most of many visits back to campus. They showed me where I could find what, made sure I never got lost, and, best of all, extended friendship and good cheer.

Christopher Fielder (Experian) and Steve Moore (Claritas) were most accommodating when it came to my requests for materials and interviews related to their bucketing operations. So, too, was Kathy Grannis at the National Retail Federation, who paved the way into the NRF's BIG Show. I'm also grateful to David Rabjohns and the folks at MotiveQuest—in particular, Kirsten Recknagel, the company's estimable and gracious director of research—for their hospitality and generous assistance.

Barbara Sylk and Ann Mashburn, two longtime friends of my wife, were kind enough to put me in touch with far-flung friends of theirs who, with frankness and self-effacing humor, responded to various survey questions and willingly bared their shopping souls—usually on the condition that I would keep their identities and confessions secret from their spouses and partners.

As for the idea that led to this book, credit or blame falls to Bruce Nichols, a terrific editor and all-around good guy, who pitched the notion over lunch one day. The project then passed to Martin Beiser at Free Press, also an all-around good guy, who put up with me for the long haul. And, once again, I am indebted to the entire Free Press team—as committed, creative, and supportive as a writer can ever hope for: Martha Levin, Dominick Anfuso, Suzanne Donahue, Carisa Hays, and Nicole Kalian, among many others.

Michael Solomon, Lisa Grunwald Adler, Betsy Carter, and Marilyn Johnson—dear friends, funny, too—issued exceedingly useful editorial suggestions whenever I called out for help. And I can't be effusive enough when it comes to praising Chris Jerome, who lent aid, comfort, humor, and, of course, her ever-sharp copy editor's eye.

And then there is the Indomitable One: my agent, Esther Newberg.

Finally, I commend my kids, Ned and Katherine, for their encouragement, but even more for their maturing awareness that, to paraphrase

Robert Louis Stevenson, the world is filled with wondrous things—which doesn't mean a student's allowance is sufficient to afford all of them. And, through the beginning, the middle, and the end of this adventure, there was Linda. Sure, she wound up with a dress and a forty-dollar necklace, but her patience and love are beyond payback.

INDEX